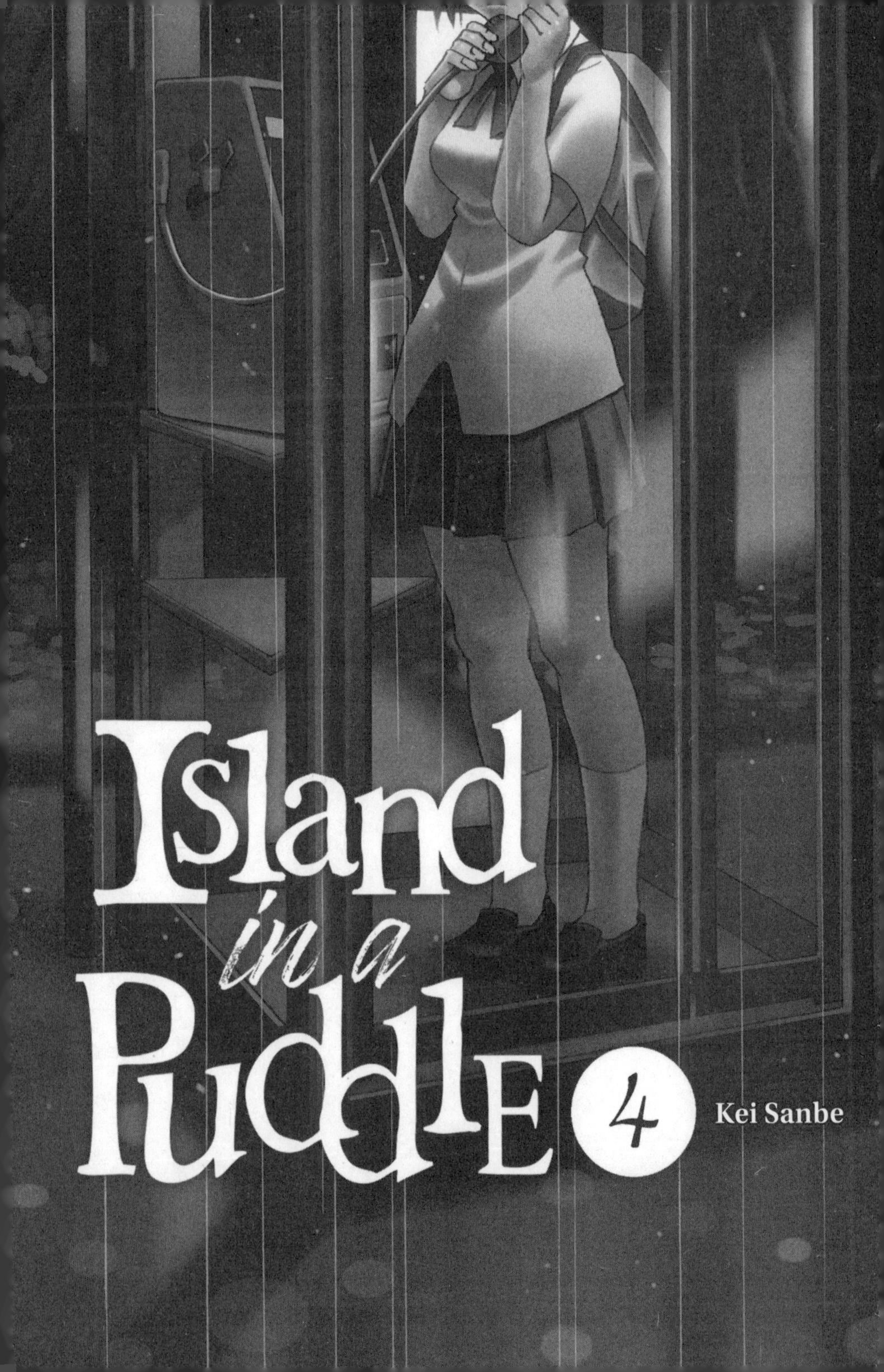
Island
in a
Puddle
4
Kei Sanbe

CONTENTS

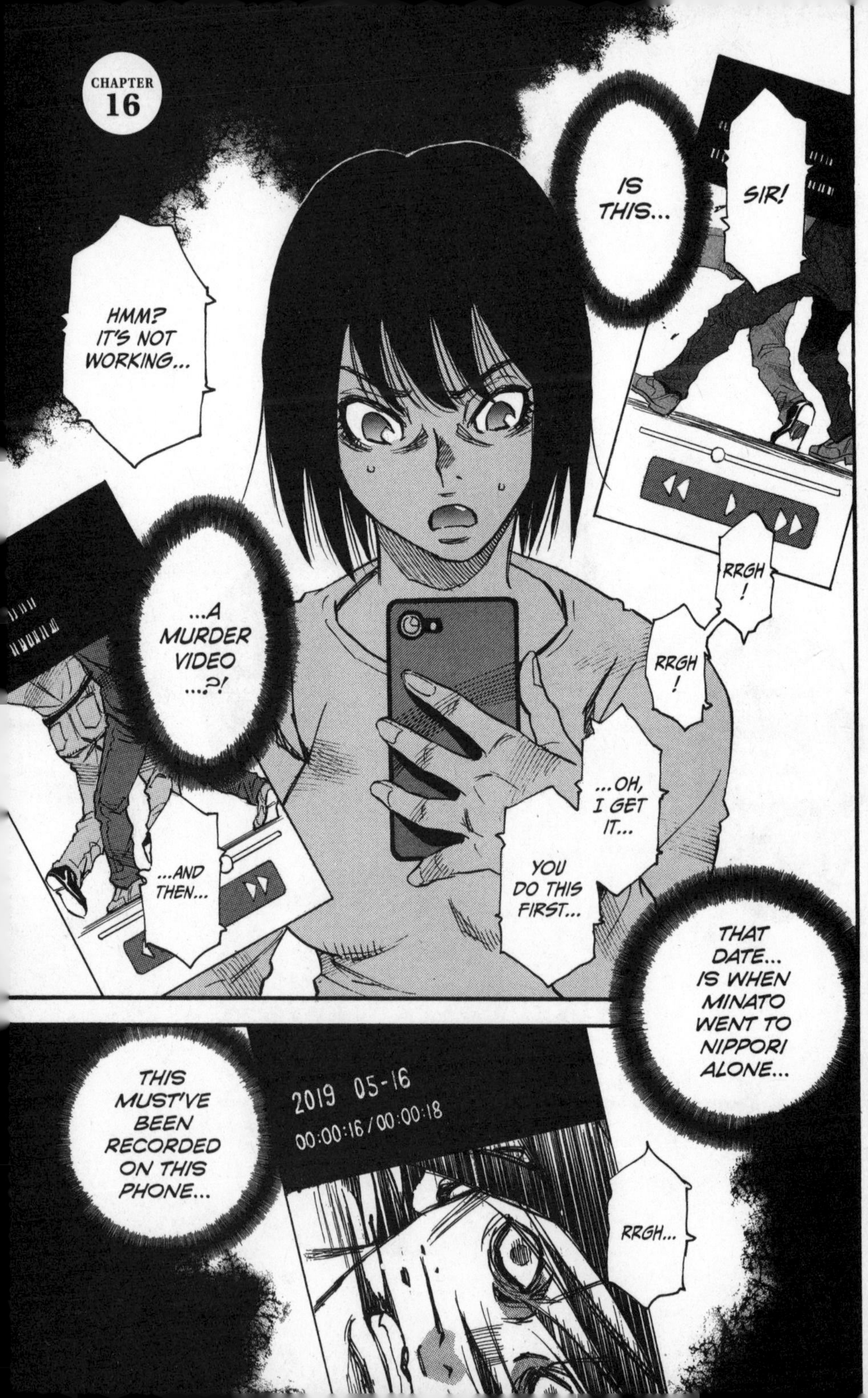
CHAPTER 16
SIR!
IS THIS...
HMM? IT'S NOT WORKING...
RRGH!
RRGH!
...A MURDER VIDEO ...?!
...OH, I GET IT...
YOU DO THIS FIRST...
...AND THEN...
THAT DATE... IS WHEN MINATO WENT TO NIPPORI ALONE...
2019 05-16
00:00:16 / 00:00:18
THIS MUST'VE BEEN RECORDED ON THIS PHONE...
RRGH...

CHAPTER 16

Let's Find Mom

THAT'S...
...NOT MINATO.

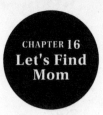

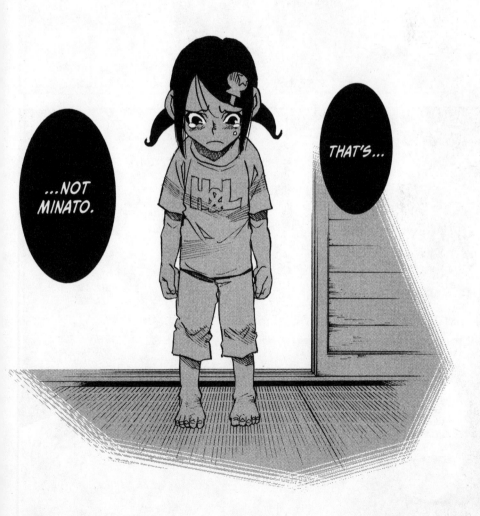

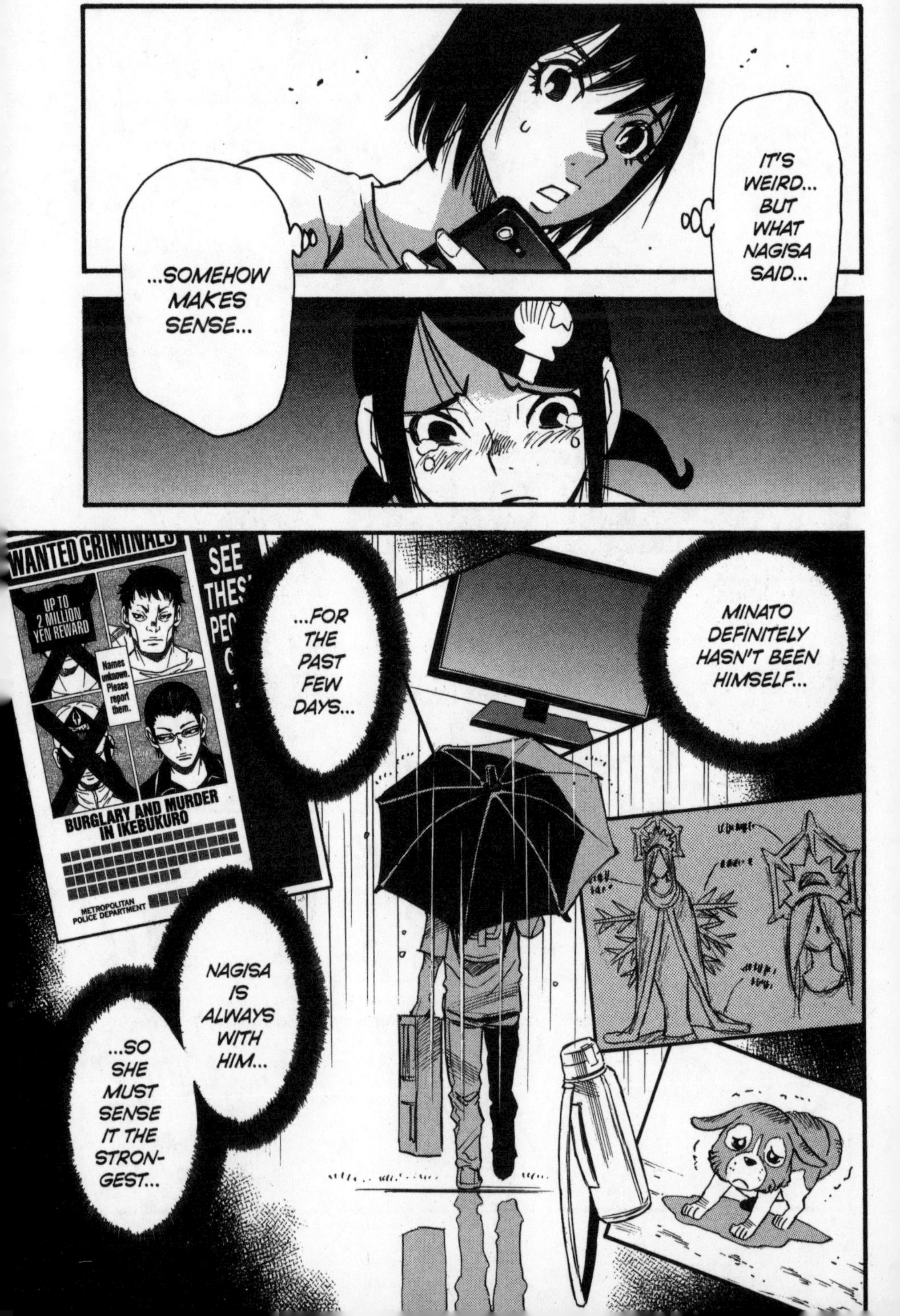
IT'S WEIRD... BUT WHAT NAGISA SAID...
...SOMEHOW MAKES SENSE...
MINATO DEFINITELY HASN'T BEEN HIMSELF...
...FOR THE PAST FEW DAYS...
WANTED CRIMINALS
UP TO 2 MILLION YEN REWARD
Names unknown. Please report them.
BURGLARY AND MURDER IN IKEBUKURO
METROPOLITAN POLICE DEPARTMENT
SEE
NAGISA IS ALWAYS WITH HIM...
...SO SHE MUST SENSE IT THE STRONGEST...

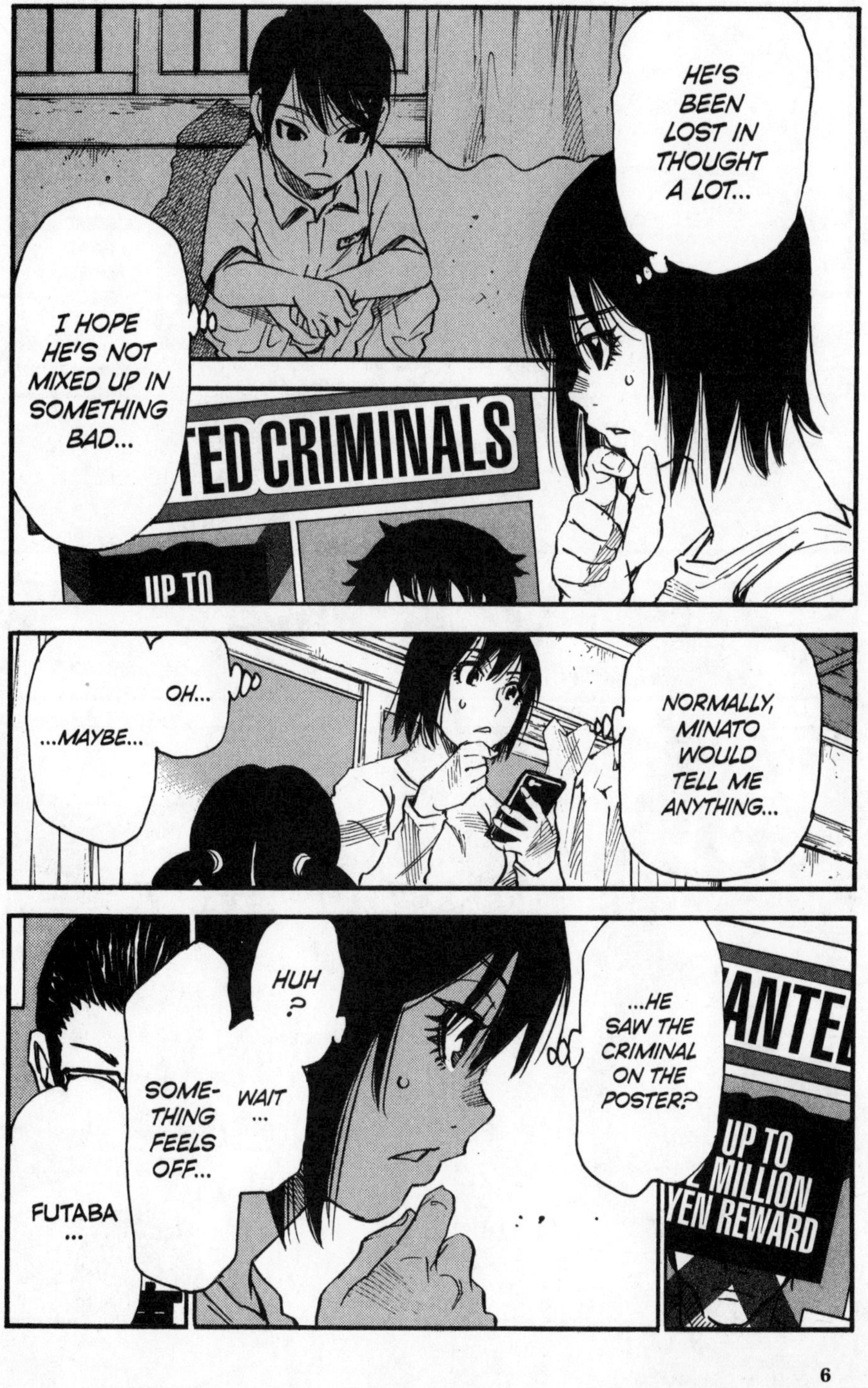
HE'S BEEN LOST IN THOUGHT A LOT...
I HOPE HE'S NOT MIXED UP IN SOMETHING BAD...
CRIMINALS
NORMALLY, MINATO WOULD TELL ME ANYTHING...
OH...
...MAYBE...
...HE SAW THE CRIMINAL ON THE POSTER?
UP TO
MILLION
YEN REWARD
HUH?
WAIT...
SOME-THING FEELS OFF...
FUTABA...

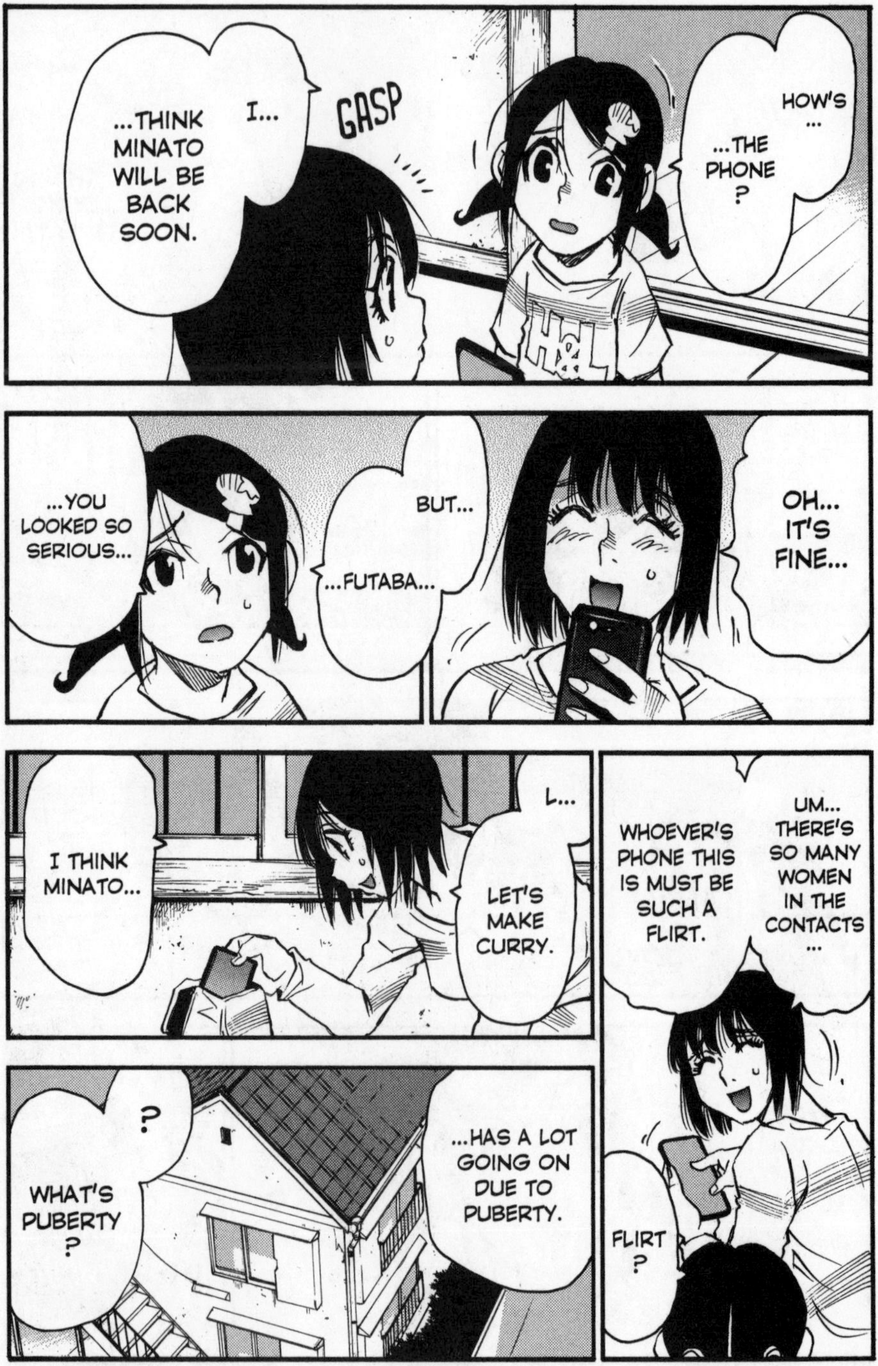
HOW'S... ...THE PHONE?
GASP
I... ...THINK MINATO WILL BE BACK SOON.
OH... IT'S FINE...
BUT... ...FUTABA...
...YOU LOOKED SO SERIOUS...
UM... THERE'S SO MANY WOMEN IN THE CONTACTS...
WHOEVER'S PHONE THIS IS MUST BE SUCH A FLIRT.
FLIRT?
I... LET'S MAKE CURRY.
I THINK MINATO...
...HAS A LOT GOING ON DUE TO PUBERTY.
?
WHAT'S PUBERTY?

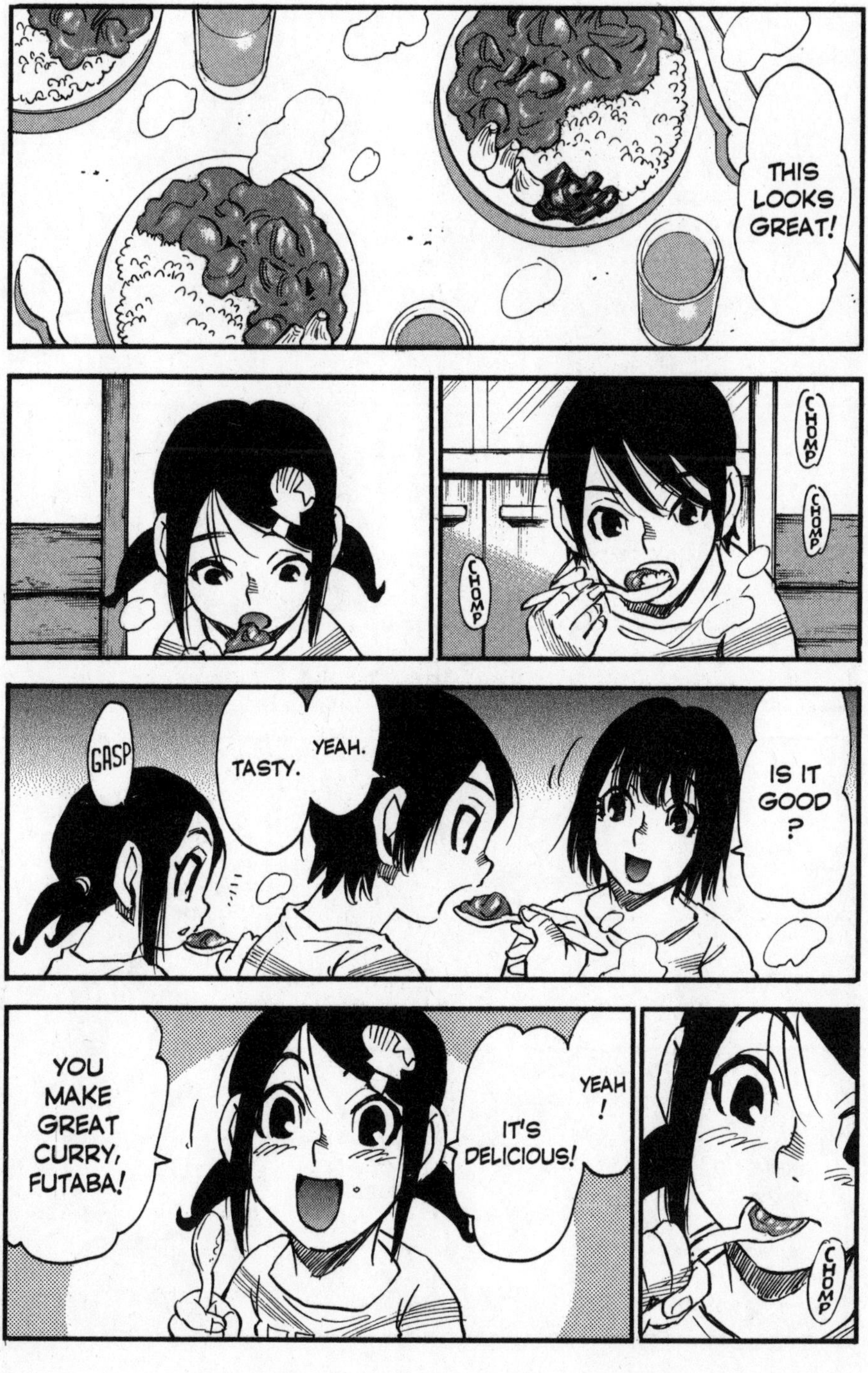
THIS LOOKS GREAT!
CHOMP
CHOMP
CHOMP
IS IT GOOD?
YEAH.
TASTY.
GASP
CHOMP
YEAH!
IT'S DELICIOUS!
YOU MAKE GREAT CURRY, FUTABA!

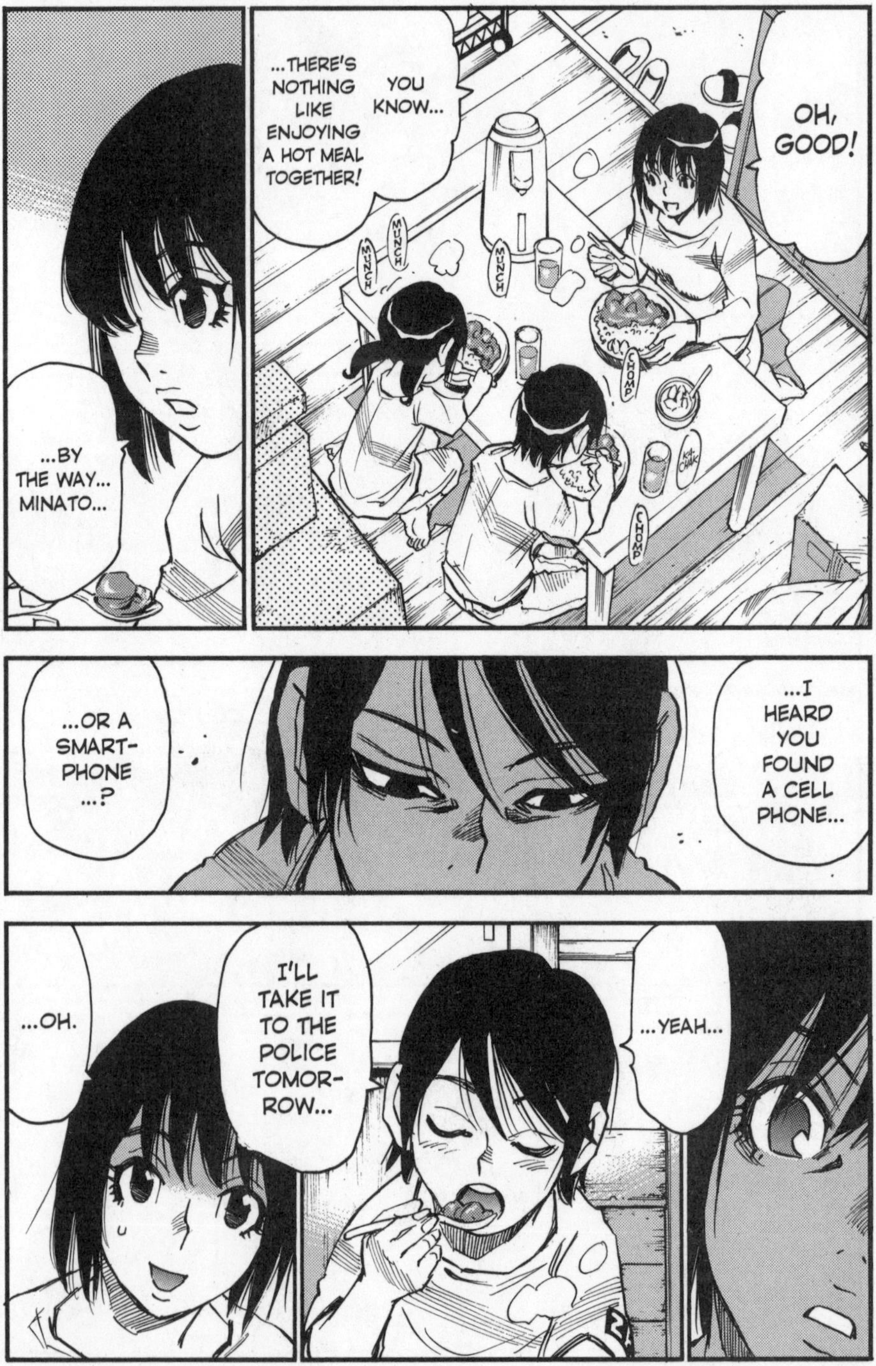
OH, GOOD!
YOU KNOW...
...THERE'S NOTHING LIKE ENJOYING A HOT MEAL TOGETHER!
MUNCH
MUNCH
MUNCH
CHOMP
KA-CHAK
CHOMP
...BY THE WAY... MINATO...
...I HEARD YOU FOUND A CELL PHONE...
...OR A SMART-PHONE ...?
...YEAH...
I'LL TAKE IT TO THE POLICE TOMOR-ROW...
...OH.

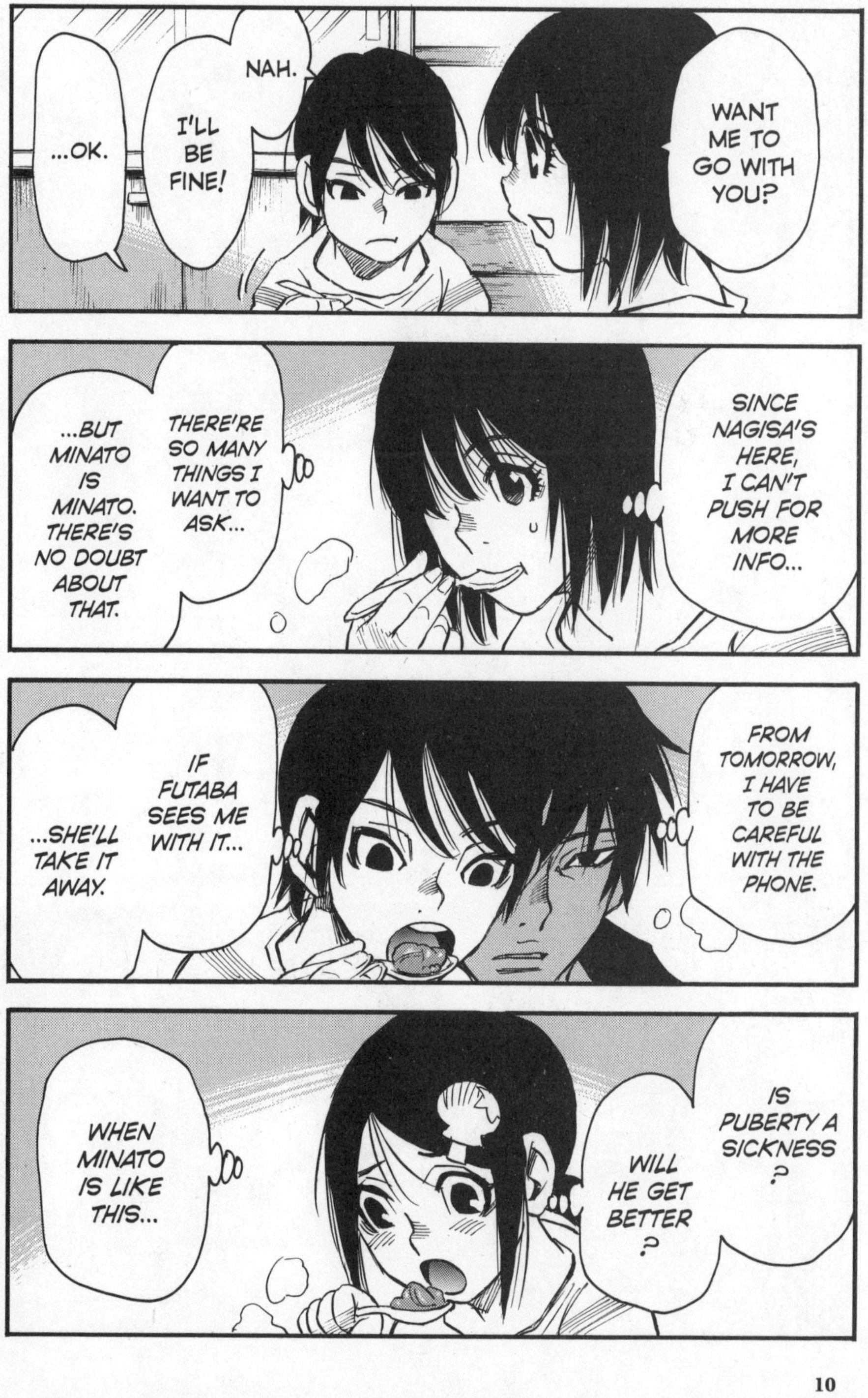
WANT ME TO GO WITH YOU?
NAH. I'LL BE FINE!
...OK.
SINCE NAGISA'S HERE, I CAN'T PUSH FOR MORE INFO...
THERE'RE SO MANY THINGS I WANT TO ASK...
...BUT MINATO IS MINATO. THERE'S NO DOUBT ABOUT THAT.
FROM TOMORROW, I HAVE TO BE CAREFUL WITH THE PHONE.
IF FUTABA SEES ME WITH IT...
...SHE'LL TAKE IT AWAY.
IS PUBERTY A SICKNESS?
WILL HE GET BETTER?
WHEN MINATO IS LIKE THIS...

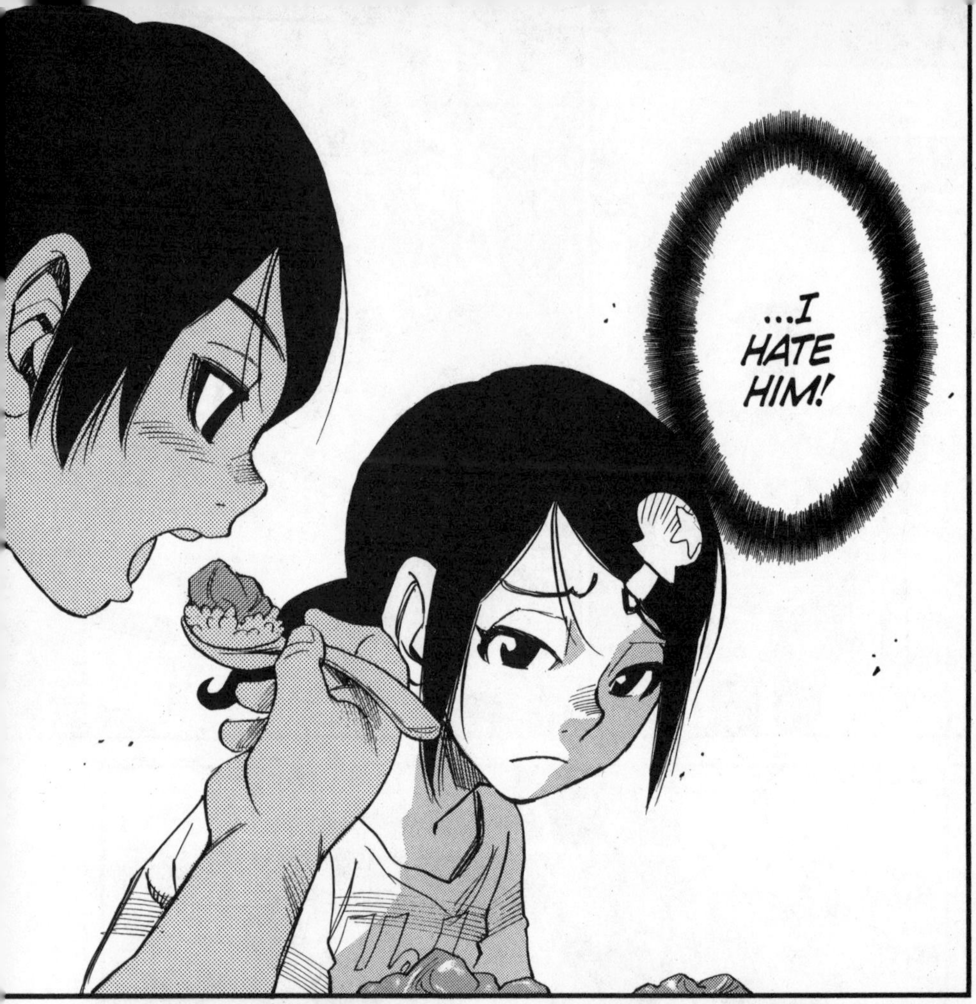
...I HATE HIM!

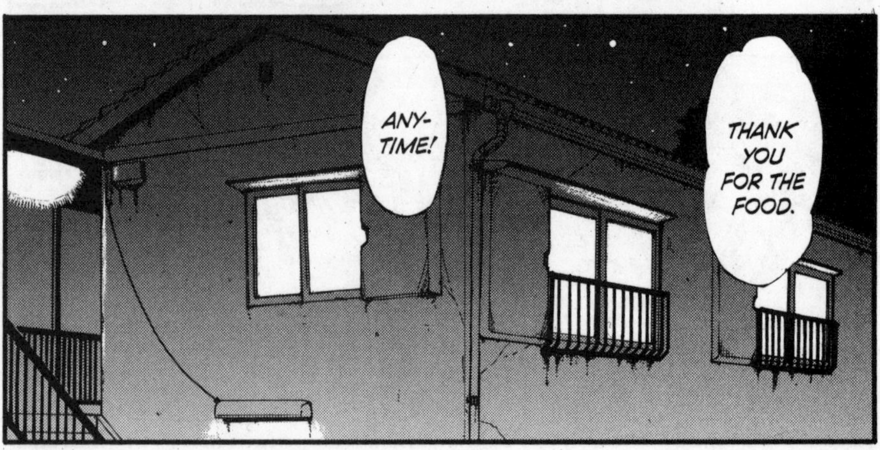
THANK YOU FOR THE FOOD.
ANY-TIME!

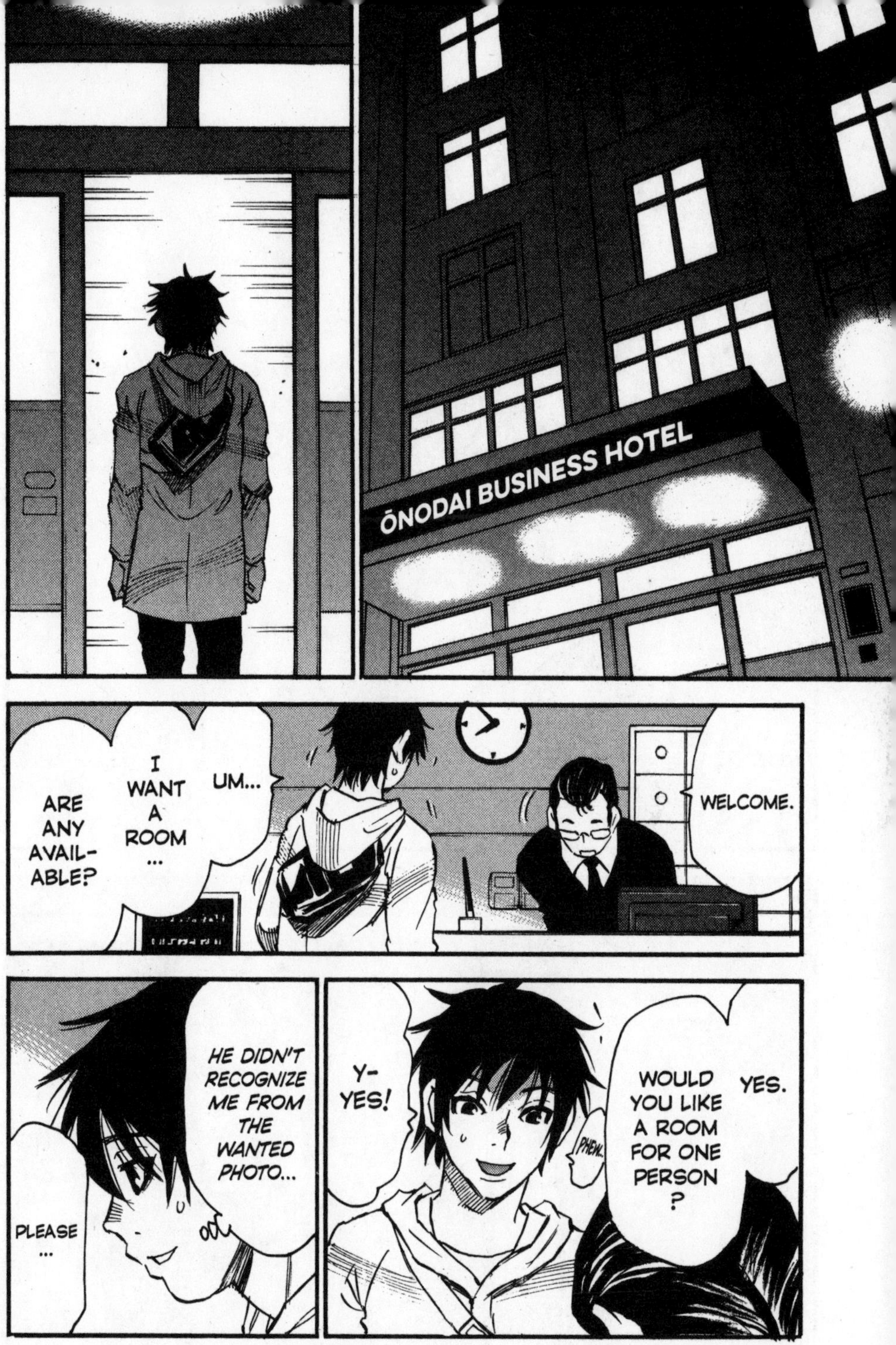
ŌNODAI BUSINESS HOTEL
WELCOME.
UM...
I WANT A ROOM ...
ARE ANY AVAIL-ABLE?
YES.
WOULD YOU LIKE A ROOM FOR ONE PERSON ?
PHEW...
Y-YES!
HE DIDN'T RECOGNIZE ME FROM THE WANTED PHOTO...
PLEASE ...

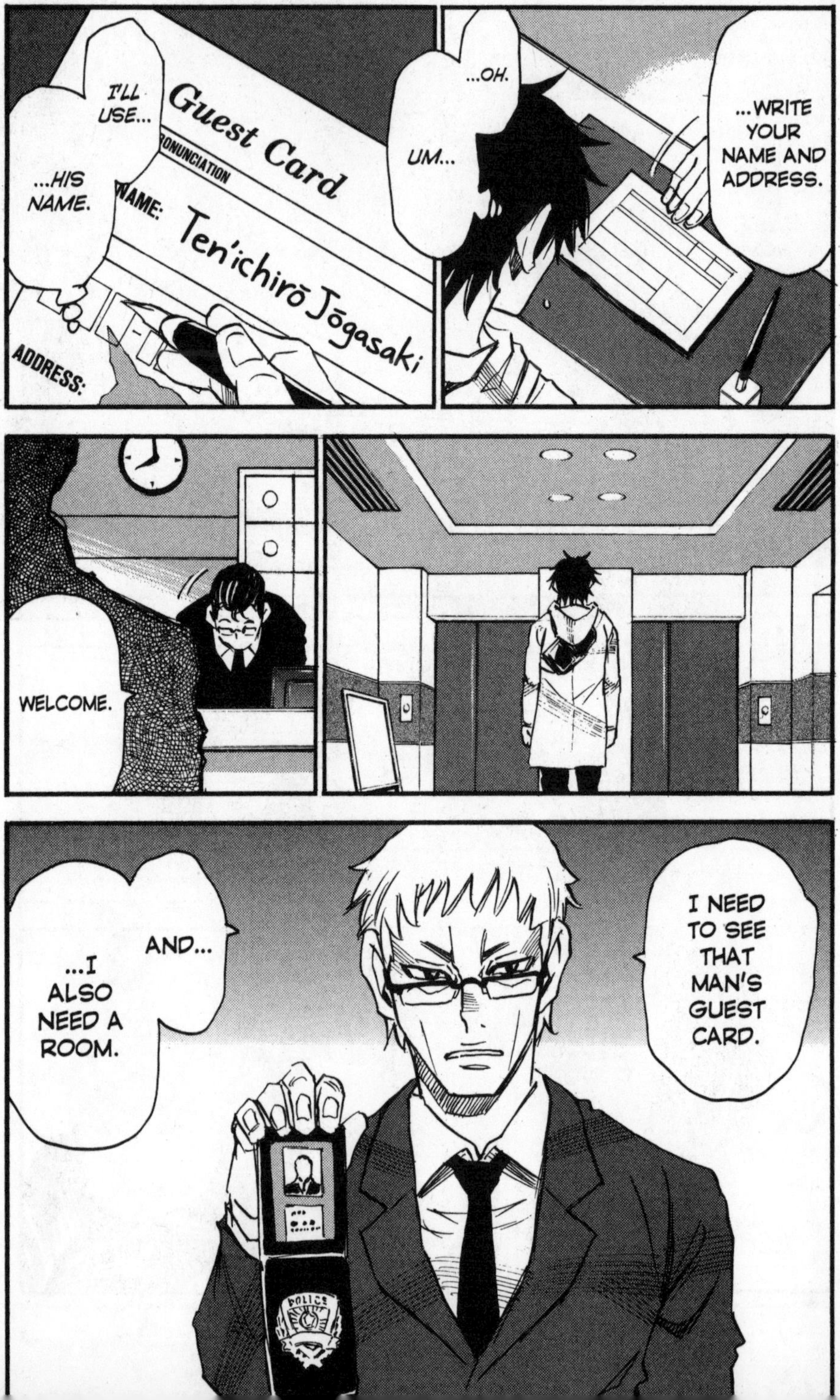
...WRITE YOUR NAME AND ADDRESS.
...OH.
UM...
Guest Card
RONUNCIATION
NAME: Ten'ichirō Jōgasaki
ADDRESS:
I'LL USE...
...HIS NAME.
WELCOME.
I NEED TO SEE THAT MAN'S GUEST CARD.
AND...
...I ALSO NEED A ROOM.

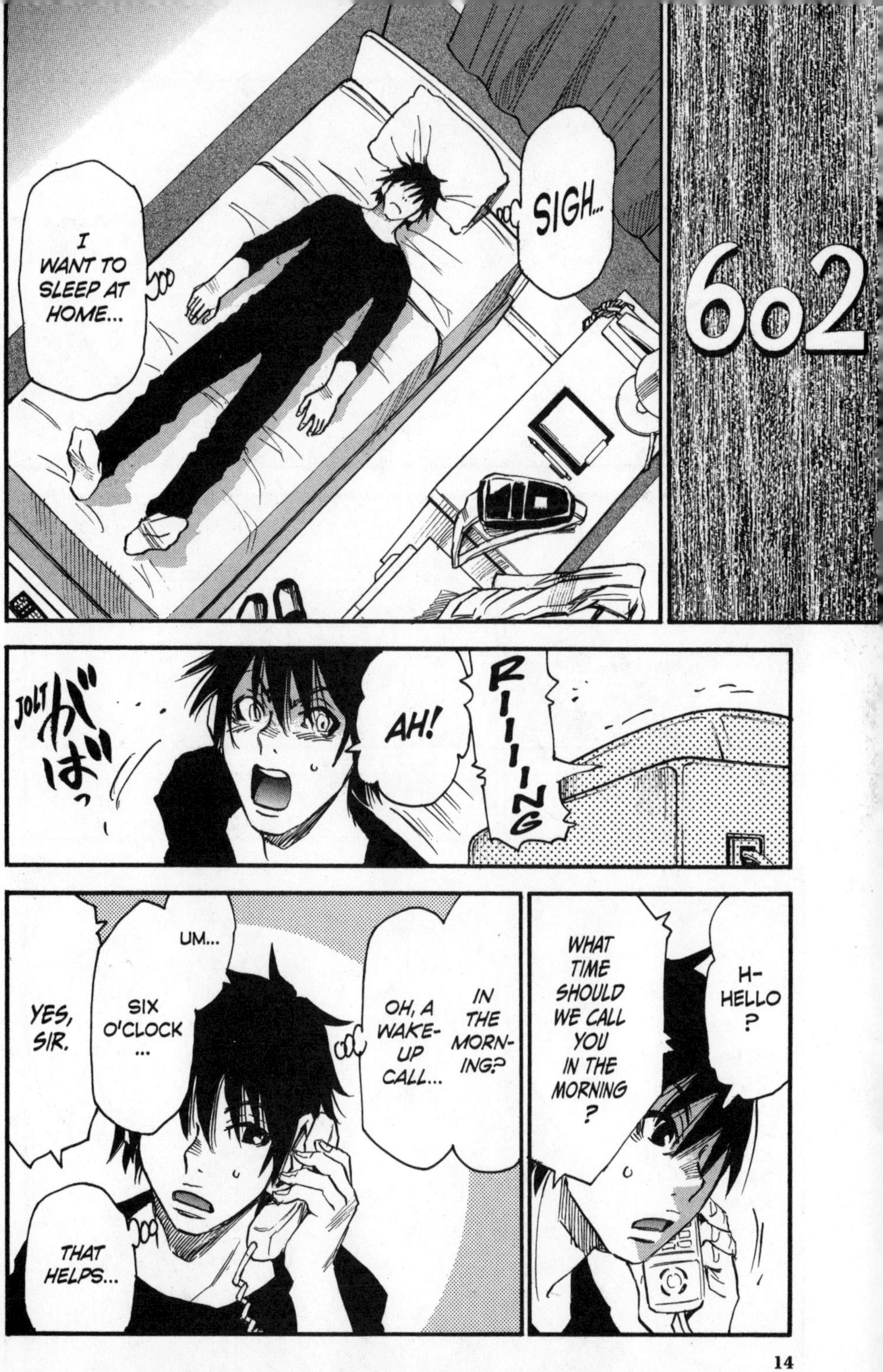
602
SIGH...
I WANT TO SLEEP AT HOME...
RIIIING
AH!
JOLT
がばっ
H-HELLO?
WHAT TIME SHOULD WE CALL YOU IN THE MORNING?
IN THE MORNING?
OH, A WAKE-UP CALL...
UM...
SIX O'CLOCK...
YES, SIR.
THAT HELPS...

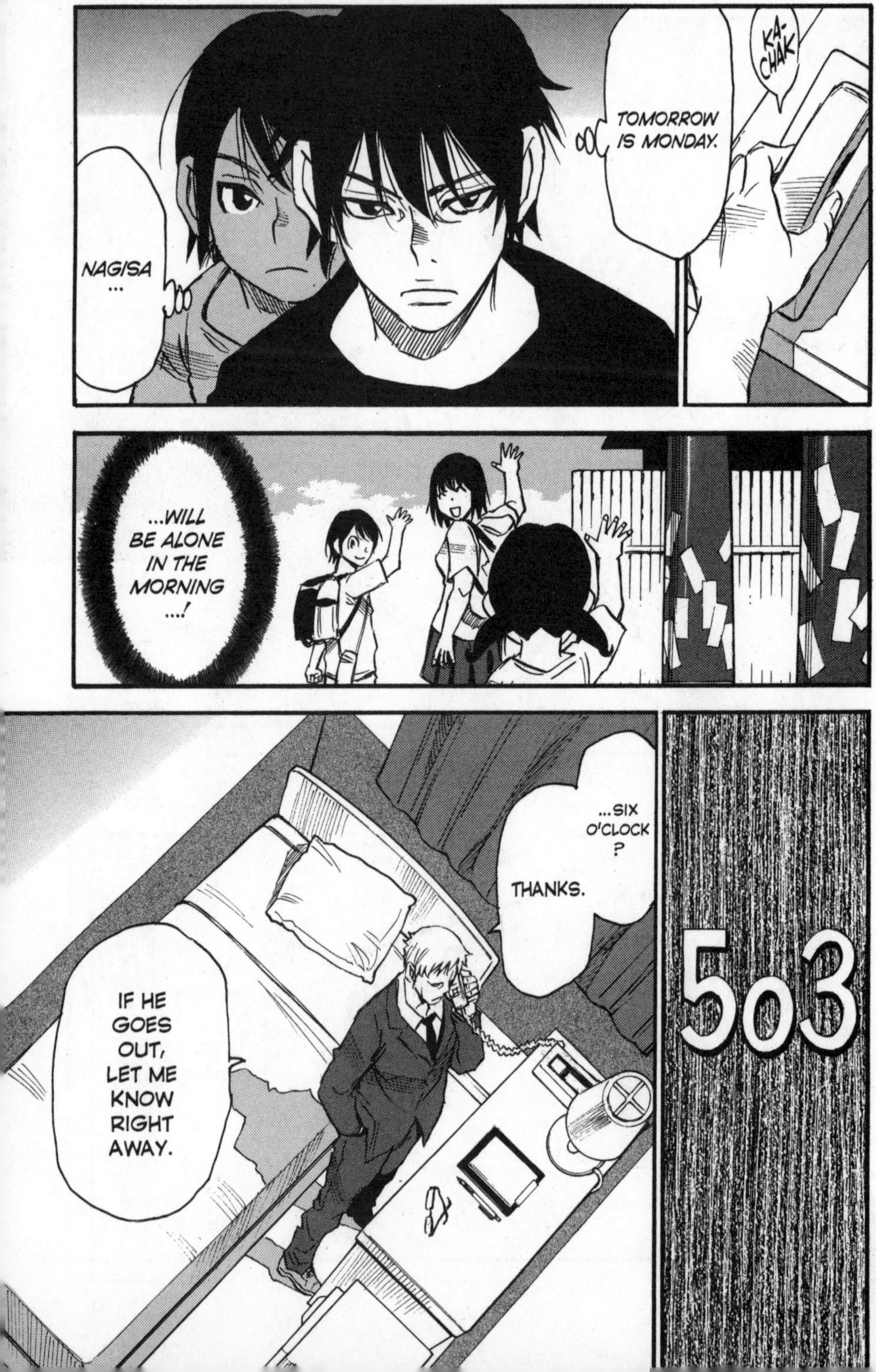
KA-CHAK
TOMORROW IS MONDAY.
NAGISA ...
...WILL BE ALONE IN THE MORNING ...!
5o3
...SIX O'CLOCK ?
THANKS.
IF HE GOES OUT, LET ME KNOW RIGHT AWAY.

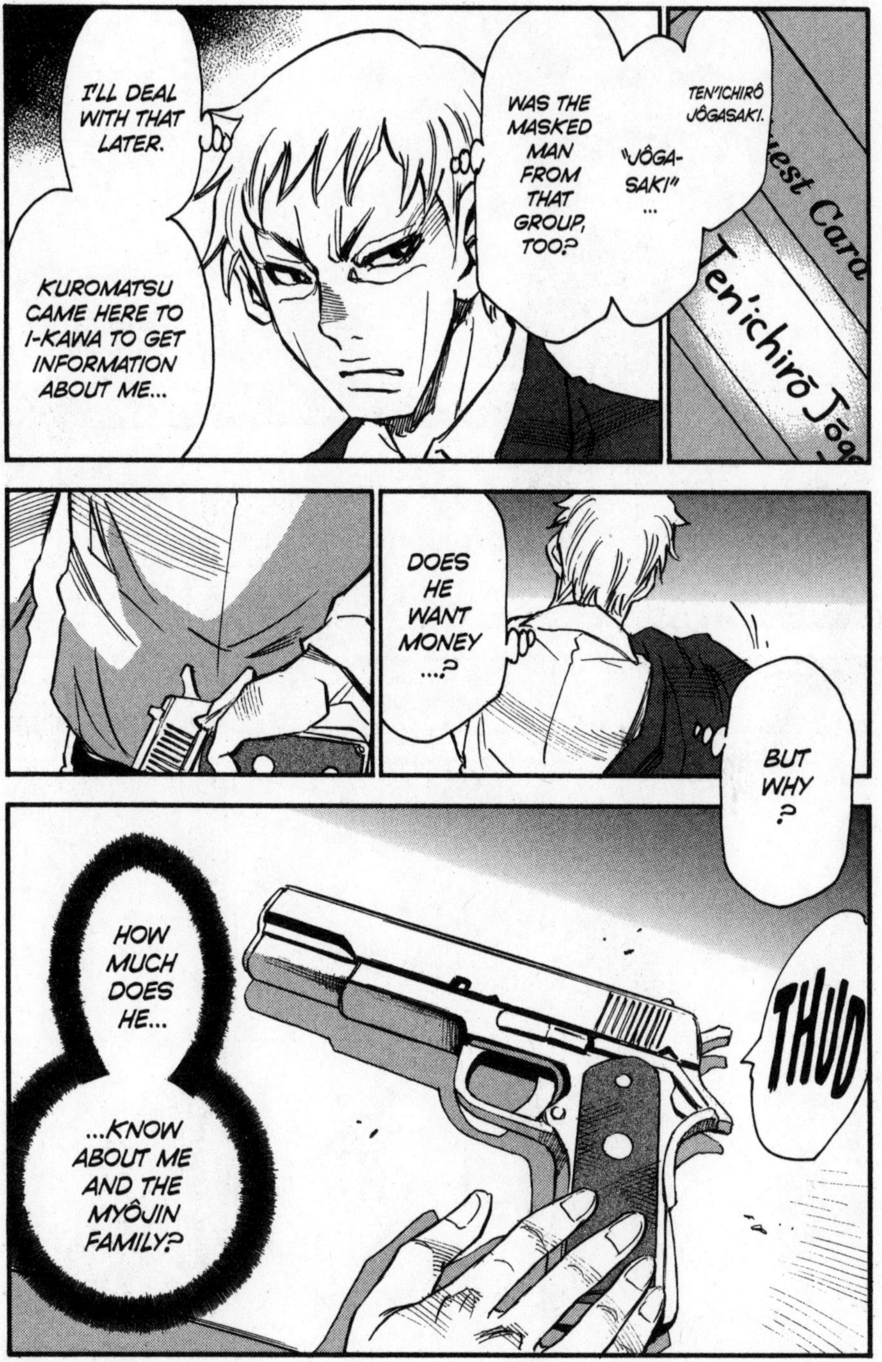

TEN'ICHIRÔ JÔGASAKI.
"JÔGA-SAKI" ...
WAS THE MASKED MAN FROM THAT GROUP, TOO?
I'LL DEAL WITH THAT LATER.
KUROMATSU CAME HERE TO I-KAWA TO GET INFORMATION ABOUT ME...
DOES HE WANT MONEY ...?
BUT WHY ?
THUD
HOW MUCH DOES HE...
...KNOW ABOUT ME AND THE MYÔJIN FAMILY?

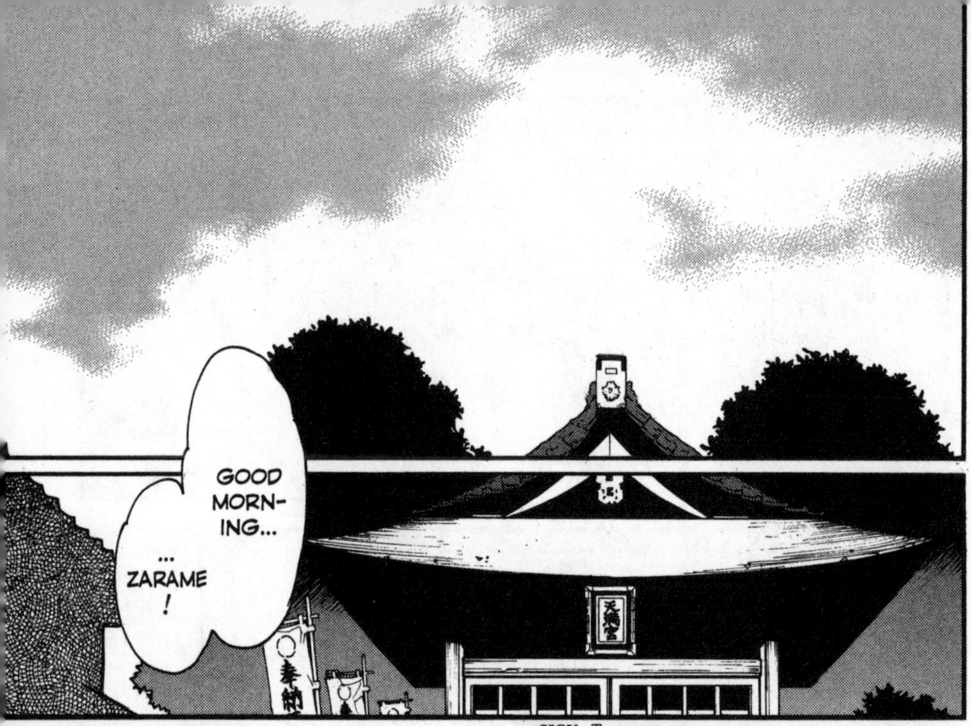
GOOD MORNING... ...ZARAME!

SIGN: *Tenmangu.*

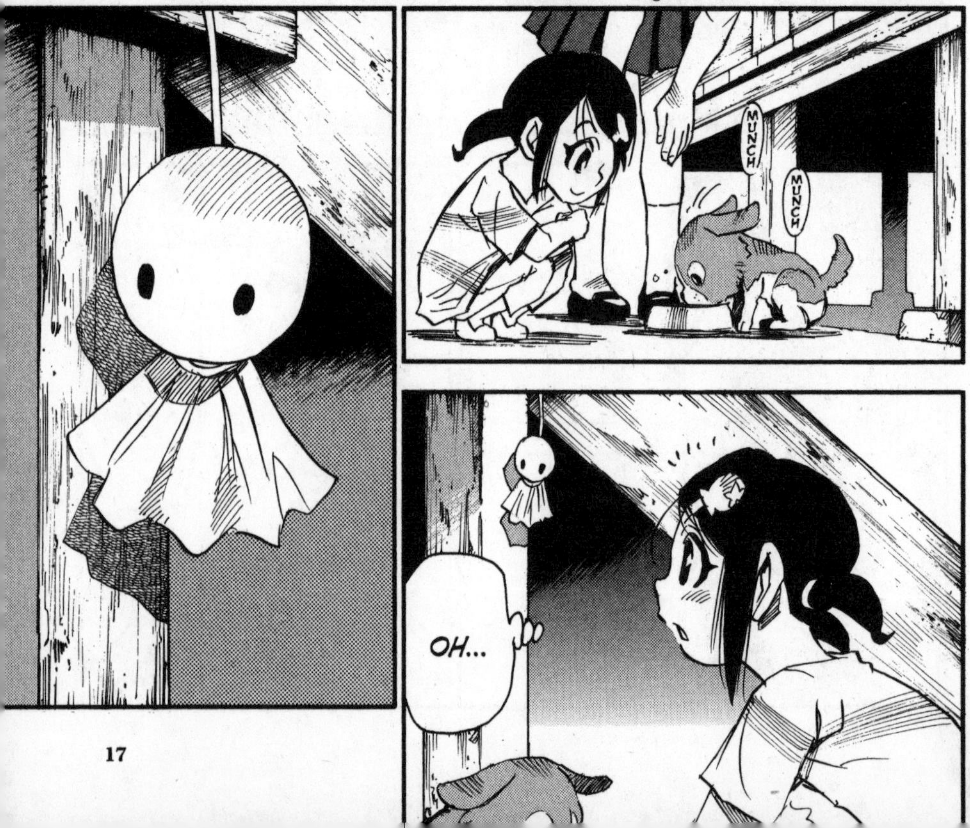
MUNCH
MUNCH
OH...

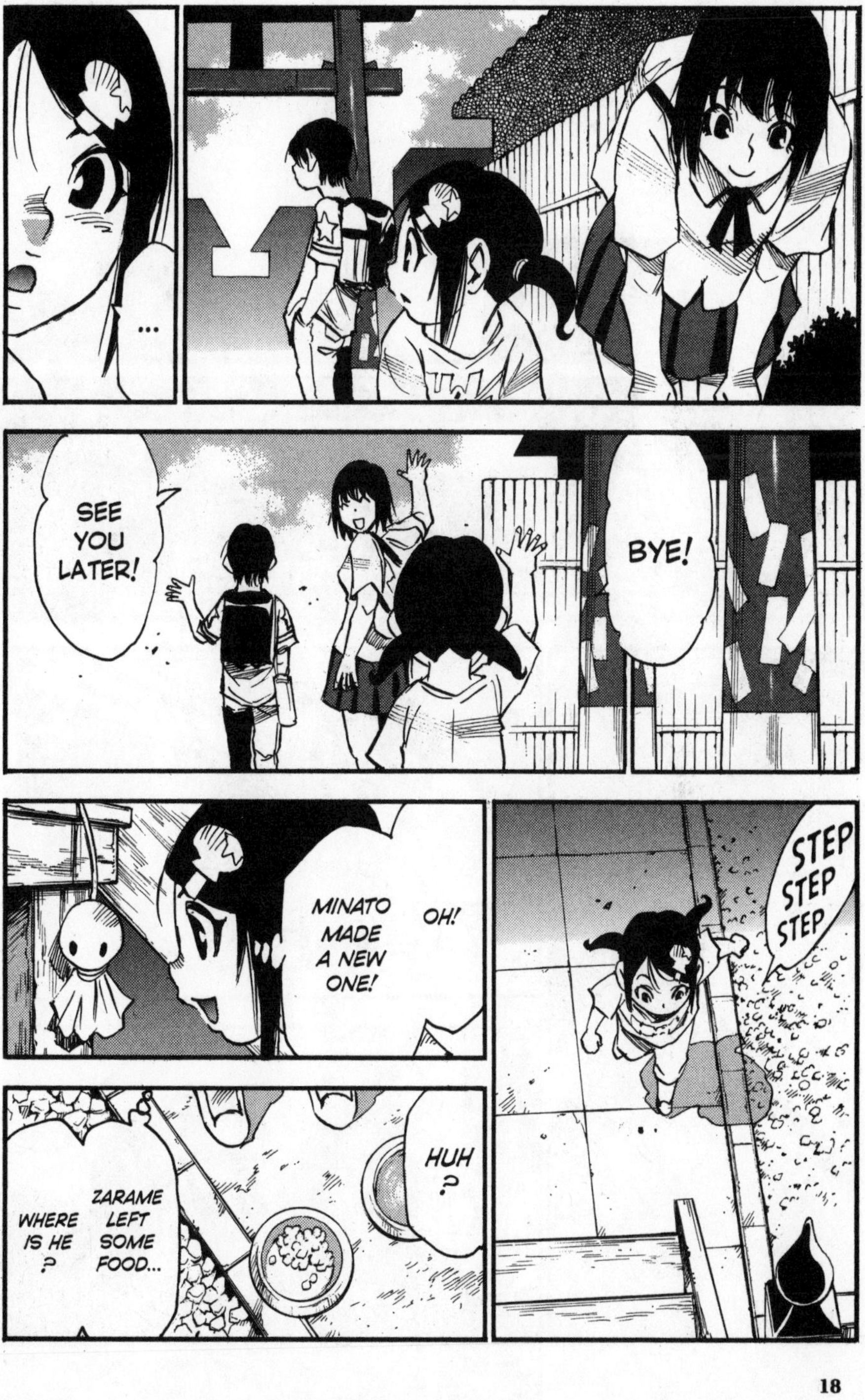
...
BYE!
SEE YOU LATER!
STEP STEP STEP
OH!
MINATO MADE A NEW ONE!
HUH?
ZARAME LEFT SOME FOOD...
WHERE IS HE?

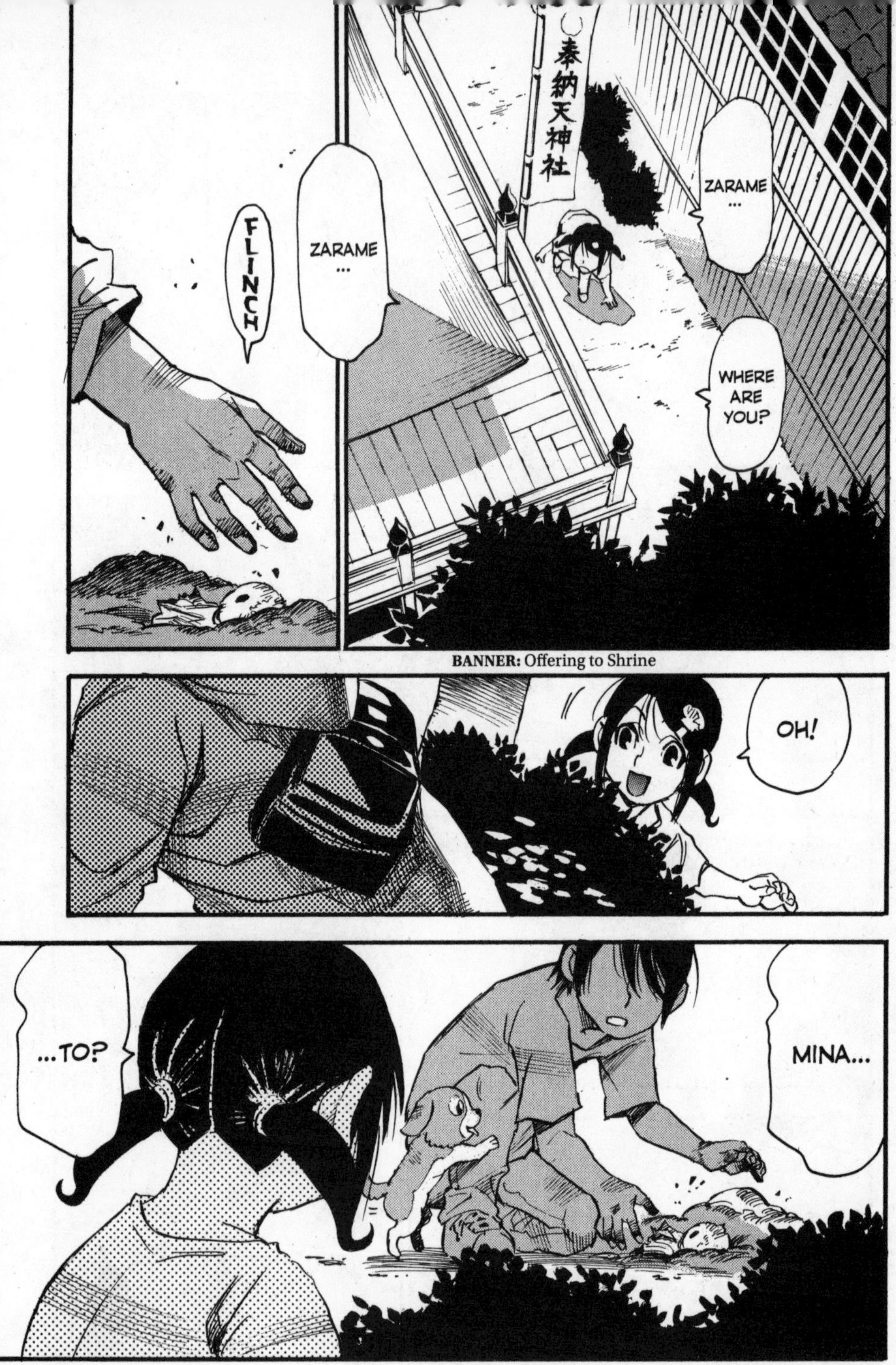
奉納天神社
ZARAME ...
WHERE ARE YOU?
ZARAME ...
FLINCH
OH!
MINA...
...TO?

BANNER: Offering to Shrine

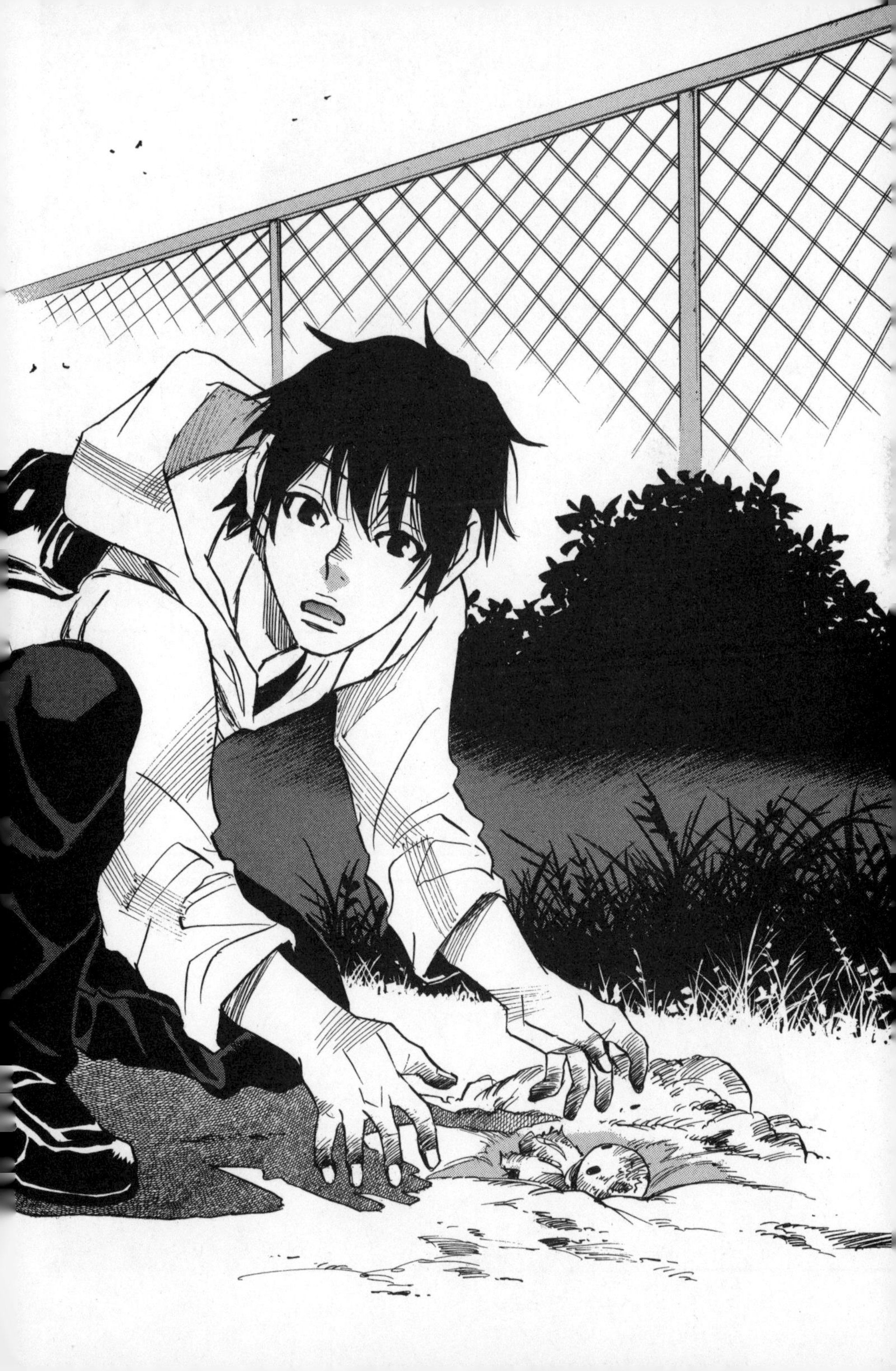

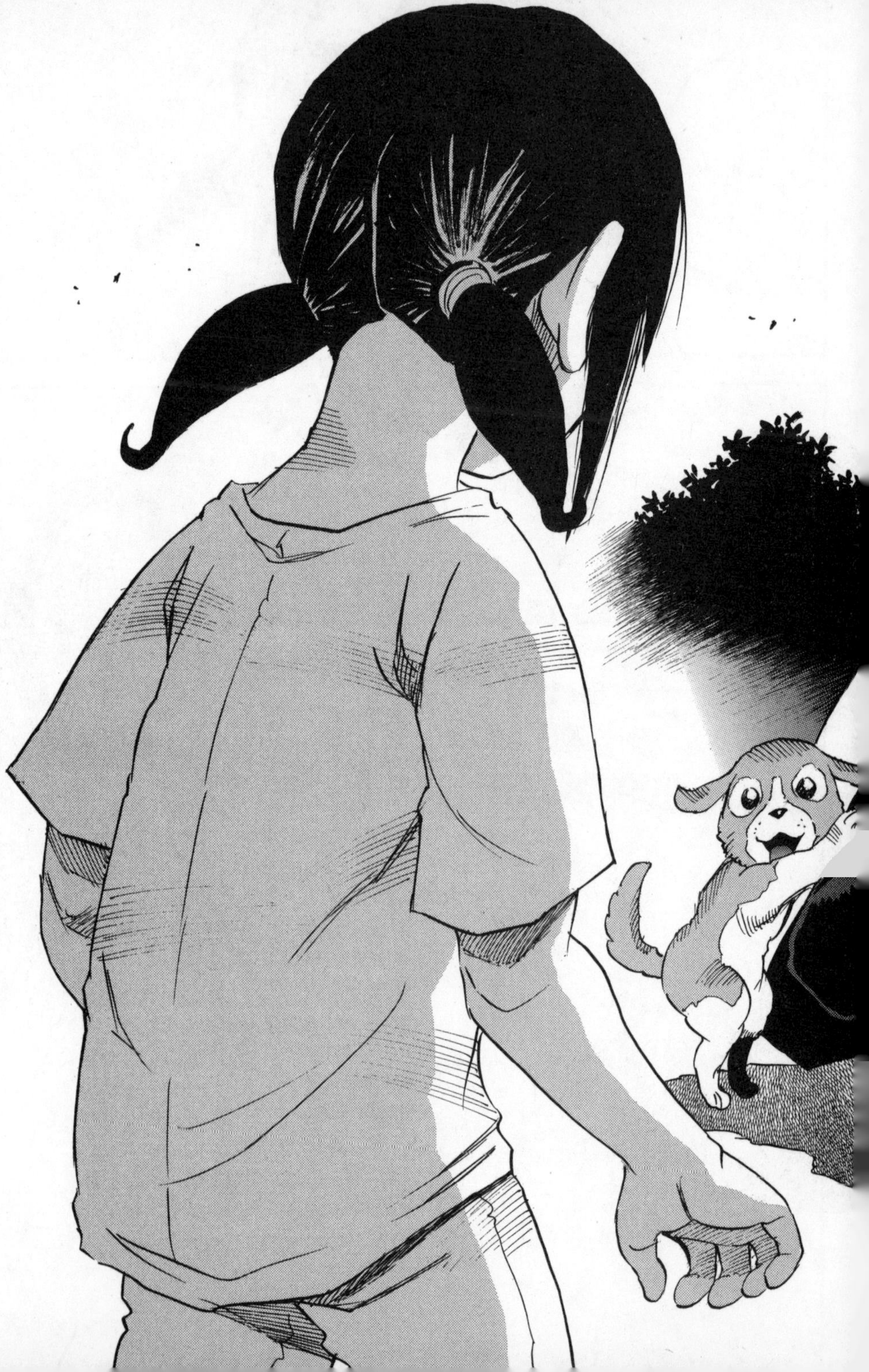

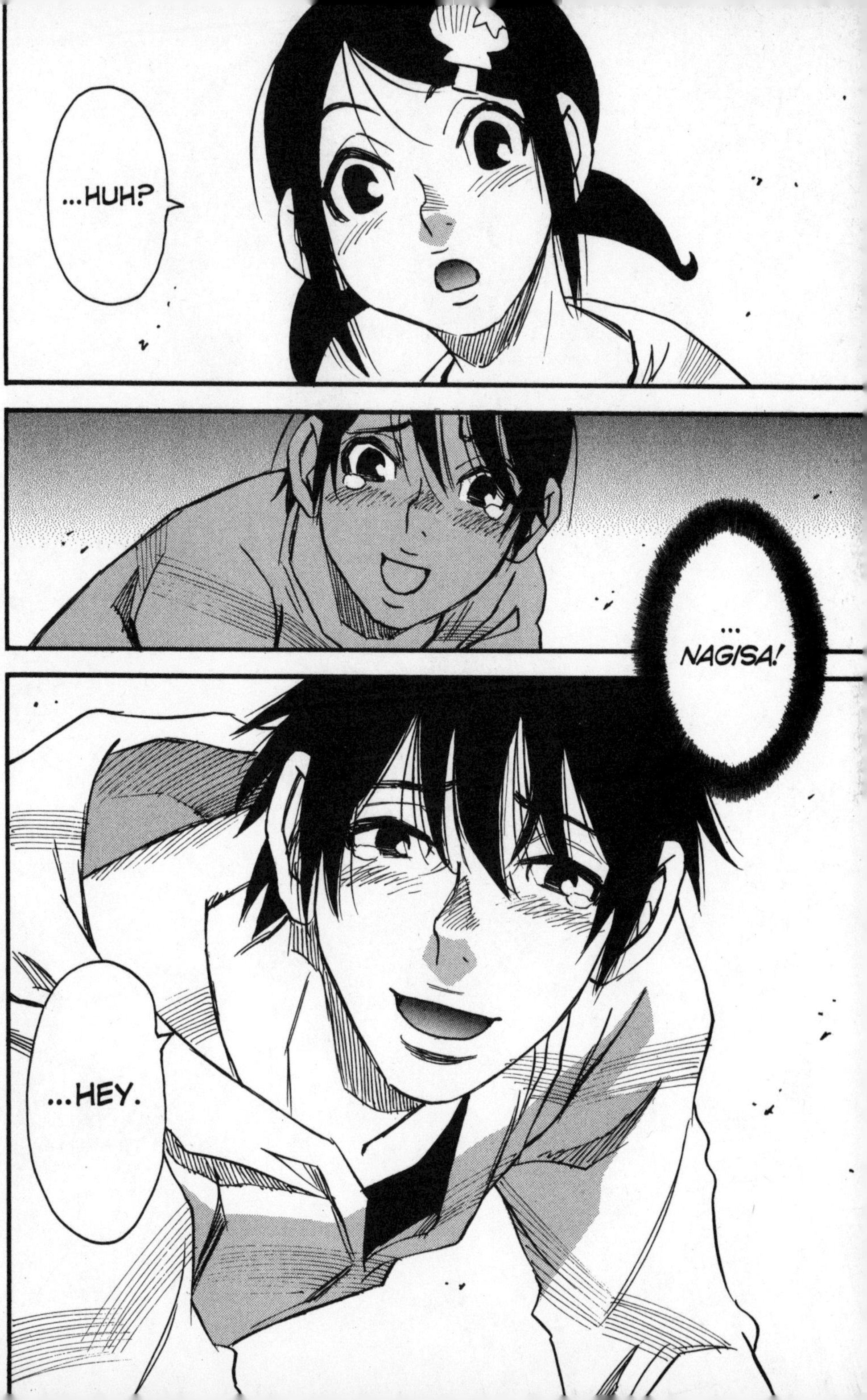
...HUH?
...NAGISA!
...HEY.

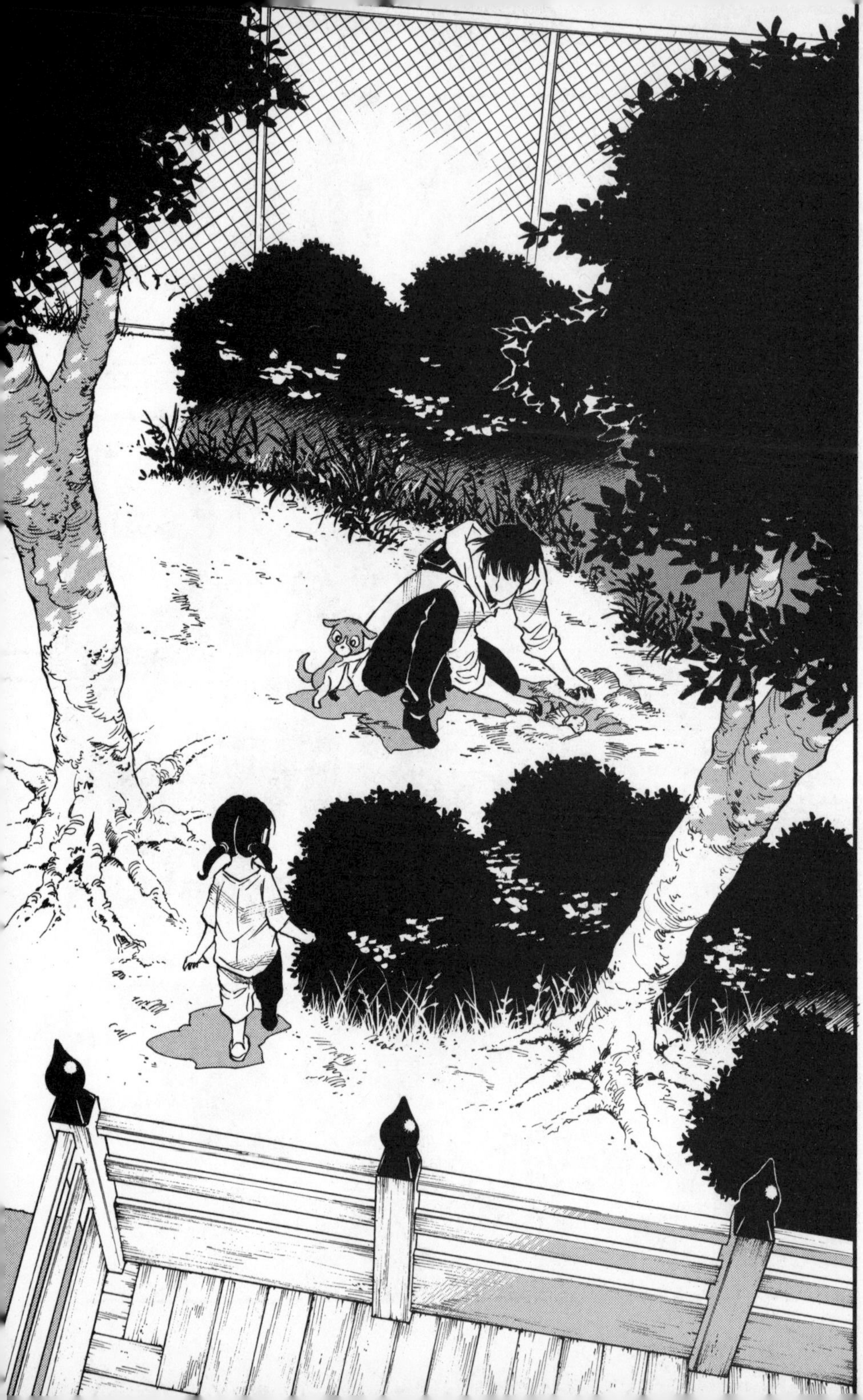

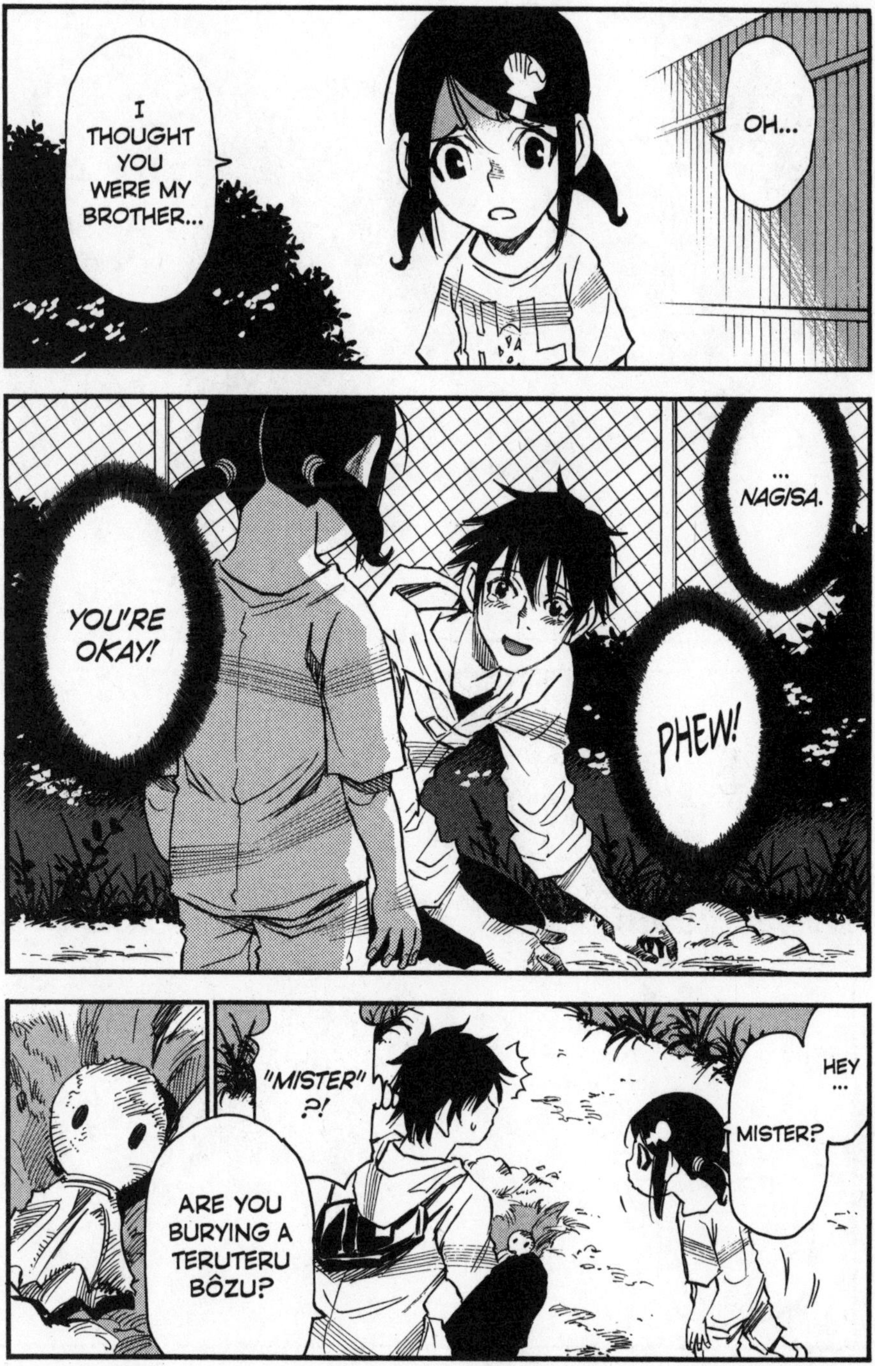
OH...
I THOUGHT YOU WERE MY BROTHER...
... NAGISA.
PHEW!
YOU'RE OKAY!
HEY ... MISTER?
"MISTER" ?!
ARE YOU BURYING A TERUTERU BÔZU?

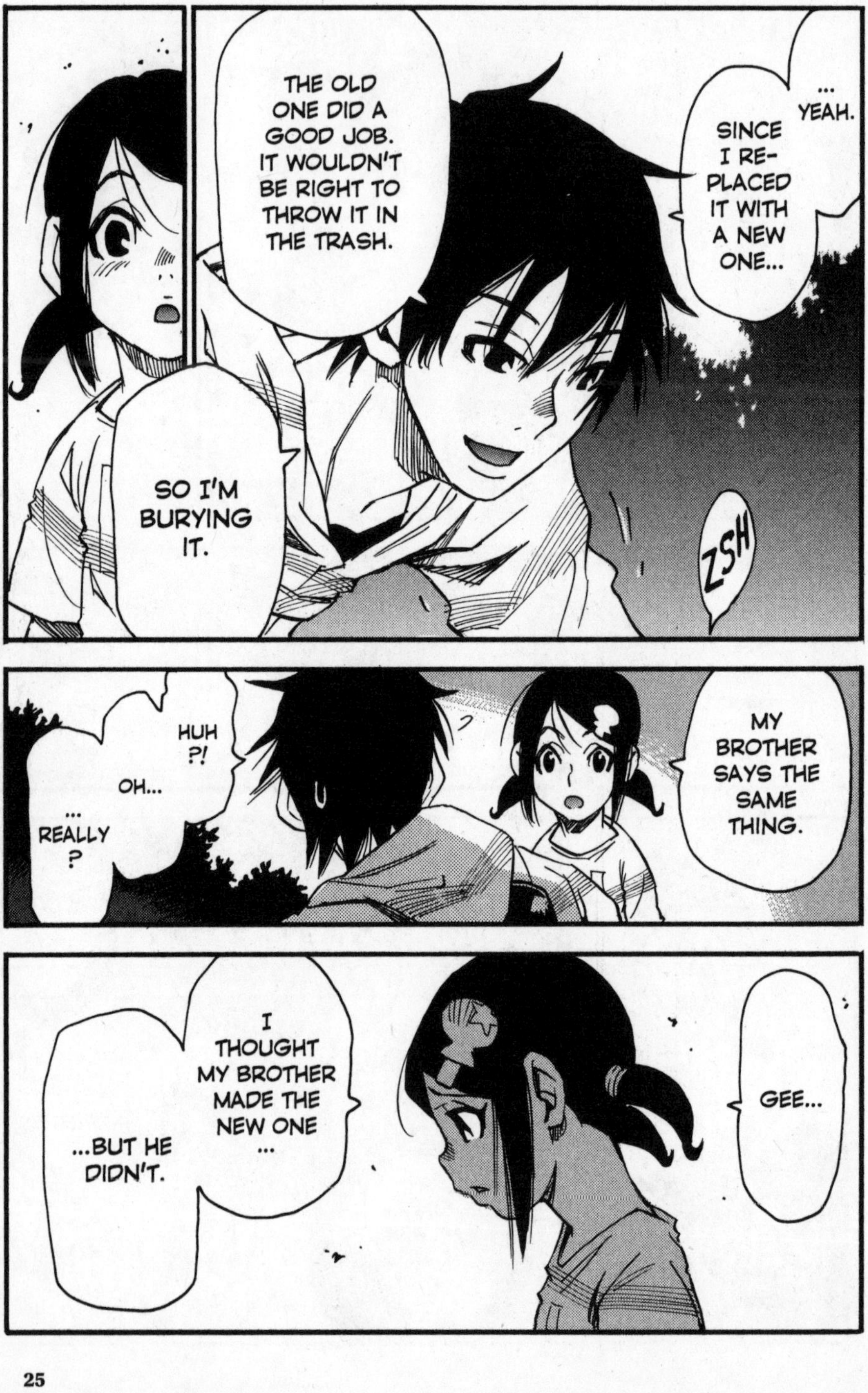
...YEAH.
SINCE I RE-PLACED IT WITH A NEW ONE...
THE OLD ONE DID A GOOD JOB. IT WOULDN'T BE RIGHT TO THROW IT IN THE TRASH.
ZSH
SO I'M BURYING IT.
MY BROTHER SAYS THE SAME THING.
HUH?!
OH...
...REALLY?
GEE...
I THOUGHT MY BROTHER MADE THE NEW ONE...
...BUT HE DIDN'T.

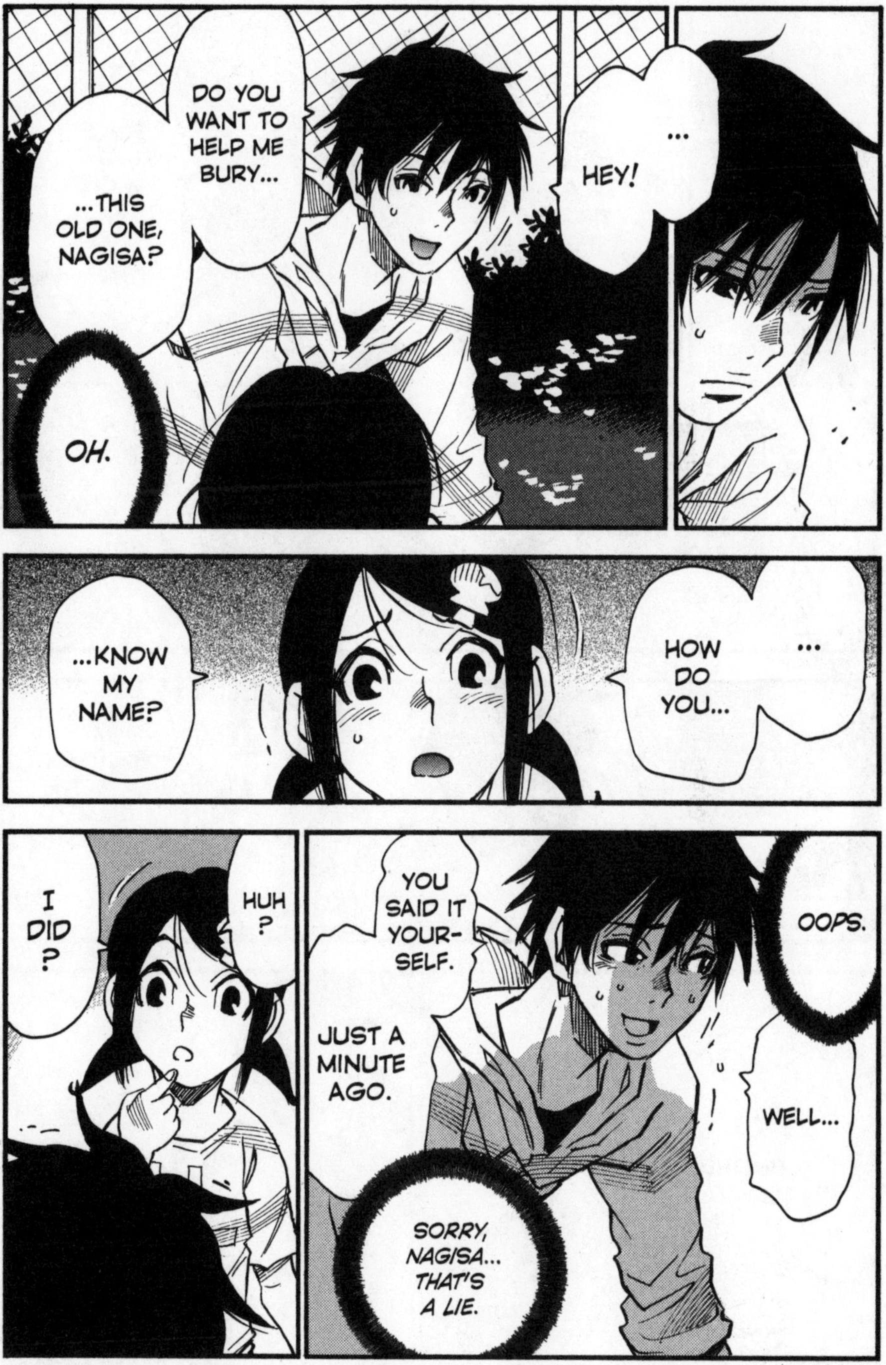
...
HEY!
DO YOU WANT TO HELP ME BURY...
...THIS OLD ONE, NAGISA?
OH.
...
HOW DO YOU...
...KNOW MY NAME?
OOPS.
YOU SAID IT YOURSELF.
WELL...
JUST A MINUTE AGO.
SORRY, NAGISA... THAT'S A LIE.
HUH?
I DID?

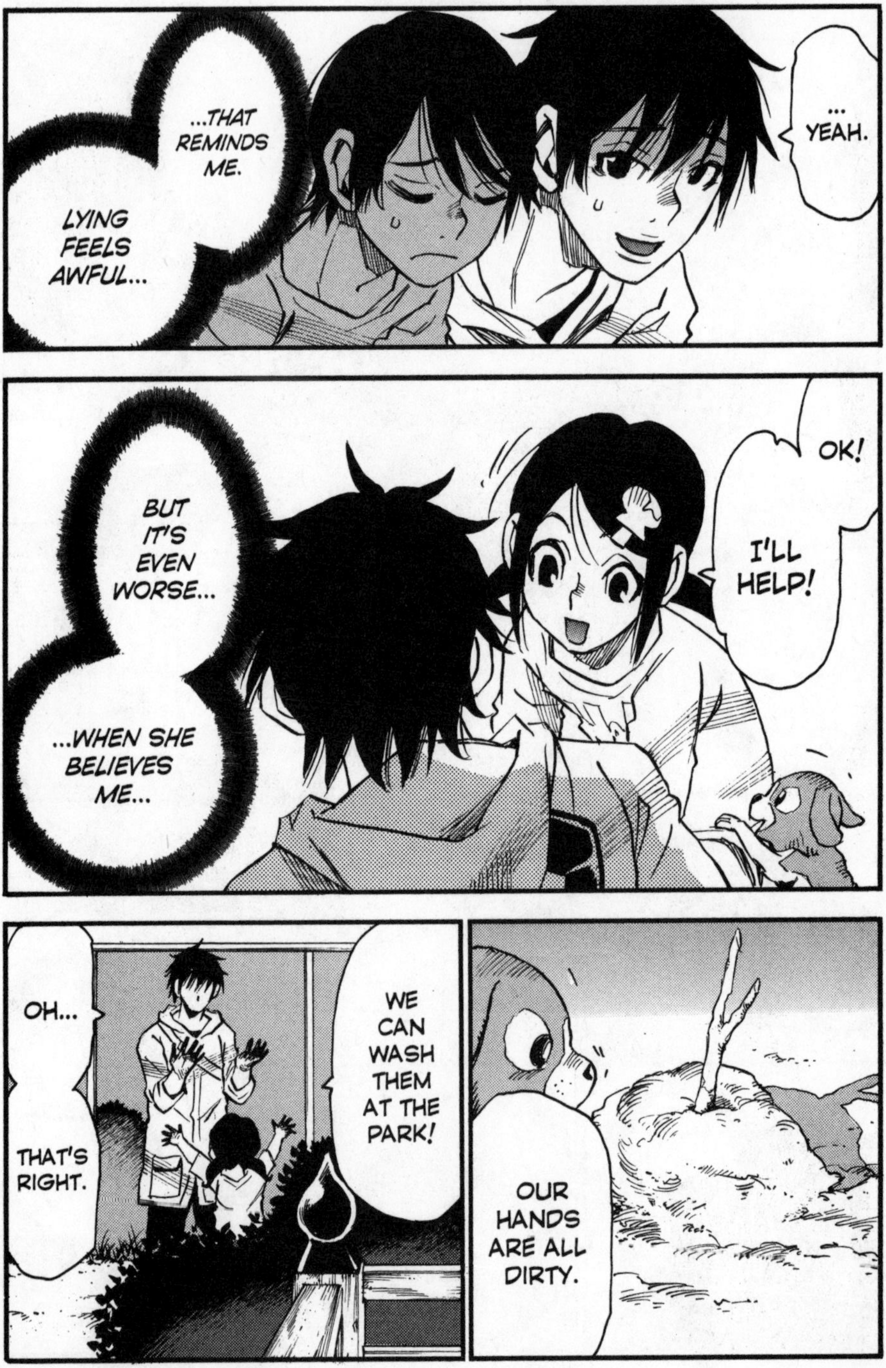
... YEAH.
...THAT REMINDS ME.
LYING FEELS AWFUL...
OK!
I'LL HELP!
BUT IT'S EVEN WORSE...
...WHEN SHE BELIEVES ME...
OUR HANDS ARE ALL DIRTY.
WE CAN WASH THEM AT THE PARK!
OH...
THAT'S RIGHT.

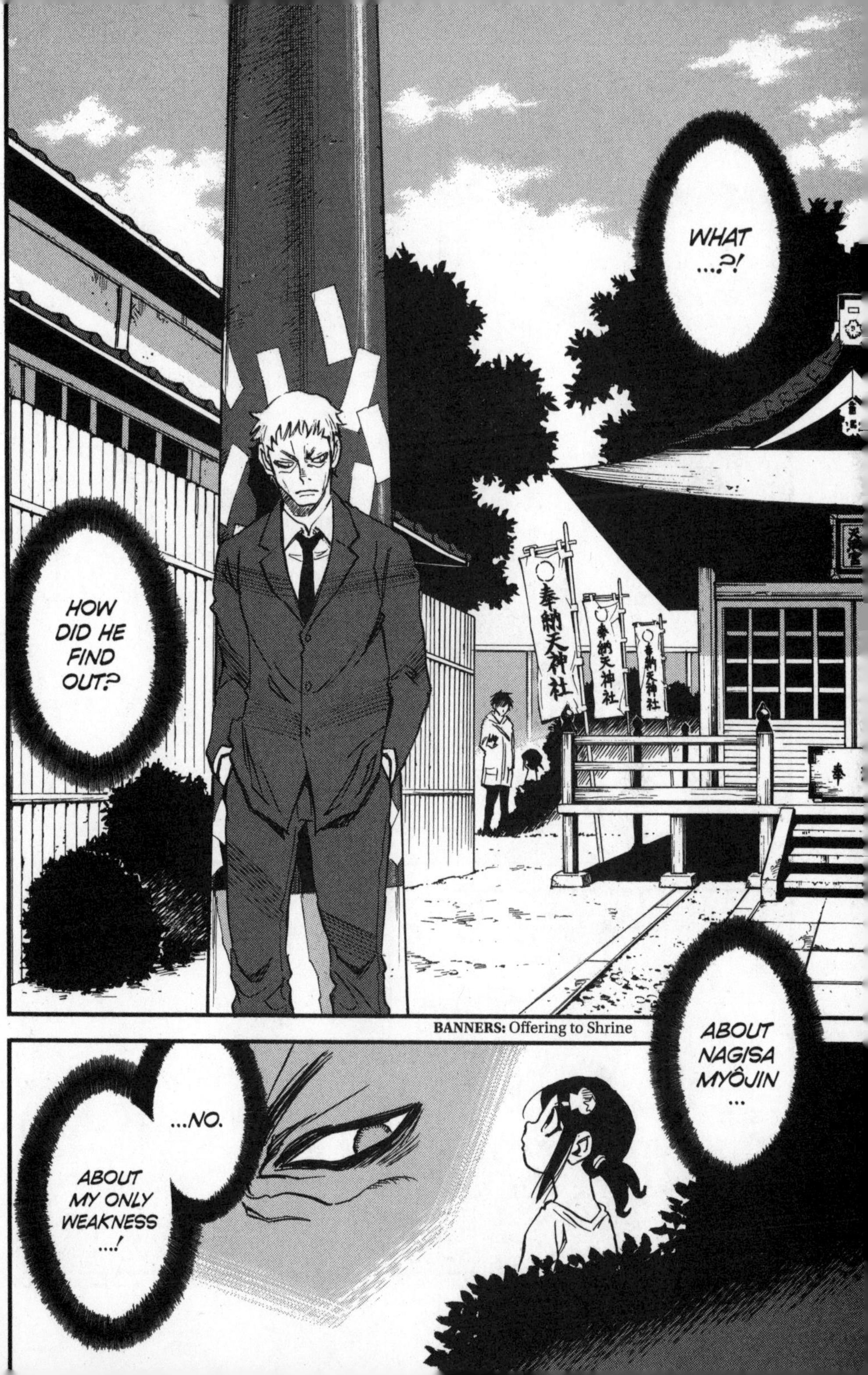
WHAT ...?!
奉納天神社
奉納天神社
奉納天神社
HOW DID HE FIND OUT?
ABOUT NAGISA MYÔJIN ...
...NO.
ABOUT MY ONLY WEAKNESS ...!
BANNERS: Offering to Shrine

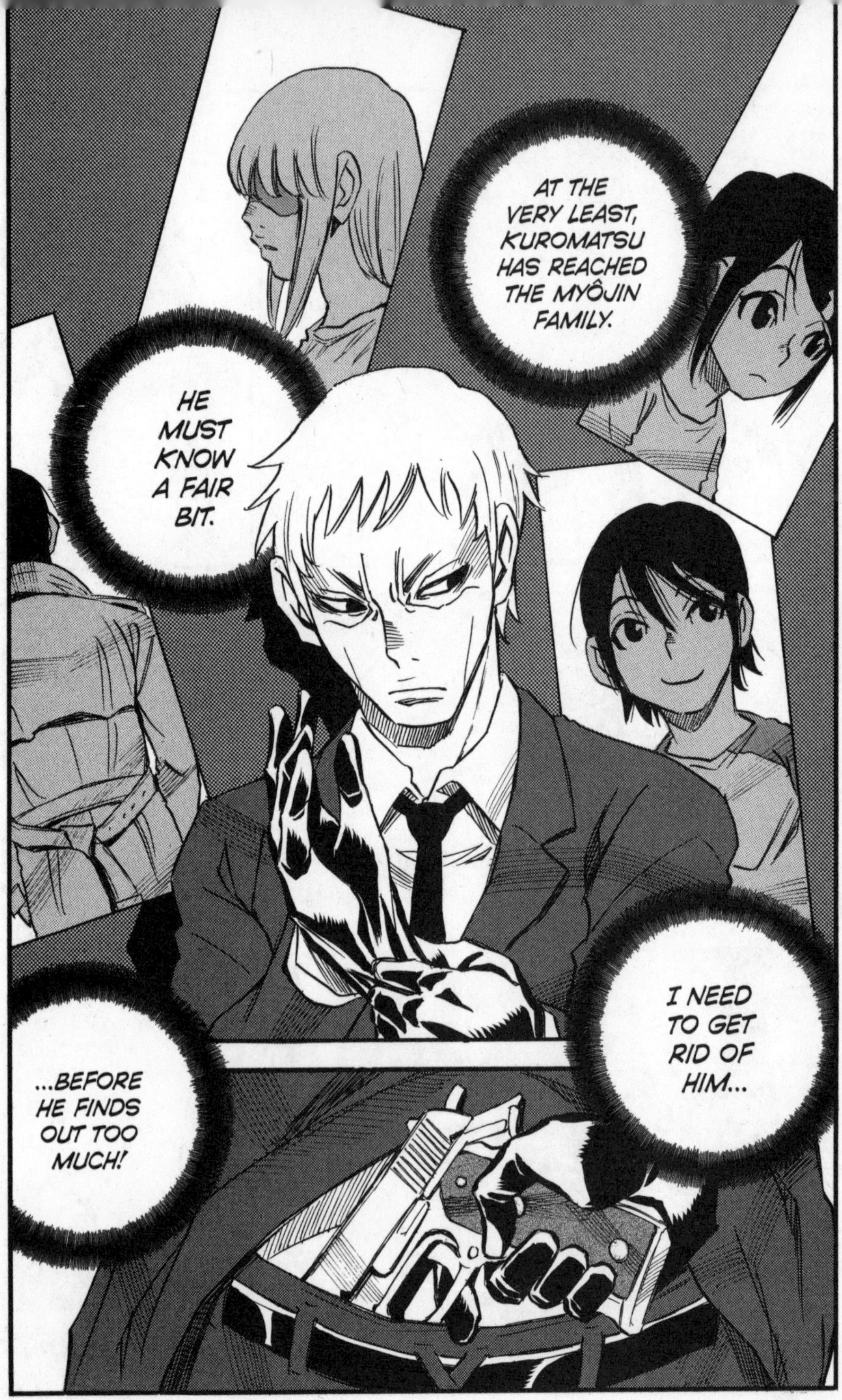
AT THE VERY LEAST, KUROMATSU HAS REACHED THE MYÔJIN FAMILY.
HE MUST KNOW A FAIR BIT.
I NEED TO GET RID OF HIM...
...BEFORE HE FINDS OUT TOO MUCH!

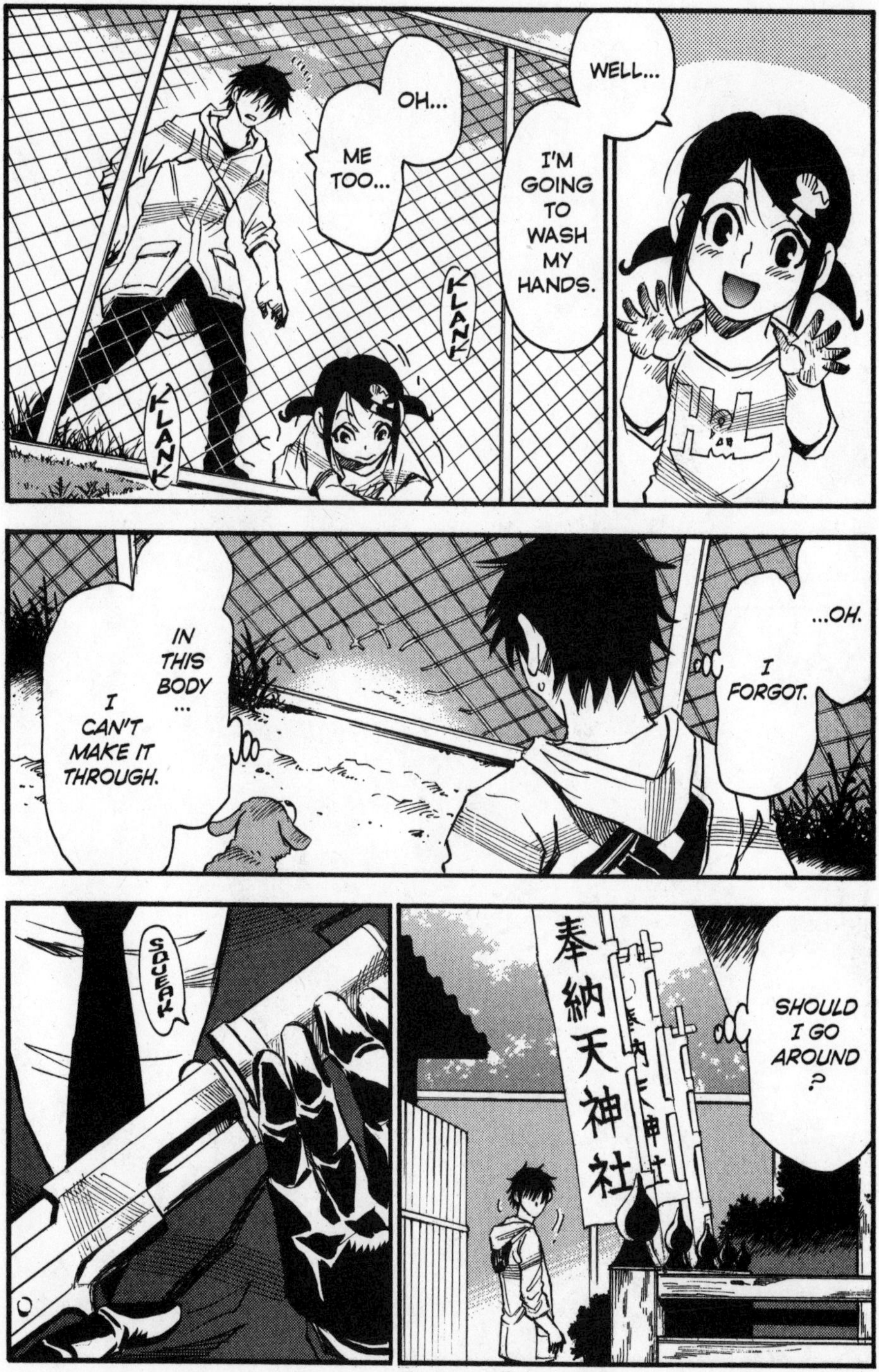
WELL...
I'M GOING TO WASH MY HANDS.
OH...
ME TOO...
KLANK
KLANK
...OH.
I FORGOT.
IN THIS BODY...
I CAN'T MAKE IT THROUGH.
SHOULD I GO AROUND?
奉納天神社
SQUEAK

BANNERS: Offering to Shrine

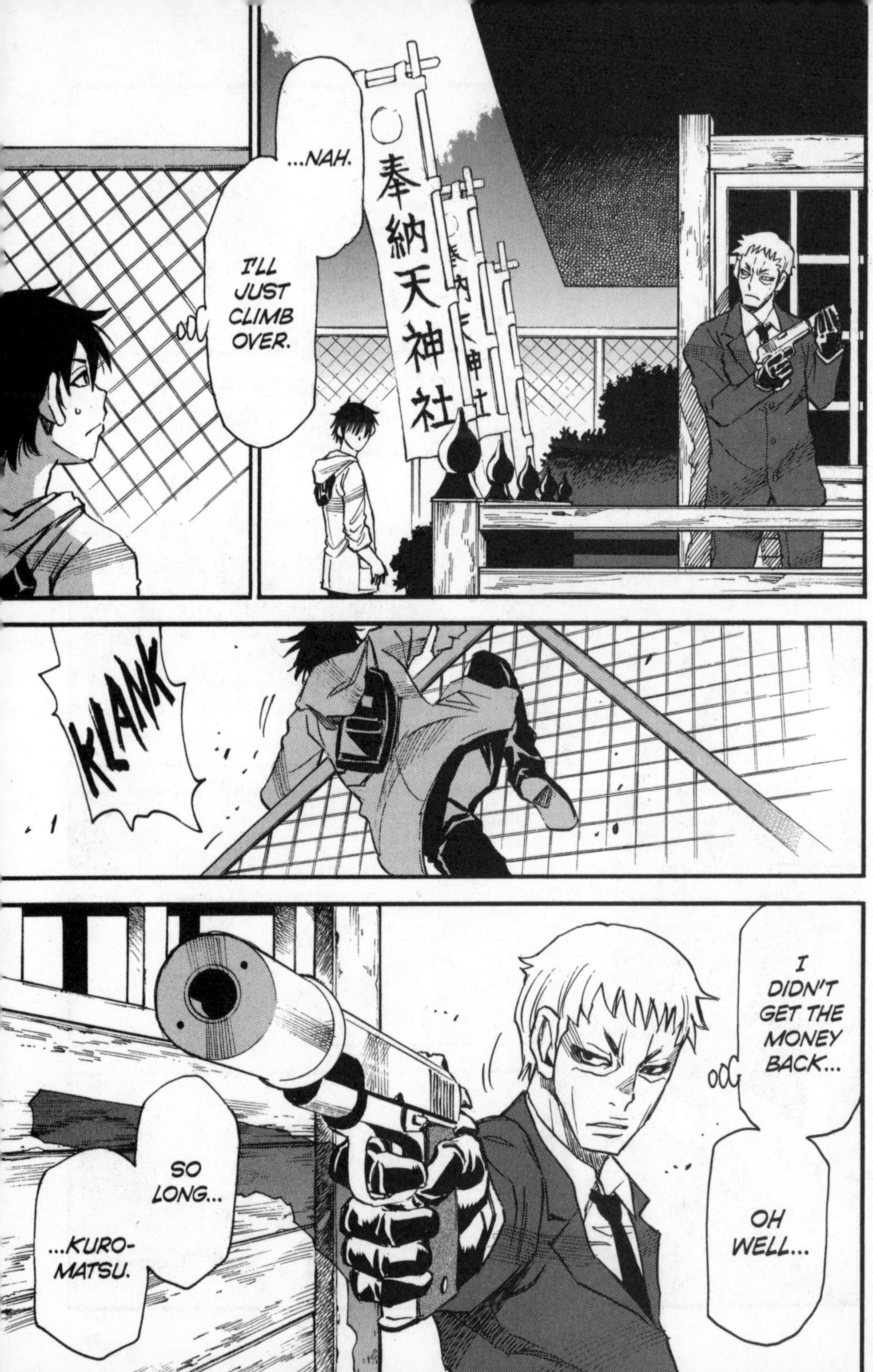
...NAH.
I'LL JUST CLIMB OVER.
奉納天神社
KLANK
I DIDN'T GET THE MONEY BACK...
...
OH WELL...
...
SO LONG...
...KURO-MATSU.

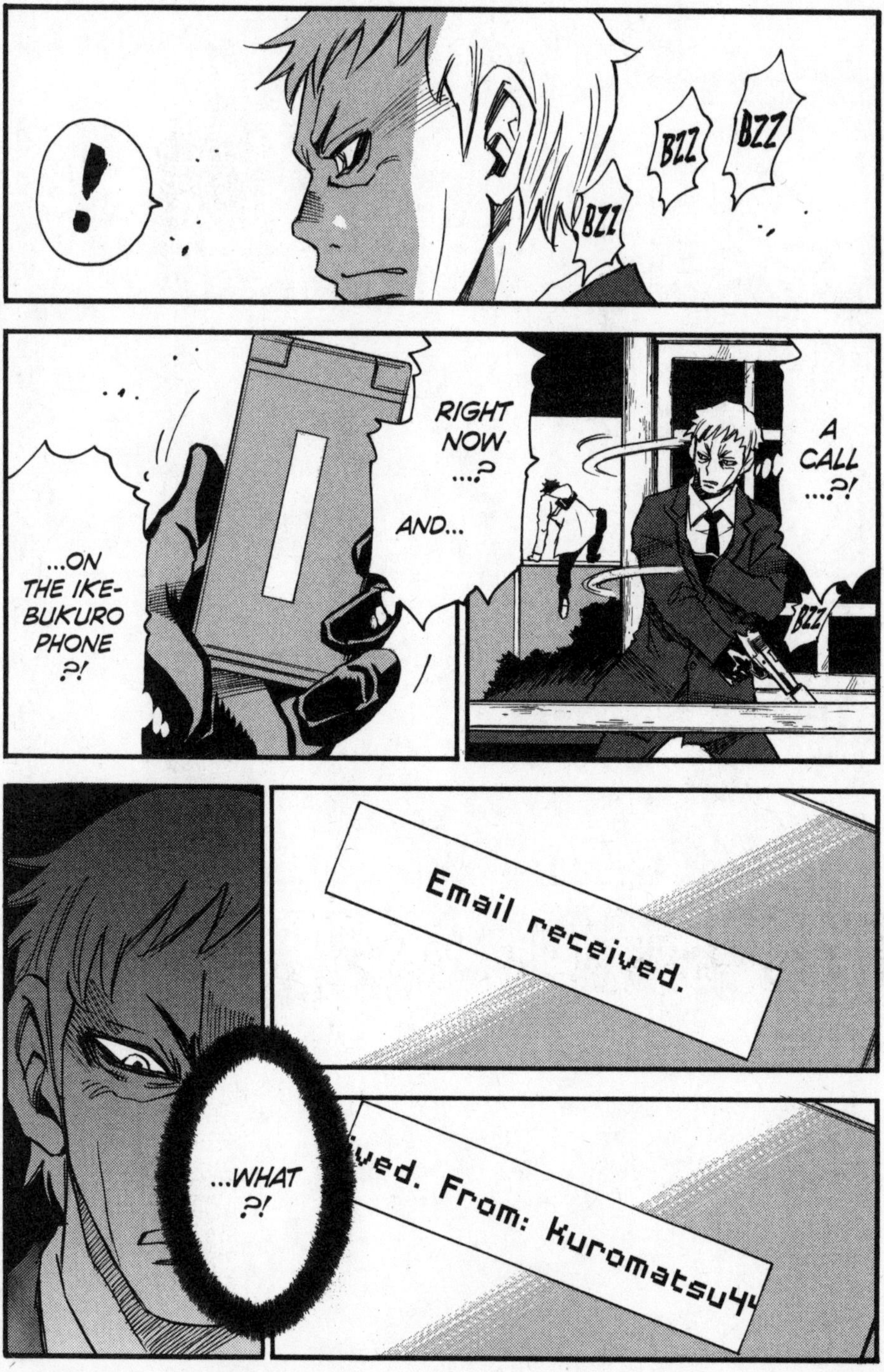
BZZ
BZZ
BZZ
!
A CALL ...?!
BZZ
RIGHT NOW ...?
AND...
...ON THE IKE-BUKURO PHONE ?!
Email received.
ived. From: Kuromatsu44
...WHAT ?!

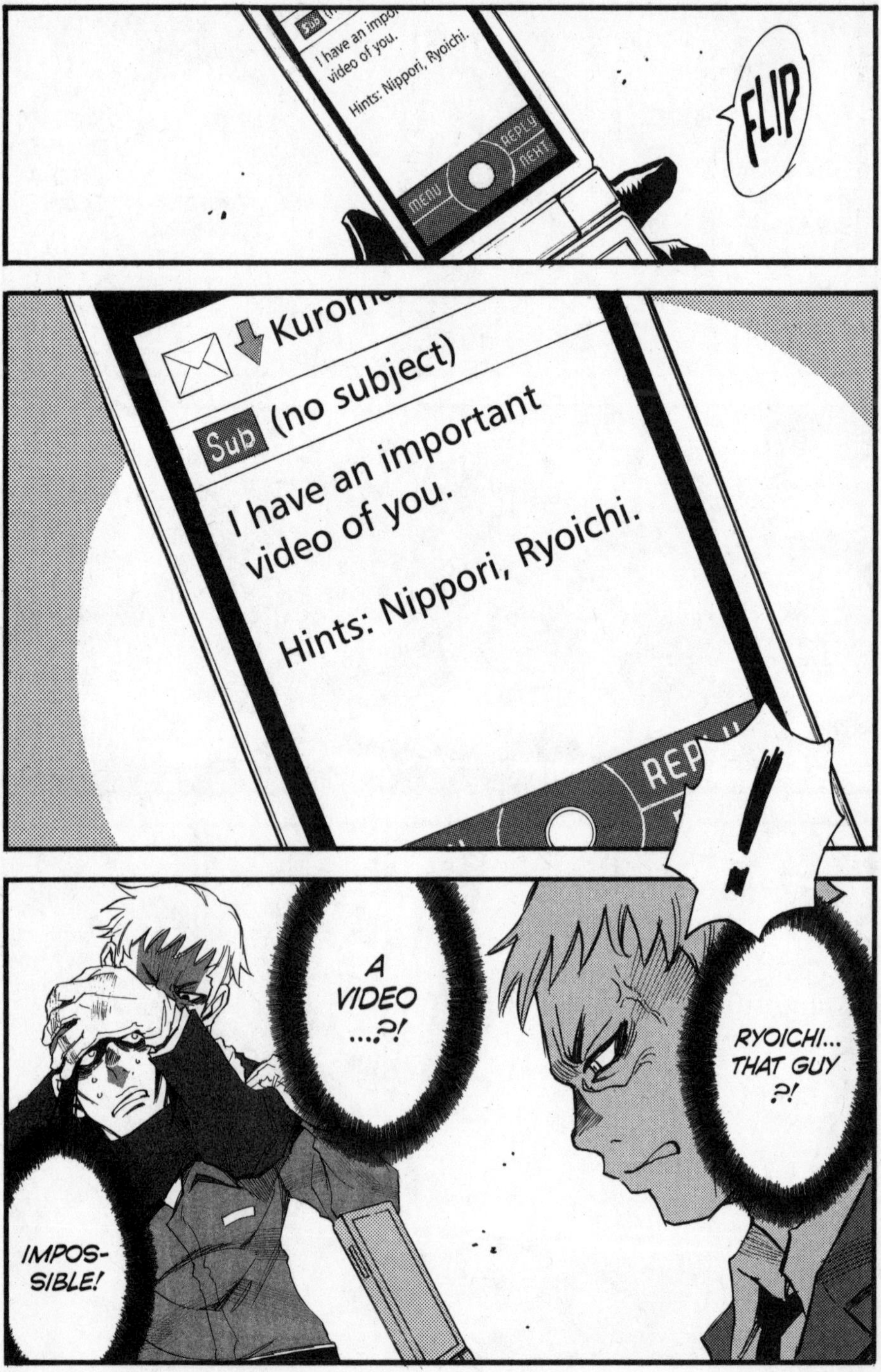
FLIP
I have an impo
video of you.
Hints: Nippori, Ryoichi.
REPLY
NEXT
MENU
(no subject)
Sub
I have an important
video of you.
Hints: Nippori, Ryoichi.
!
RYOICHI... THAT GUY ?!
A VIDEO ...?!
IMPOS-SIBLE!

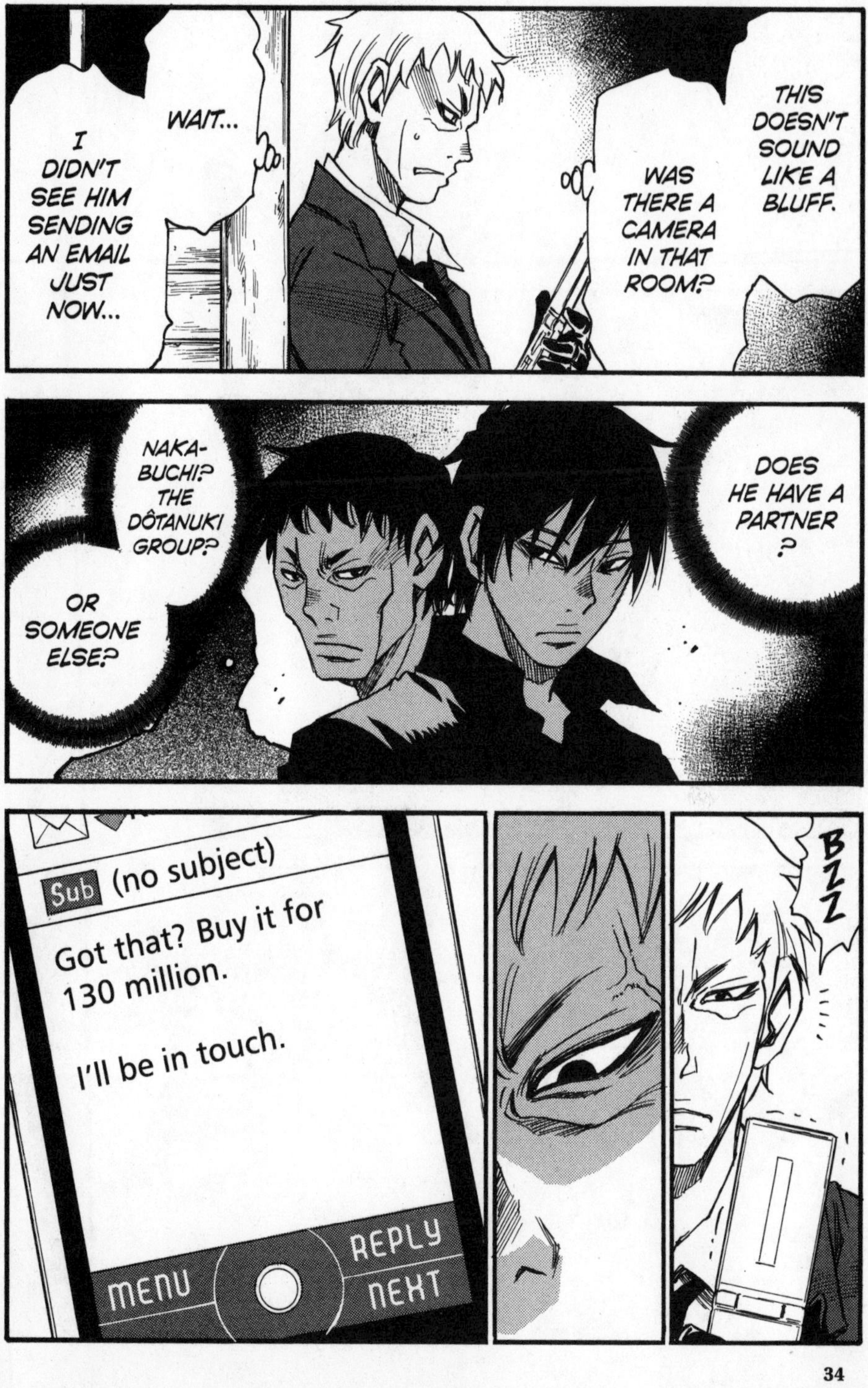
THIS DOESN'T SOUND LIKE A BLUFF.
WAS THERE A CAMERA IN THAT ROOM?
WAIT...
I DIDN'T SEE HIM SENDING AN EMAIL JUST NOW...
DOES HE HAVE A PARTNER?
NAKA-BUCHI? THE DÔTANUKI GROUP?
OR SOMEONE ELSE?
BZZ
Sub (no subject)
Got that? Buy it for 130 million.
I'll be in touch.
REPLY
MENU
NEXT

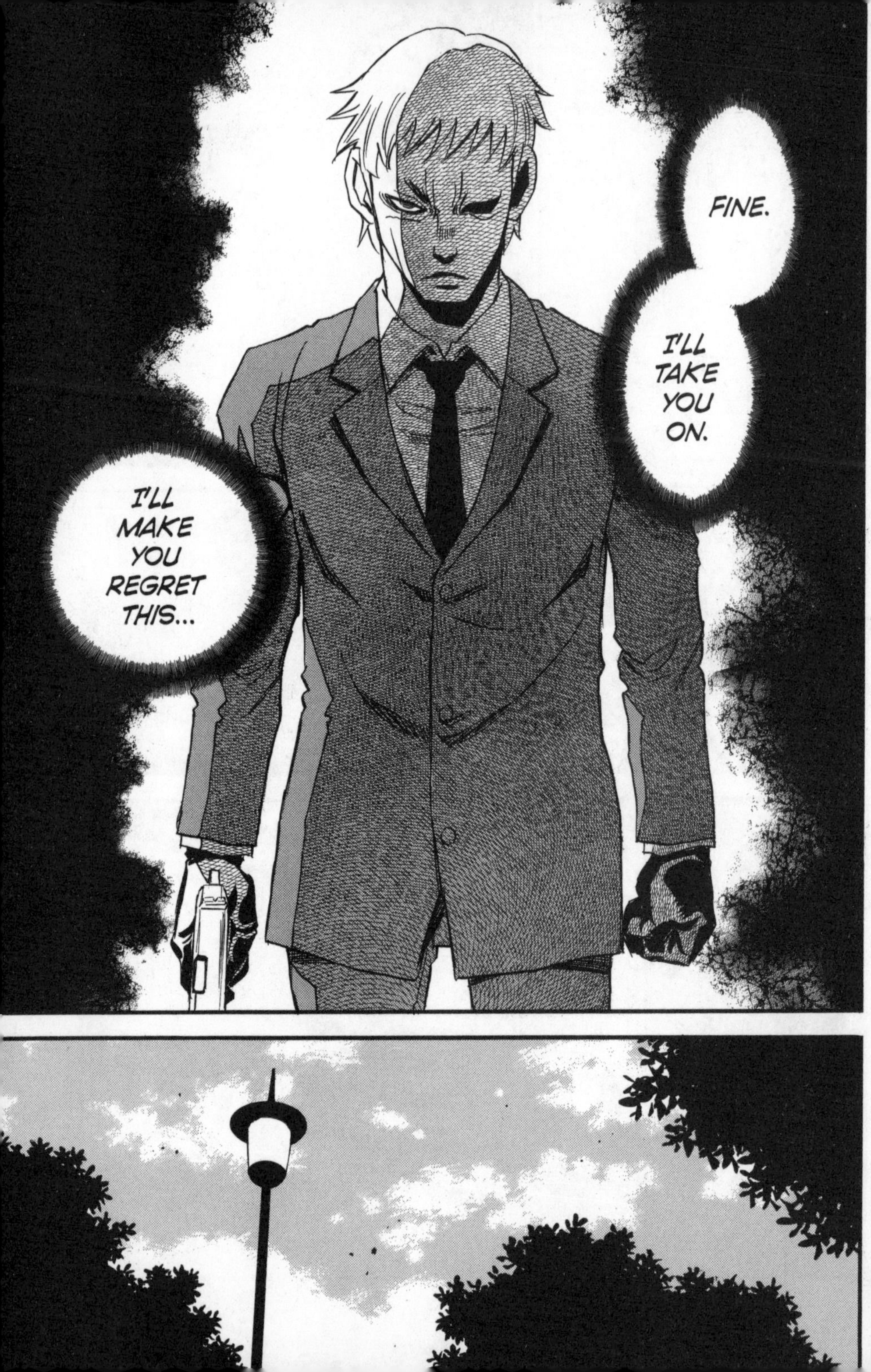
FINE.
I'LL TAKE YOU ON.
I'LL MAKE YOU REGRET THIS...

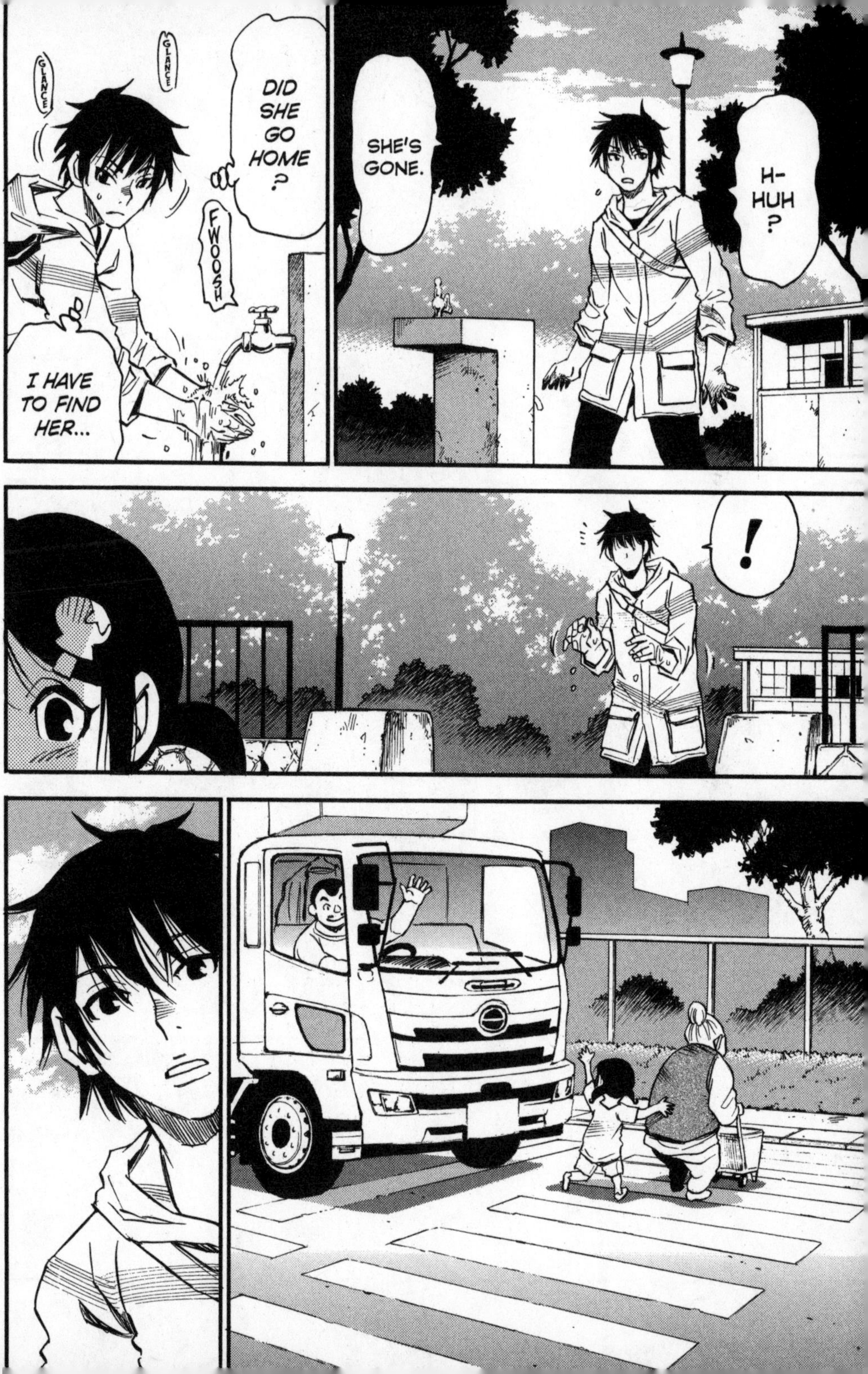
H-HUH?
SHE'S GONE.
DID SHE GO HOME?
GLANCE
GLANCE
FWOOSH
I HAVE TO FIND HER...
!

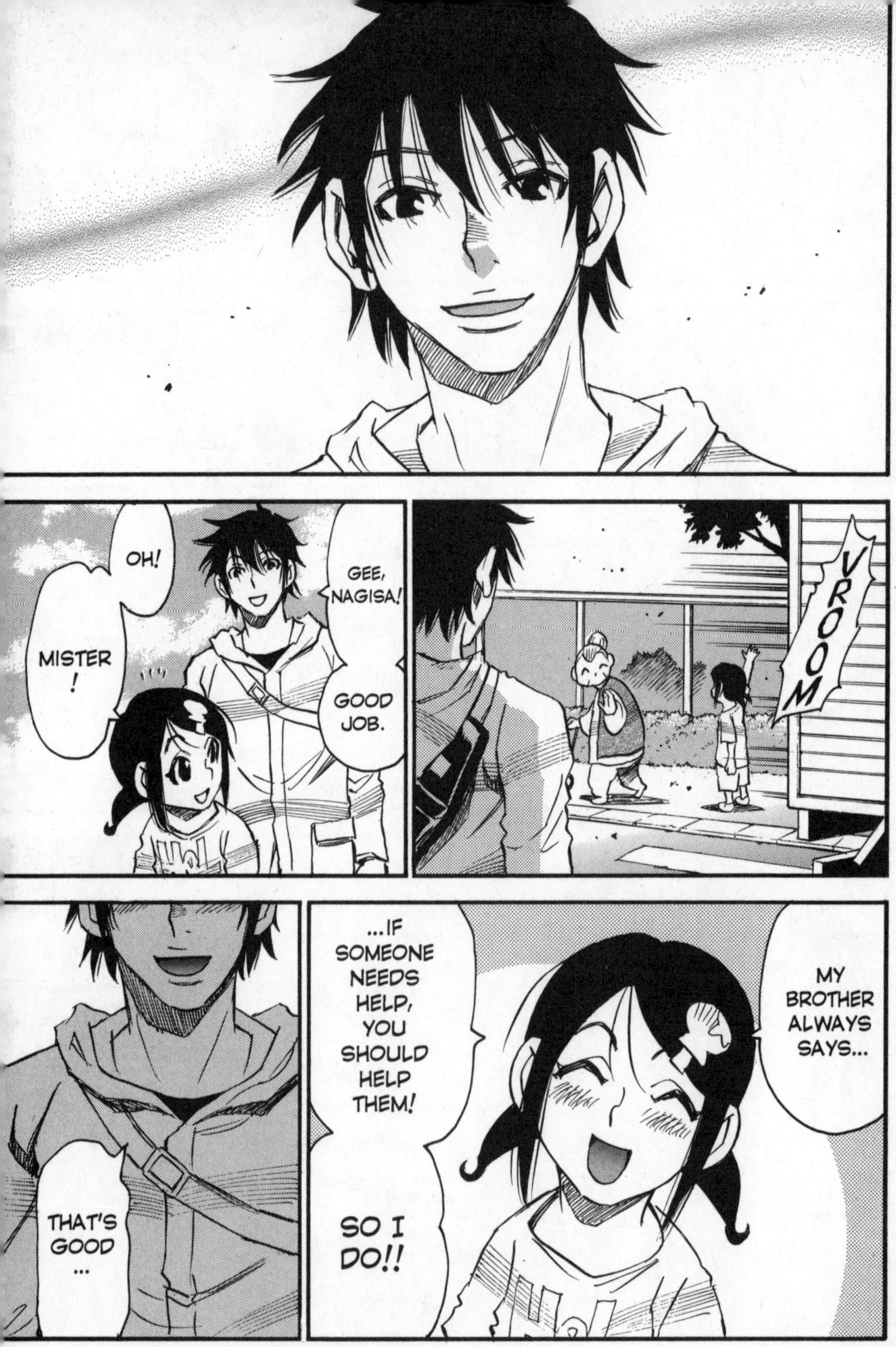
...
VROOM
GEE, NAGISA!
GOOD JOB.
OH!
MISTER!
MY BROTHER ALWAYS SAYS...
...IF SOMEONE NEEDS HELP, YOU SHOULD HELP THEM!
SO I DO!!
THAT'S GOOD ...

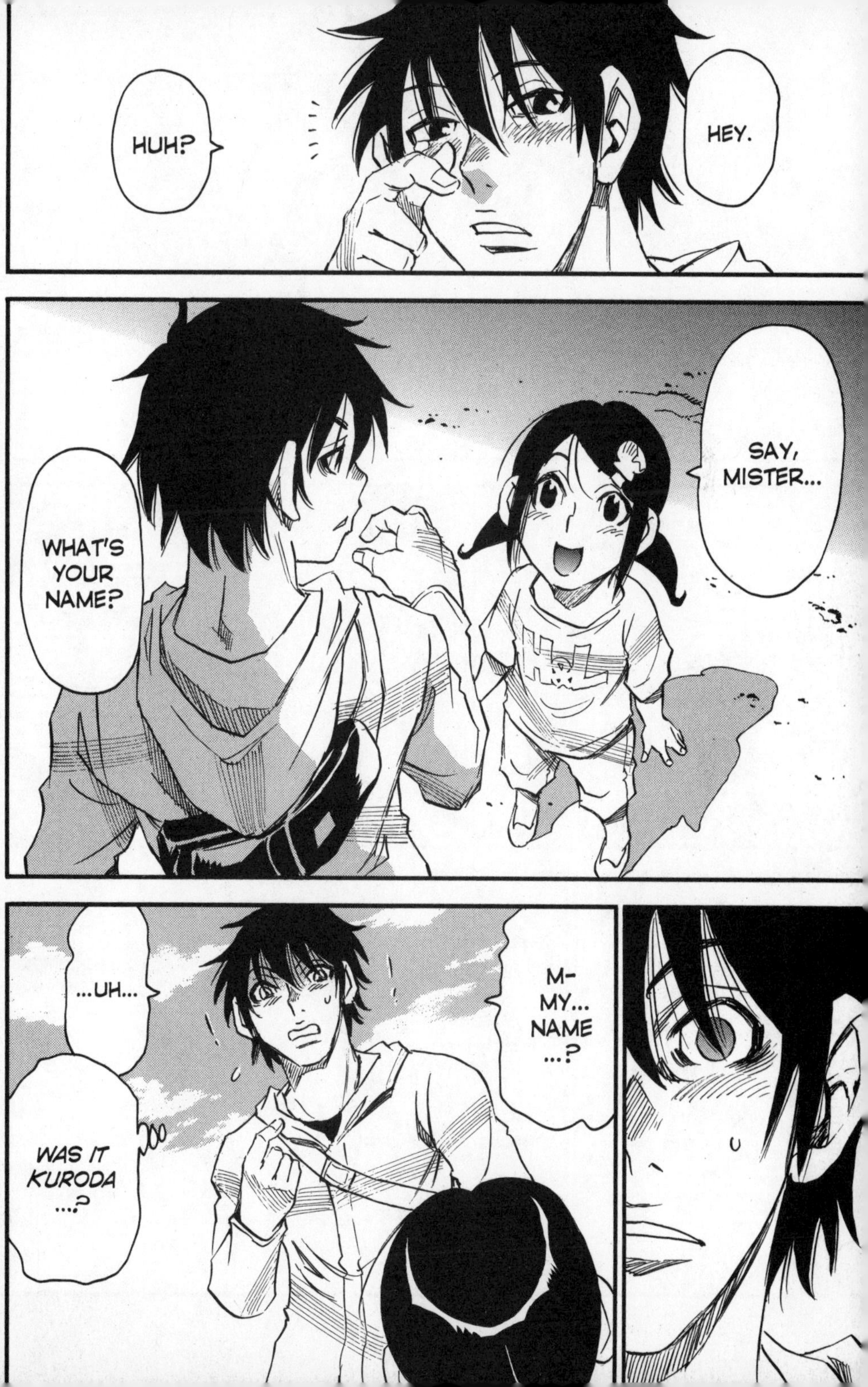
HEY.
HUH?
SAY, MISTER...
WHAT'S YOUR NAME?
M- MY... NAME ...?
...UH...
WAS IT KURODA ...?

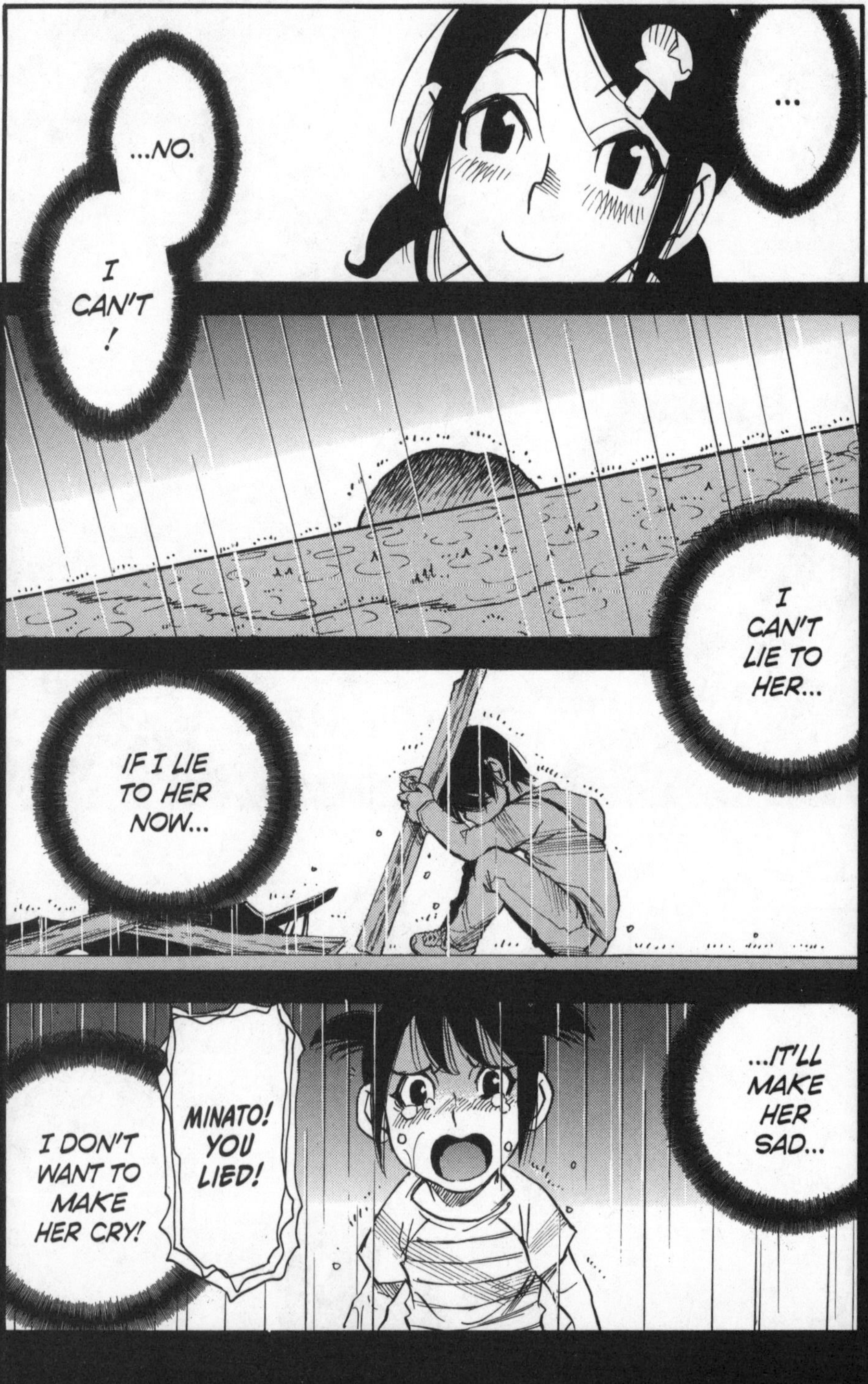
...
...NO.
I CAN'T!
I CAN'T LIE TO HER...
IF I LIE TO HER NOW...
...IT'LL MAKE HER SAD...
MINATO! YOU LIED!
I DON'T WANT TO MAKE HER CRY!

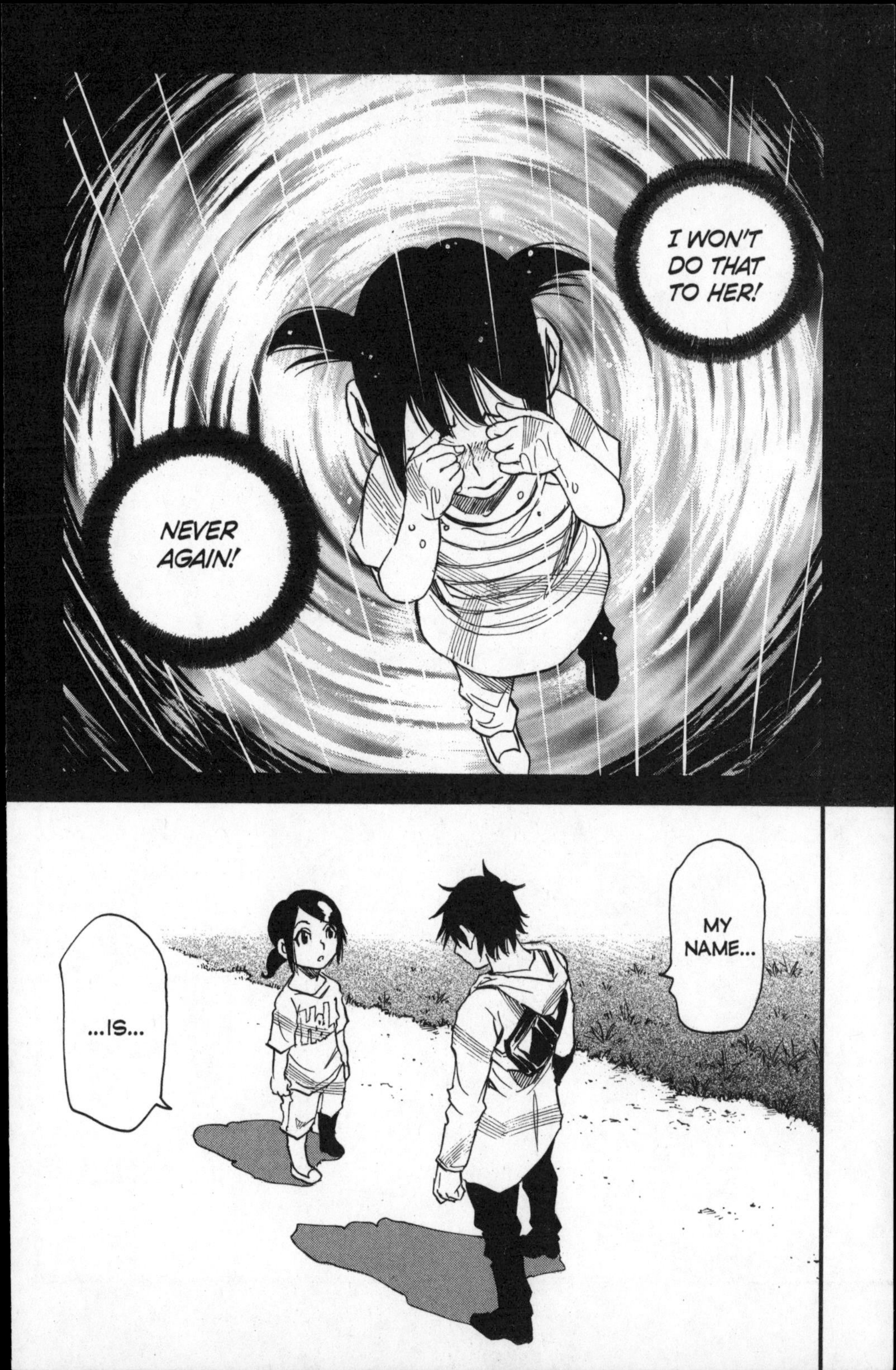
I WON'T DO THAT TO HER!
NEVER AGAIN!
MY NAME...
...IS...

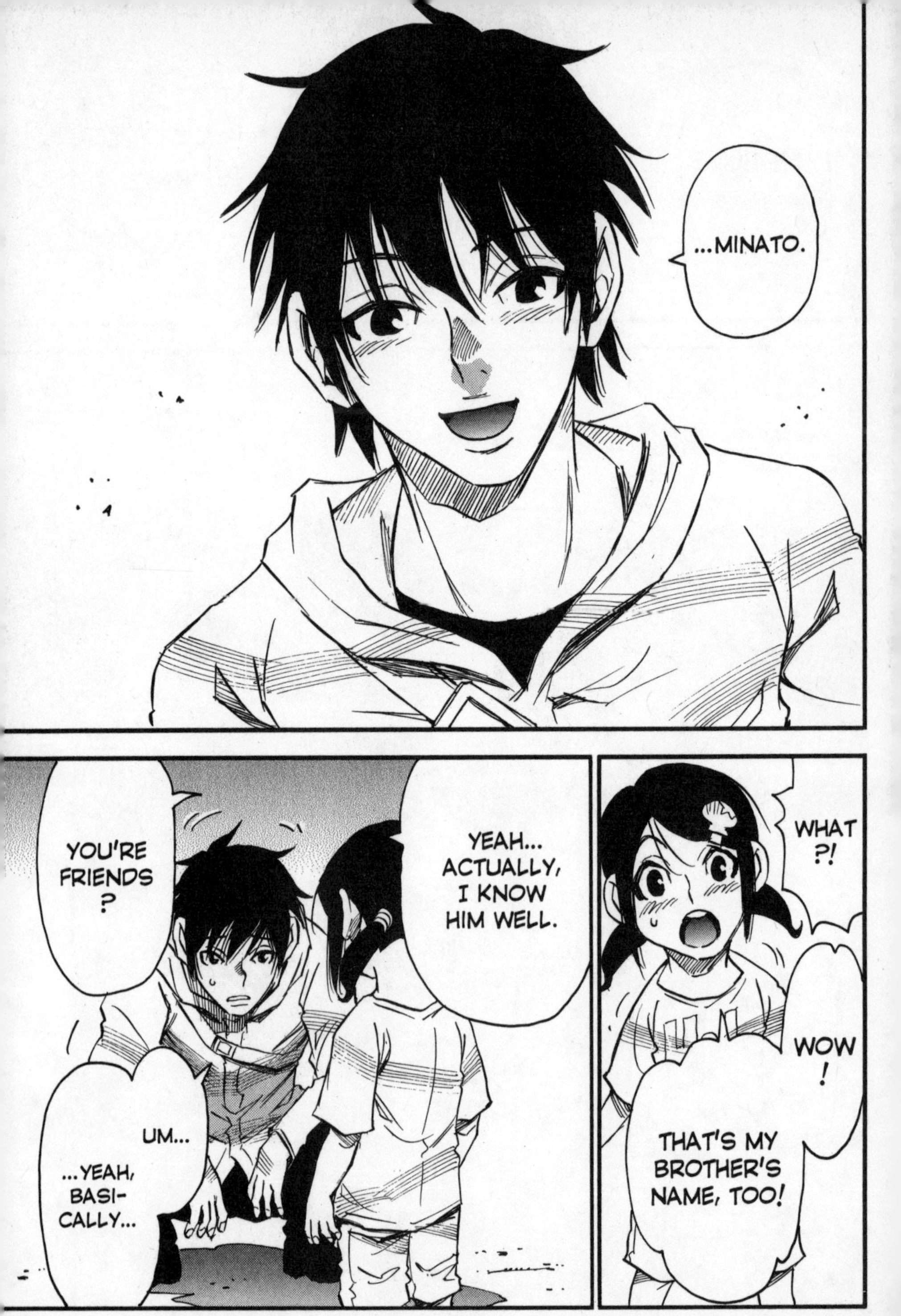
...MINATO.
WHAT ?!
WOW !
THAT'S MY BROTHER'S NAME, TOO!
YEAH... ACTUALLY, I KNOW HIM WELL.
YOU'RE FRIENDS ?
UM...
...YEAH, BASI- CALLY...

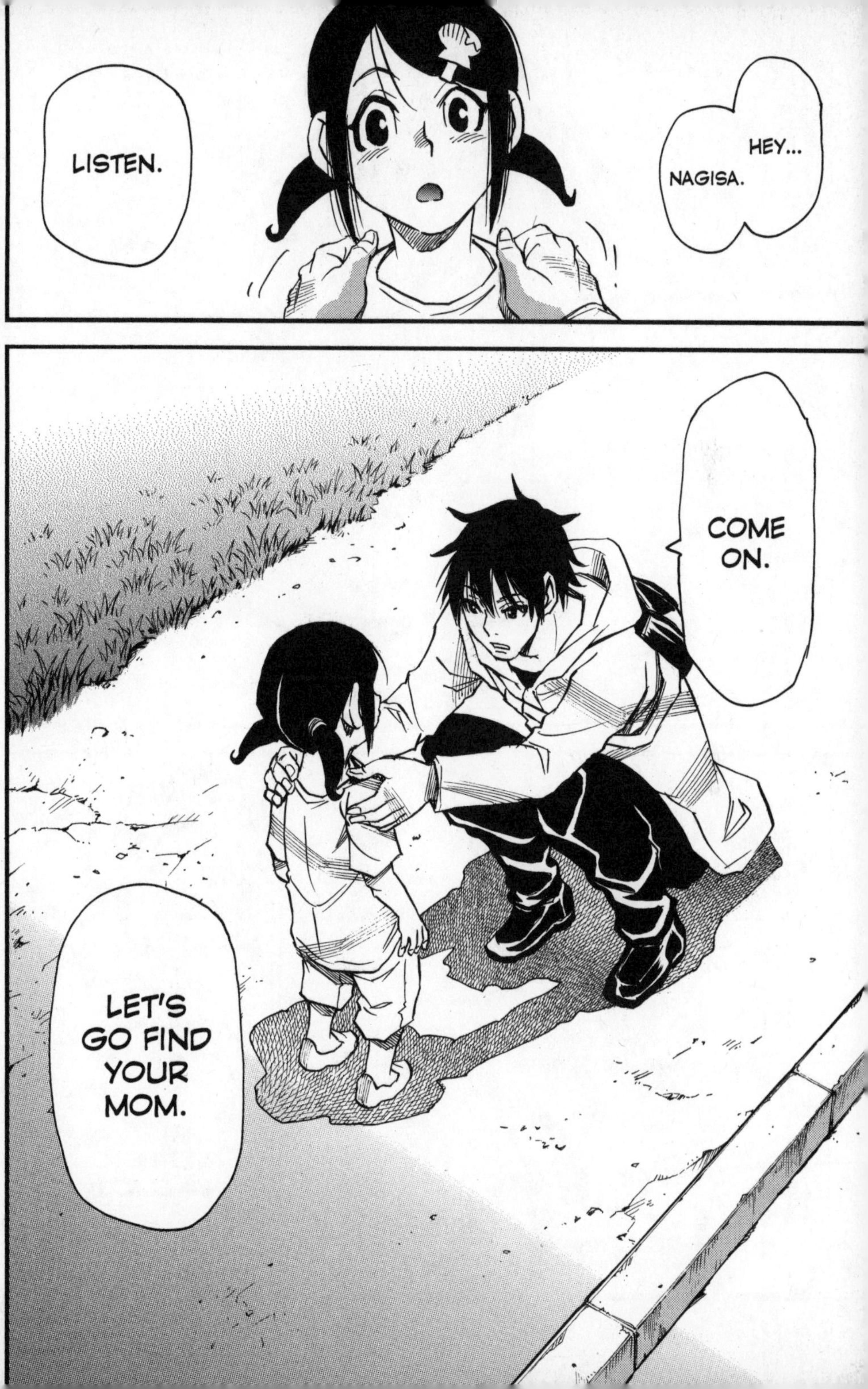
HEY... NAGISA.
LISTEN.
COME ON.
LET'S GO FIND YOUR MOM.

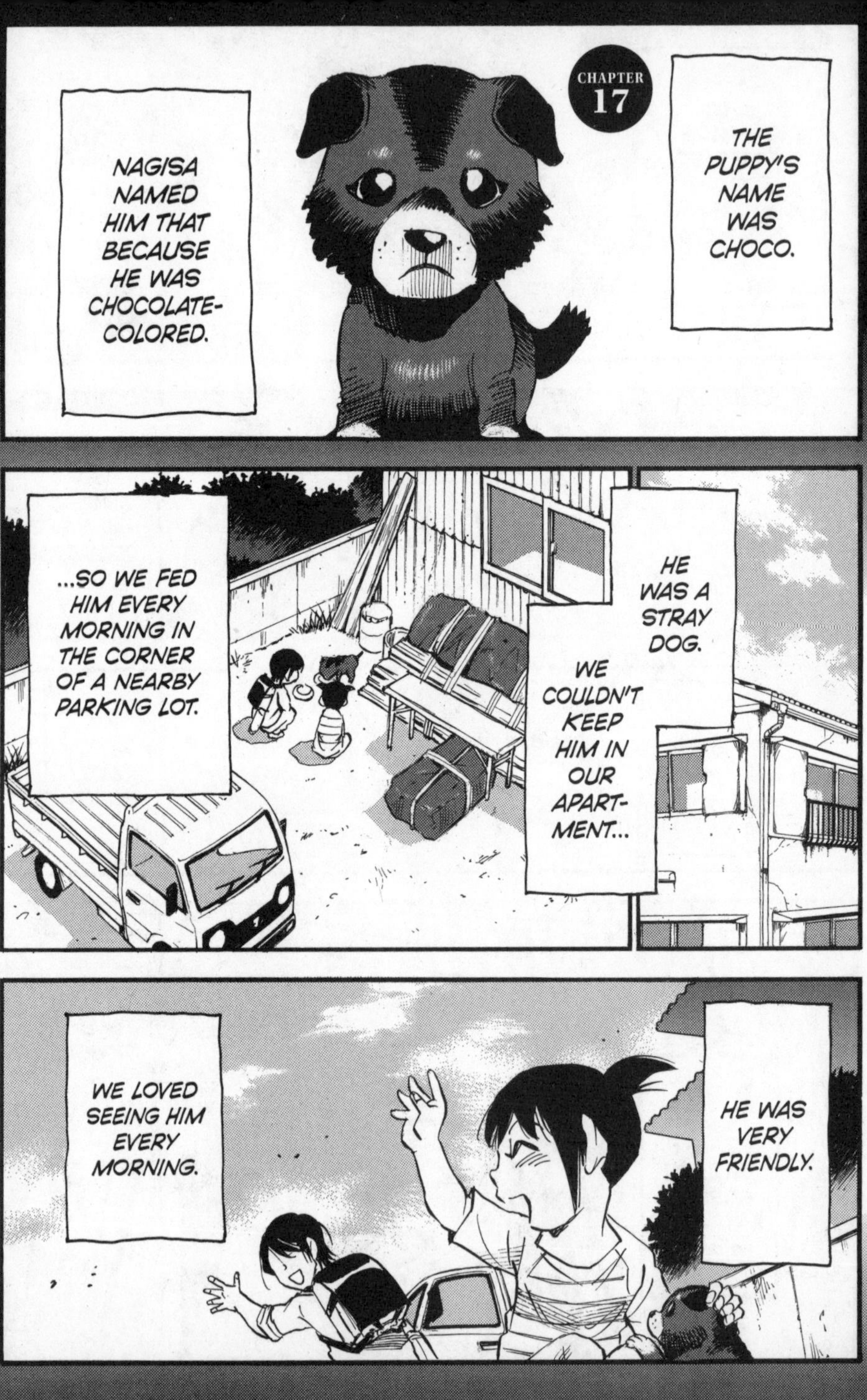
CHAPTER 17
THE PUPPY'S NAME WAS CHOCO.
NAGISA NAMED HIM THAT BECAUSE HE WAS CHOCOLATE-COLORED.
HE WAS A STRAY DOG.
WE COULDN'T KEEP HIM IN OUR APARTMENT...
...SO WE FED HIM EVERY MORNING IN THE CORNER OF A NEARBY PARKING LOT.
HE WAS VERY FRIENDLY.
WE LOVED SEEING HIM EVERY MORNING.

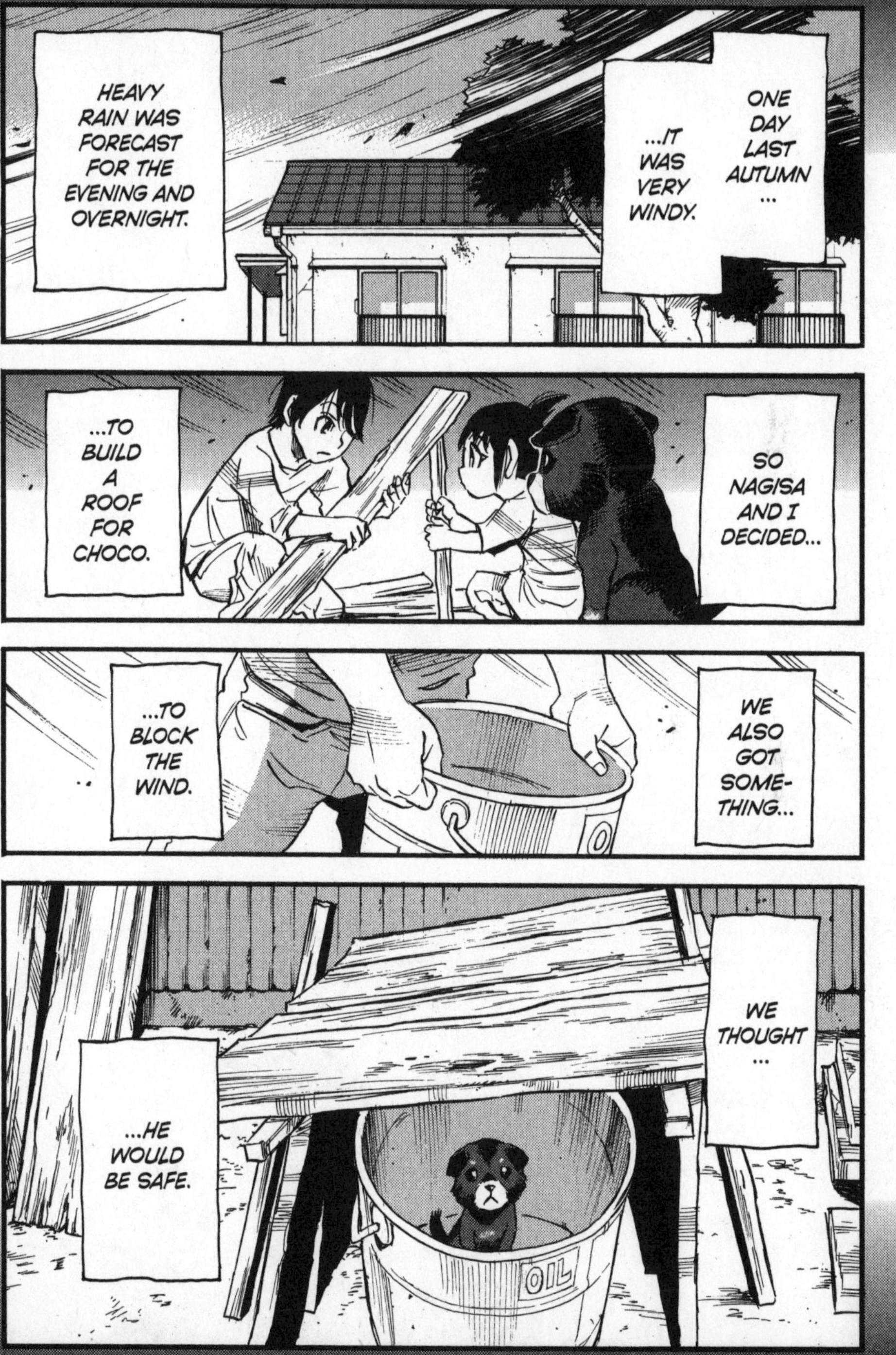
ONE DAY LAST AUTUMN ...
...IT WAS VERY WINDY.
HEAVY RAIN WAS FORECAST FOR THE EVENING AND OVERNIGHT.
SO NAGISA AND I DECIDED...
...TO BUILD A ROOF FOR CHOCO.
WE ALSO GOT SOME-THING...
...TO BLOCK THE WIND.
WE THOUGHT ...
...HE WOULD BE SAFE.
OIL

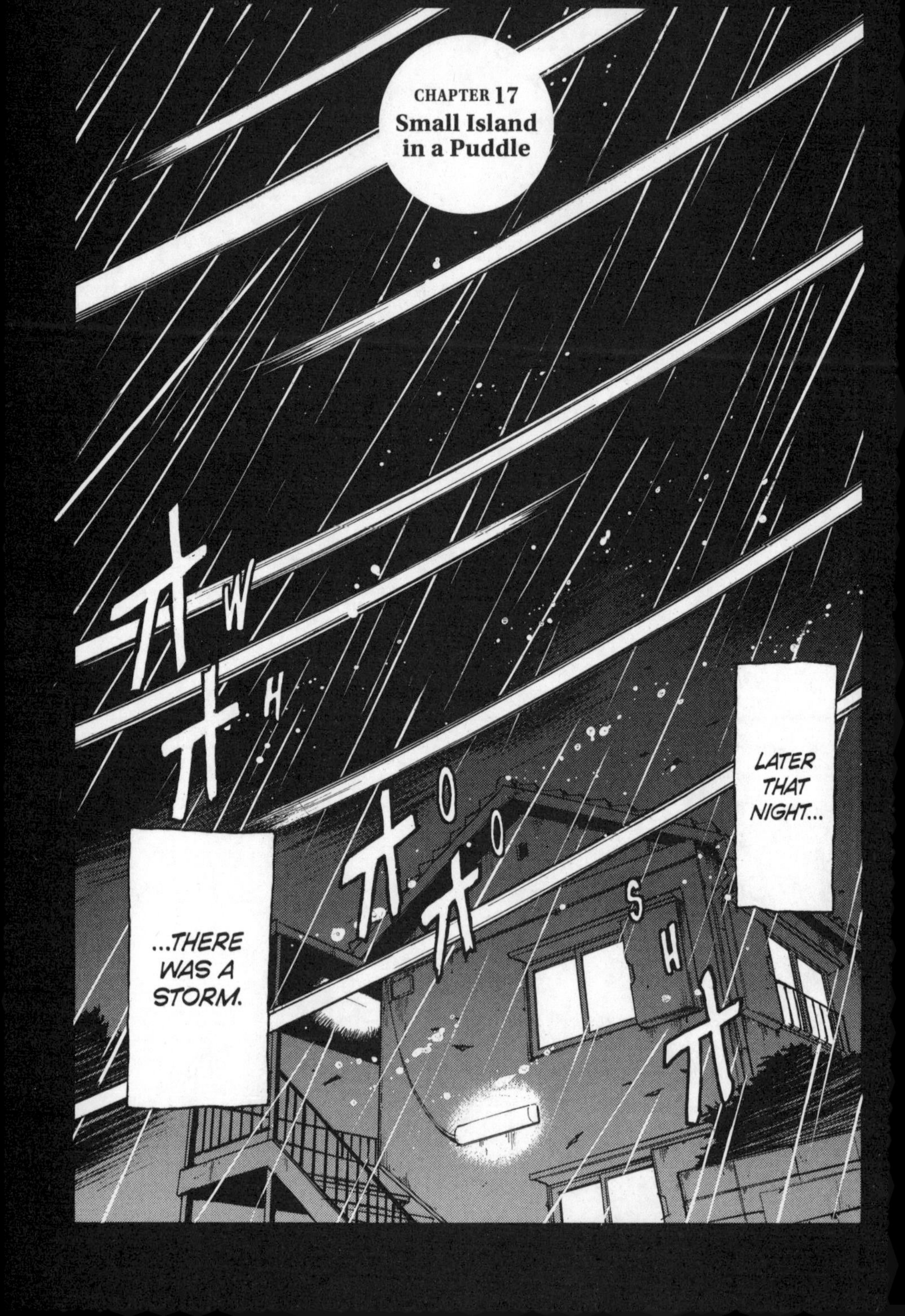
CHAPTER 17
Small Island in a Puddle
LATER THAT NIGHT...
WHOOSH
...THERE WAS A STORM.

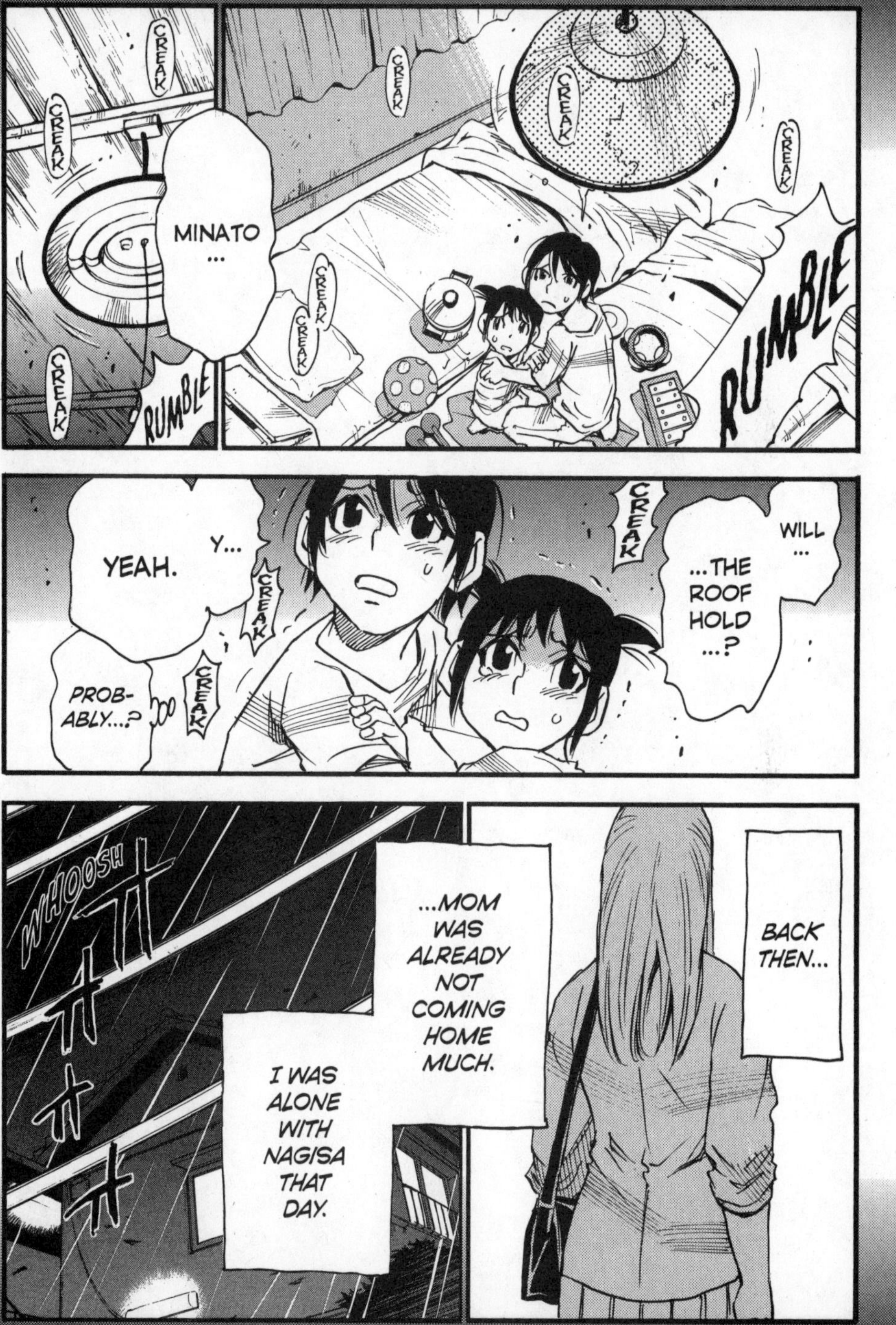
CREAK
CREAK
CREAK
MINATO
...
CREAK
CREAK
RUMBLE
CREAK
CREAK
RUMBLE
WILL
...
...THE
ROOF
HOLD
...?
Y...
YEAH.
CREAK
CREAK
PROB-
ABLY...?
CREAK
BACK
THEN...
...MOM
WAS
ALREADY
NOT
COMING
HOME
MUCH.
I WAS
ALONE
WITH
NAGISA
THAT
DAY.
WHOOSH

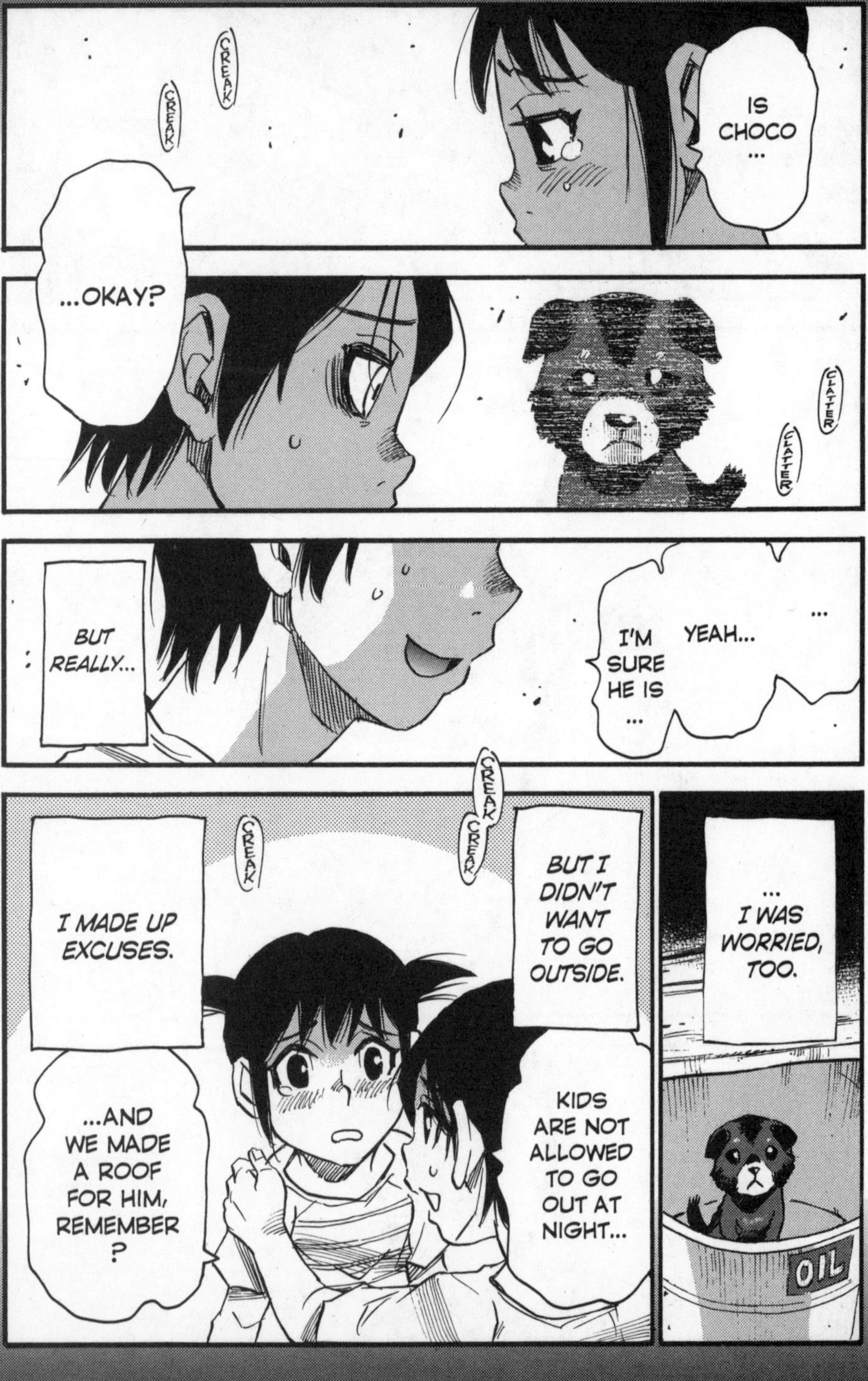
IS CHOCO ...
CREAK
CREAK
...OKAY?
CLATTER
CLATTER
... YEAH... I'M SURE HE IS ...
BUT REALLY...
... I WAS WORRIED, TOO.
OIL
BUT I DIDN'T WANT TO GO OUTSIDE.
CREAK
CREAK
CREAK
I MADE UP EXCUSES.
KIDS ARE NOT ALLOWED TO GO OUT AT NIGHT...
...AND WE MADE A ROOF FOR HIM, REMEMBER?

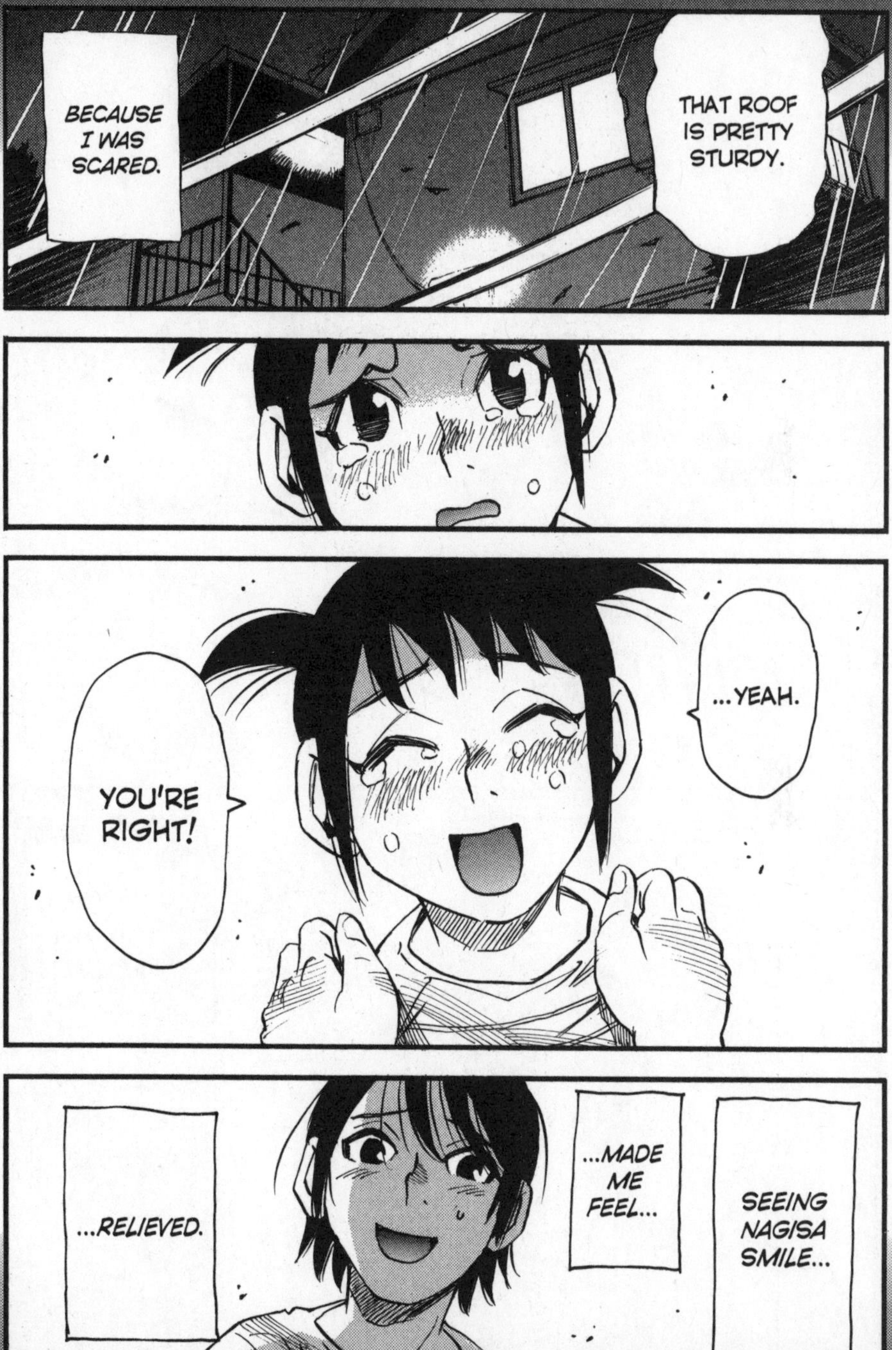
THAT ROOF IS PRETTY STURDY.
BECAUSE I WAS SCARED.
...YEAH.
YOU'RE RIGHT!
SEEING NAGISA SMILE...
...MADE ME FEEL...
...RELIEVED.

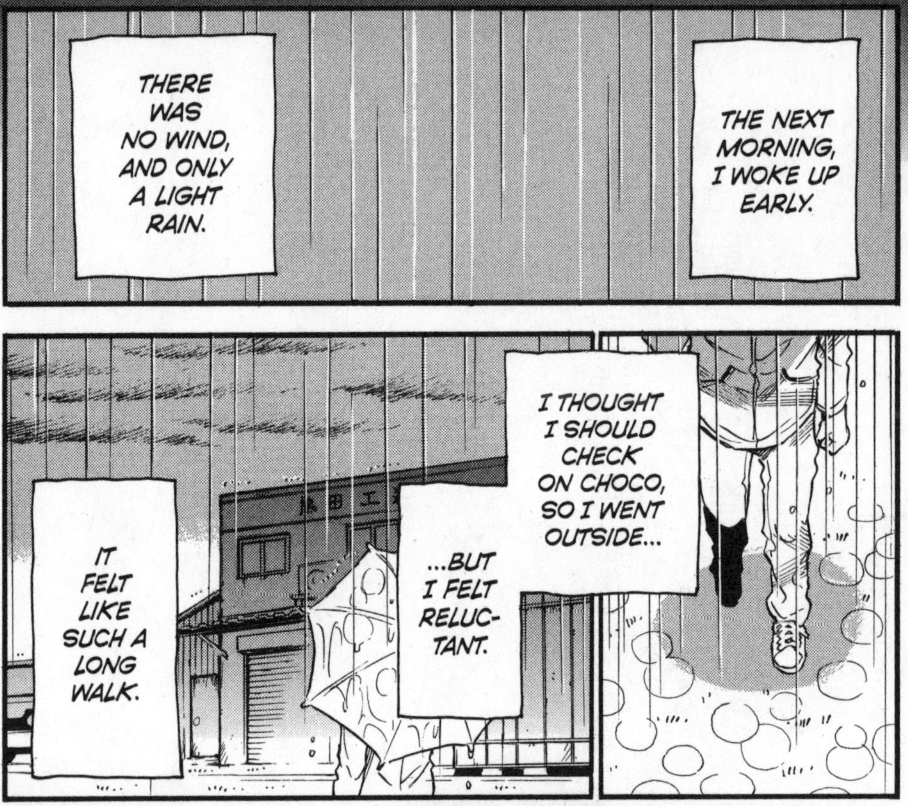
THE NEXT MORNING, I WOKE UP EARLY.
THERE WAS NO WIND, AND ONLY A LIGHT RAIN.
I THOUGHT I SHOULD CHECK ON CHOCO, SO I WENT OUTSIDE...
...BUT I FELT RELUCTANT.
IT FELT LIKE SUCH A LONG WALK.

SIGN: Tsuruta Industries

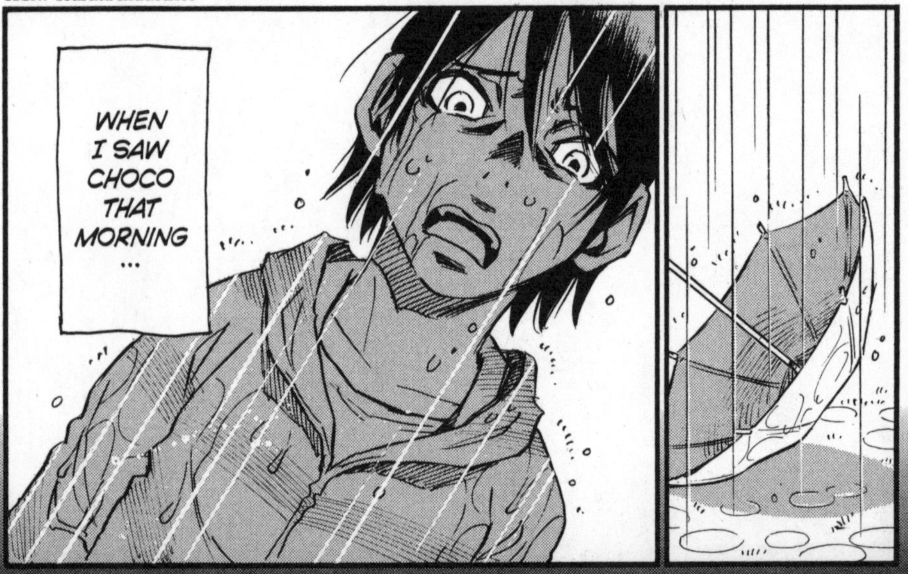
WHEN I SAW CHOCO THAT MORNING...

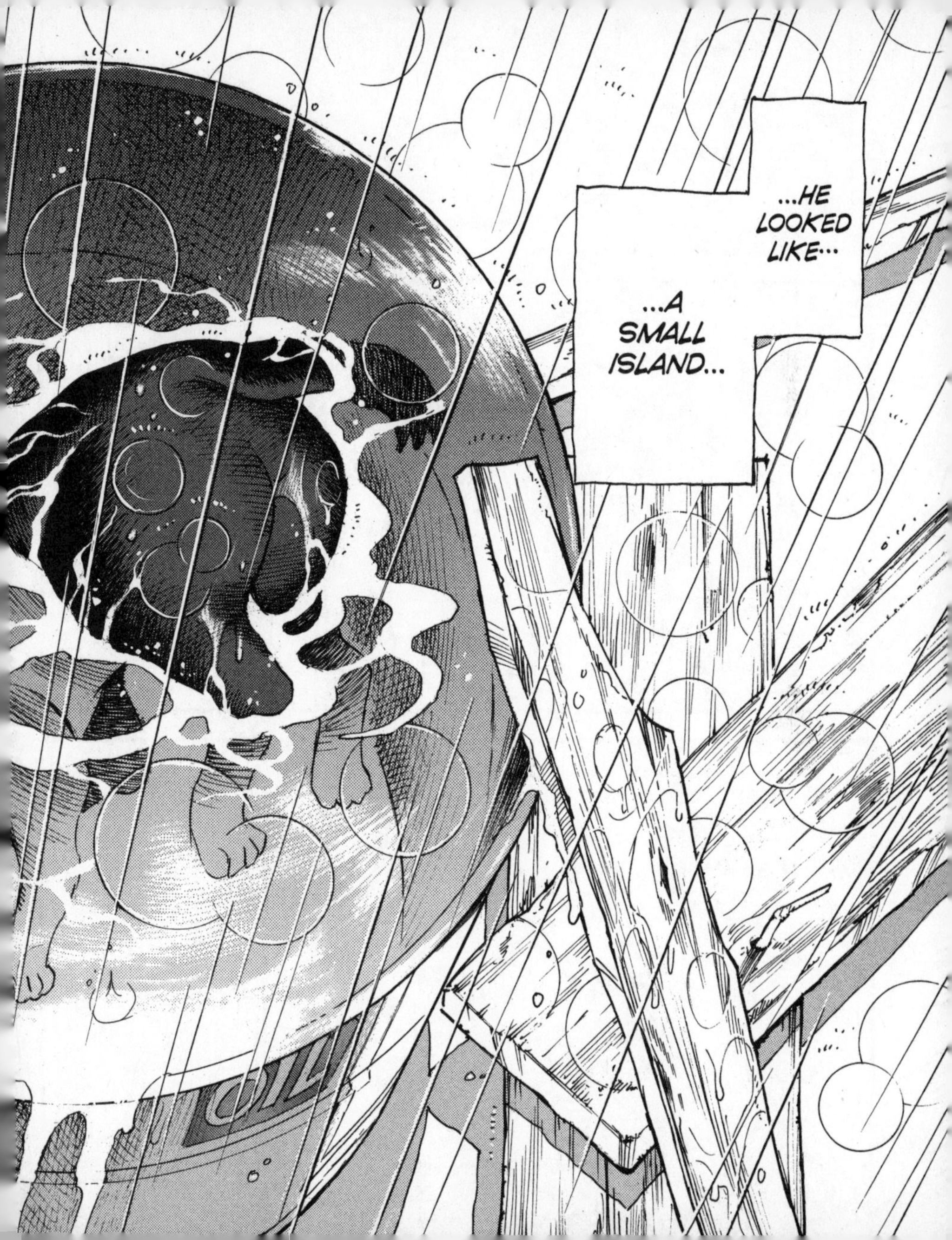
...HE LOOKED LIKE...
...A SMALL ISLAND...

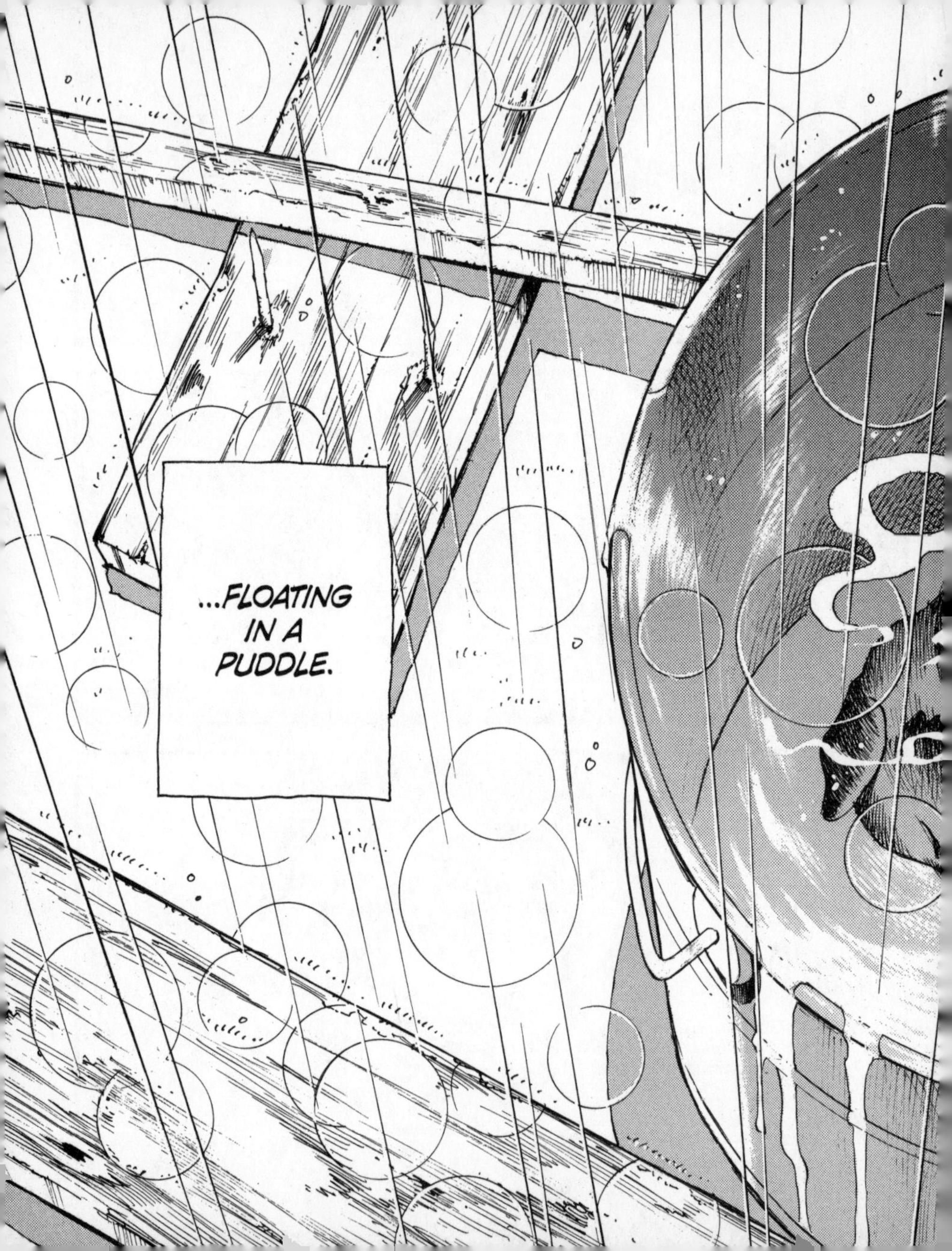
...FLOATING IN A PUDDLE.

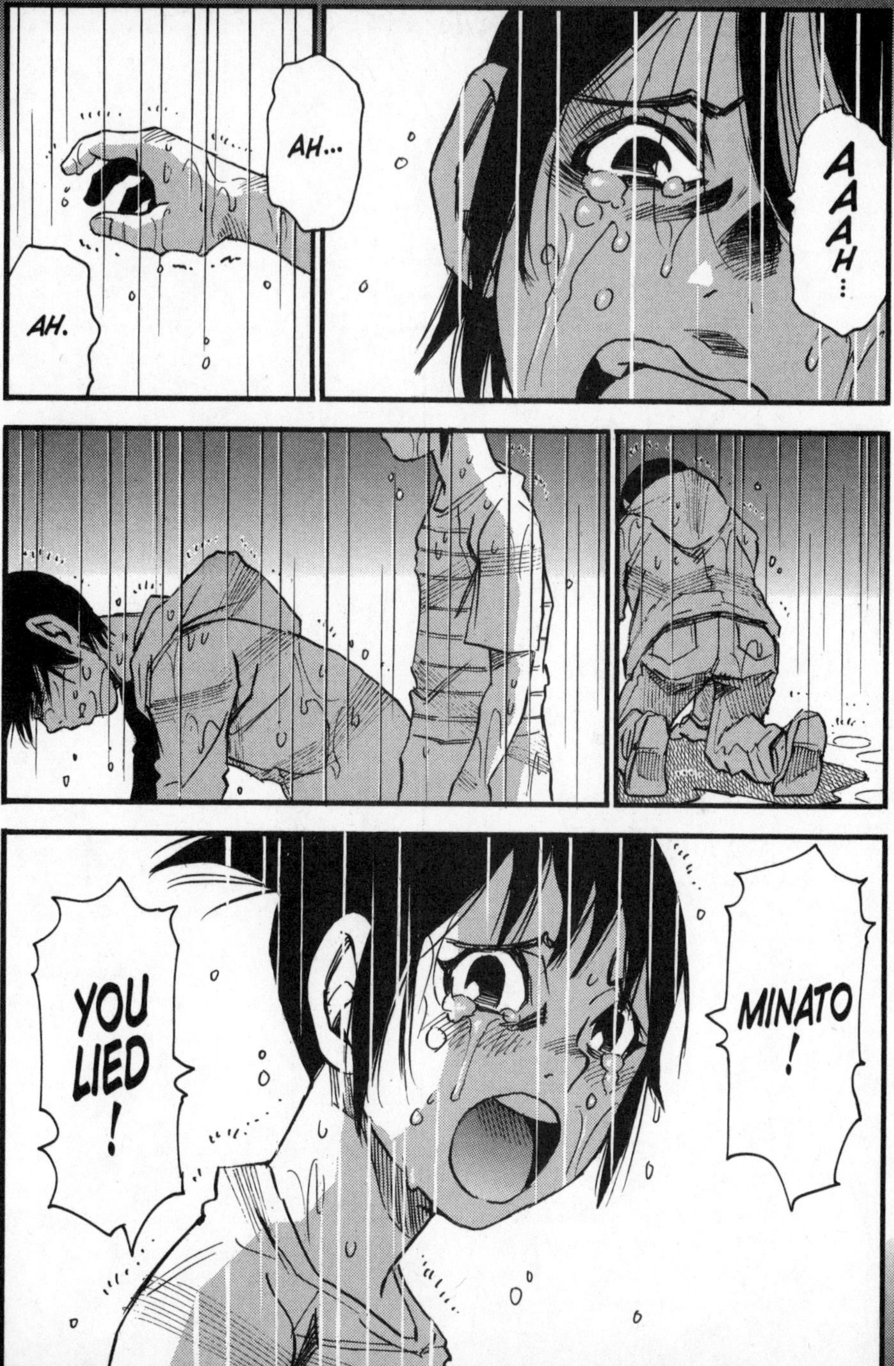
AAAAH...
AH...
AH.
MINATO!
YOU LIED!

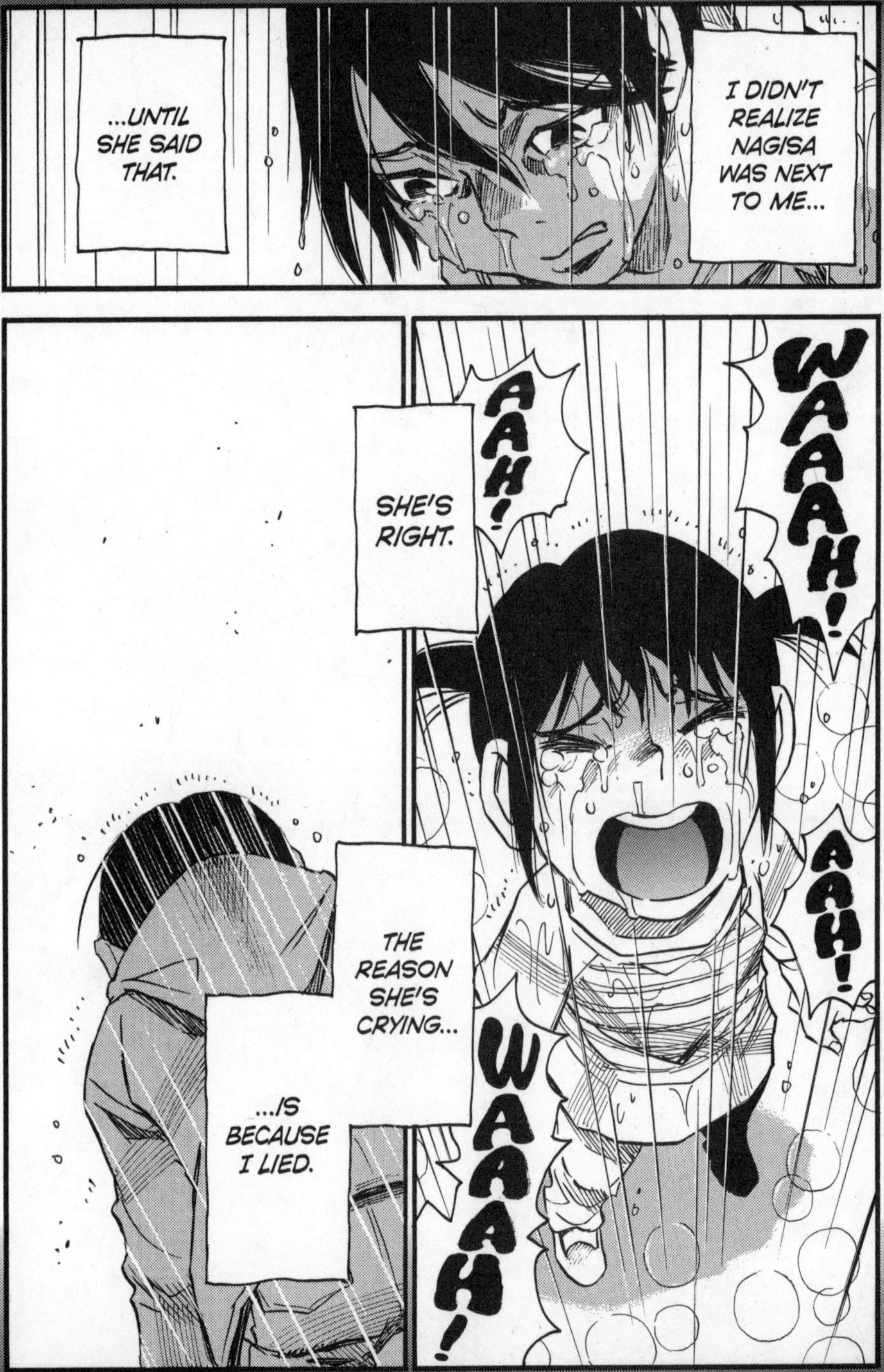
I DIDN'T REALIZE NAGISA WAS NEXT TO ME...
...UNTIL SHE SAID THAT.
WAAAAH!
AAH!
SHE'S RIGHT.
AAH!
WAAAAH!
THE REASON SHE'S CRYING...
...IS BECAUSE I LIED.

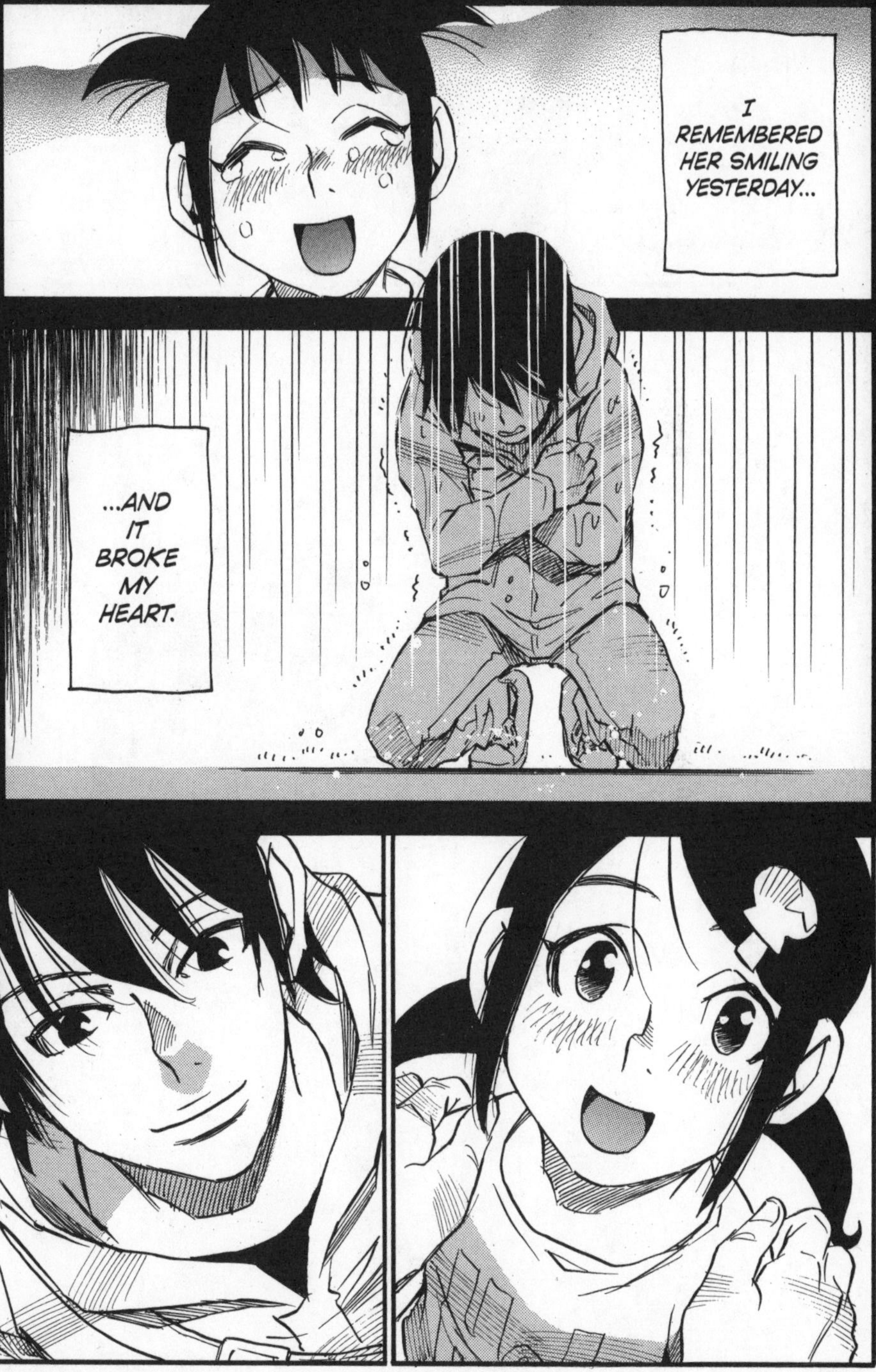
I REMEMBERED HER SMILING YESTERDAY...
...AND IT BROKE MY HEART.

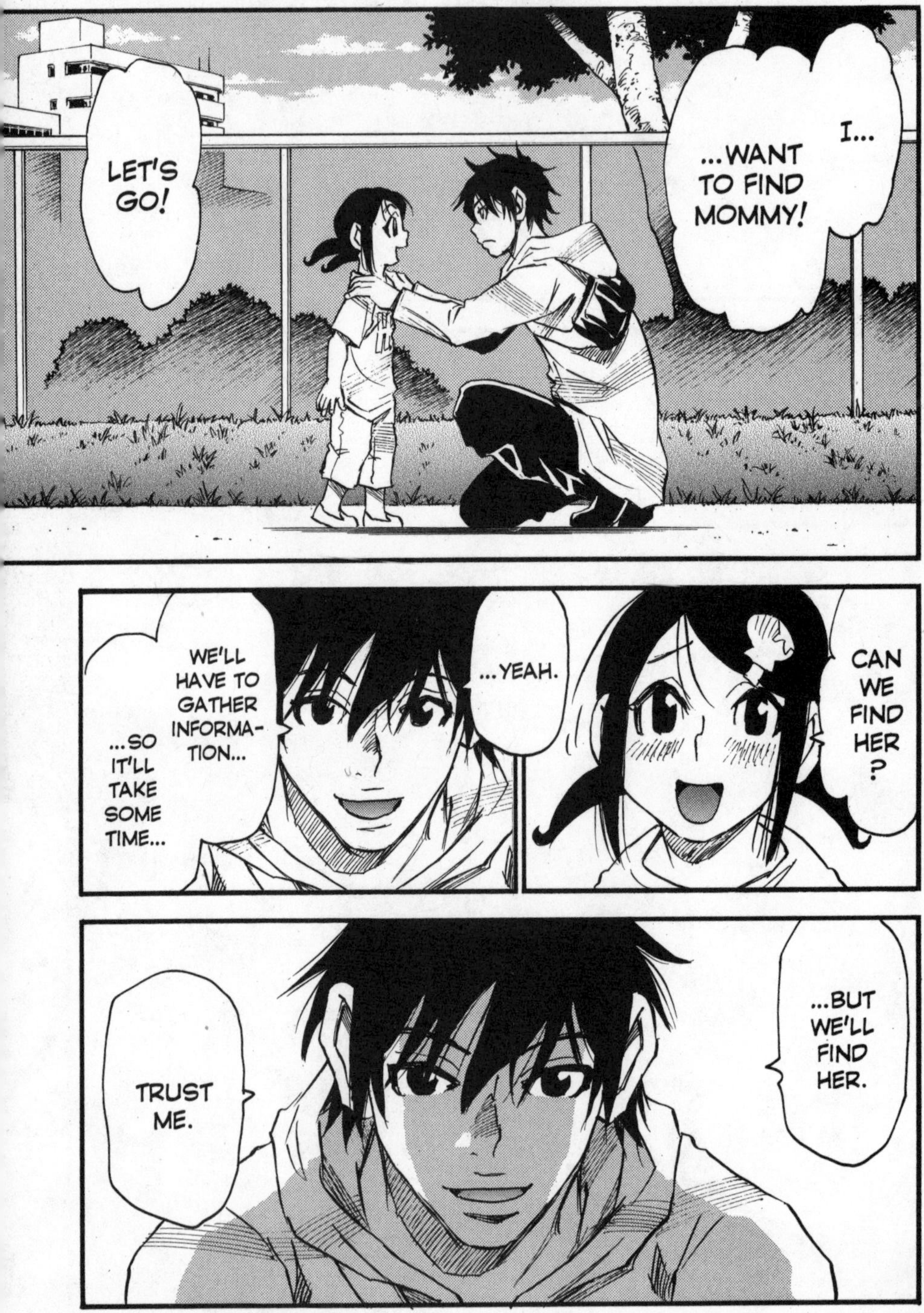
I...
...WANT TO FIND MOMMY!
LET'S GO!
CAN WE FIND HER?
...YEAH.
WE'LL HAVE TO GATHER INFORMATION...
...SO IT'LL TAKE SOME TIME...
...BUT WE'LL FIND HER.
TRUST ME.

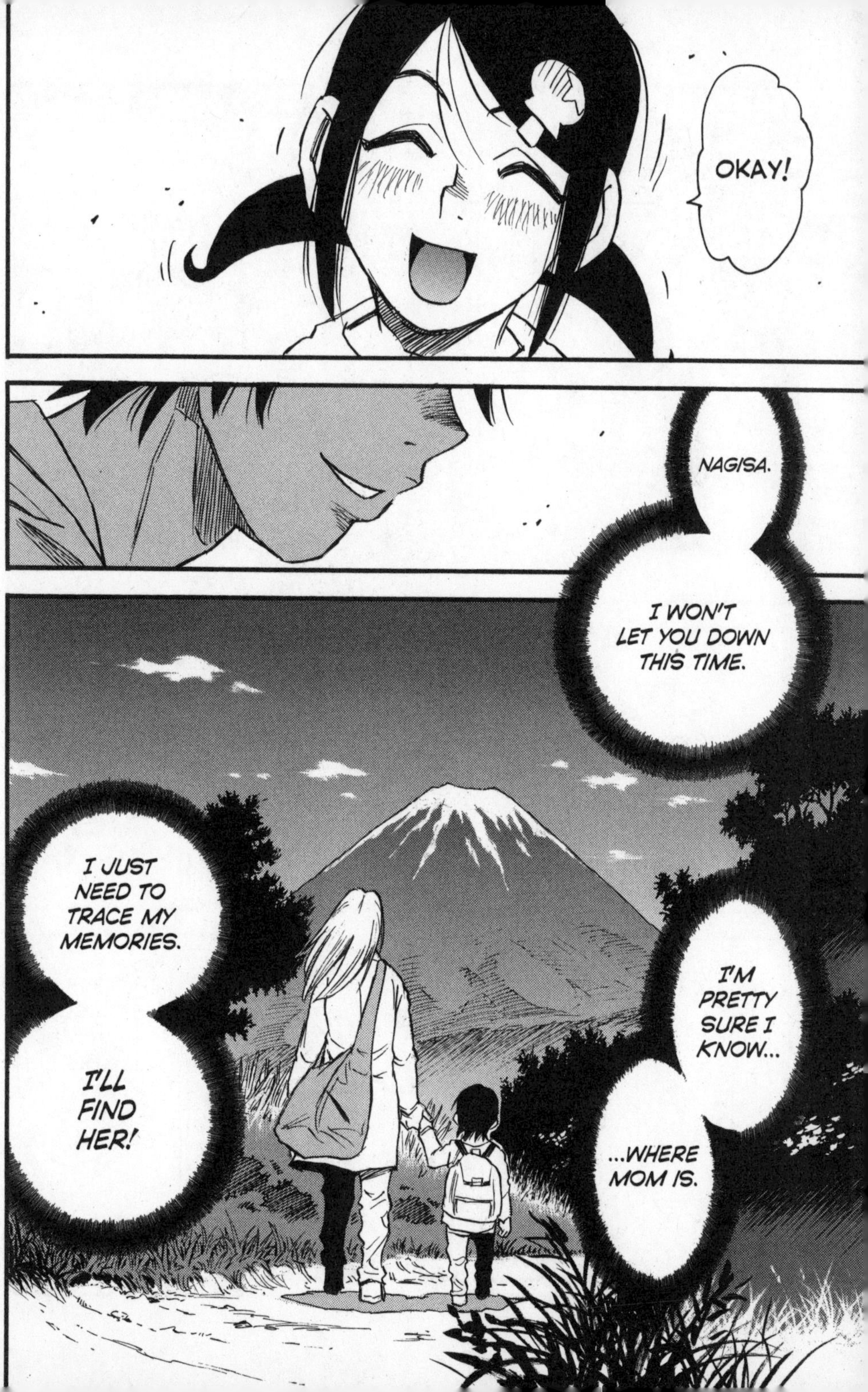
OKAY!
NAGISA.
I WON'T LET YOU DOWN THIS TIME.
I'M PRETTY SURE I KNOW...
...WHERE MOM IS.
I JUST NEED TO TRACE MY MEMORIES.
I'LL FIND HER!

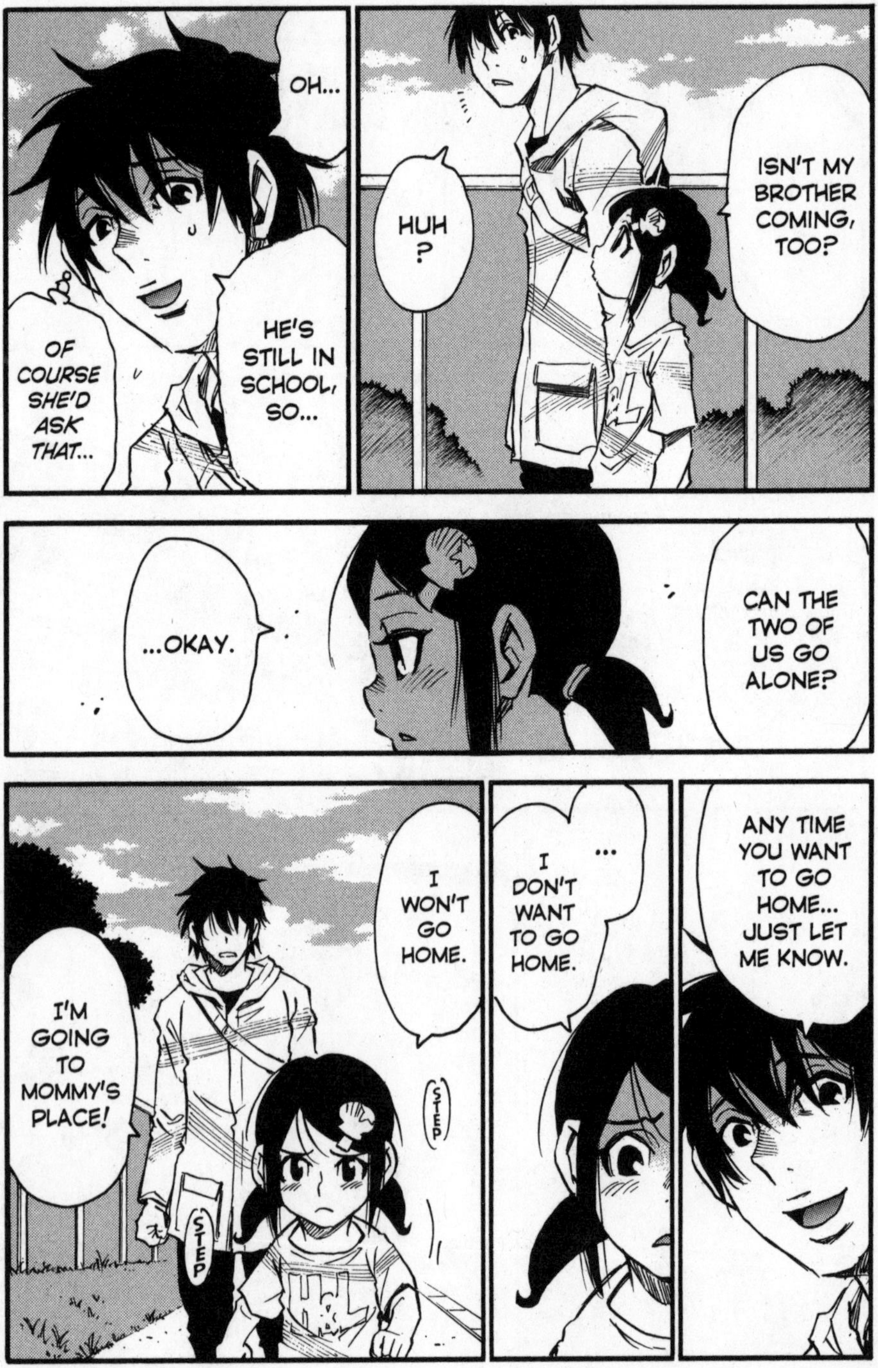
ISN'T MY BROTHER COMING, TOO?
HUH?
OH...
HE'S STILL IN SCHOOL, SO...
OF COURSE SHE'D ASK THAT...
CAN THE TWO OF US GO ALONE?
...OKAY.
ANY TIME YOU WANT TO GO HOME... JUST LET ME KNOW.
...
I DON'T WANT TO GO HOME.
I WON'T GO HOME.
STEP
I'M GOING TO MOMMY'S PLACE!
STEP

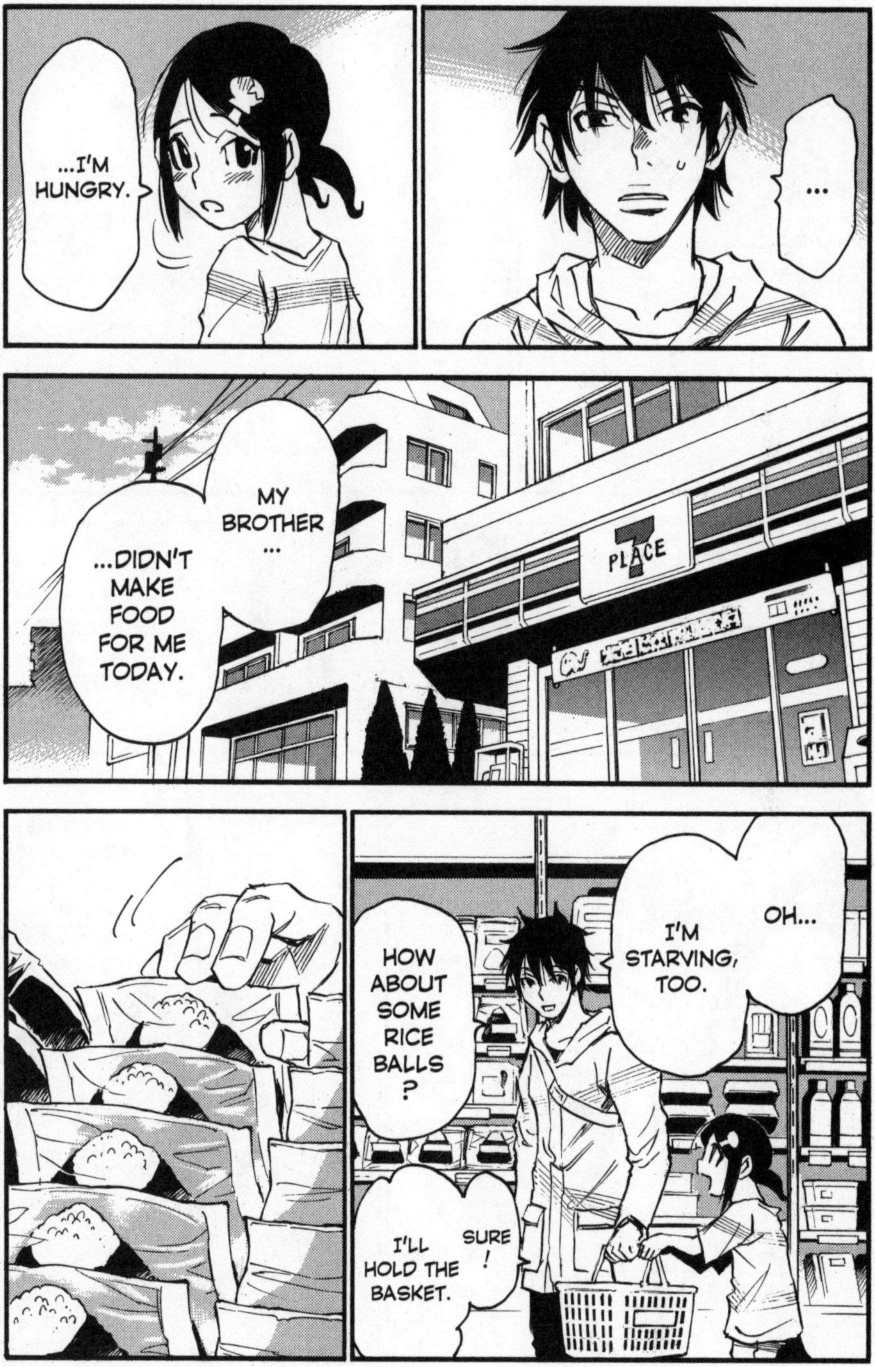
...
...I'M HUNGRY.
MY BROTHER ...
...DIDN'T MAKE FOOD FOR ME TODAY.
PLACE 7
OH...
I'M STARVING, TOO.
HOW ABOUT SOME RICE BALLS?
SURE!
I'LL HOLD THE BASKET.

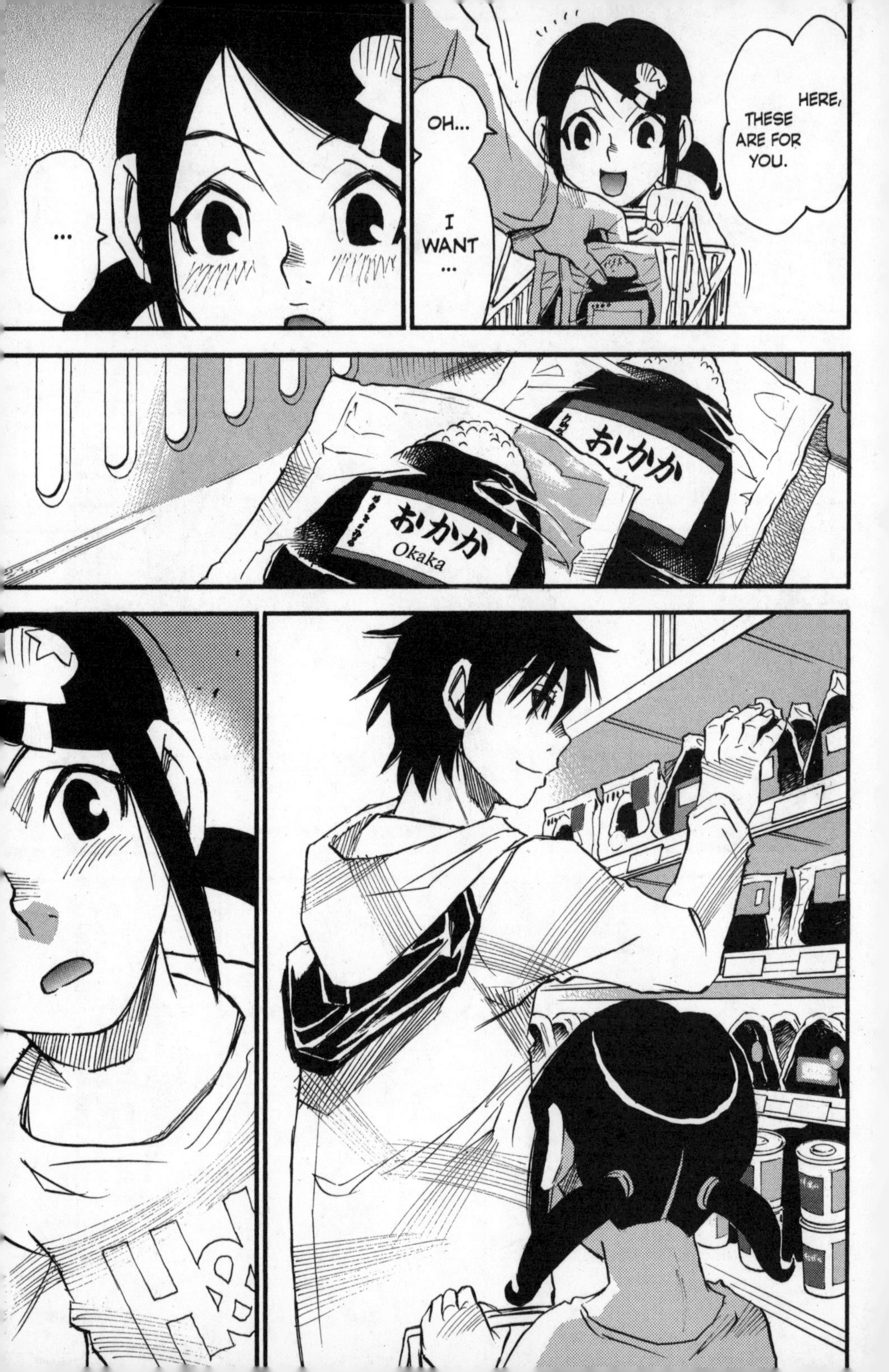
HERE, THESE ARE FOR YOU.
OH...
I WANT ...
...
おかか
おかか
Okaka

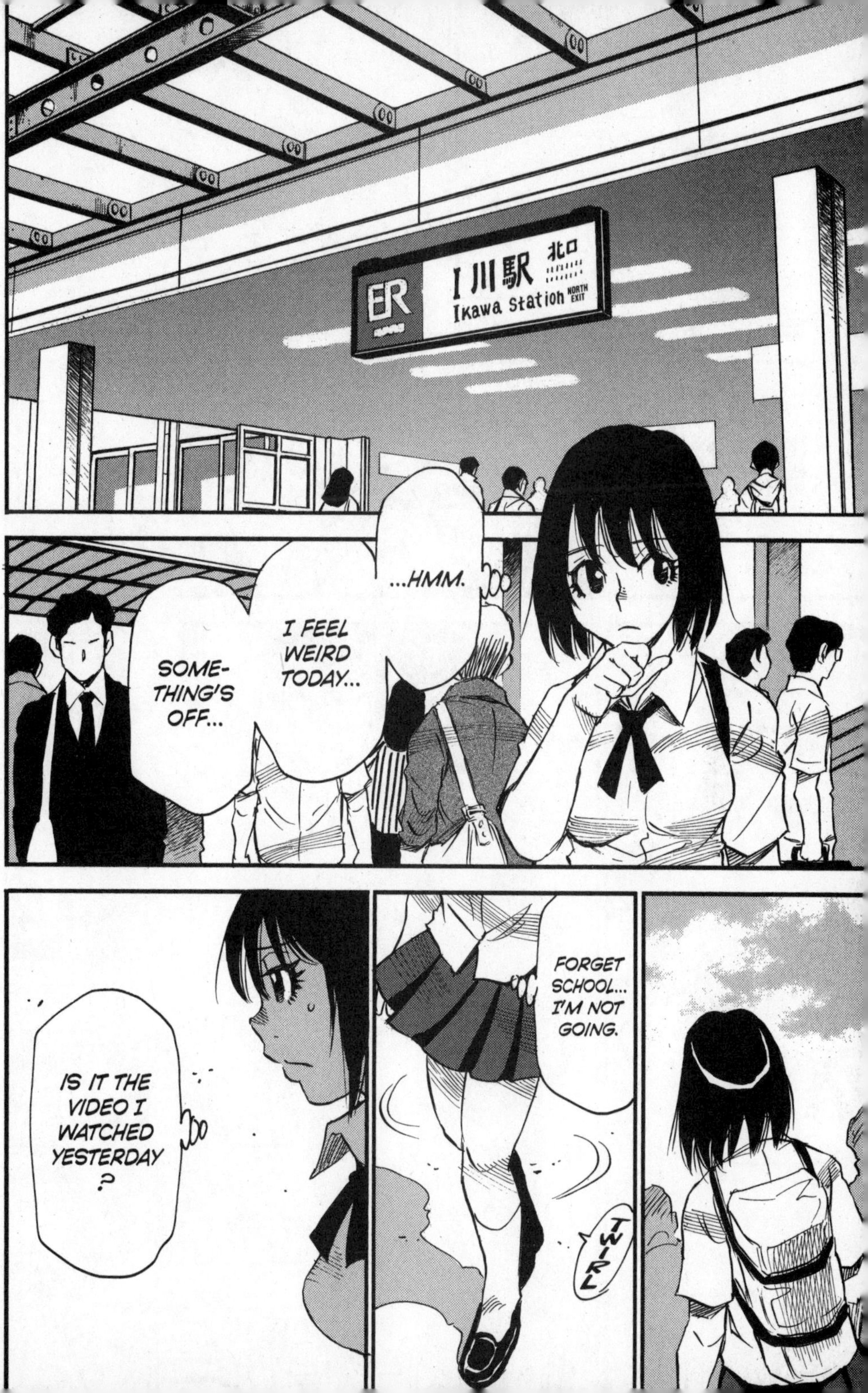
ER
I川駅
北口
Ikawa Station
NORTH EXIT
...HMM.
I FEEL WEIRD TODAY...
SOME-THING'S OFF...
FORGET SCHOOL... I'M NOT GOING.
TWIRL
IS IT THE VIDEO I WATCHED YESTERDAY?

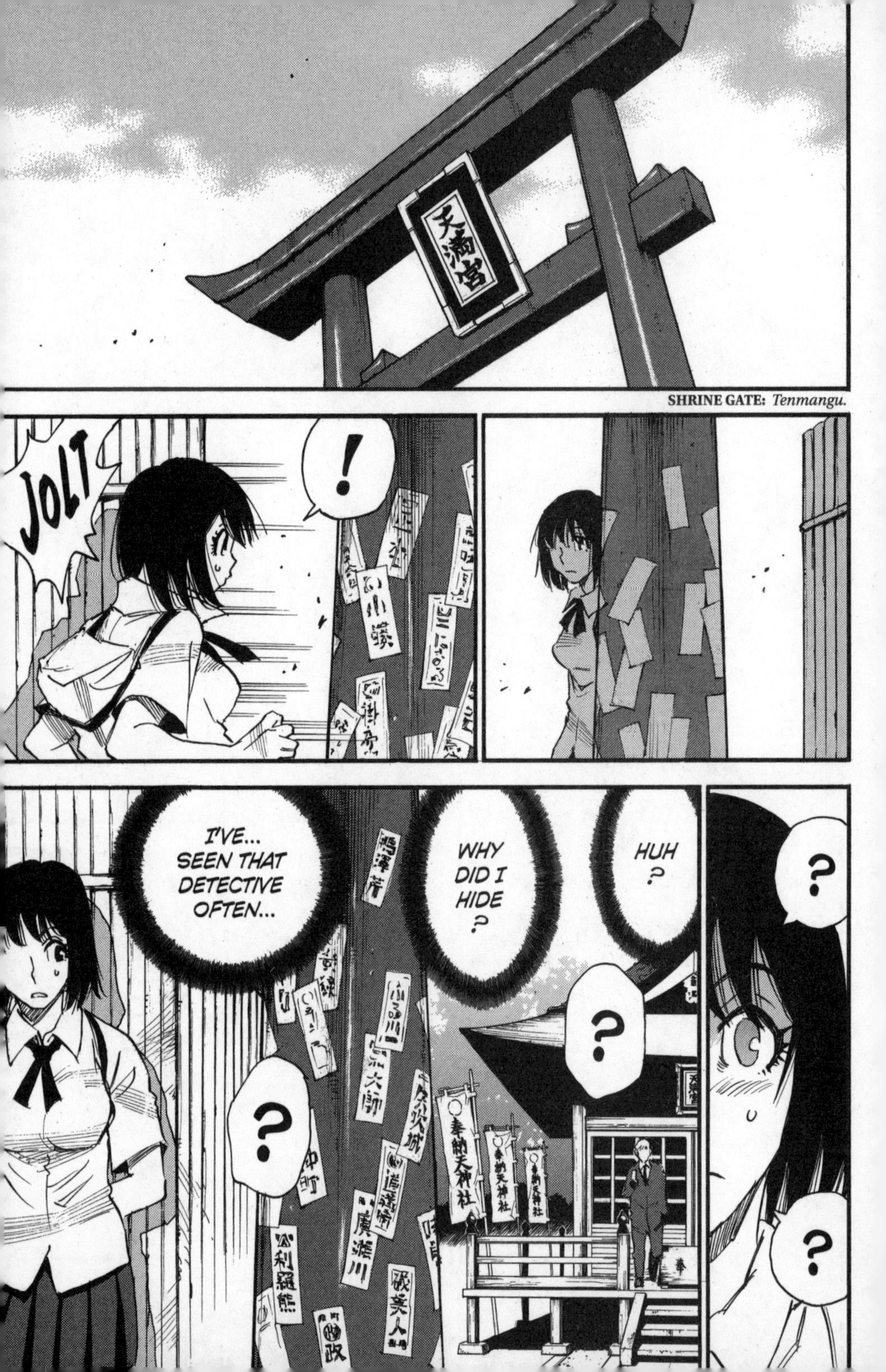

天満宮
JOLT
!
?
?
HUH?
WHY DID I HIDE?
?
I'VE... SEEN THAT DETECTIVE OFTEN...
?

SHRINE GATE: *Tenmangu.*

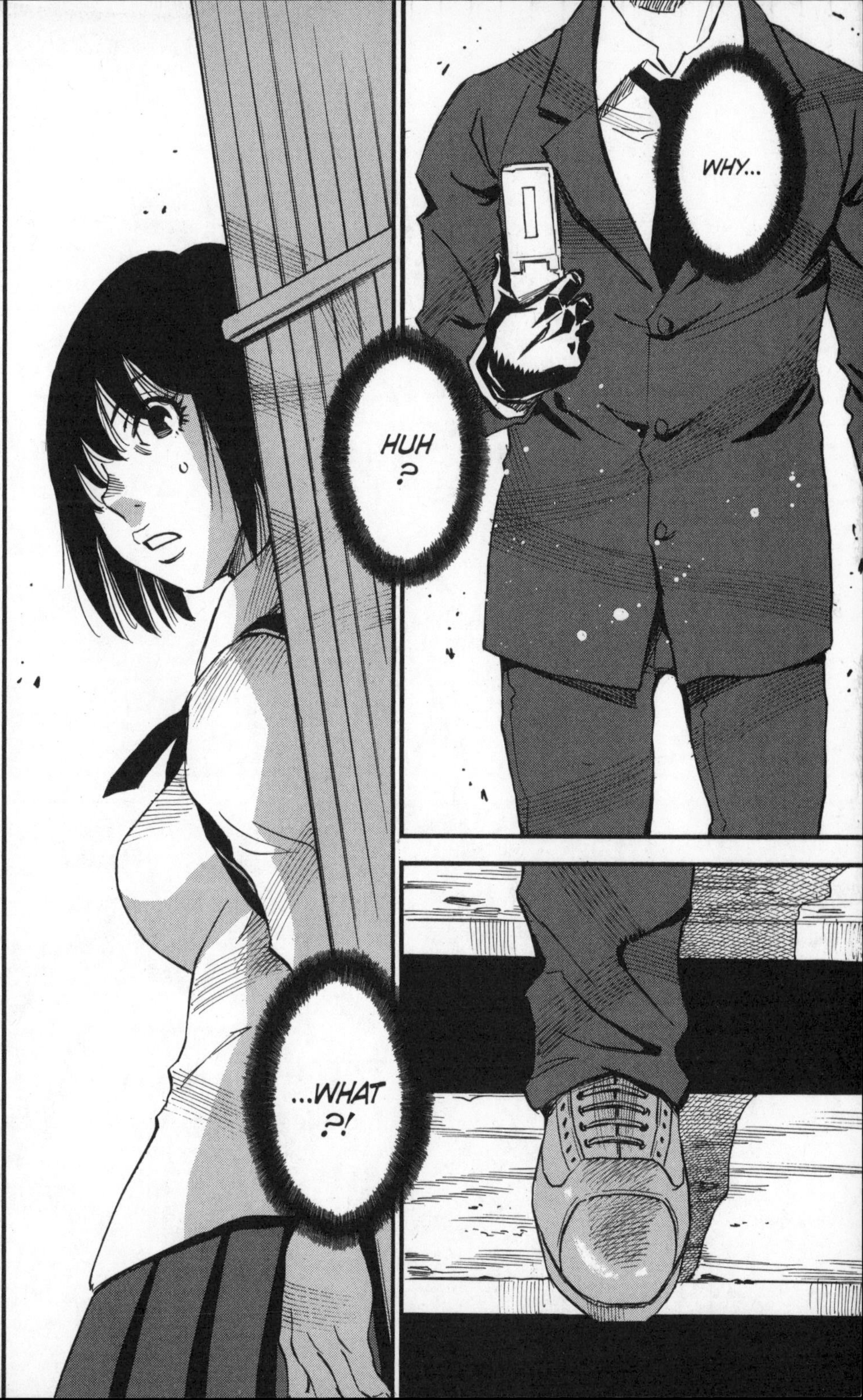
WHY...
HUH ?
...WHAT ?!

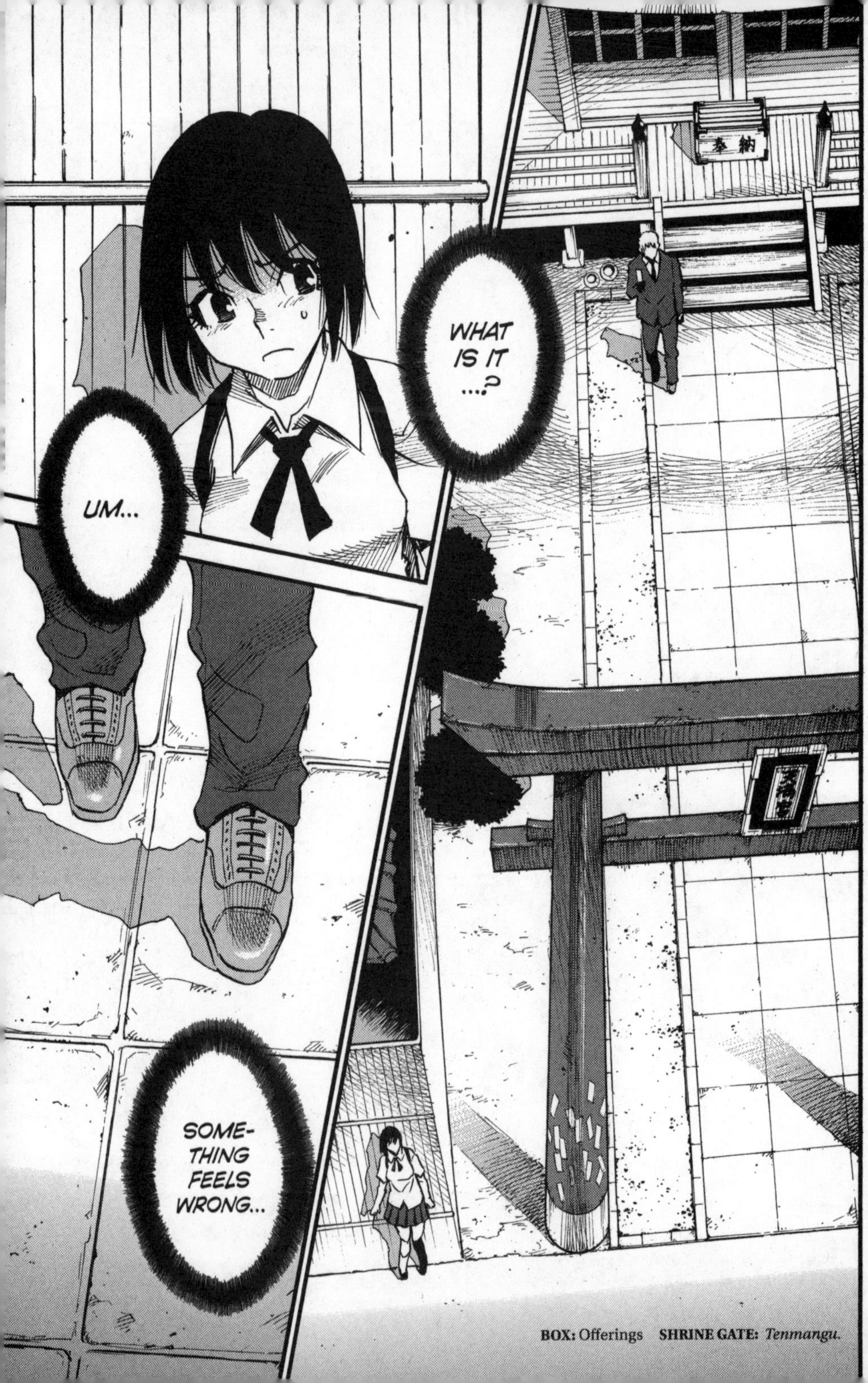
WHAT IS IT ...?
UM...
SOME-THING FEELS WRONG...

BOX: Offerings **SHRINE GATE:** *Tenmangu.*

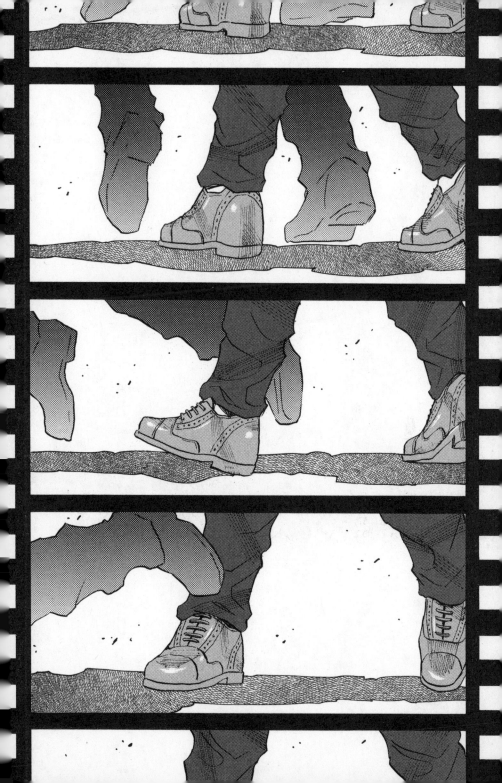

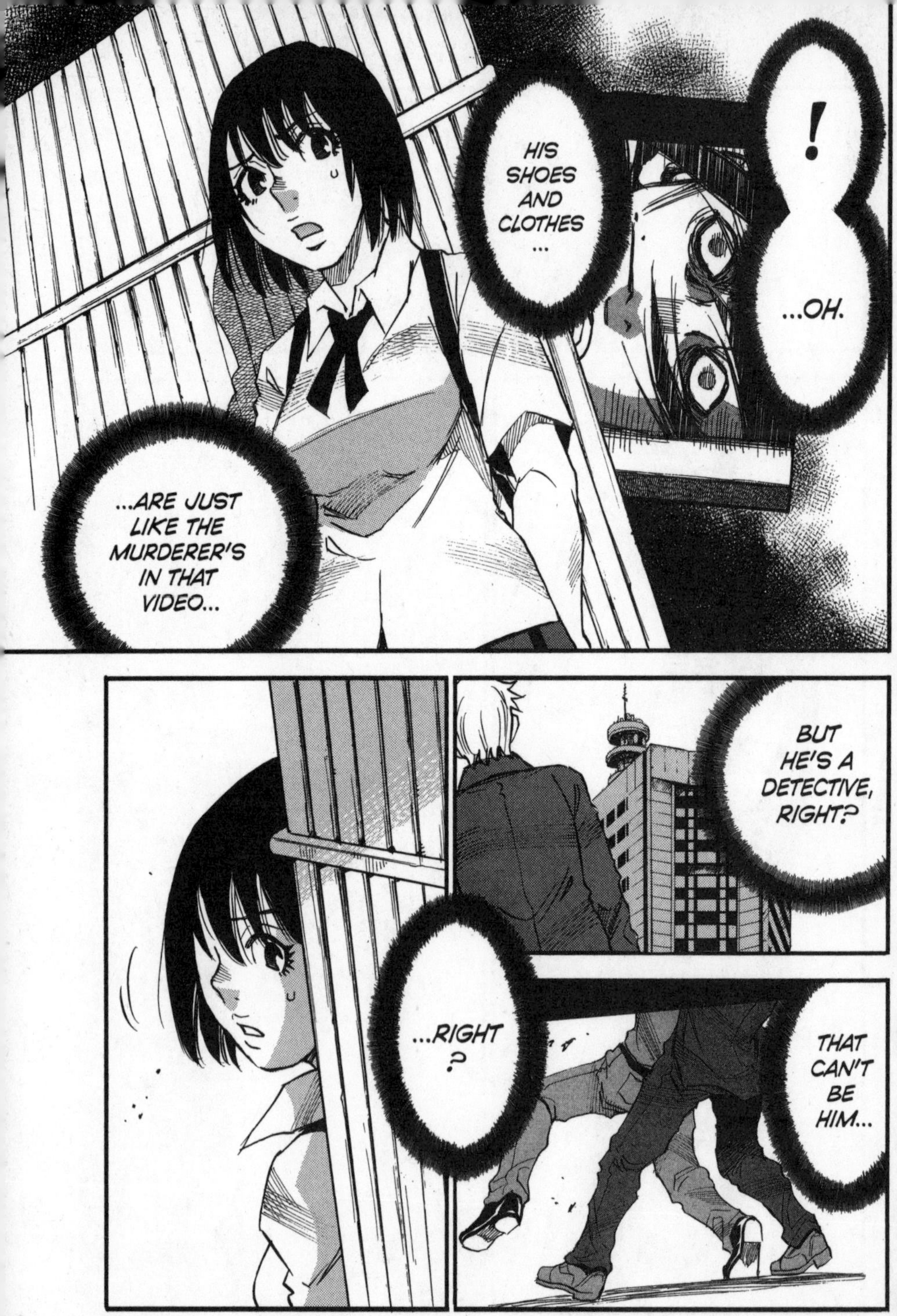
!
...OH.
HIS SHOES AND CLOTHES ...
...ARE JUST LIKE THE MURDERER'S IN THAT VIDEO...
BUT HE'S A DETECTIVE, RIGHT?
THAT CAN'T BE HIM...
...RIGHT ?

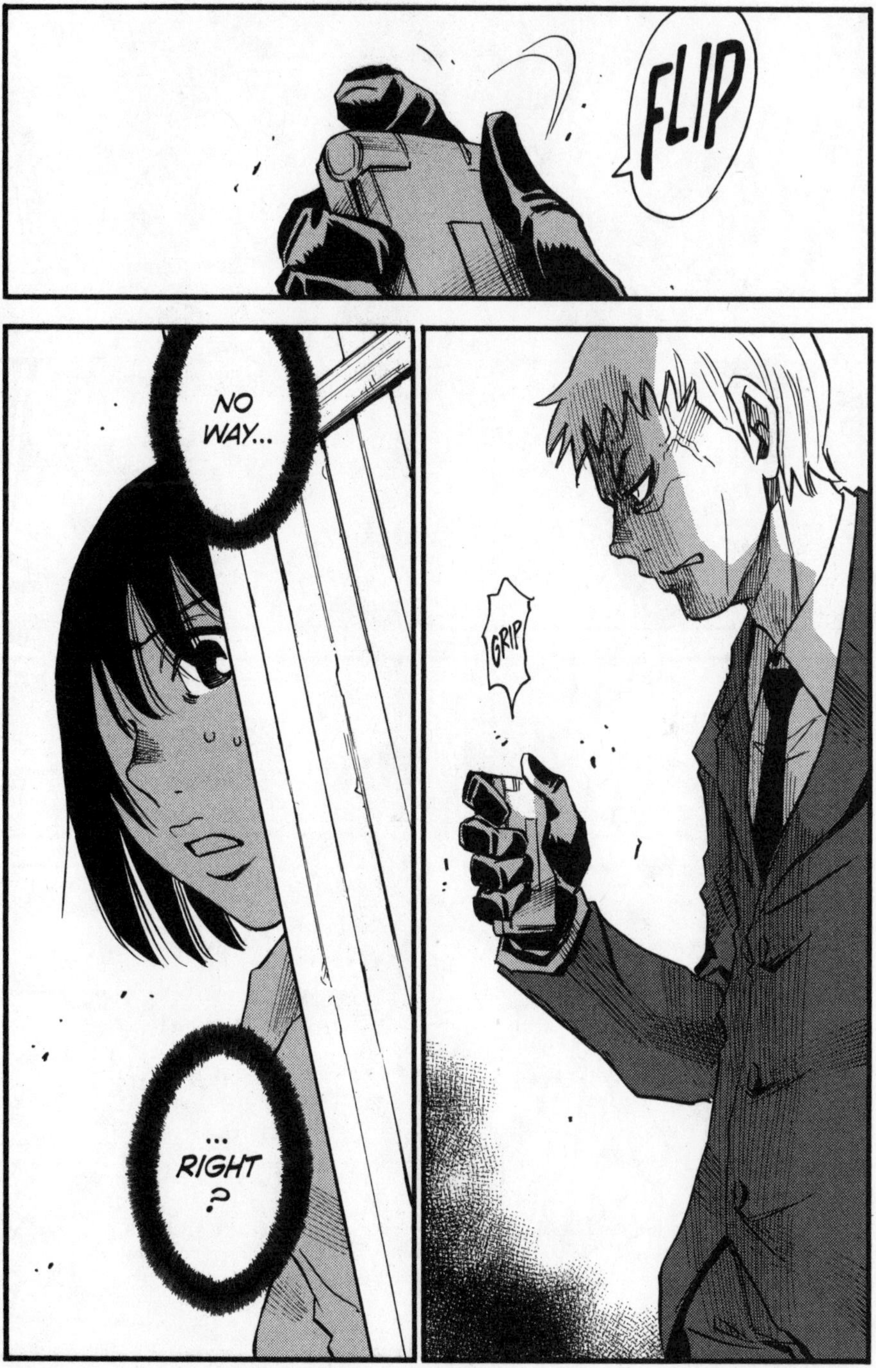
FLIP
GRIP
NO WAY...
...RIGHT?

ZSH
ZSH
ZSH
ZSH
ZSH
ZSH
社
KLANG
BANNER: Offering to Shrine
LEAP
...

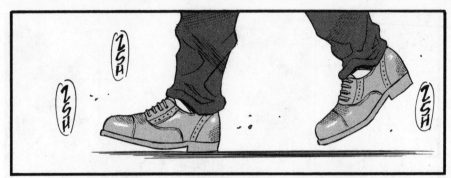

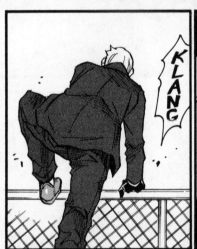

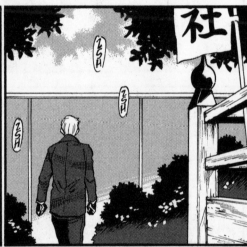

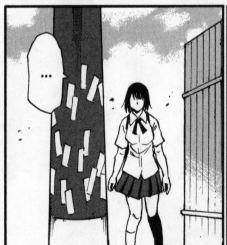

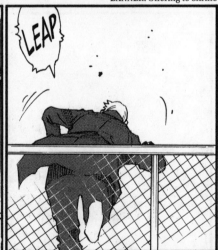

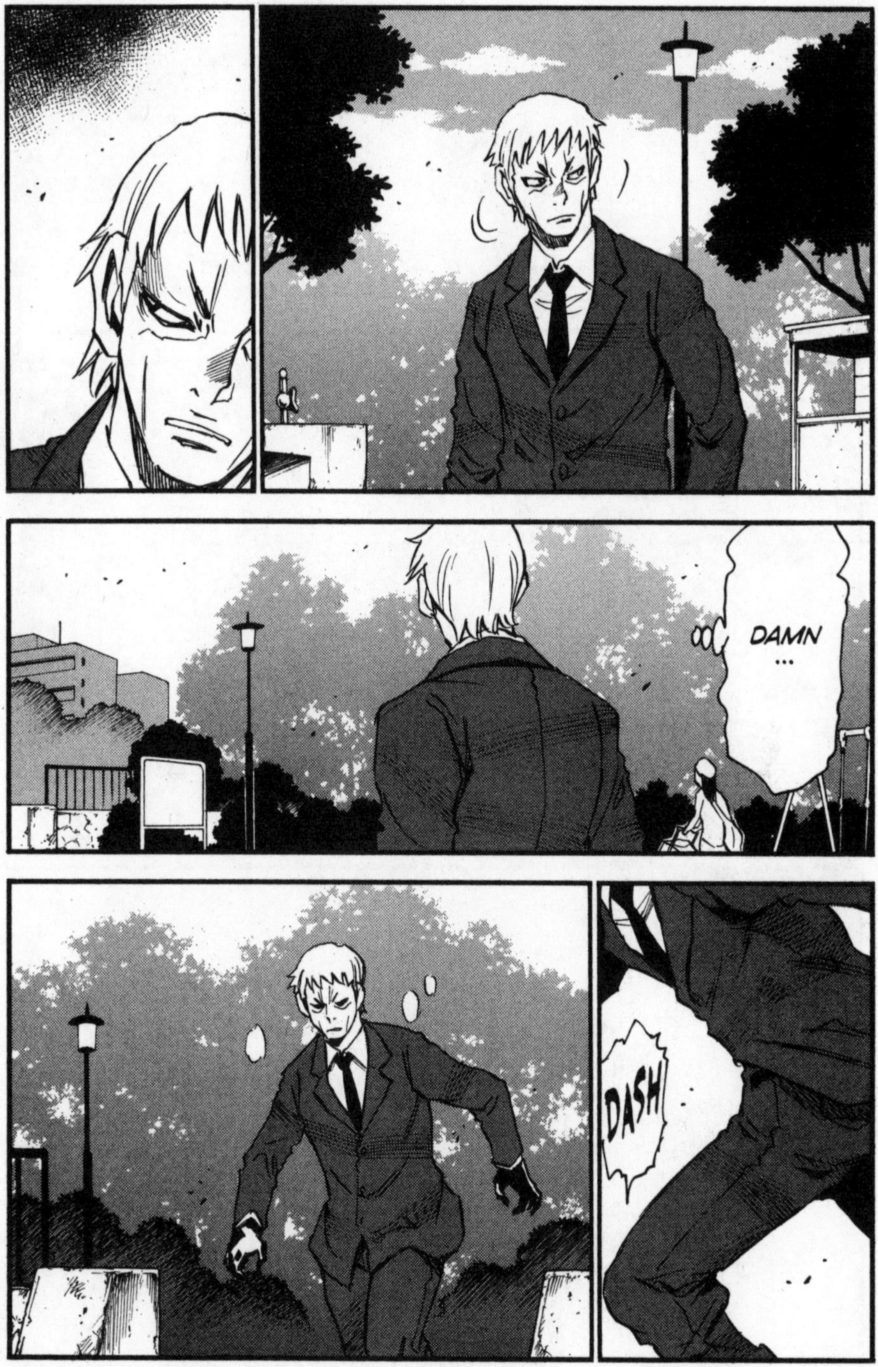
DAMN
...
DASH

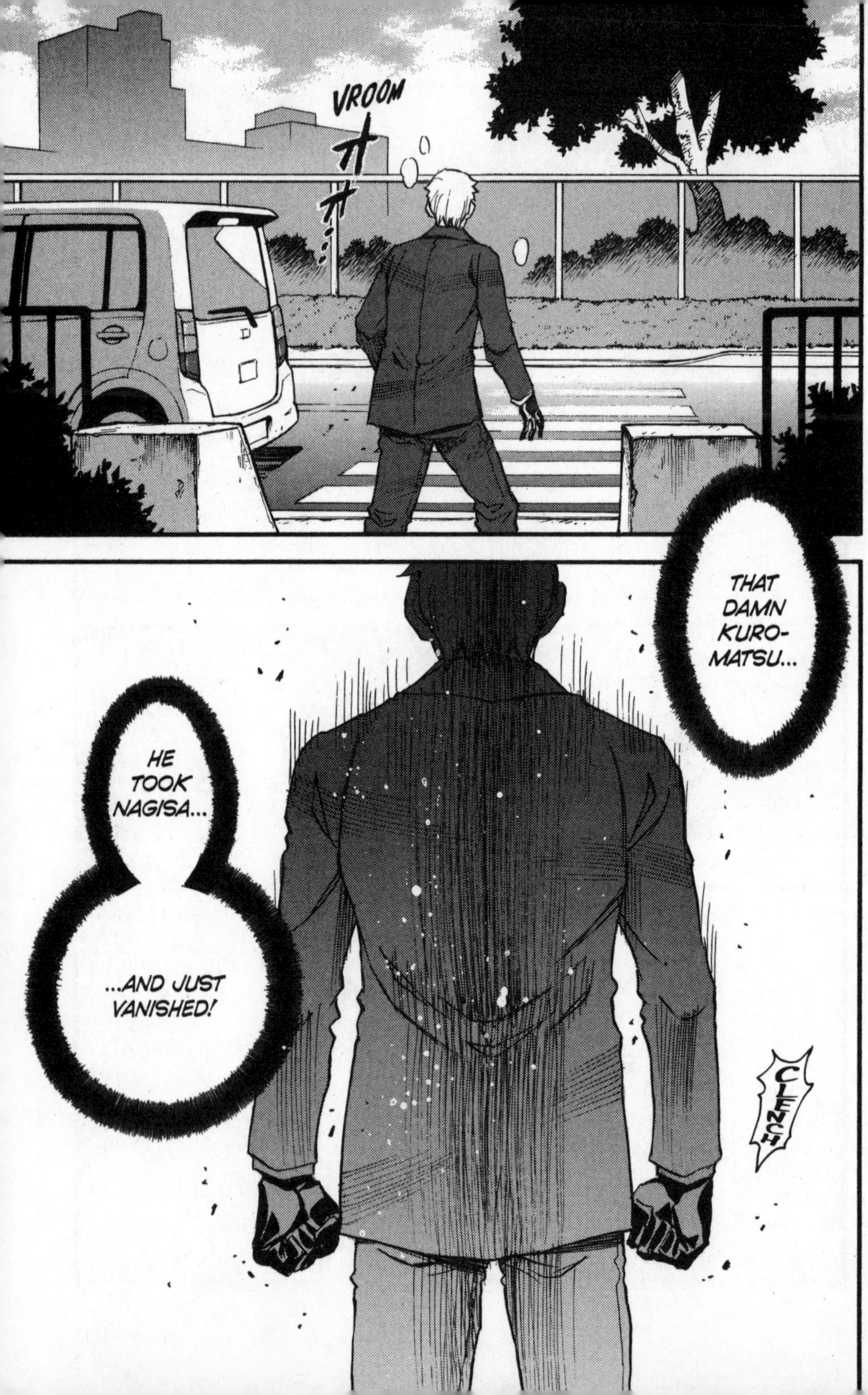
VROOM
THAT DAMN KURO-MATSU...
HE TOOK NAGISA...
...AND JUST VANISHED!
CLENCH

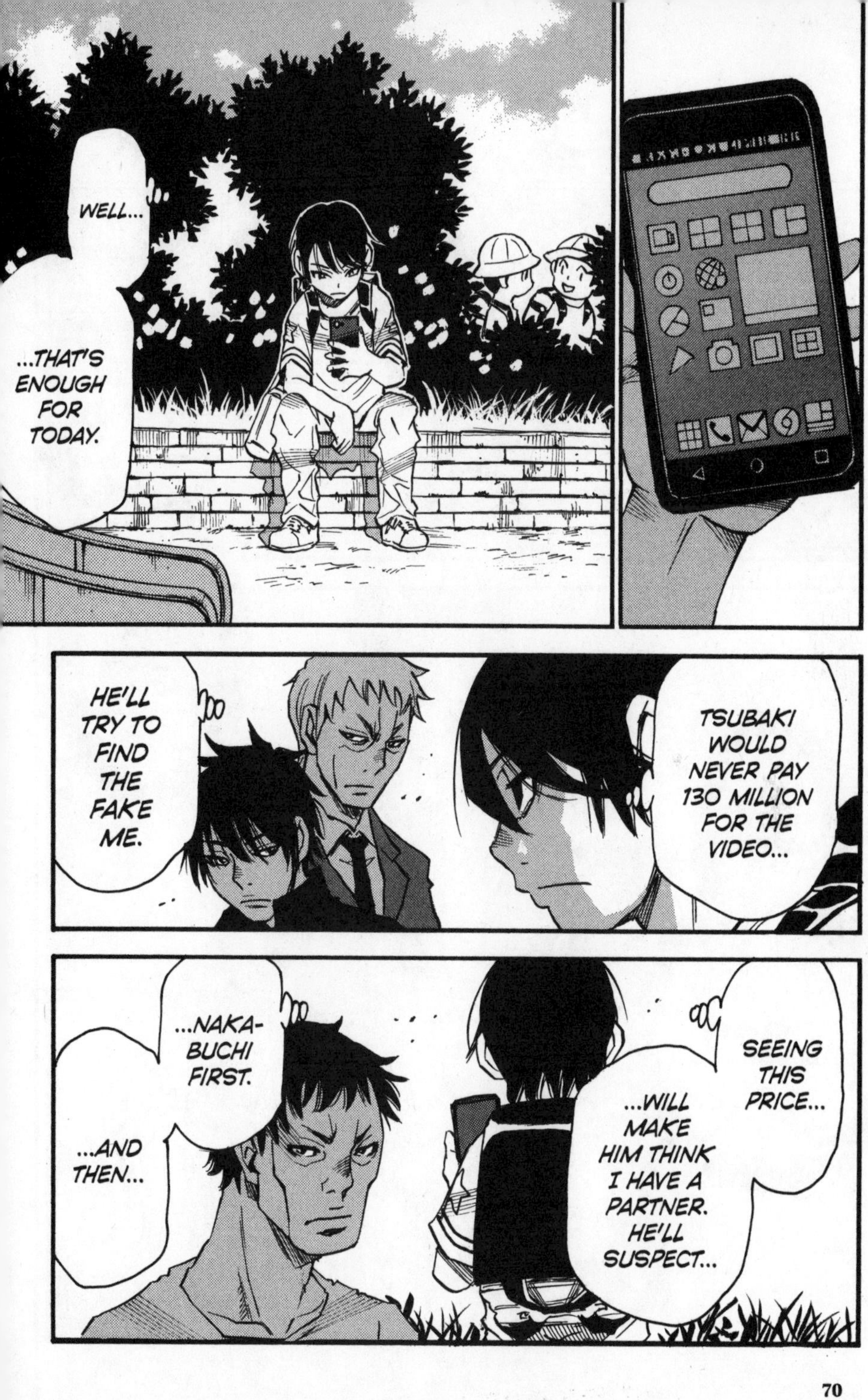
WELL...
...THAT'S ENOUGH FOR TODAY.
TSUBAKI WOULD NEVER PAY 130 MILLION FOR THE VIDEO...
HE'LL TRY TO FIND THE FAKE ME.
SEEING THIS PRICE...
...WILL MAKE HIM THINK I HAVE A PARTNER. HE'LL SUSPECT...
...NAKA-BUCHI FIRST.
...AND THEN...

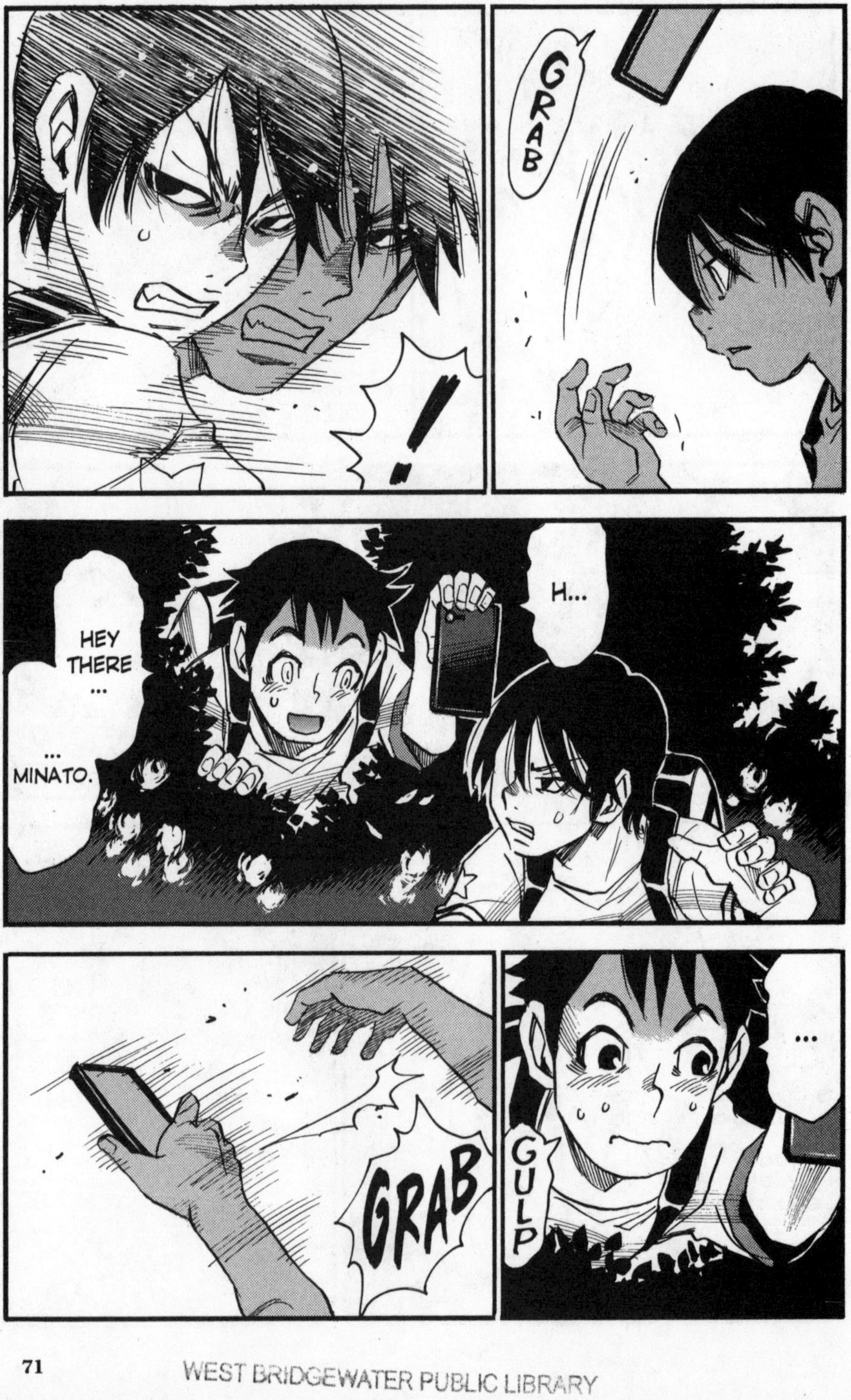
GRAB
!
H...
HEY THERE ...
... MINATO.
...
GULP
GRAB

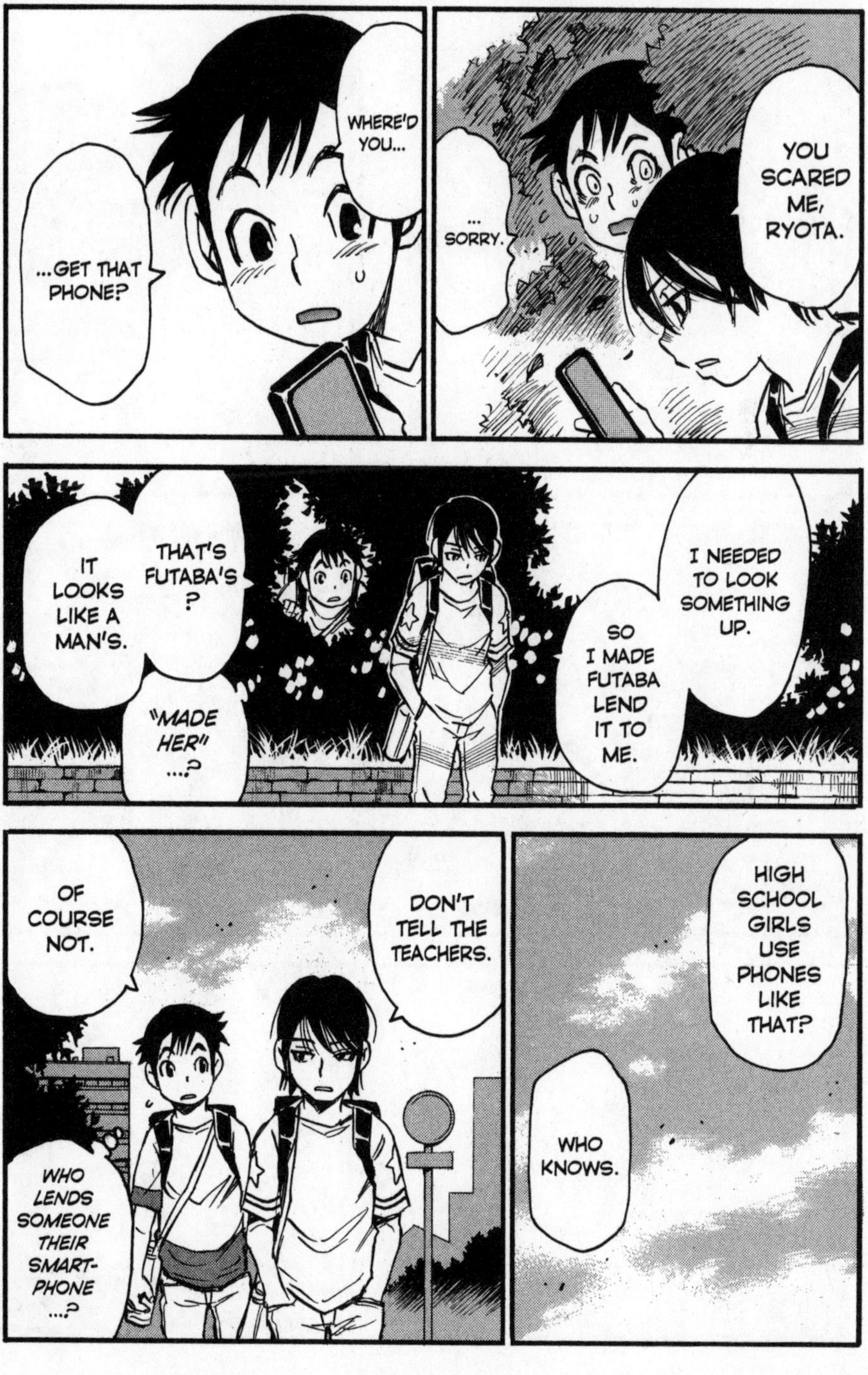
YOU SCARED ME, RYOTA.
... SORRY.
WHERE'D YOU...
...GET THAT PHONE?
I NEEDED TO LOOK SOMETHING UP.
SO I MADE FUTABA LEND IT TO ME.
THAT'S FUTABA'S?
IT LOOKS LIKE A MAN'S.
"MADE HER" ...?
HIGH SCHOOL GIRLS USE PHONES LIKE THAT?
WHO KNOWS.
DON'T TELL THE TEACHERS.
OF COURSE NOT.
WHO LENDS SOMEONE THEIR SMART-PHONE ...?

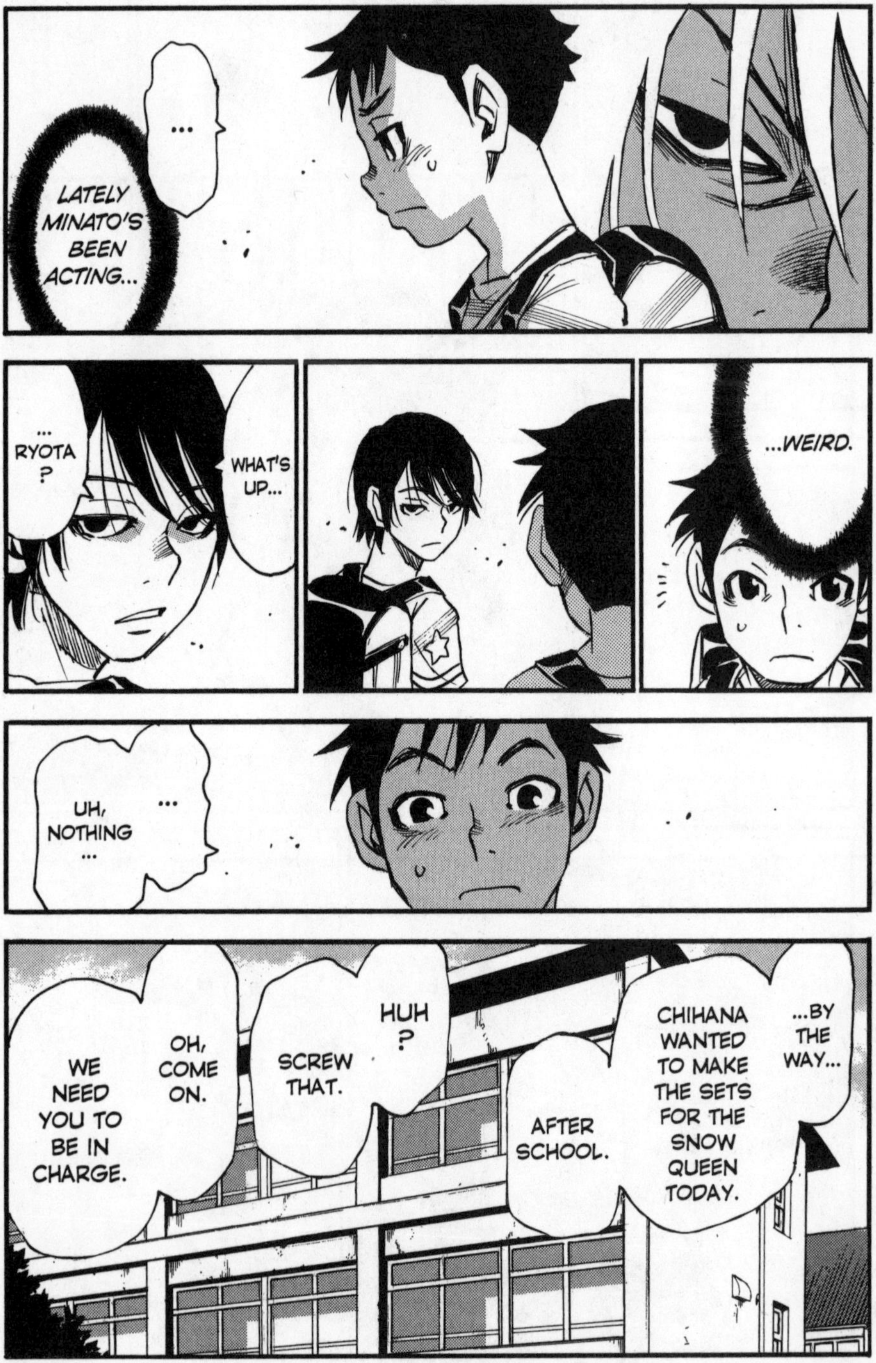
...
LATELY MINATO'S BEEN ACTING...
...WEIRD.
WHAT'S UP...
... RYOTA ?
UH, NOTHING ... ...
...BY THE WAY...
CHIHANA WANTED TO MAKE THE SETS FOR THE SNOW QUEEN TODAY.
AFTER SCHOOL.
HUH ?
SCREW THAT.
OH, COME ON.
WE NEED YOU TO BE IN CHARGE.

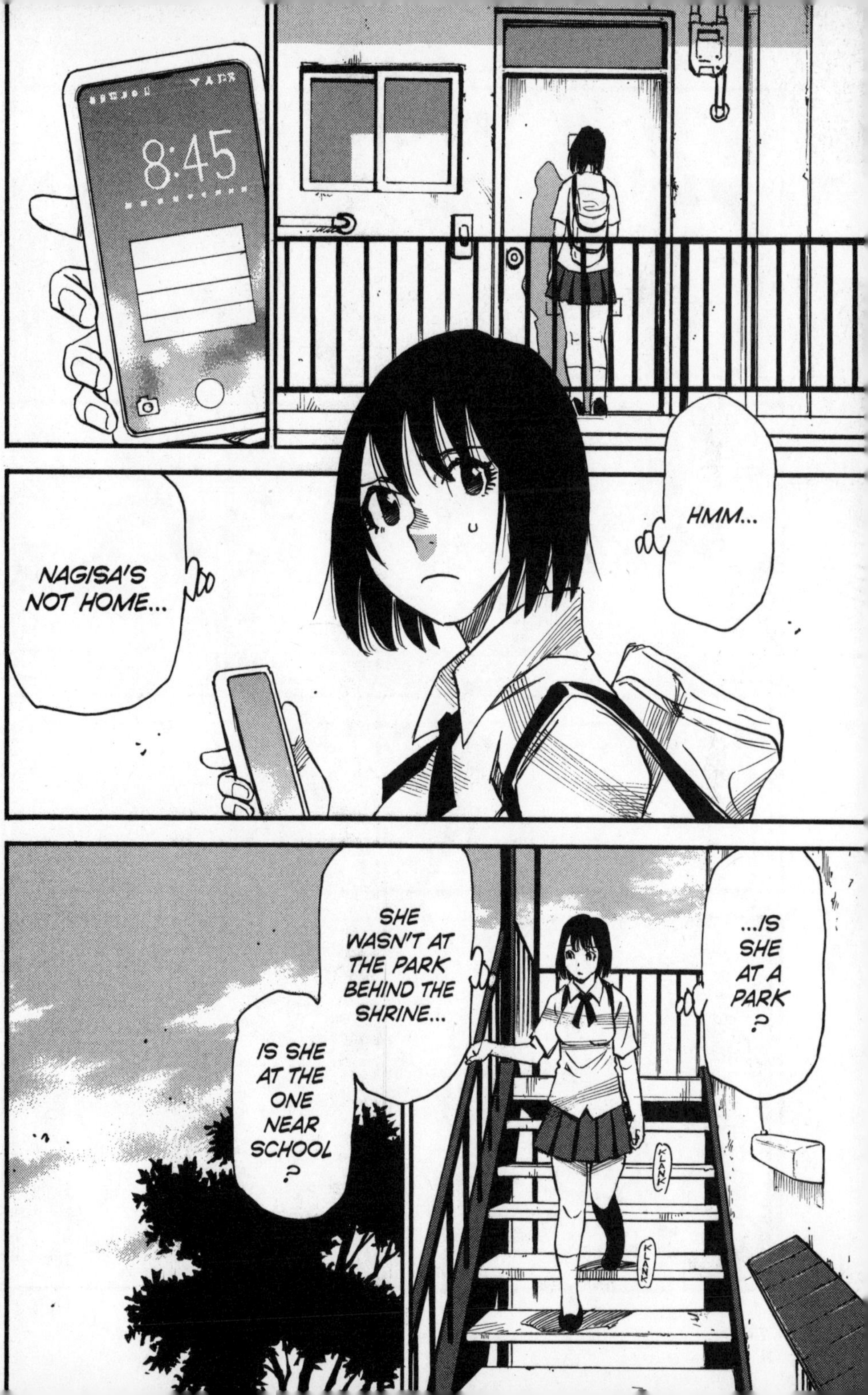
8:45
HMM...
NAGISA'S NOT HOME...
...IS SHE AT A PARK?
SHE WASN'T AT THE PARK BEHIND THE SHRINE...
IS SHE AT THE ONE NEAR SCHOOL?
KLANK
KLANK

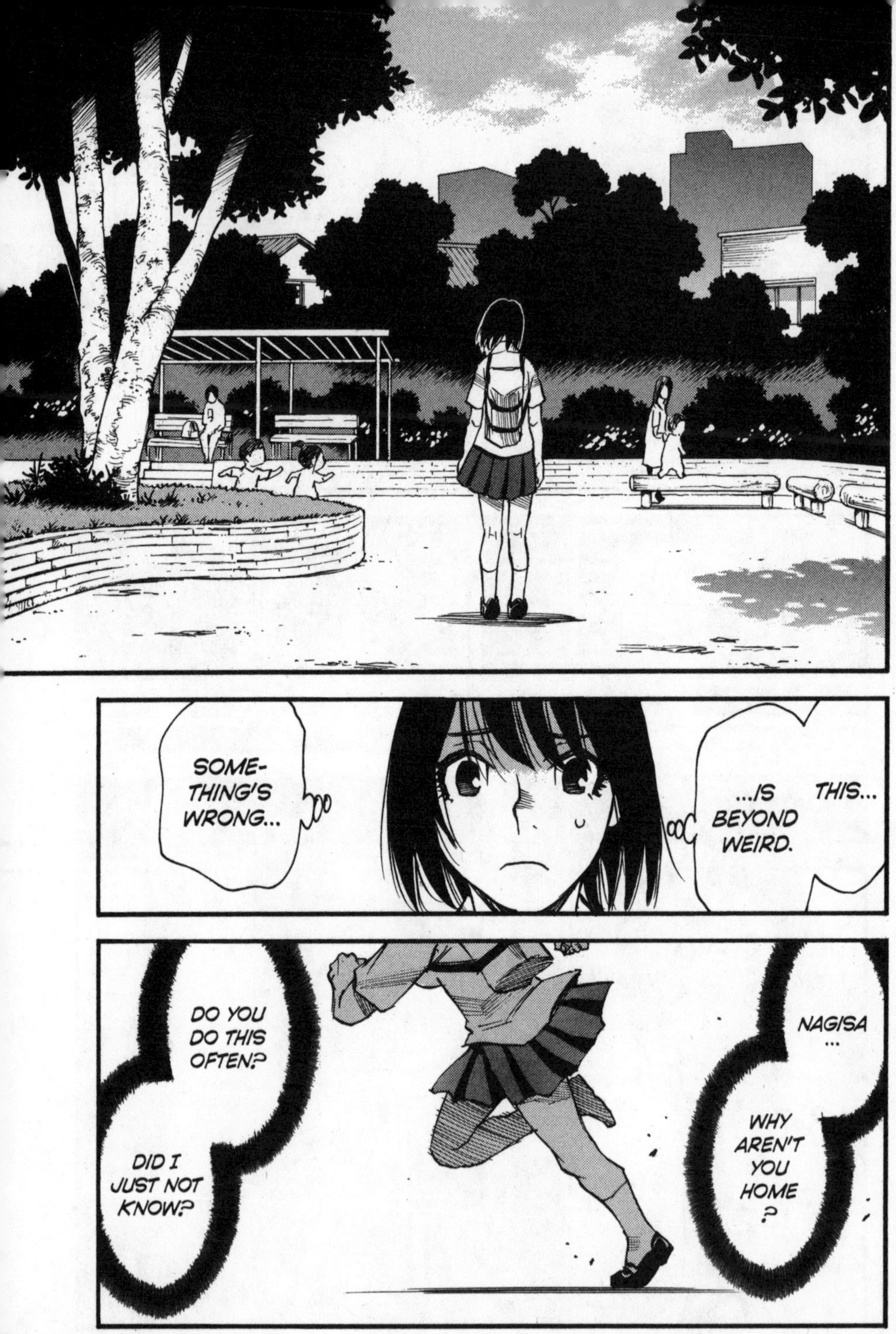
THIS...
...IS BEYOND WEIRD.
SOME-THING'S WRONG...
NAGISA ...
WHY AREN'T YOU HOME ?
DO YOU DO THIS OFTEN?
DID I JUST NOT KNOW?

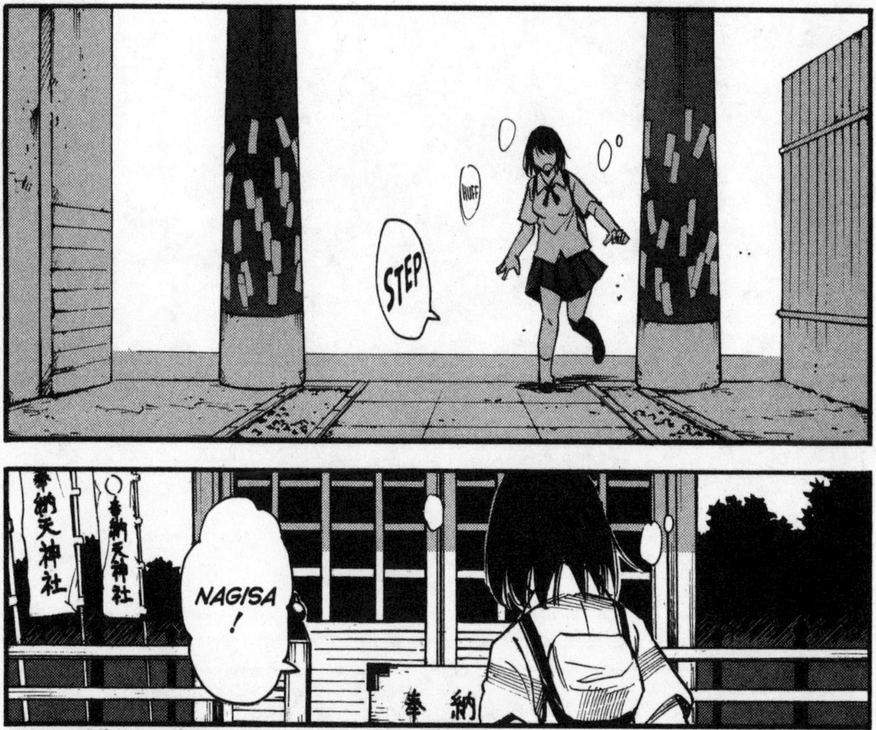
HUFF
STEP
NAGISA!

BANNER: Offering to Shrine

BOX: Offerings

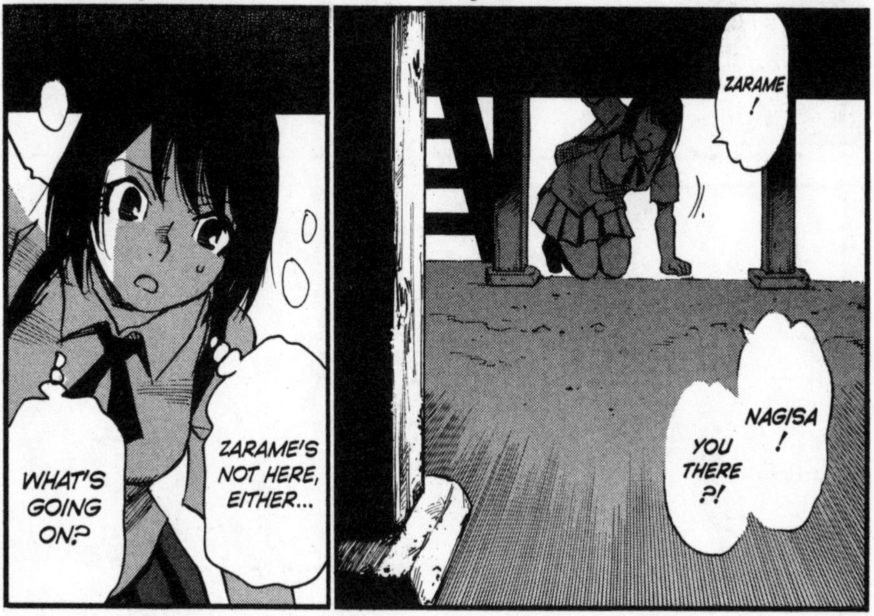
ZARAME!
NAGISA! YOU THERE?!
ZARAME'S NOT HERE, EITHER...
WHAT'S GOING ON?

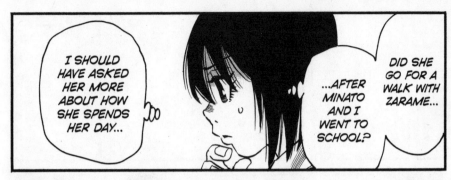

DID SHE GO FOR A WALK WITH ZARAME...
...AFTER MINATO AND I WENT TO SCHOOL?
I SHOULD HAVE ASKED HER MORE ABOUT HOW SHE SPENDS HER DAY...
IF SHE'S ON A WALK...
...WOULD A YOUNG CHILD STAY IN THE AREA SHE KNOWS?
LIKE NEAR THE APARTMENT AND THE SHRINE?
IF ZARAME IS LEADING THE WAY, I'LL NEVER FIND THEM...
OH NO...
...HUH?

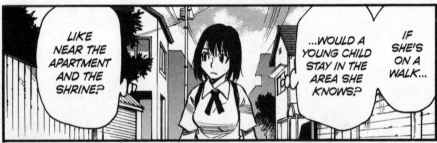

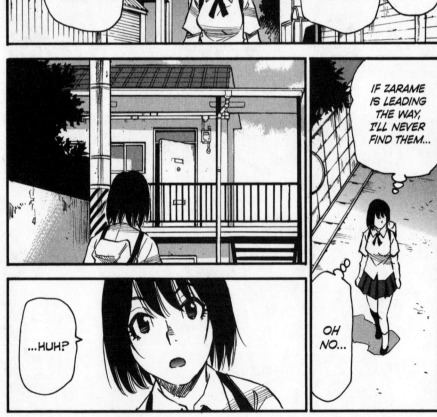

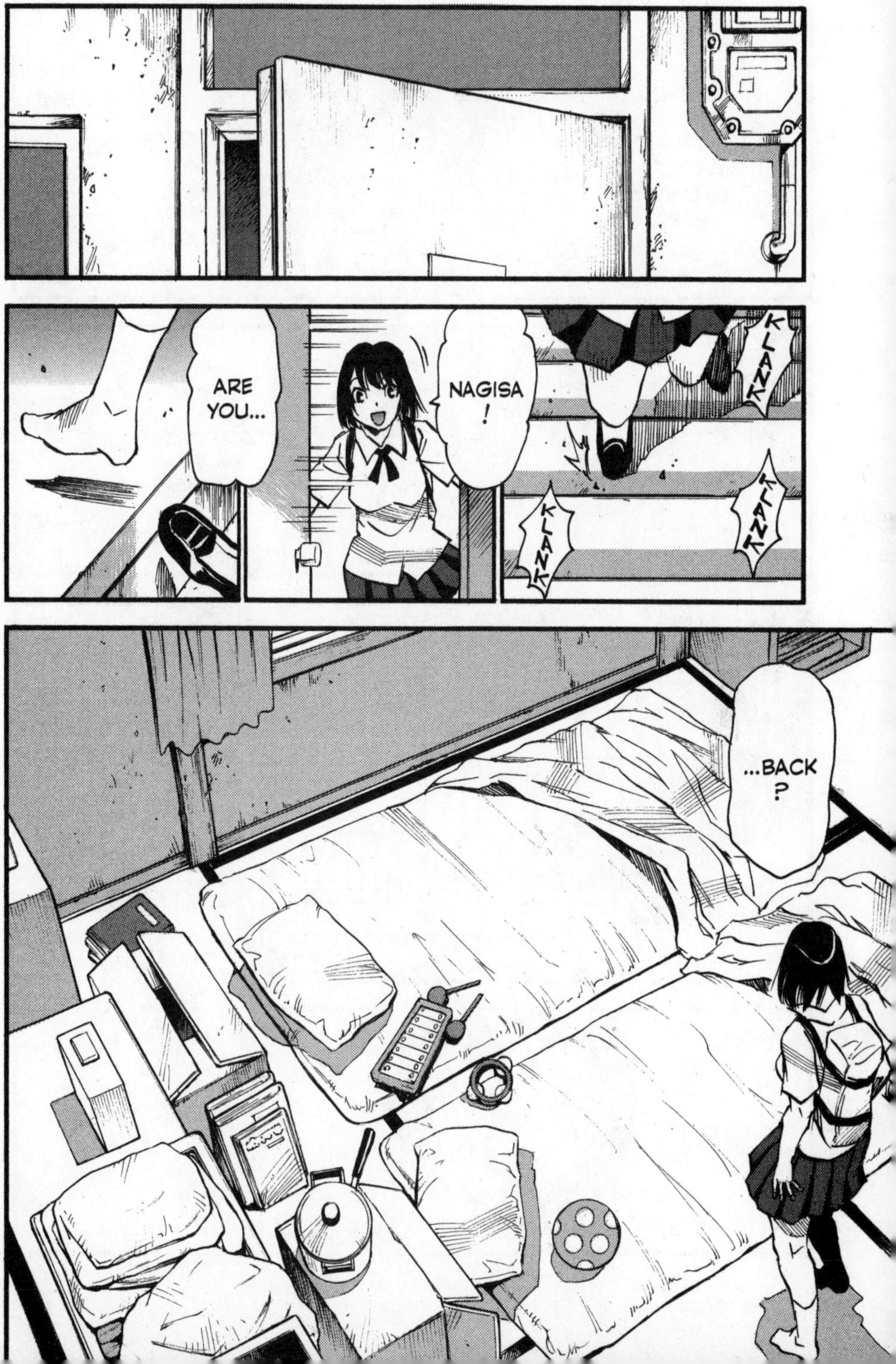
KLANK
KLANK
KLANK
NAGISA!
ARE YOU...
...BACK?

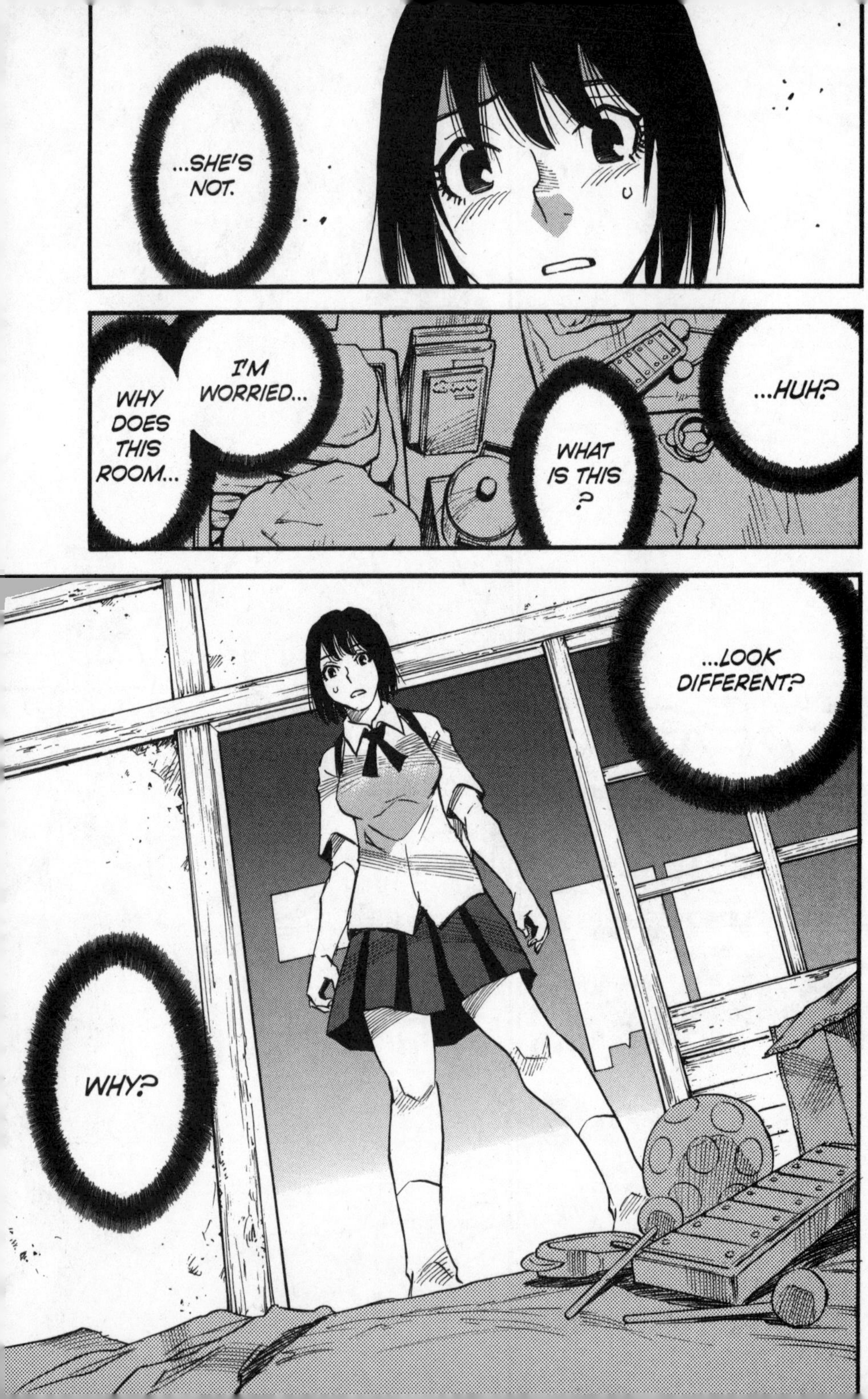
...SHE'S NOT.
...HUH?
WHAT IS THIS ?
I'M WORRIED...
WHY DOES THIS ROOM...
...LOOK DIFFERENT?
WHY?

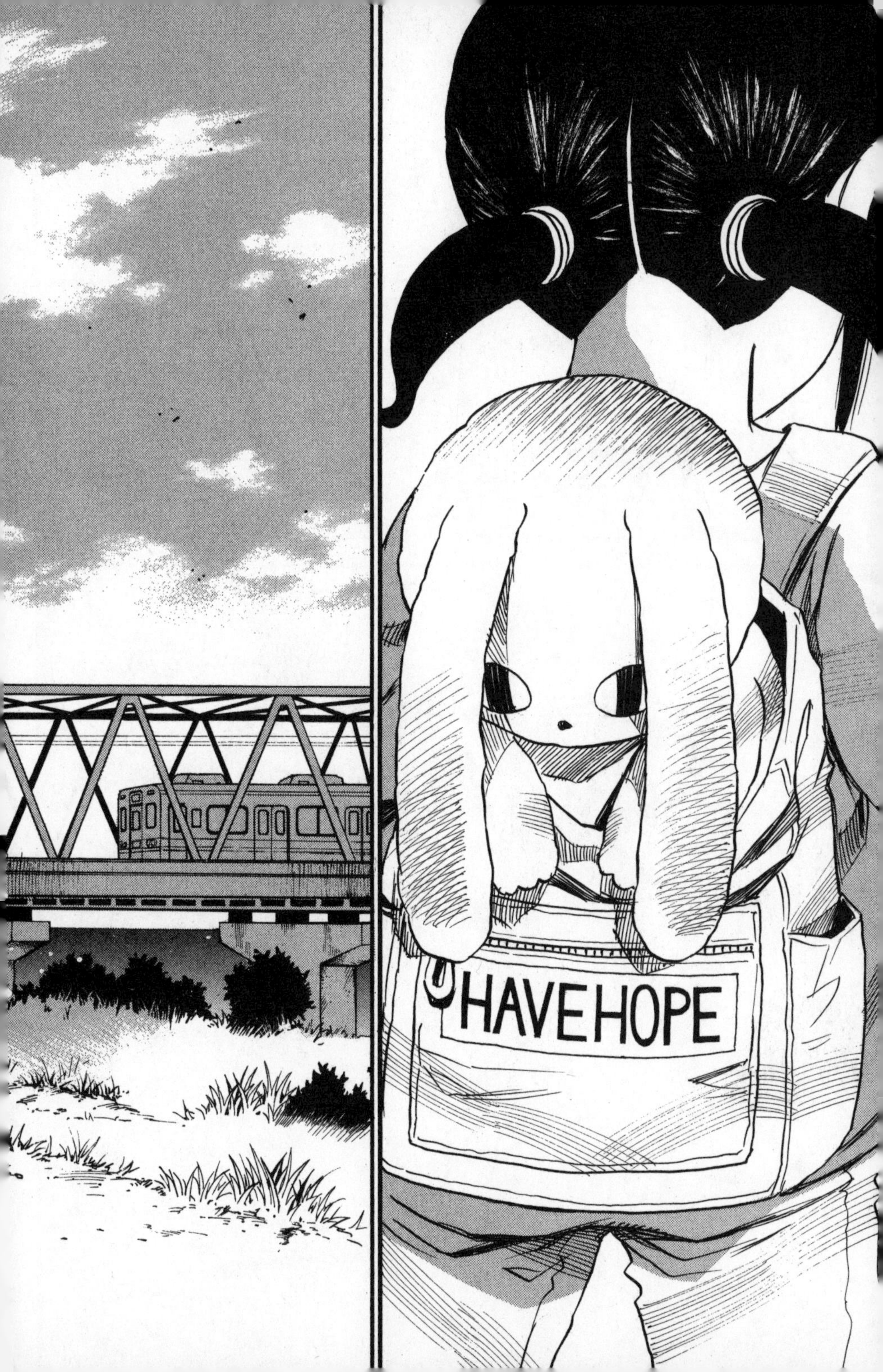
HAVE HOPE

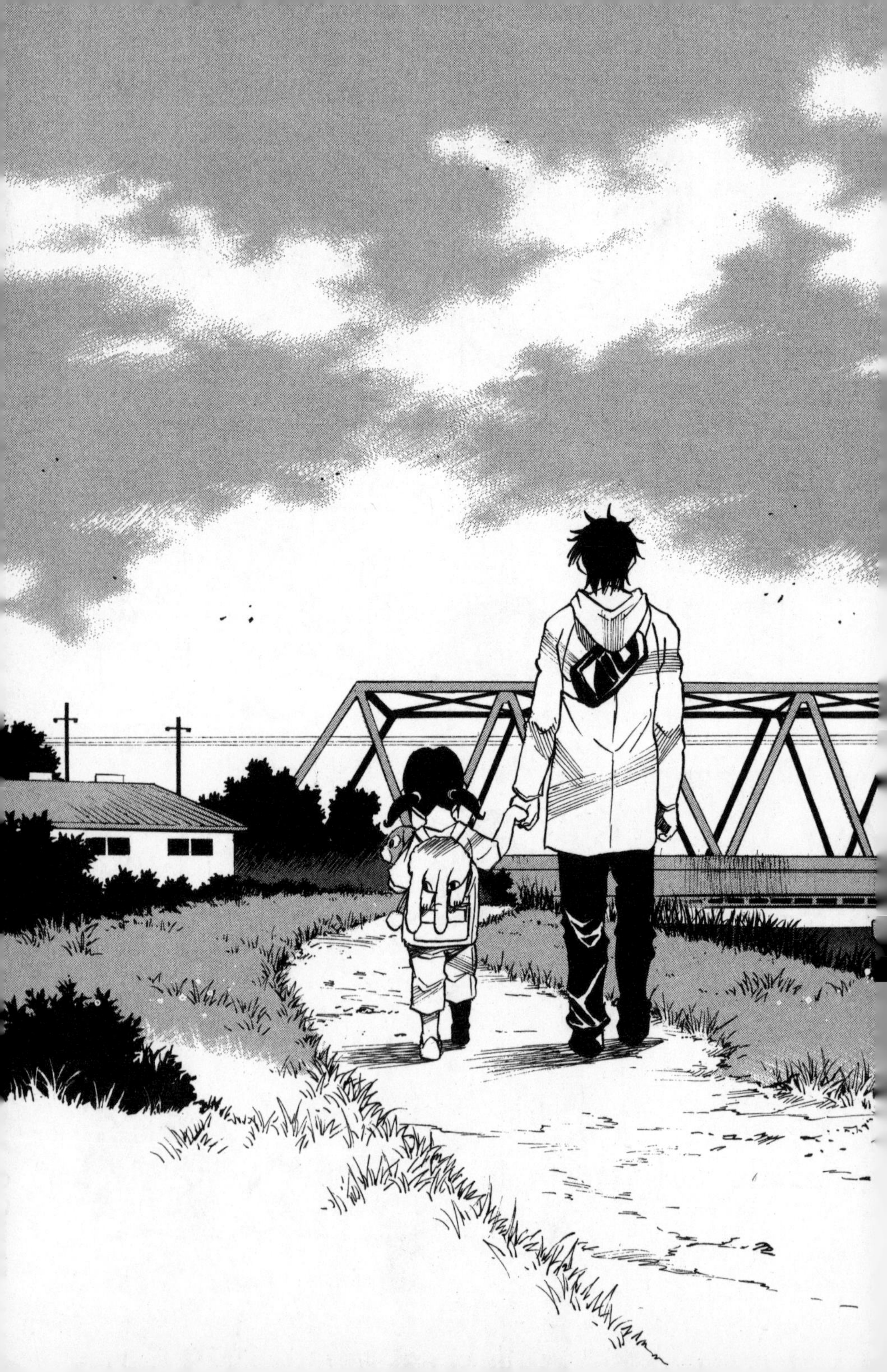

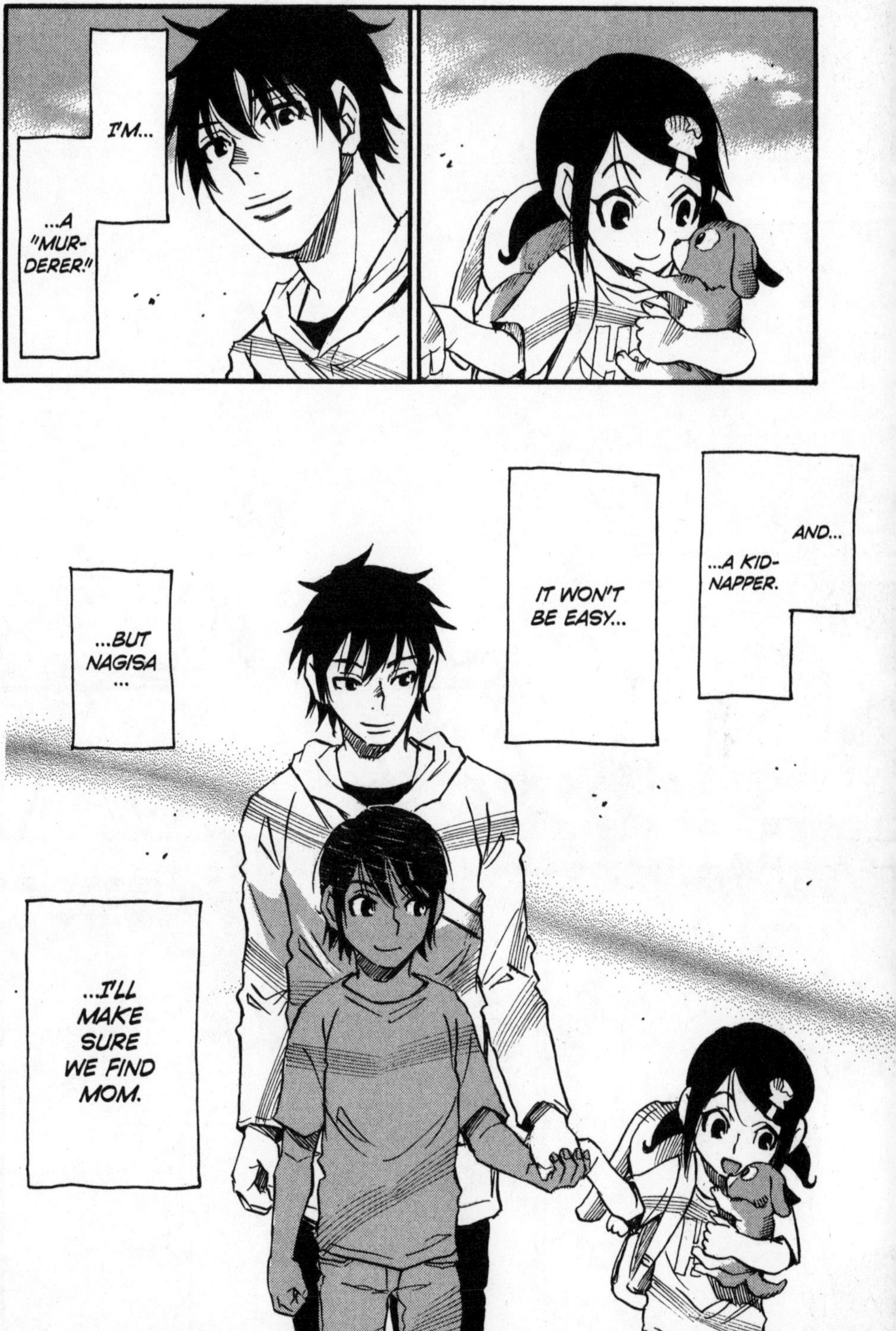
I'M...
...A "MUR-DERER!"
AND...
...A KID-NAPPER.
IT WON'T BE EASY...
...BUT NAGISA ...
...I'LL MAKE SURE WE FIND MOM.

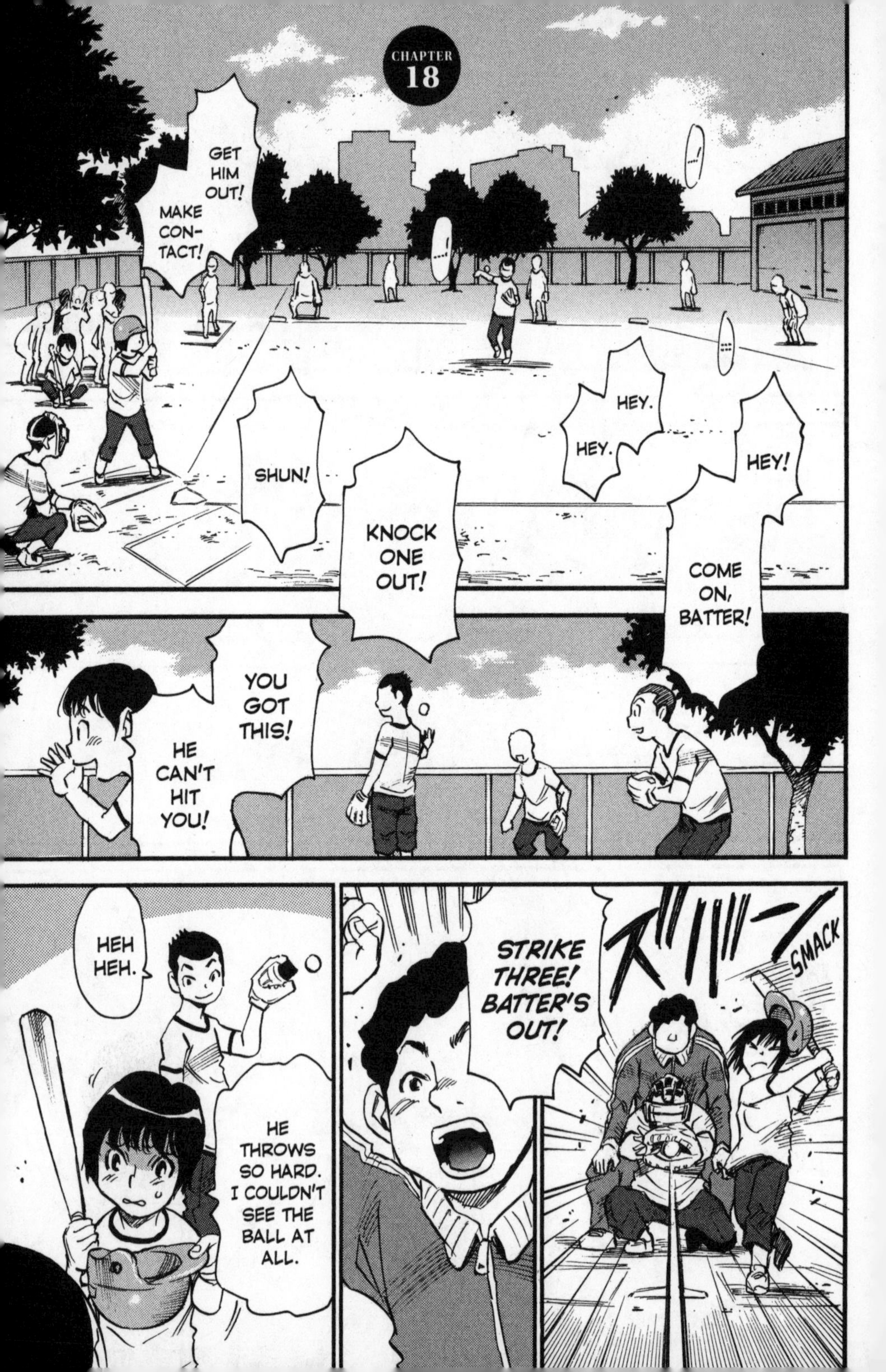
CHAPTER 18
HEY!
HEY. HEY.
COME ON, BATTER!
KNOCK ONE OUT!
SHUN!
GET HIM OUT!
MAKE CON-TACT!
YOU GOT THIS!
HE CAN'T HIT YOU!
SMACK
STRIKE THREE! BATTER'S OUT!
HEH HEH.
HE THROWS SO HARD. I COULDN'T SEE THE BALL AT ALL.

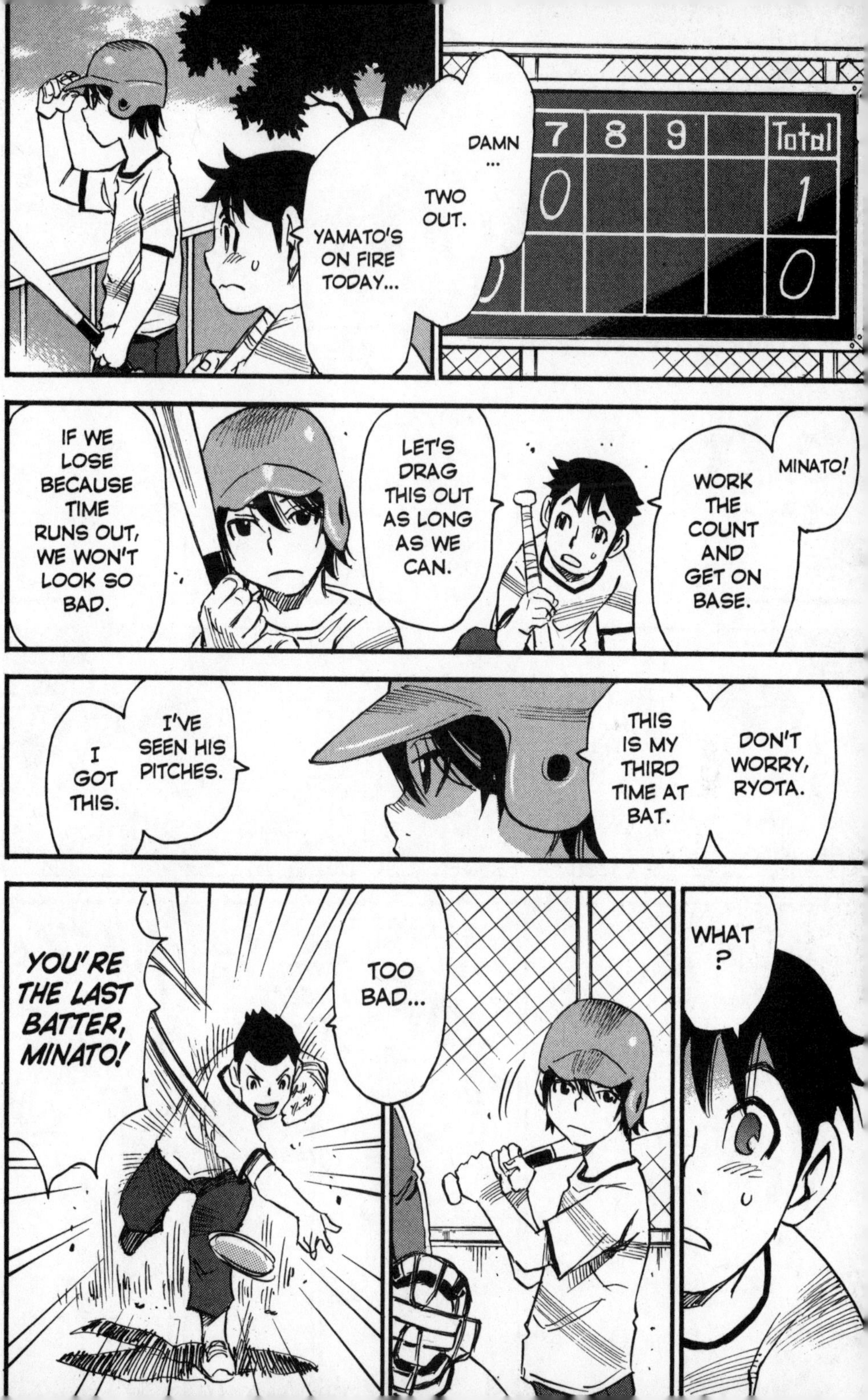
DAMN ... TWO OUT. YAMATO'S ON FIRE TODAY...
7 8 9 Total
0
1
0
MINATO! WORK THE COUNT AND GET ON BASE.
LET'S DRAG THIS OUT AS LONG AS WE CAN.
IF WE LOSE BECAUSE TIME RUNS OUT, WE WON'T LOOK SO BAD.
DON'T WORRY, RYOTA. THIS IS MY THIRD TIME AT BAT.
I'VE SEEN HIS PITCHES. I GOT THIS.
WHAT?
TOO BAD...
YOU'RE THE LAST BATTER, MINATO!

CHAPTER 18
Nobody's Looking for You

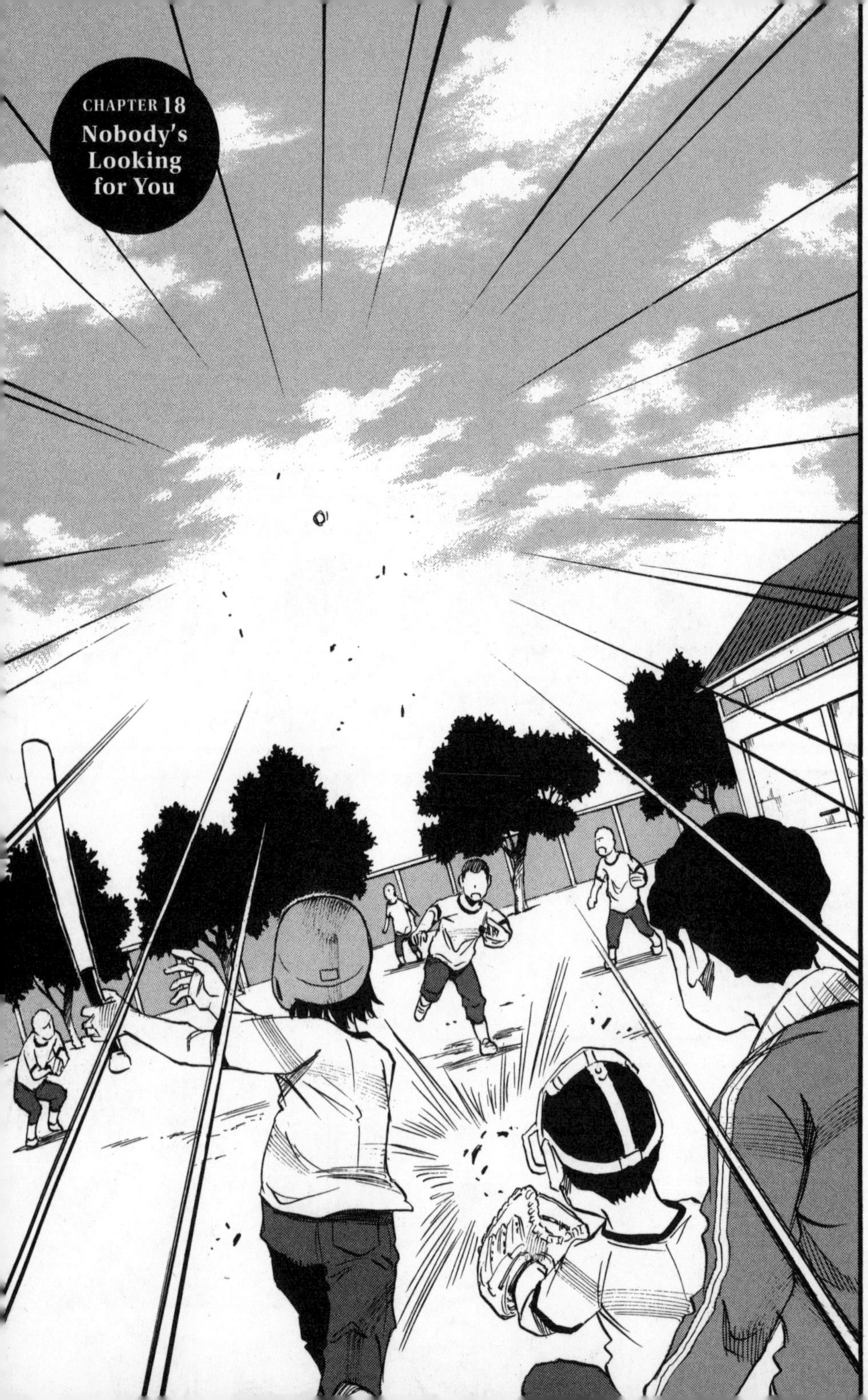

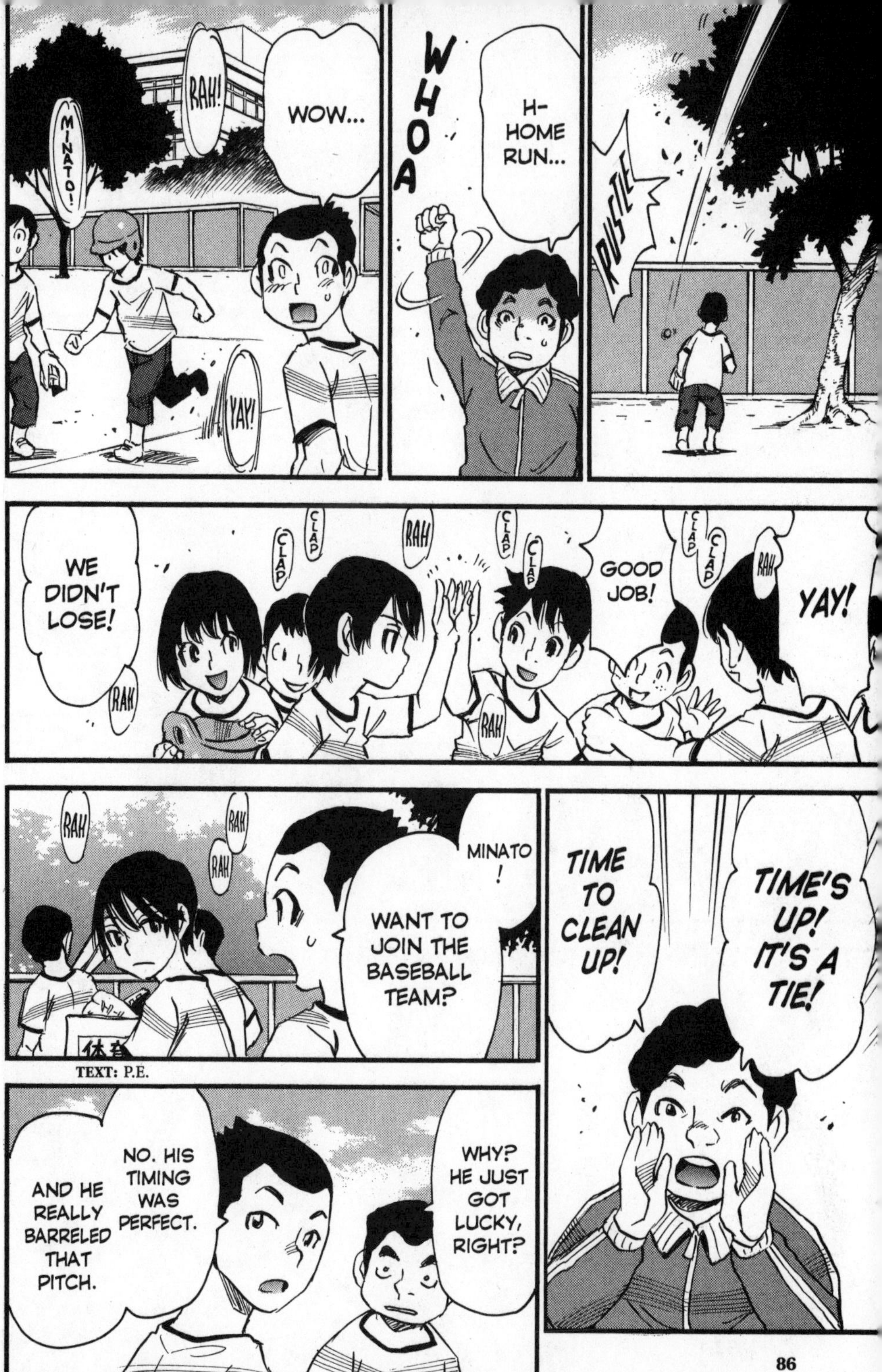
RUSTLE
WHOA
H- HOME RUN...
WOW...
RAH!
MINATO!
YAY!
YAY!
RAH
CLAP CLAP
GOOD JOB!
CLAP CLAP
RAH
CLAP CLAP
RAH
WE DIDN'T LOSE!
RAH
TIME'S UP! IT'S A TIE!
TIME TO CLEAN UP!
MINATO!
WANT TO JOIN THE BASEBALL TEAM?
RAH
RAH
RAH
TEXT: P.E.
WHY? HE JUST GOT LUCKY, RIGHT?
NO. HIS TIMING WAS PERFECT.
AND HE REALLY BARRELED THAT PITCH.

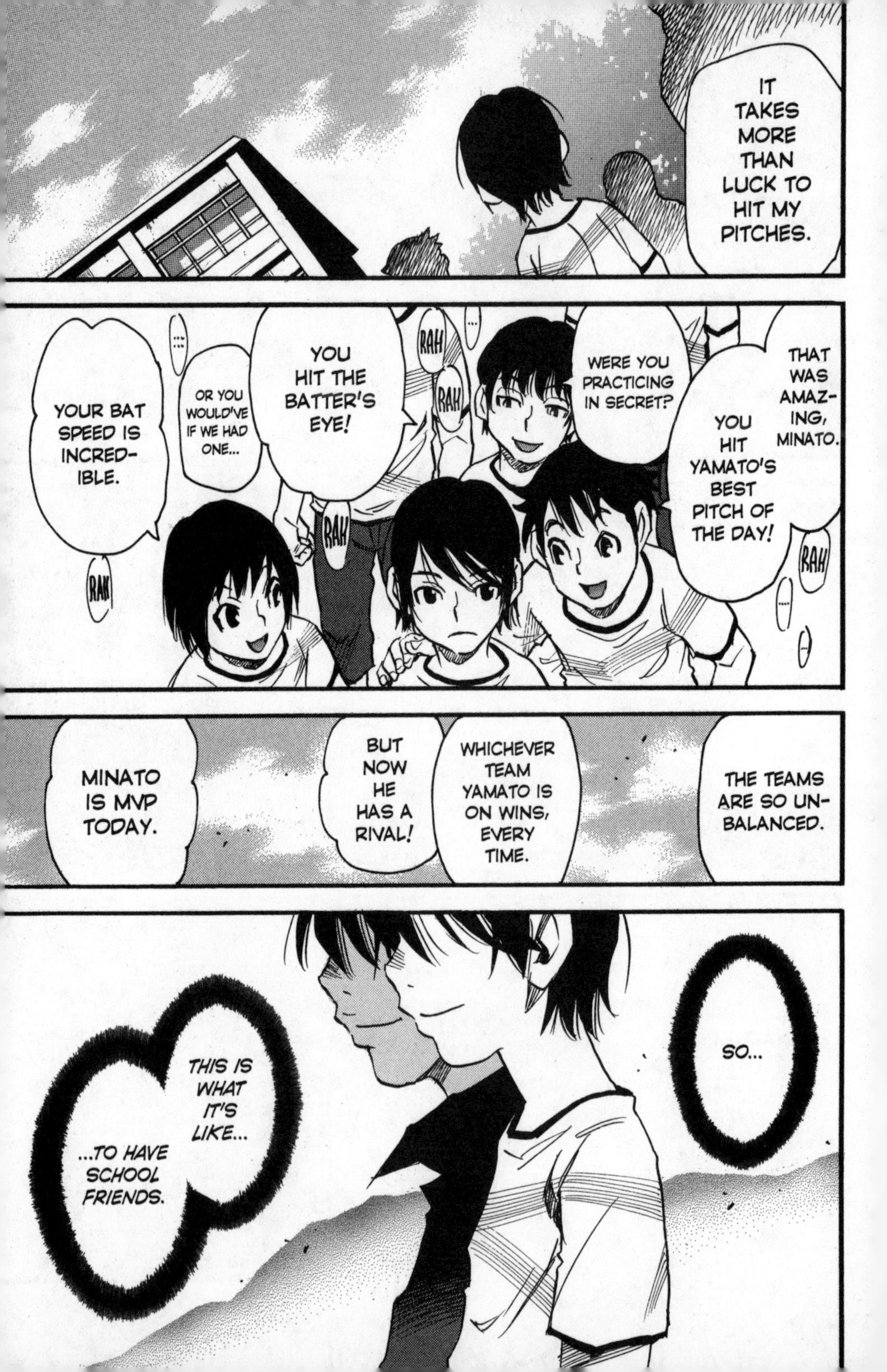
IT TAKES MORE THAN LUCK TO HIT MY PITCHES.
THAT WAS AMAZ-ING, MINATO.
YOU HIT YAMATO'S BEST PITCH OF THE DAY!
RAH
WERE YOU PRACTICING IN SECRET?
RAH
RAH
YOU HIT THE BATTER'S EYE!
RAH
OR YOU WOULD'VE IF WE HAD ONE...
YOUR BAT SPEED IS INCRED-IBLE.
RAH
THE TEAMS ARE SO UN-BALANCED.
WHICHEVER TEAM YAMATO IS ON WINS, EVERY TIME.
BUT NOW HE HAS A RIVAL!
MINATO IS MVP TODAY.
SO...
THIS IS WHAT IT'S LIKE...
...TO HAVE SCHOOL FRIENDS.

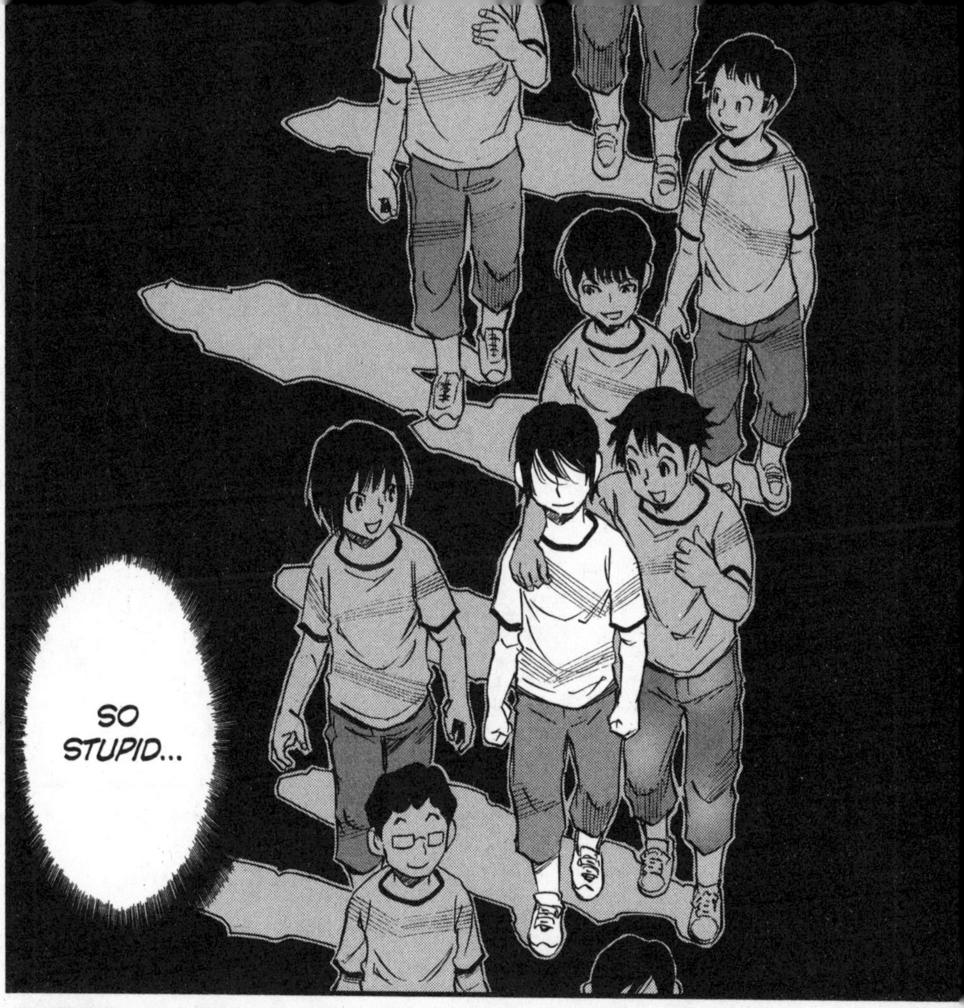
SO STUPID...

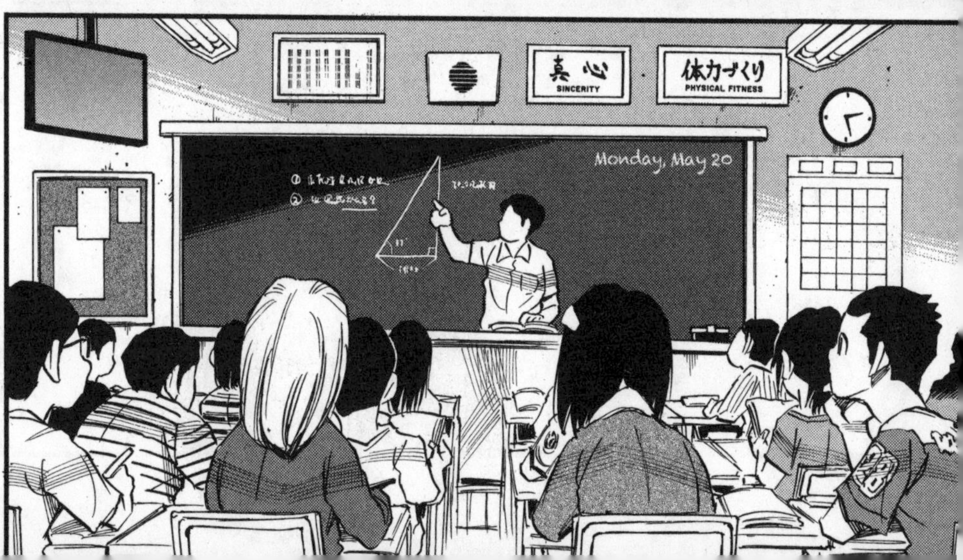
真心
SINCERITY
体力づくり
PHYSICAL FITNESS
Monday, May 20

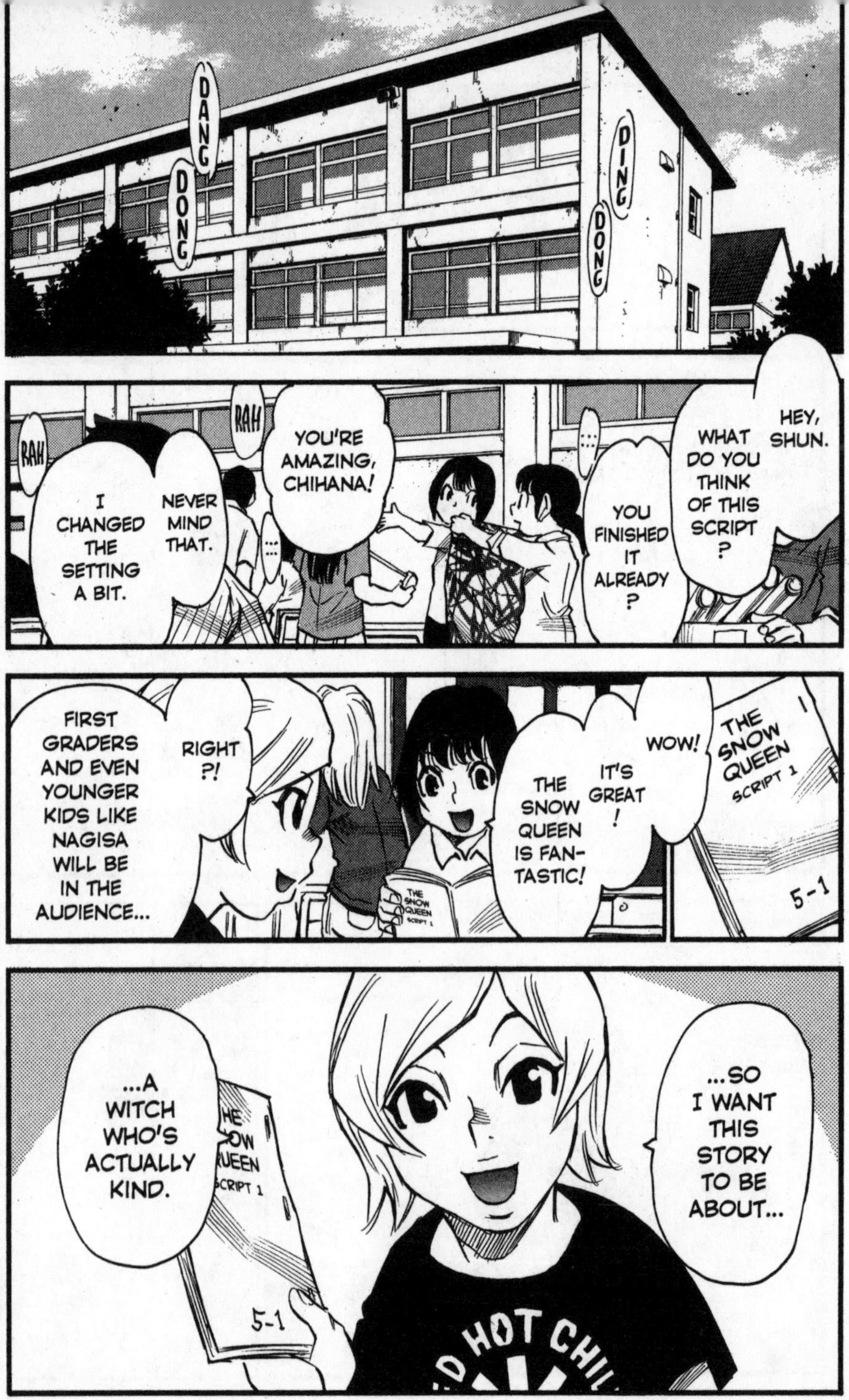
DING DONG
DANG DONG
HEY, SHUN. WHAT DO YOU THINK OF THIS SCRIPT?
YOU FINISHED IT ALREADY?
...
YOU'RE AMAZING, CHIHANA!
RAH
...
NEVER MIND THAT. I CHANGED THE SETTING A BIT.
RAH
THE SNOW QUEEN SCRIPT 1
5-1
WOW! IT'S GREAT! THE SNOW QUEEN IS FANTASTIC!
RIGHT?! FIRST GRADERS AND EVEN YOUNGER KIDS LIKE NAGISA WILL BE IN THE AUDIENCE...
...SO I WANT THIS STORY TO BE ABOUT...
...A WITCH WHO'S ACTUALLY KIND.
5-1

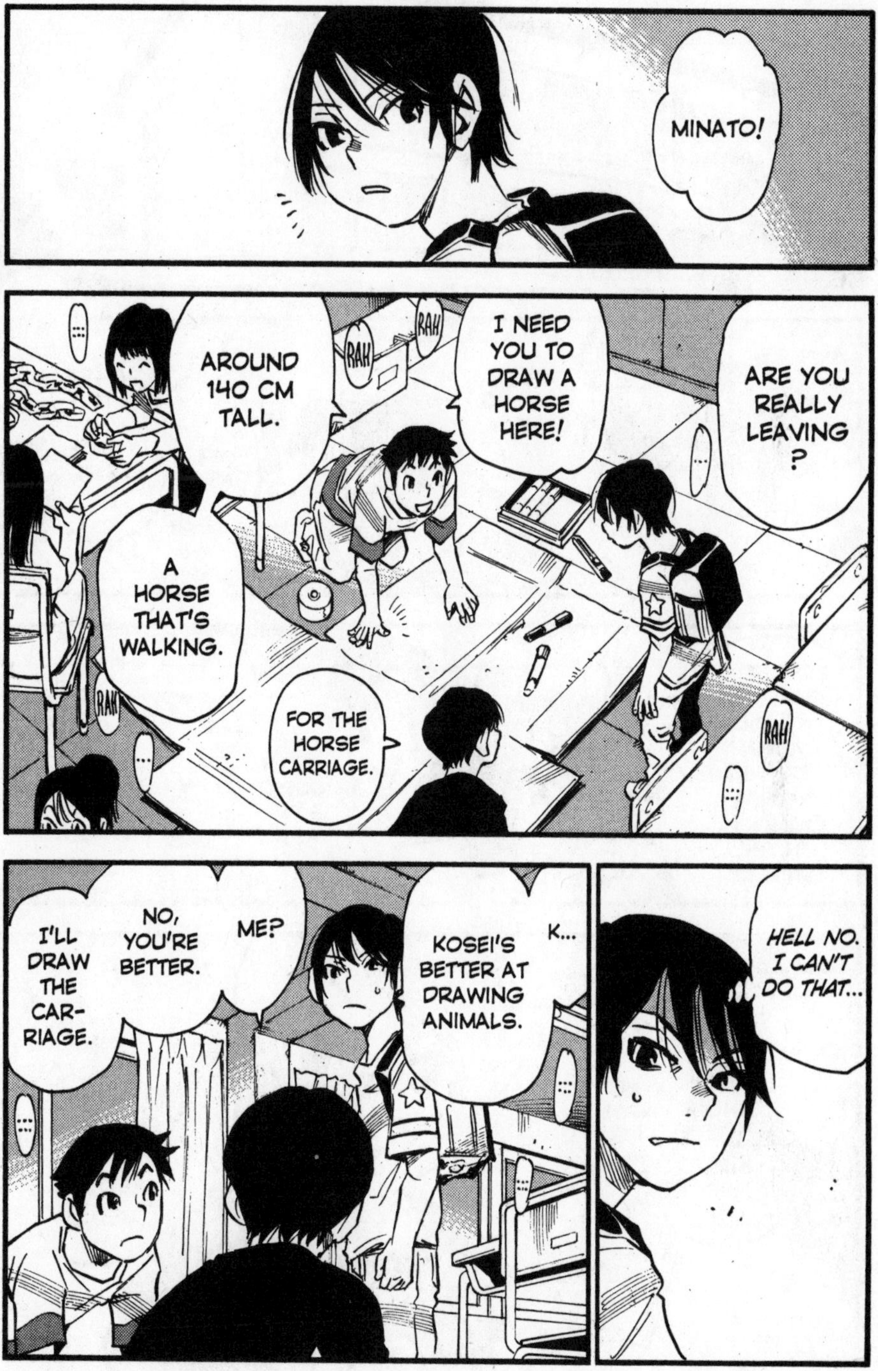
MINATO!
ARE YOU REALLY LEAVING?
...
I NEED YOU TO DRAW A HORSE HERE!
RAH
RAH
AROUND 140 CM TALL.
...
A HORSE THAT'S WALKING.
RAH
...
FOR THE HORSE CARRIAGE.
RAH
...
HELL NO. I CAN'T DO THAT...
K...
KOSEI'S BETTER AT DRAWING ANIMALS.
...
ME?
NO, YOU'RE BETTER.
I'LL DRAW THE CARRIAGE.
...

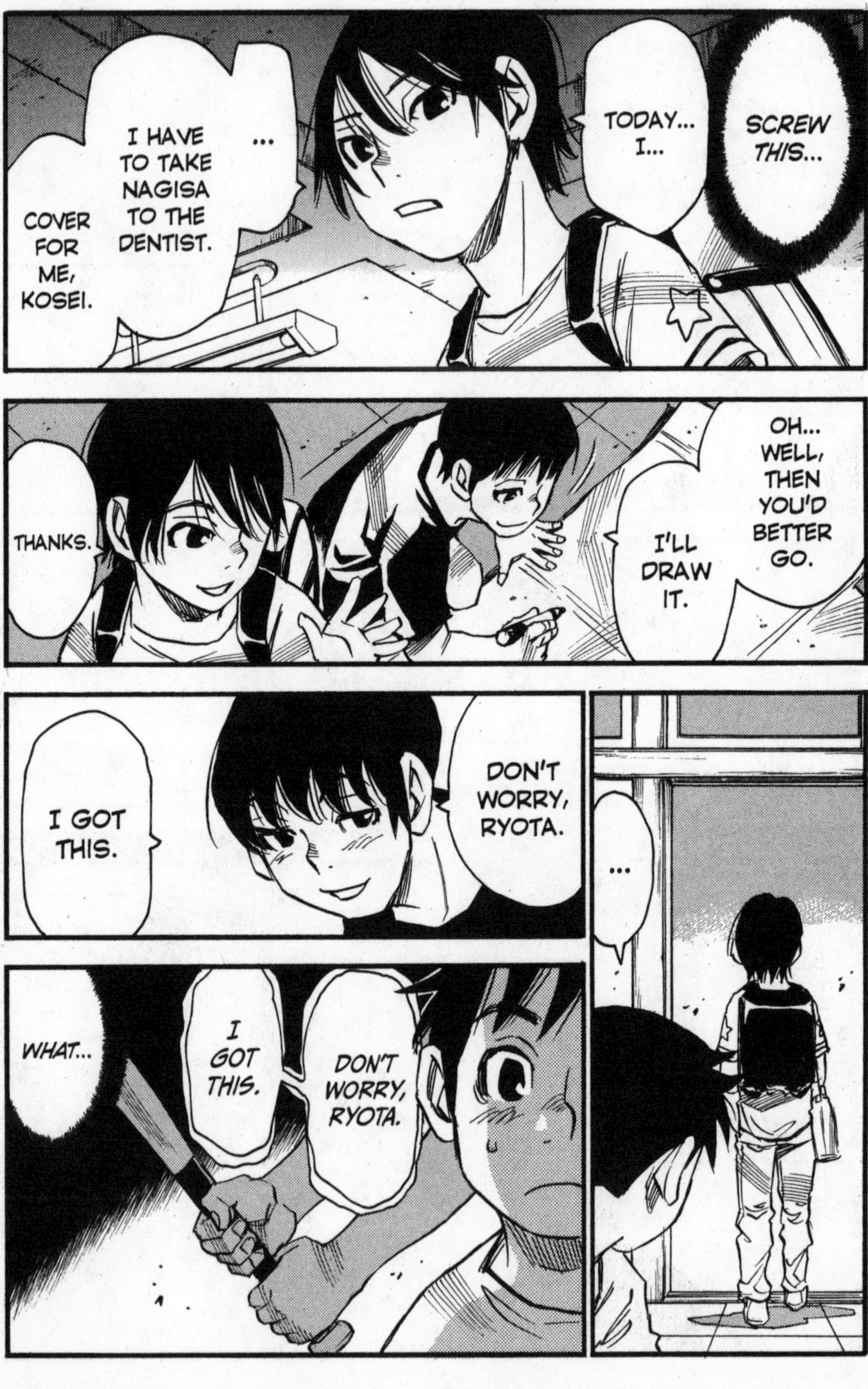
SCREW THIS...
TODAY... I...
...
I HAVE TO TAKE NAGISA TO THE DENTIST.
COVER FOR ME, KOSEI.
OH... WELL, THEN YOU'D BETTER GO.
I'LL DRAW IT.
THANKS.
...
DON'T WORRY, RYOTA.
I GOT THIS.
DON'T WORRY, RYOTA.
I GOT THIS.
WHAT...

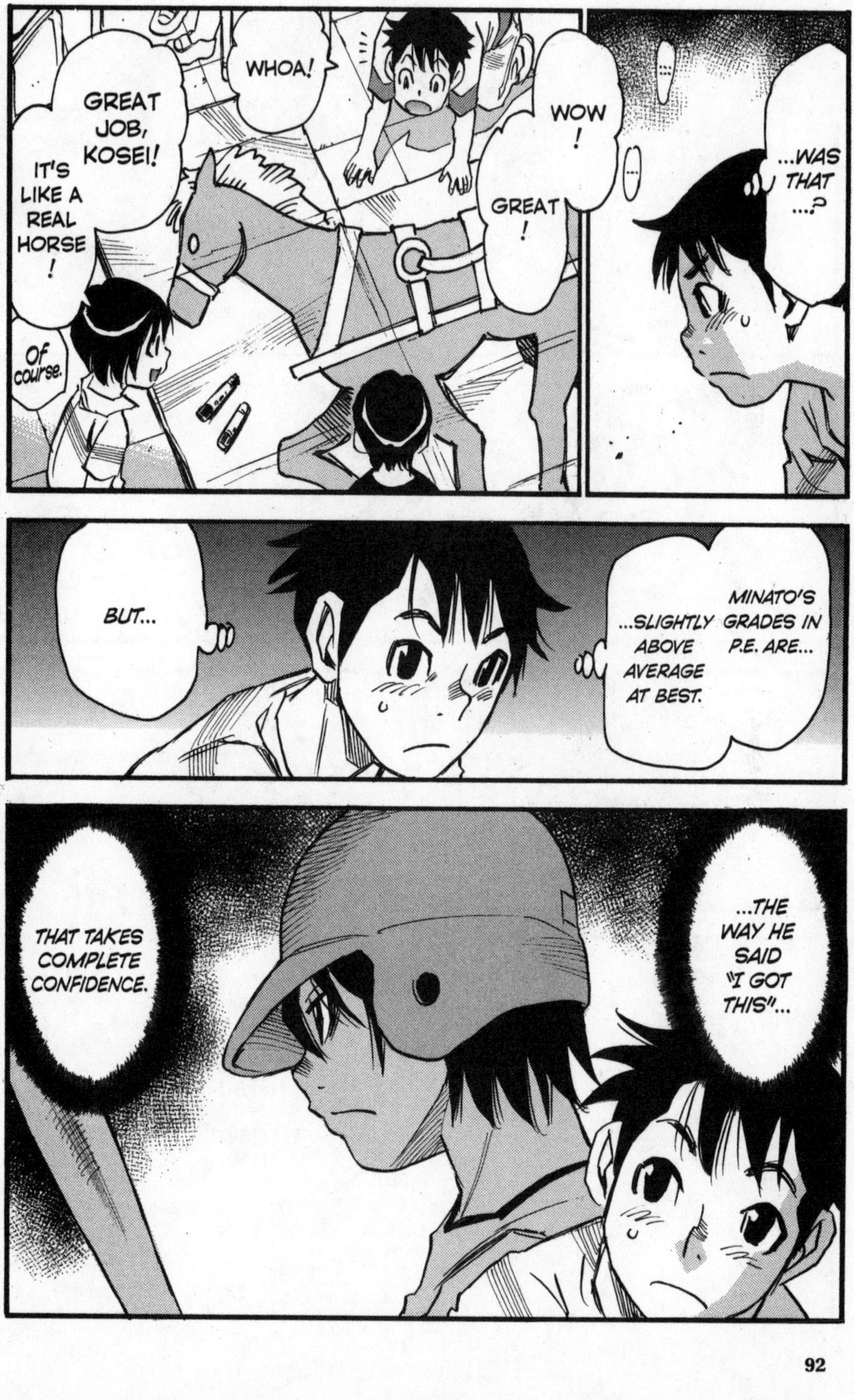

...
...
...WAS THAT ...?
WOW! GREAT!
WHOA!
GREAT JOB, KOSEI!
IT'S LIKE A REAL HORSE!
Of course.
MINATO'S GRADES IN P.E. ARE...
...SLIGHTLY ABOVE AVERAGE AT BEST.
BUT...
...THE WAY HE SAID "I GOT THIS"...
THAT TAKES COMPLETE CONFIDENCE.

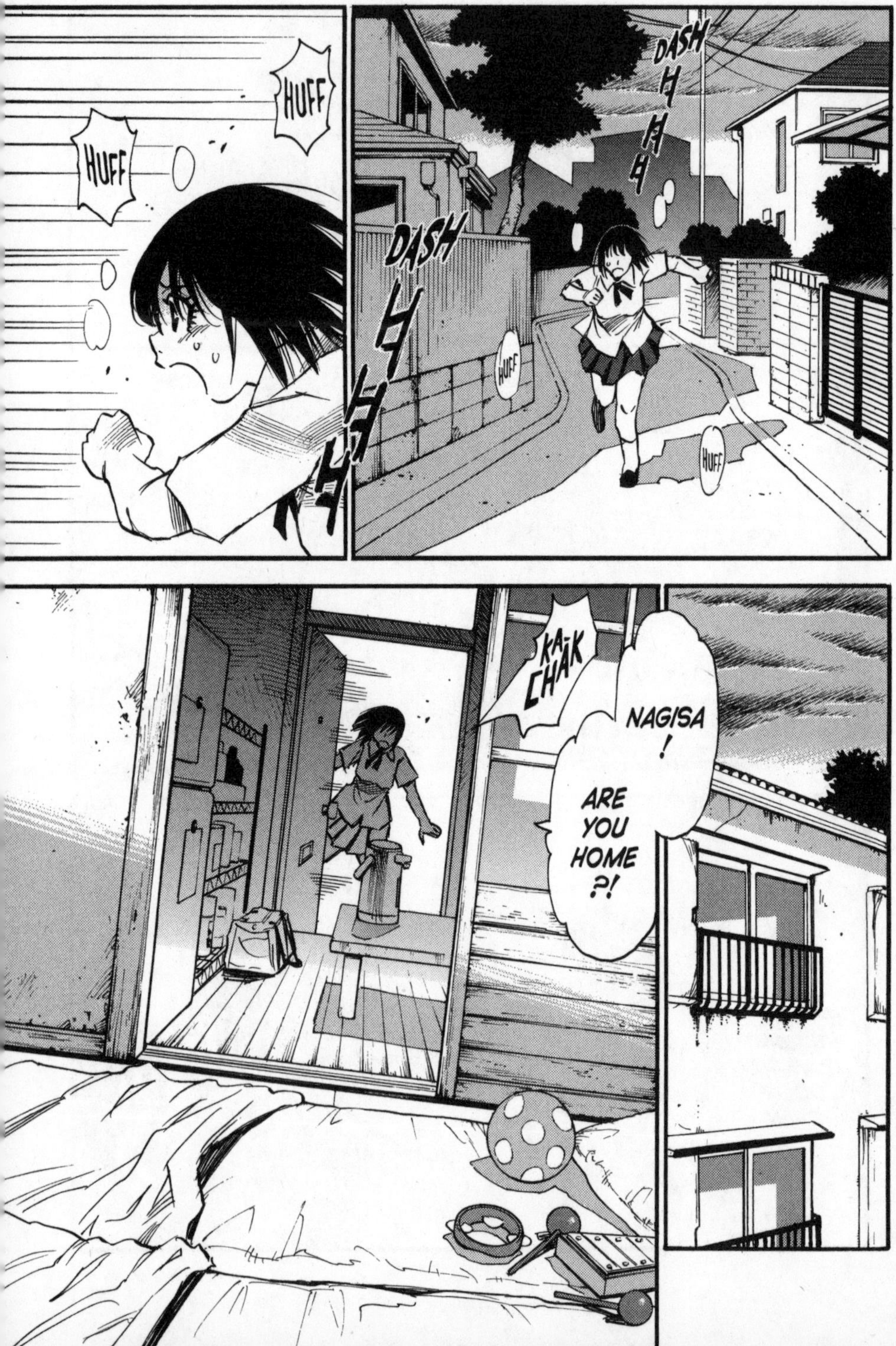
DASH
DASH
HUFF
HUFF
HUFF
HUFF
NAGISA! ARE YOU HOME?!
KA-CHAK

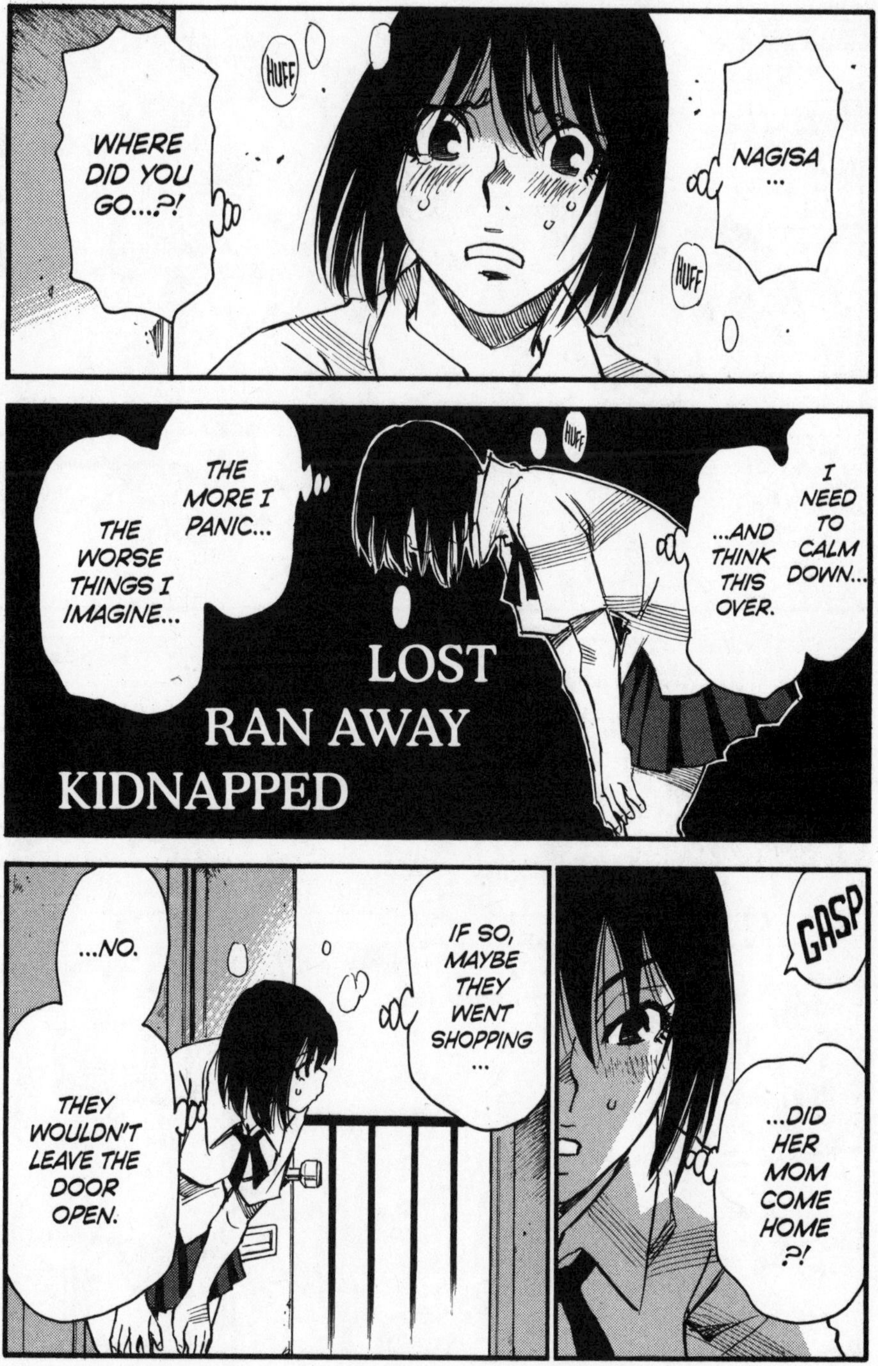
NAGISA ...
HUFF
HUFF
WHERE DID YOU GO...?!
I NEED TO CALM DOWN...
...AND THINK THIS OVER.
HUFF
THE MORE I PANIC...
THE WORSE THINGS I IMAGINE...
LOST
RAN AWAY
KIDNAPPED
GASP
...DID HER MOM COME HOME ?!
IF SO, MAYBE THEY WENT SHOPPING ...
...NO.
THEY WOULDN'T LEAVE THE DOOR OPEN.

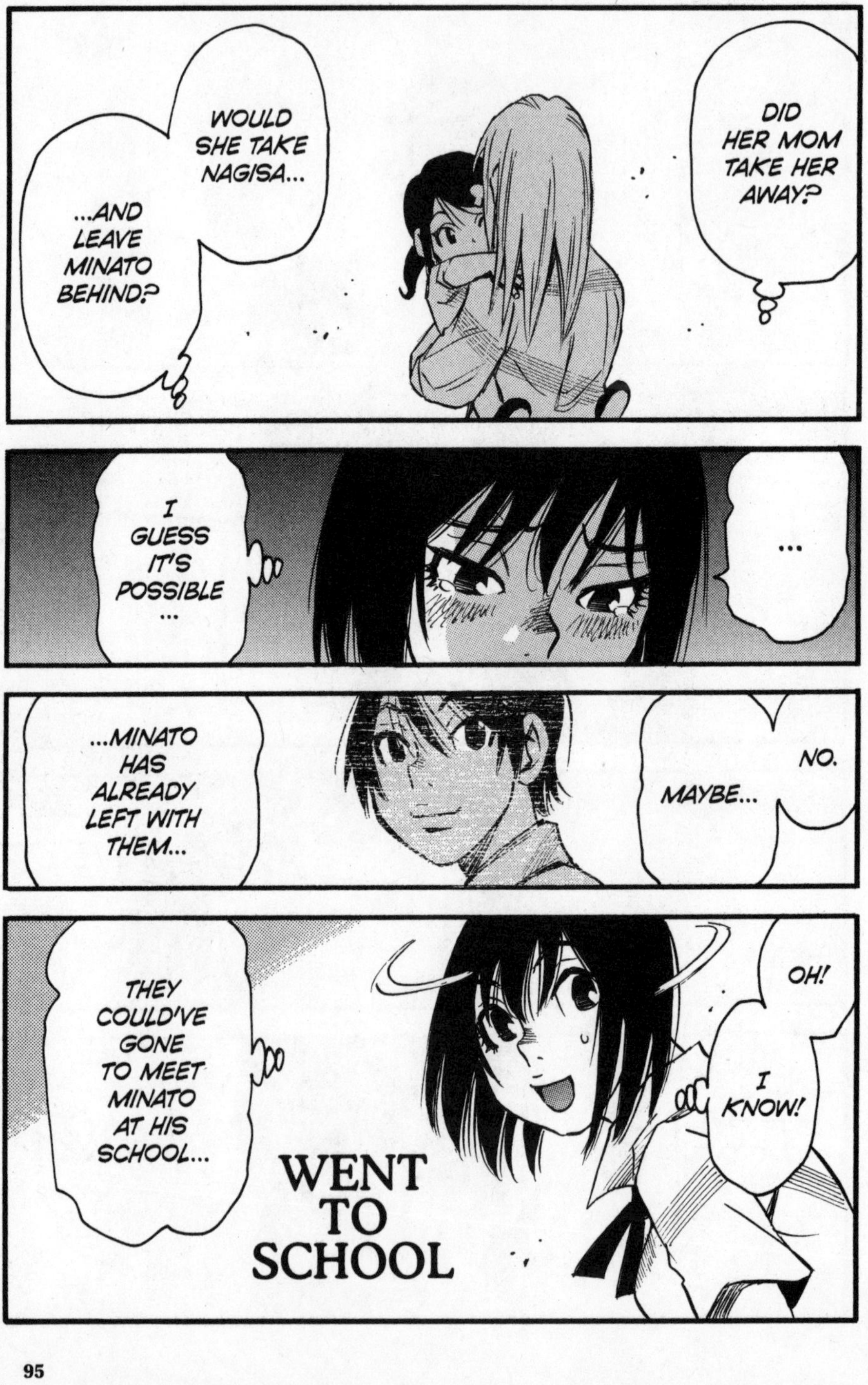
DID HER MOM TAKE HER AWAY?
WOULD SHE TAKE NAGISA...
...AND LEAVE MINATO BEHIND?
...
I GUESS IT'S POSSIBLE ...
NO.
MAYBE...
...MINATO HAS ALREADY LEFT WITH THEM...
OH!
I KNOW!
THEY COULD'VE GONE TO MEET MINATO AT HIS SCHOOL...
WENT TO SCHOOL

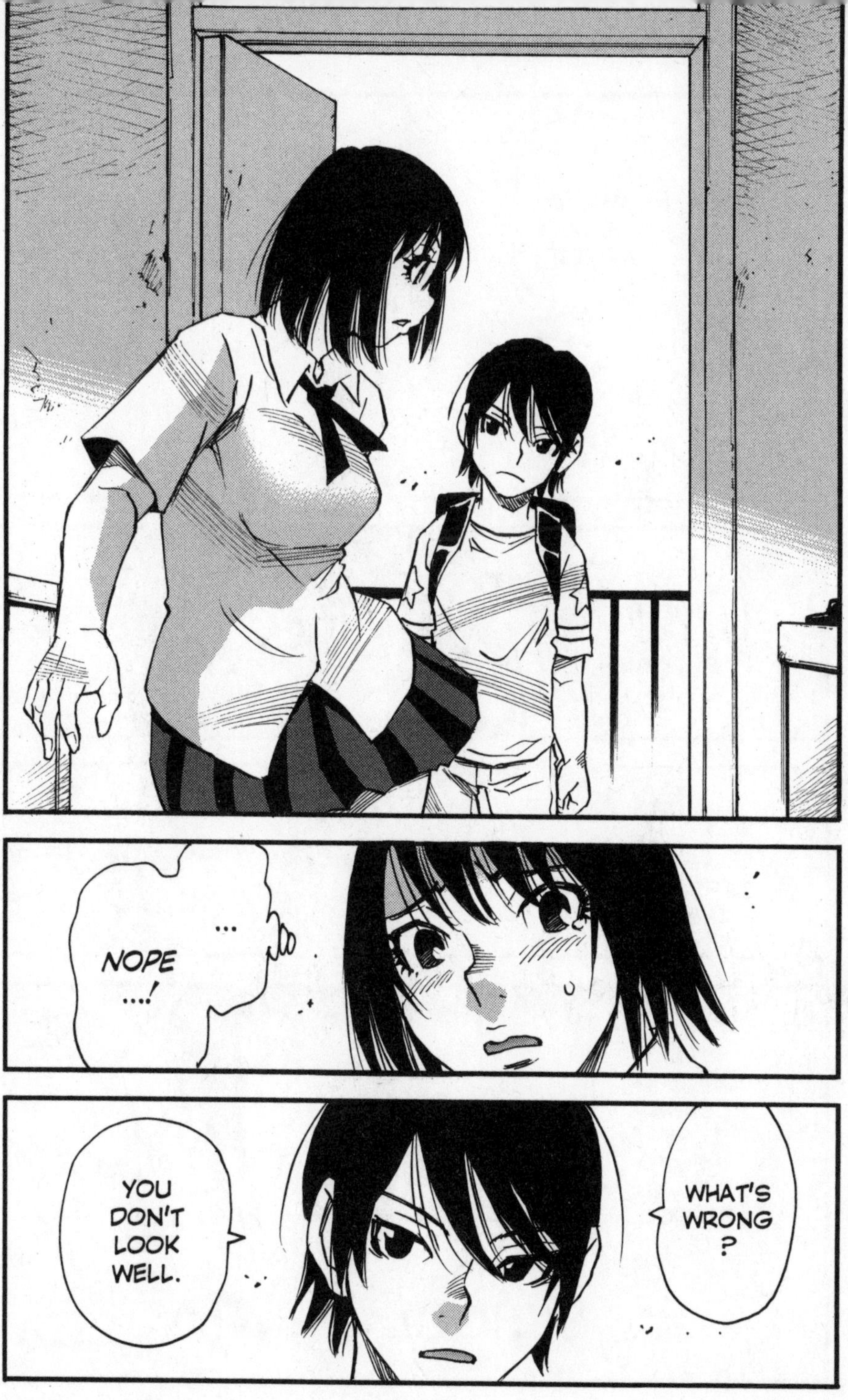
...
NOPE ....!
WHAT'S WRONG ?
YOU DON'T LOOK WELL.

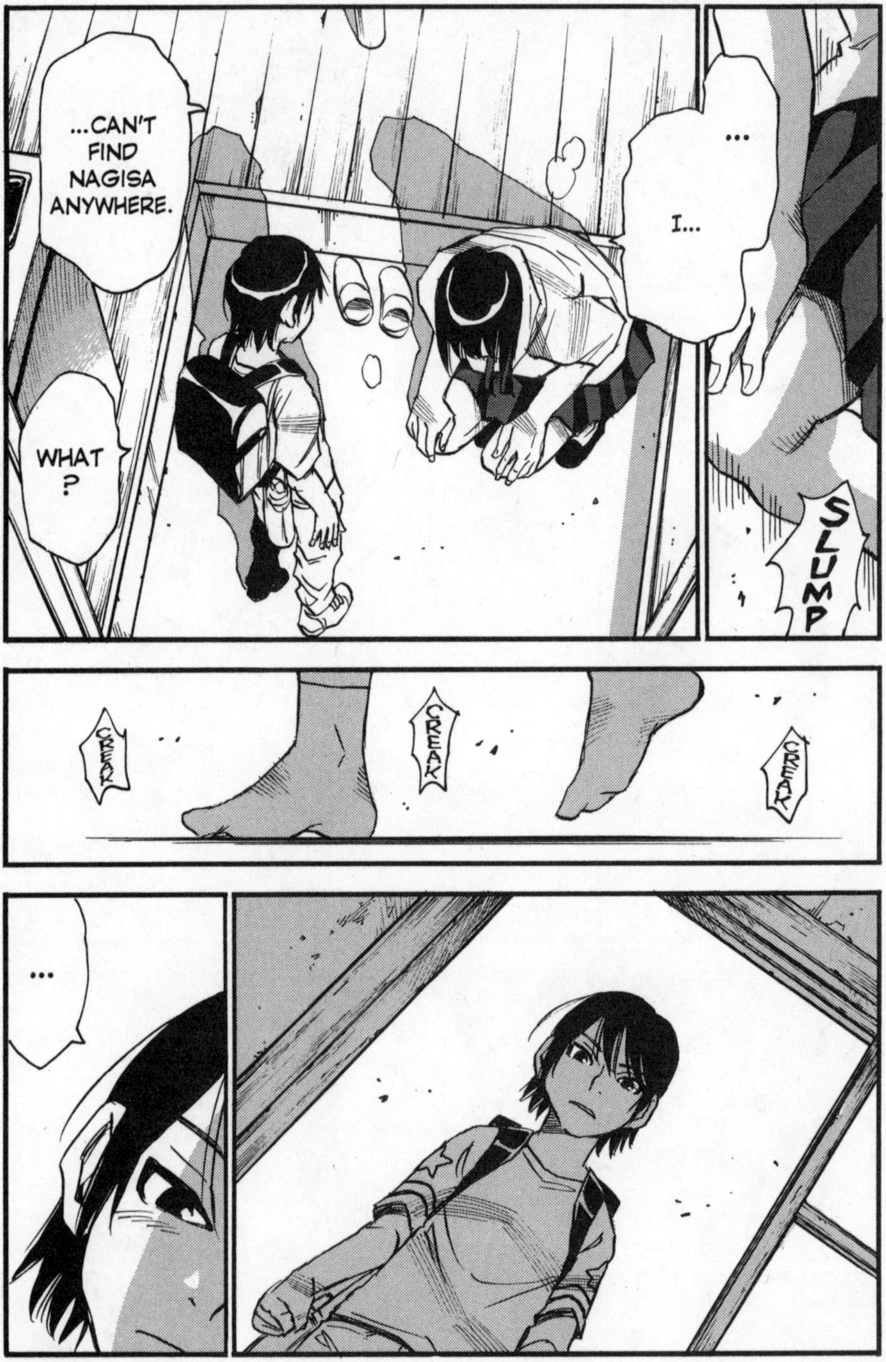
...
I...
SLUMP
...CAN'T FIND NAGISA ANYWHERE.
WHAT?
CREAK
CREAK
CREAK
...

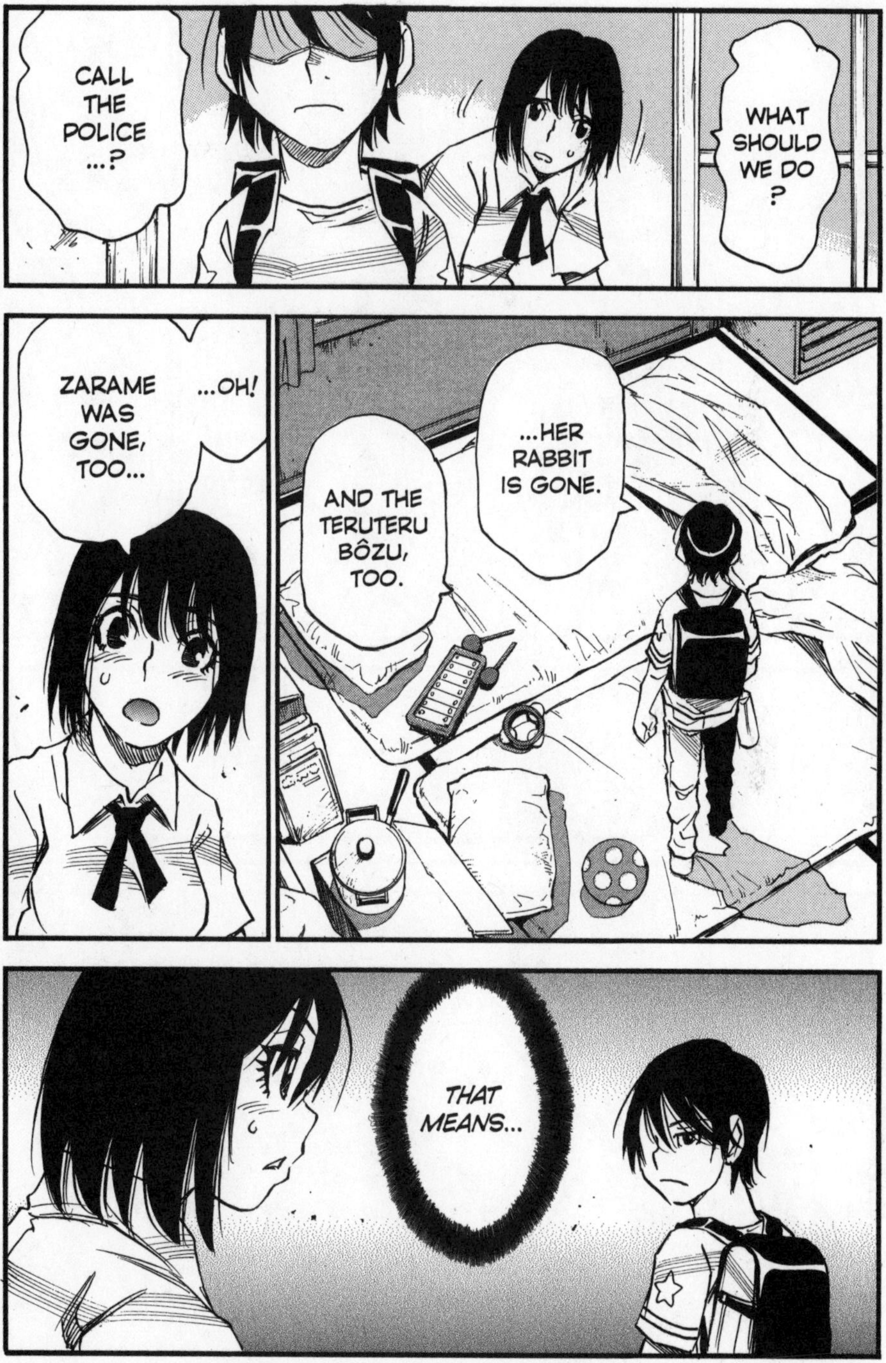
WHAT SHOULD WE DO?
CALL THE POLICE...?
...HER RABBIT IS GONE.
AND THE TERUTERU BÔZU, TOO.
...OH!
ZARAME WAS GONE, TOO...
THAT MEANS...

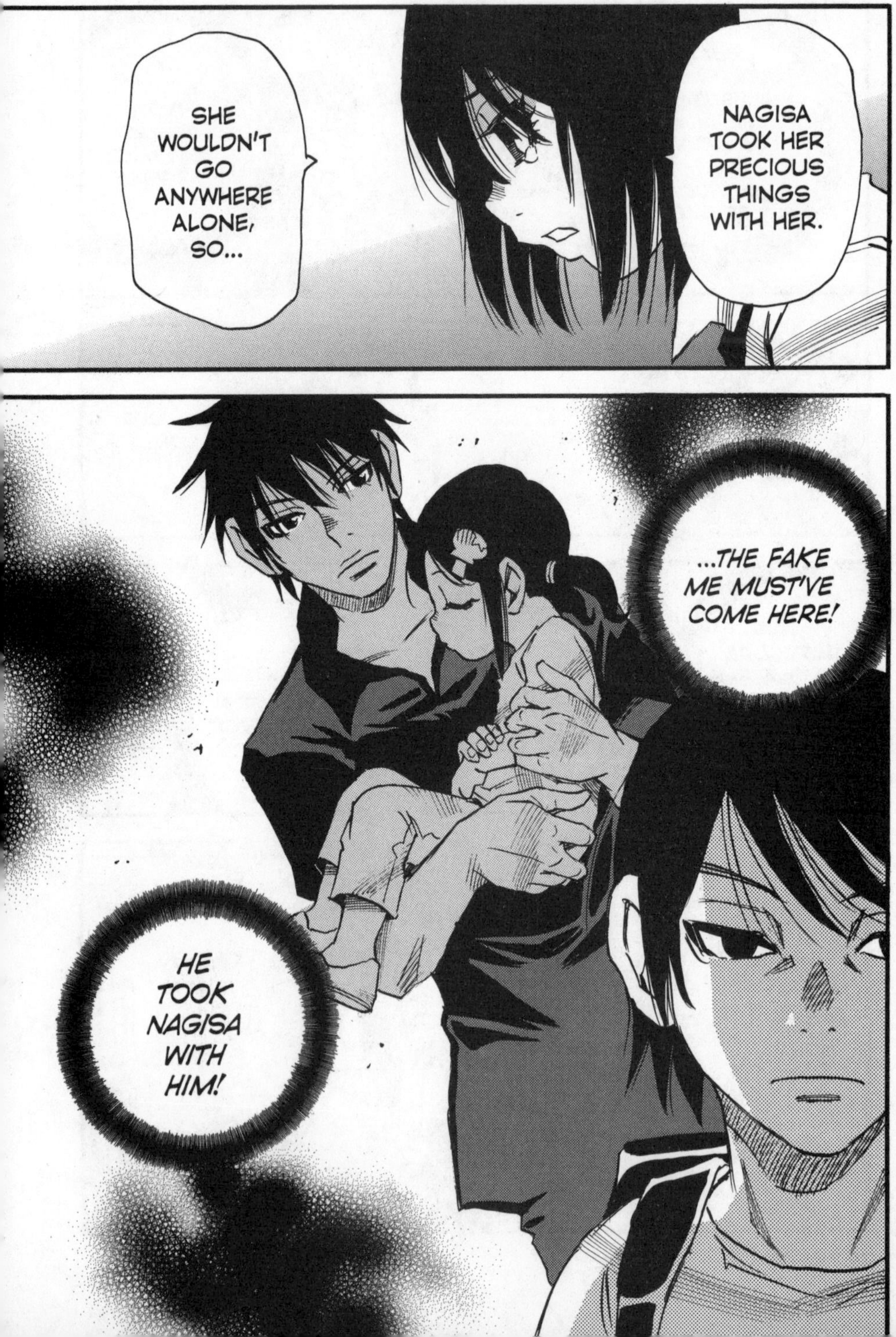
NAGISA TOOK HER PRECIOUS THINGS WITH HER.
SHE WOULDN'T GO ANYWHERE ALONE, SO...
...THE FAKE ME MUST'VE COME HERE!
HE TOOK NAGISA WITH HIM!

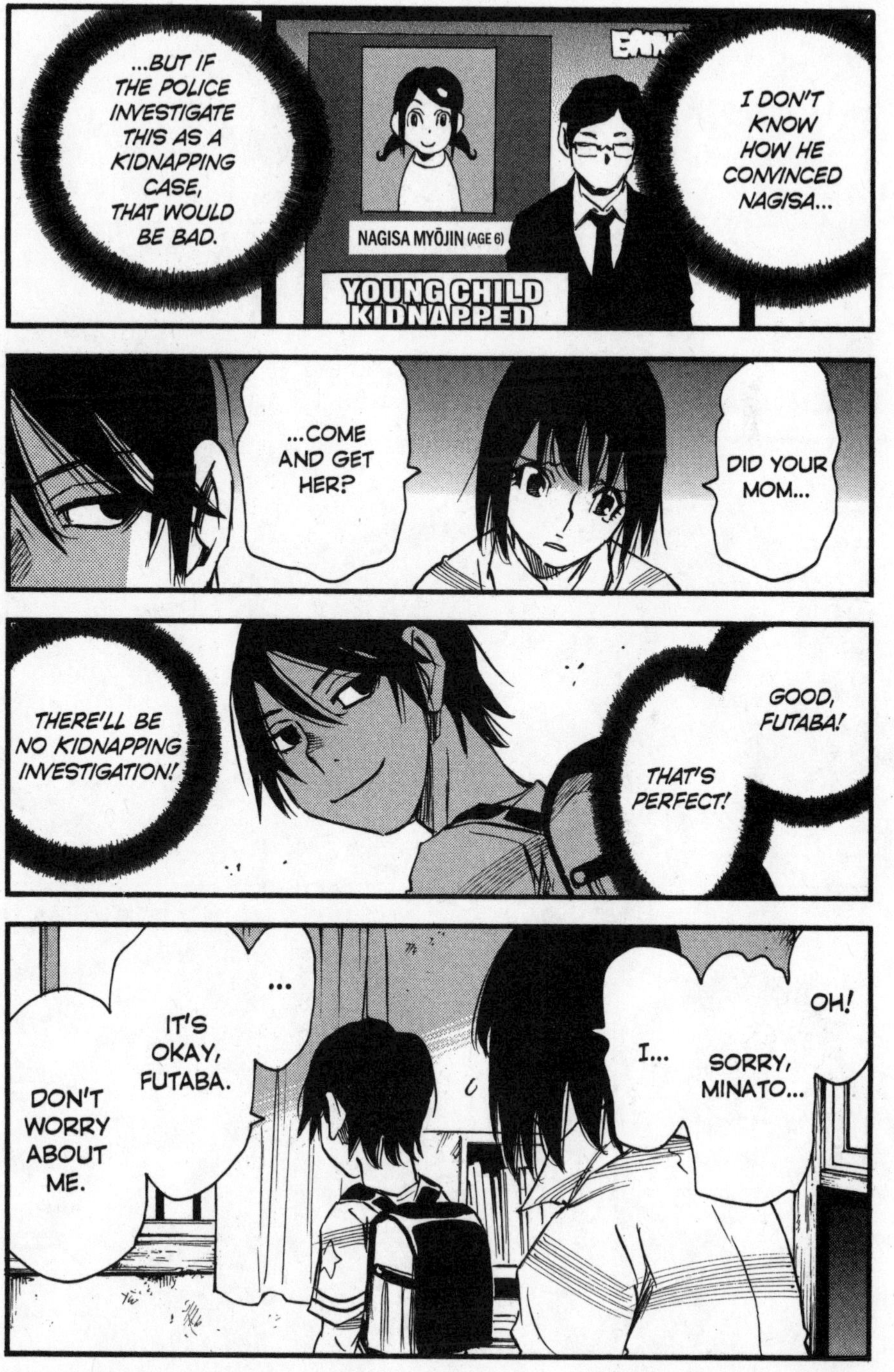
I DON'T KNOW HOW HE CONVINCED NAGISA...
NAGISA MYŌJIN (AGE 6)
YOUNG CHILD KIDNAPPED
...BUT IF THE POLICE INVESTIGATE THIS AS A KIDNAPPING CASE, THAT WOULD BE BAD.
DID YOUR MOM...
...COME AND GET HER?
GOOD, FUTABA!
THAT'S PERFECT!
THERE'LL BE NO KIDNAPPING INVESTIGATION!
OH!
SORRY, MINATO...
I...
...
IT'S OKAY, FUTABA.
DON'T WORRY ABOUT ME.

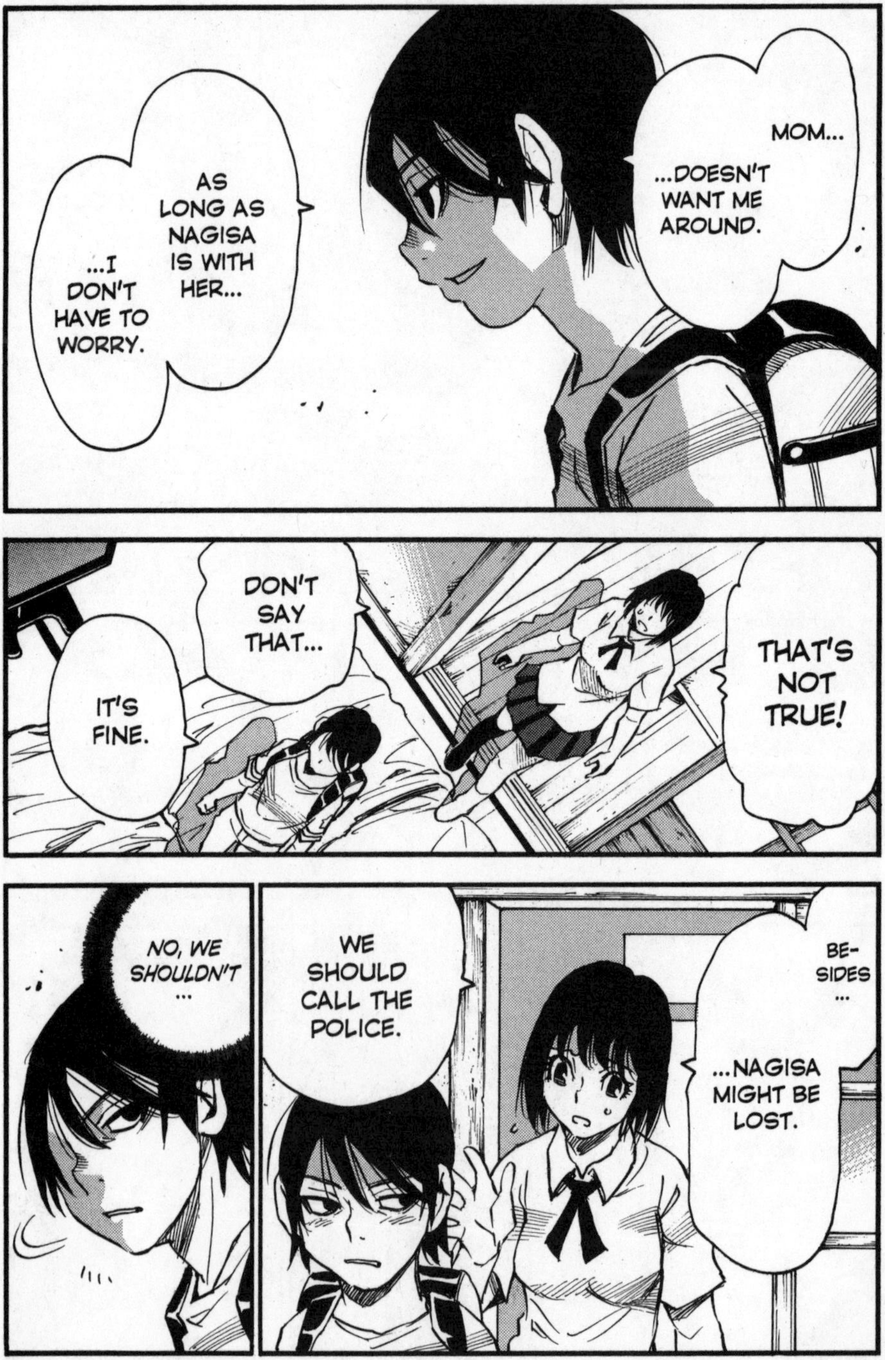
MOM...
...DOESN'T WANT ME AROUND.
AS LONG AS NAGISA IS WITH HER...
...I DON'T HAVE TO WORRY.
THAT'S NOT TRUE!
DON'T SAY THAT...
IT'S FINE.
BE-SIDES...
...NAGISA MIGHT BE LOST.
WE SHOULD CALL THE POLICE.
NO, WE SHOULDN'T...

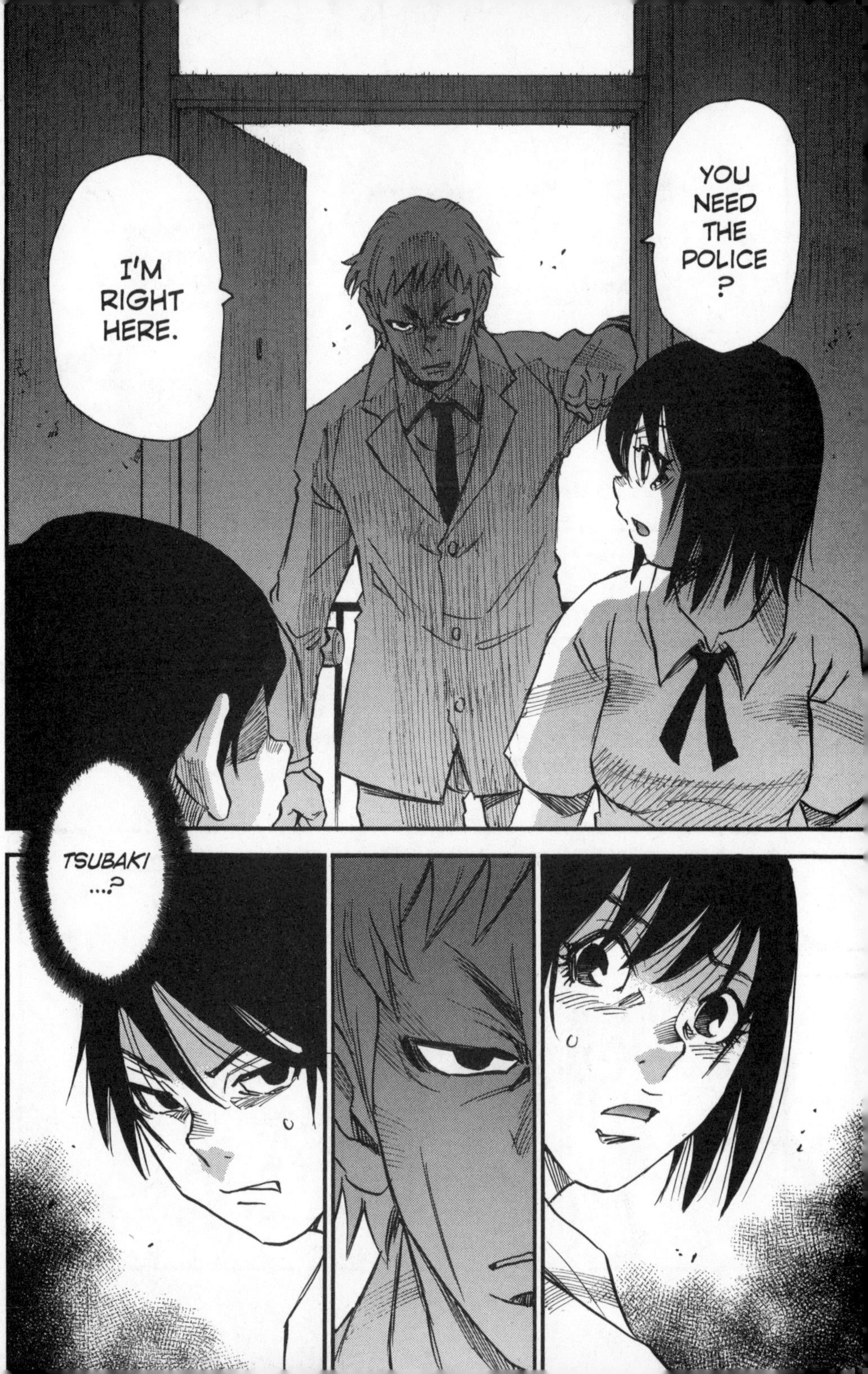
YOU NEED THE POLICE?
I'M RIGHT HERE.
TSUBAKI ...?

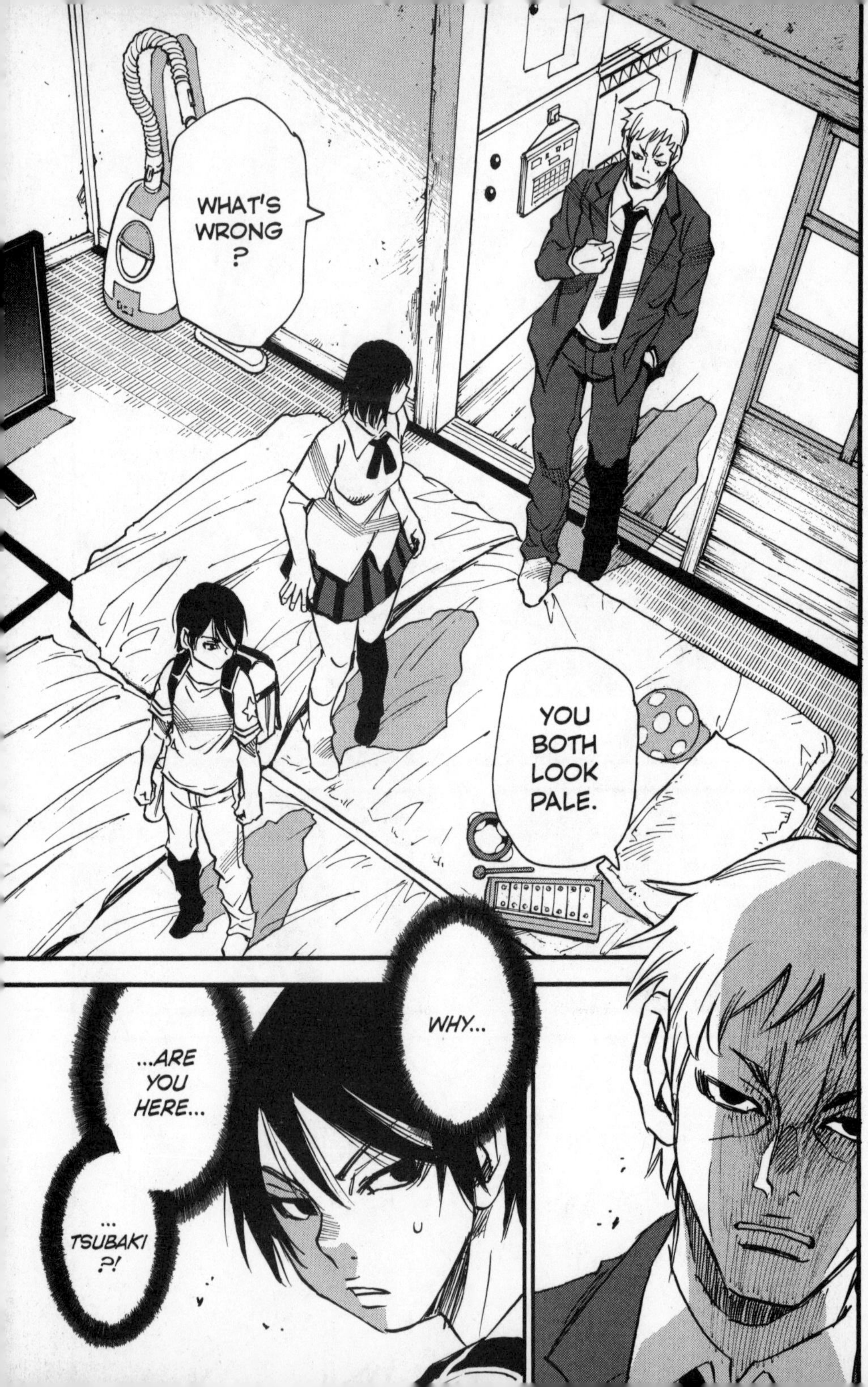
WHAT'S WRONG ?
YOU BOTH LOOK PALE.
WHY...
...ARE YOU HERE...
... TSUBAKI ?!

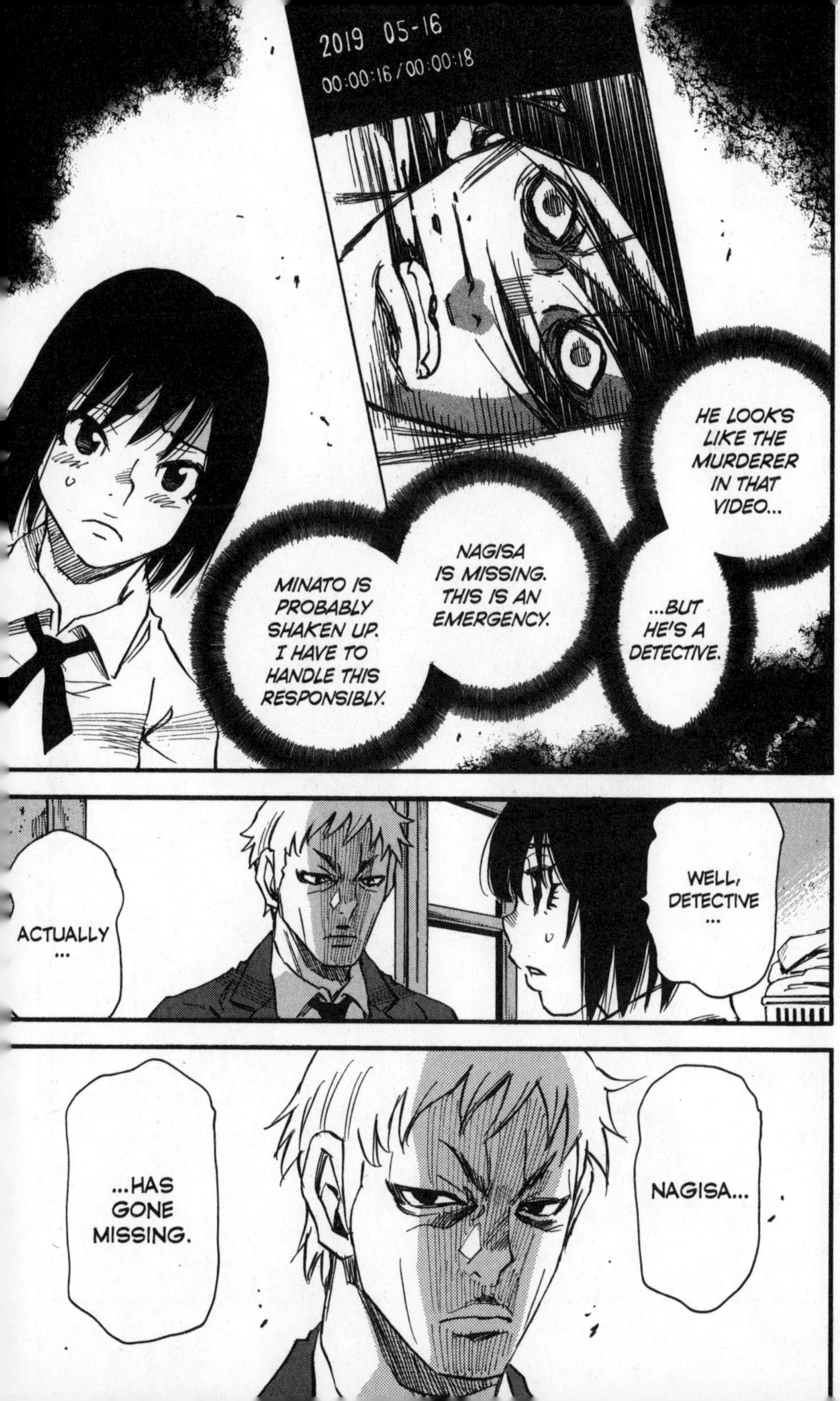

2019 05-16
00:00:16/00:00:18
HE LOOKS LIKE THE MURDERER IN THAT VIDEO...
...BUT HE'S A DETECTIVE.
NAGISA IS MISSING. THIS IS AN EMERGENCY.
MINATO IS PROBABLY SHAKEN UP. I HAVE TO HANDLE THIS RESPONSIBLY.
WELL, DETECTIVE ...
ACTUALLY ...
NAGISA...
...HAS GONE MISSING.

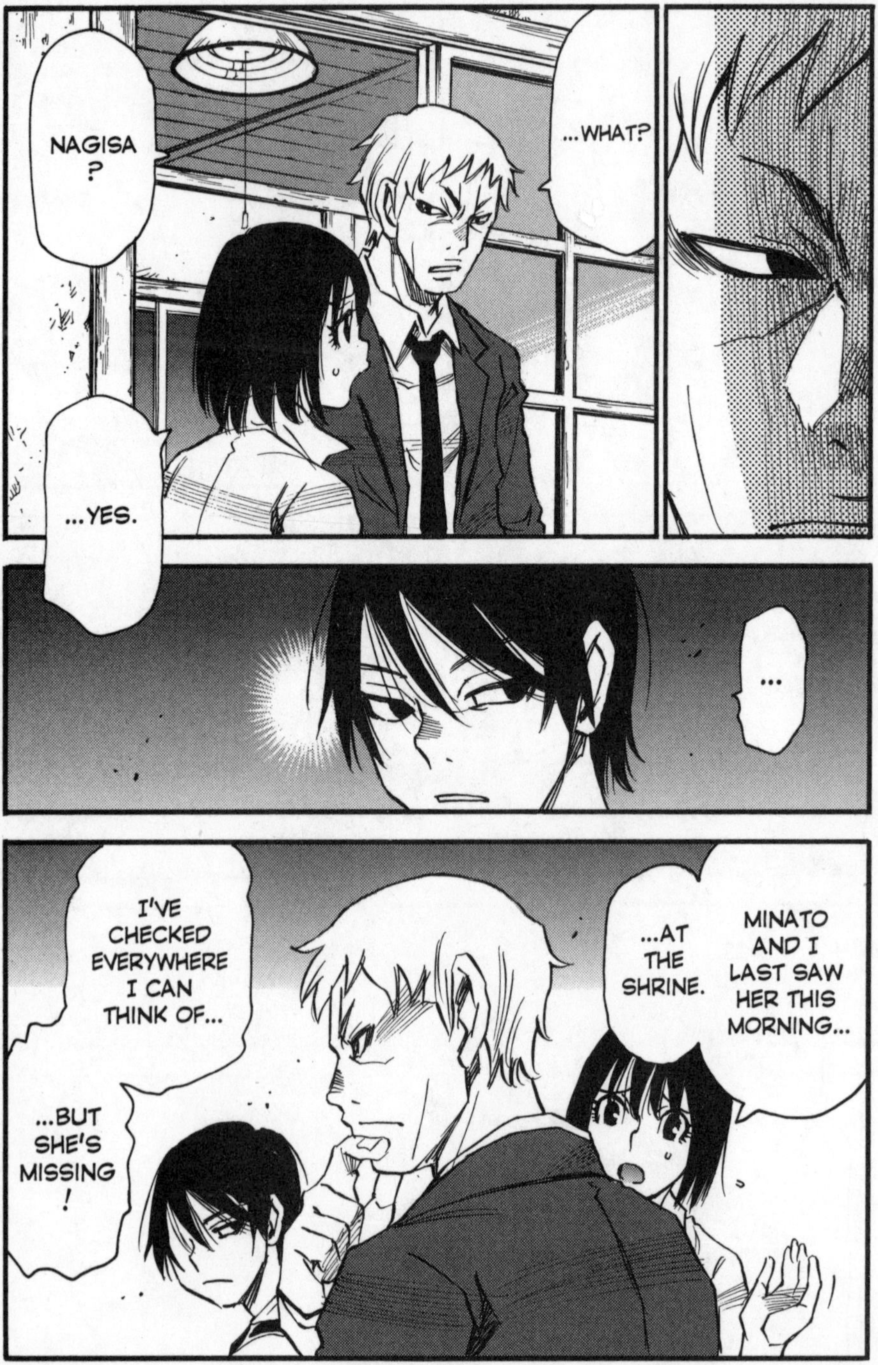
...WHAT?
NAGISA?
...YES.
...
MINATO AND I LAST SAW HER THIS MORNING...
...AT THE SHRINE.
I'VE CHECKED EVERYWHERE I CAN THINK OF...
...BUT SHE'S MISSING!

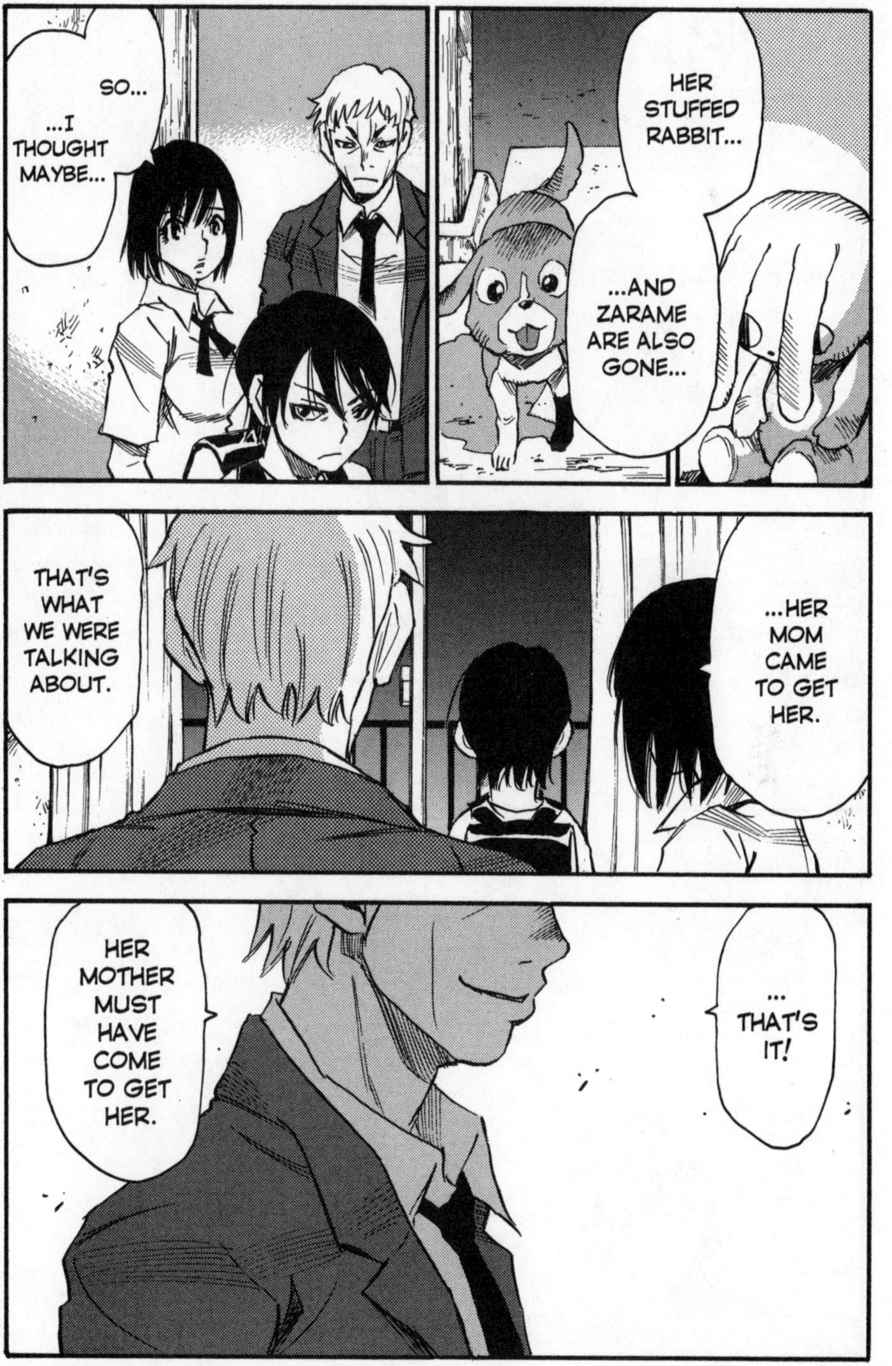
HER STUFFED RABBIT...
...AND ZARAME ARE ALSO GONE...
SO...
...I THOUGHT MAYBE...
...HER MOM CAME TO GET HER.
THAT'S WHAT WE WERE TALKING ABOUT.
... THAT'S IT!
HER MOTHER MUST HAVE COME TO GET HER.

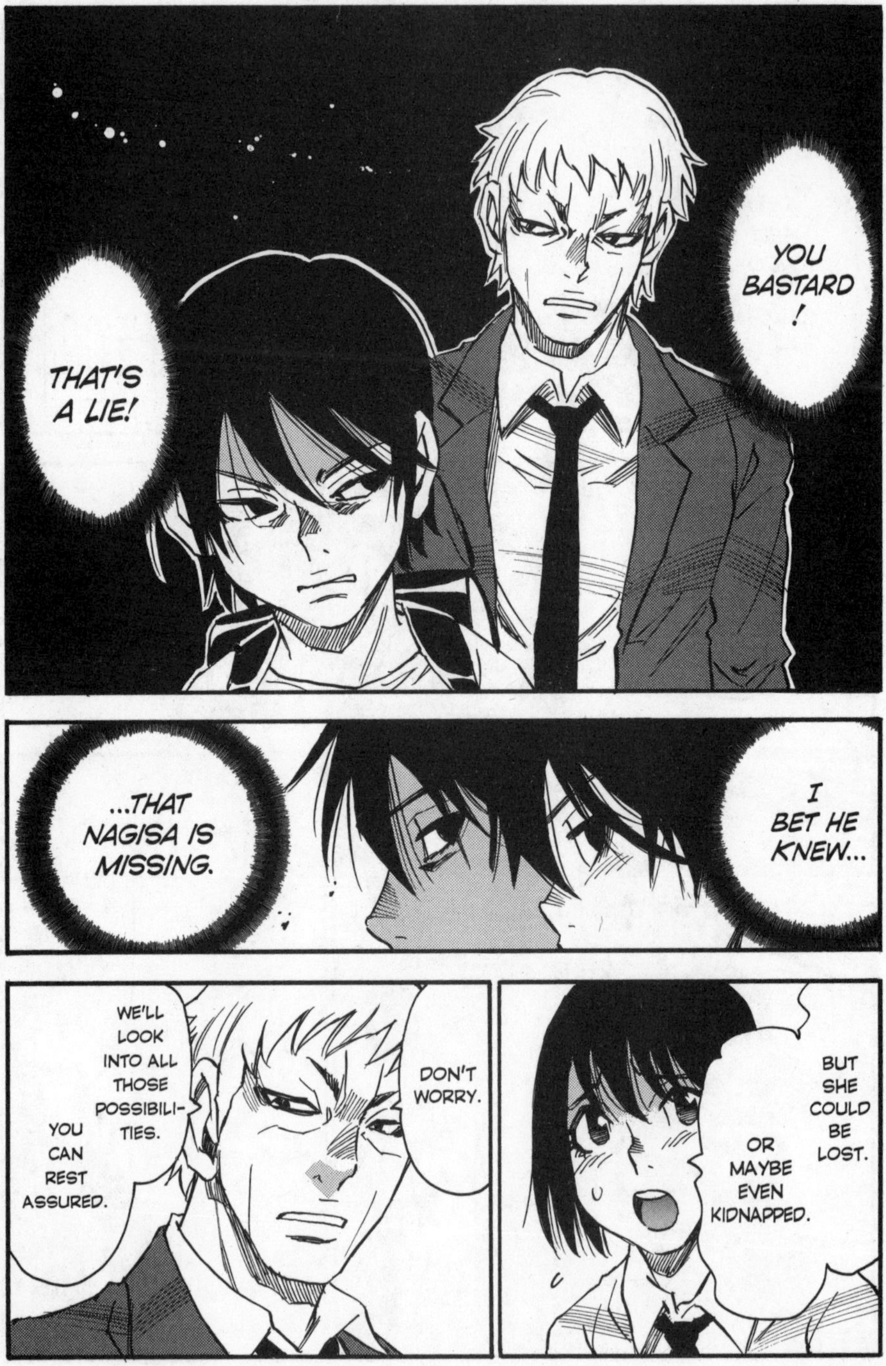
YOU BASTARD!
THAT'S A LIE!
I BET HE KNEW...
...THAT NAGISA IS MISSING.
BUT SHE COULD BE LOST.
OR MAYBE EVEN KIDNAPPED.
DON'T WORRY.
WE'LL LOOK INTO ALL THOSE POSSIBILITIES.
YOU CAN REST ASSURED.

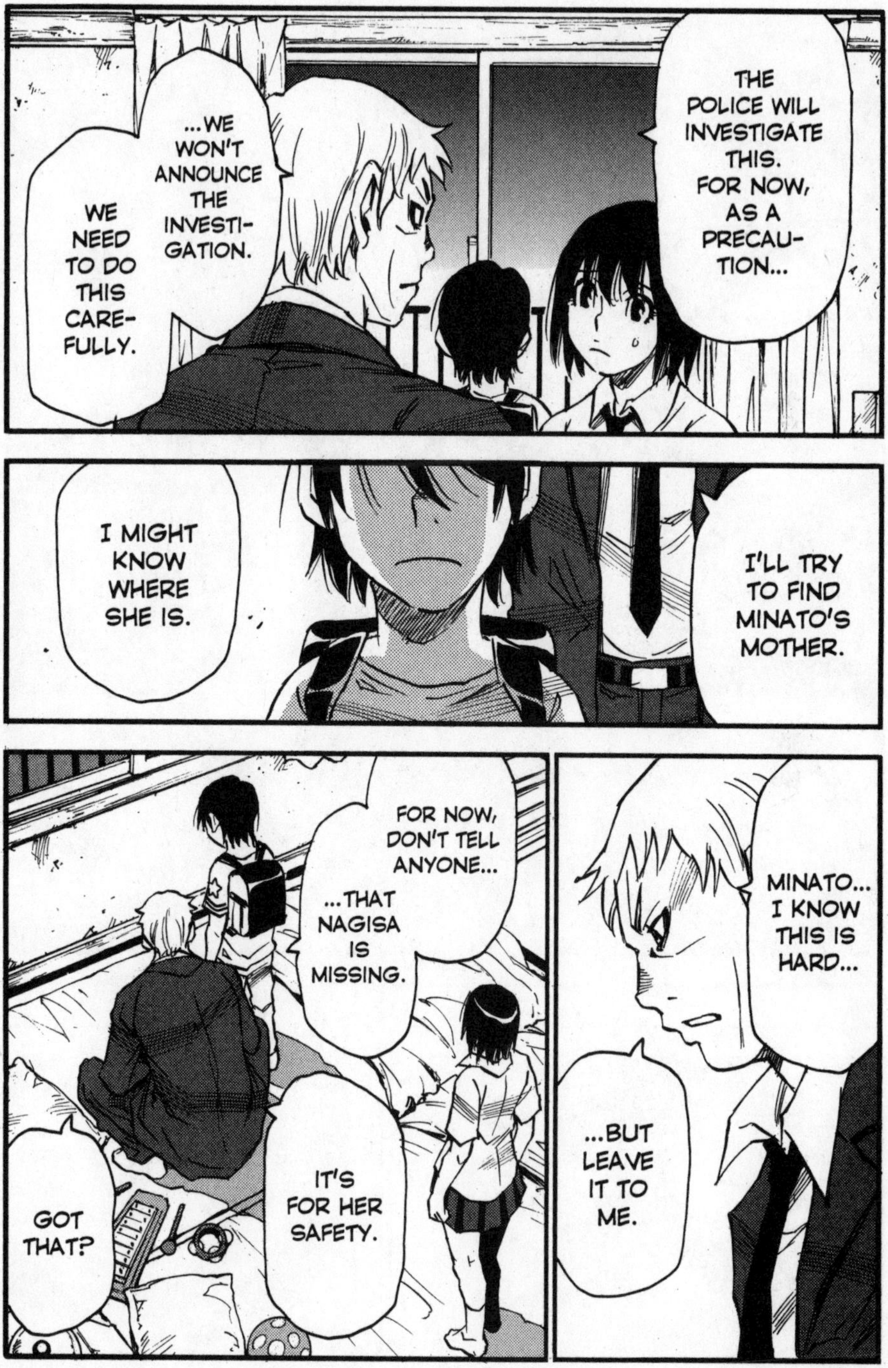
THE POLICE WILL INVESTIGATE THIS. FOR NOW, AS A PRECAUTION...
...WE WON'T ANNOUNCE THE INVESTIGATION.
WE NEED TO DO THIS CAREFULLY.
I'LL TRY TO FIND MINATO'S MOTHER.
I MIGHT KNOW WHERE SHE IS.
MINATO... I KNOW THIS IS HARD...
...BUT LEAVE IT TO ME.
FOR NOW, DON'T TELL ANYONE...
...THAT NAGISA IS MISSING.
IT'S FOR HER SAFETY.
GOT THAT?

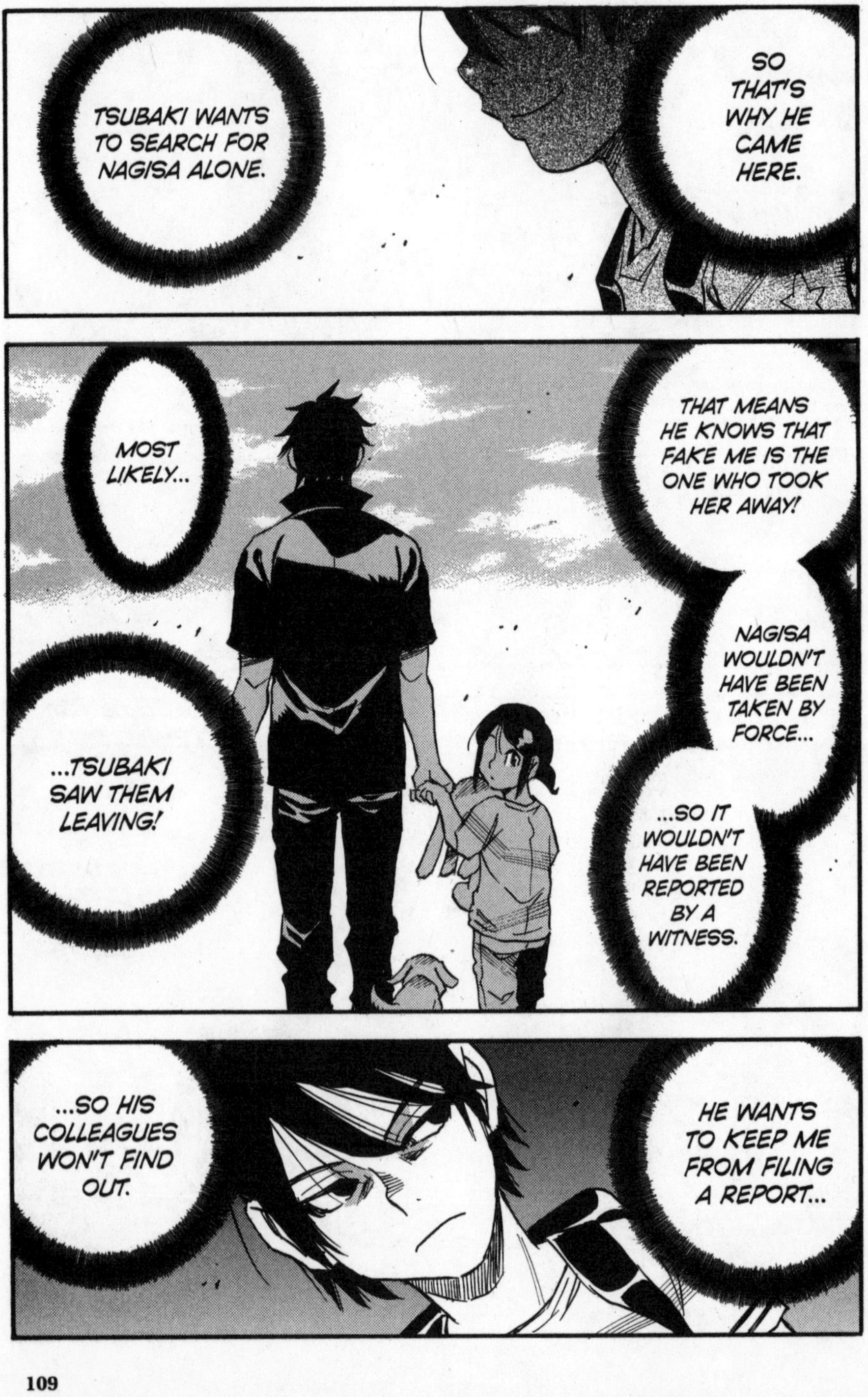
SO THAT'S WHY HE CAME HERE.
TSUBAKI WANTS TO SEARCH FOR NAGISA ALONE.
THAT MEANS HE KNOWS THAT FAKE ME IS THE ONE WHO TOOK HER AWAY!
NAGISA WOULDN'T HAVE BEEN TAKEN BY FORCE...
...SO IT WOULDN'T HAVE BEEN REPORTED BY A WITNESS.
MOST LIKELY...
...TSUBAKI SAW THEM LEAVING!
HE WANTS TO KEEP ME FROM FILING A REPORT...
...SO HIS COLLEAGUES WON'T FIND OUT.

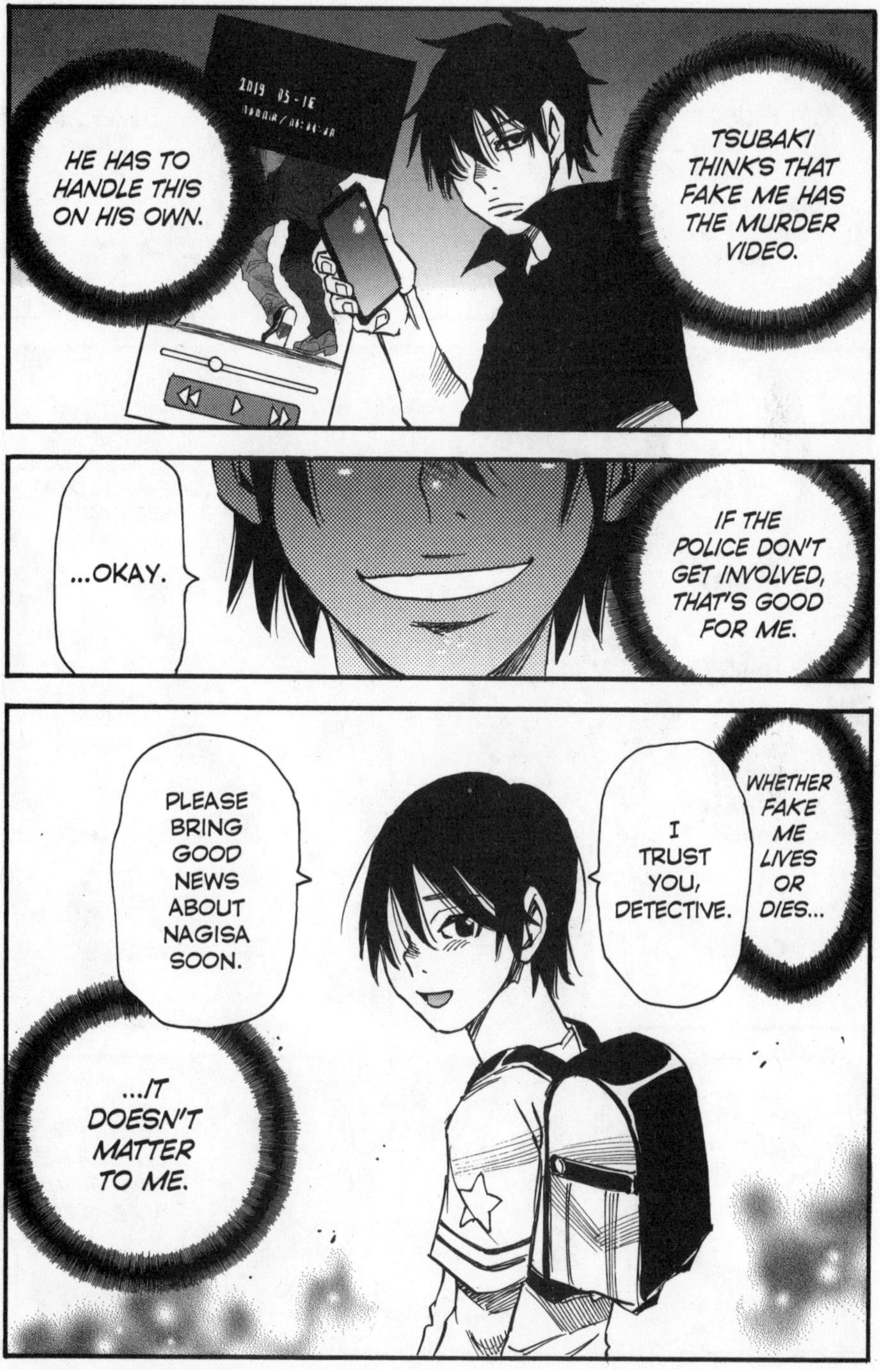
TSUBAKI THINKS THAT FAKE ME HAS THE MURDER VIDEO.
HE HAS TO HANDLE THIS ON HIS OWN.
IF THE POLICE DON'T GET INVOLVED, THAT'S GOOD FOR ME.
...OKAY.
WHETHER FAKE ME LIVES OR DIES...
I TRUST YOU, DETECTIVE.
PLEASE BRING GOOD NEWS ABOUT NAGISA SOON.
...IT DOESN'T MATTER TO ME.

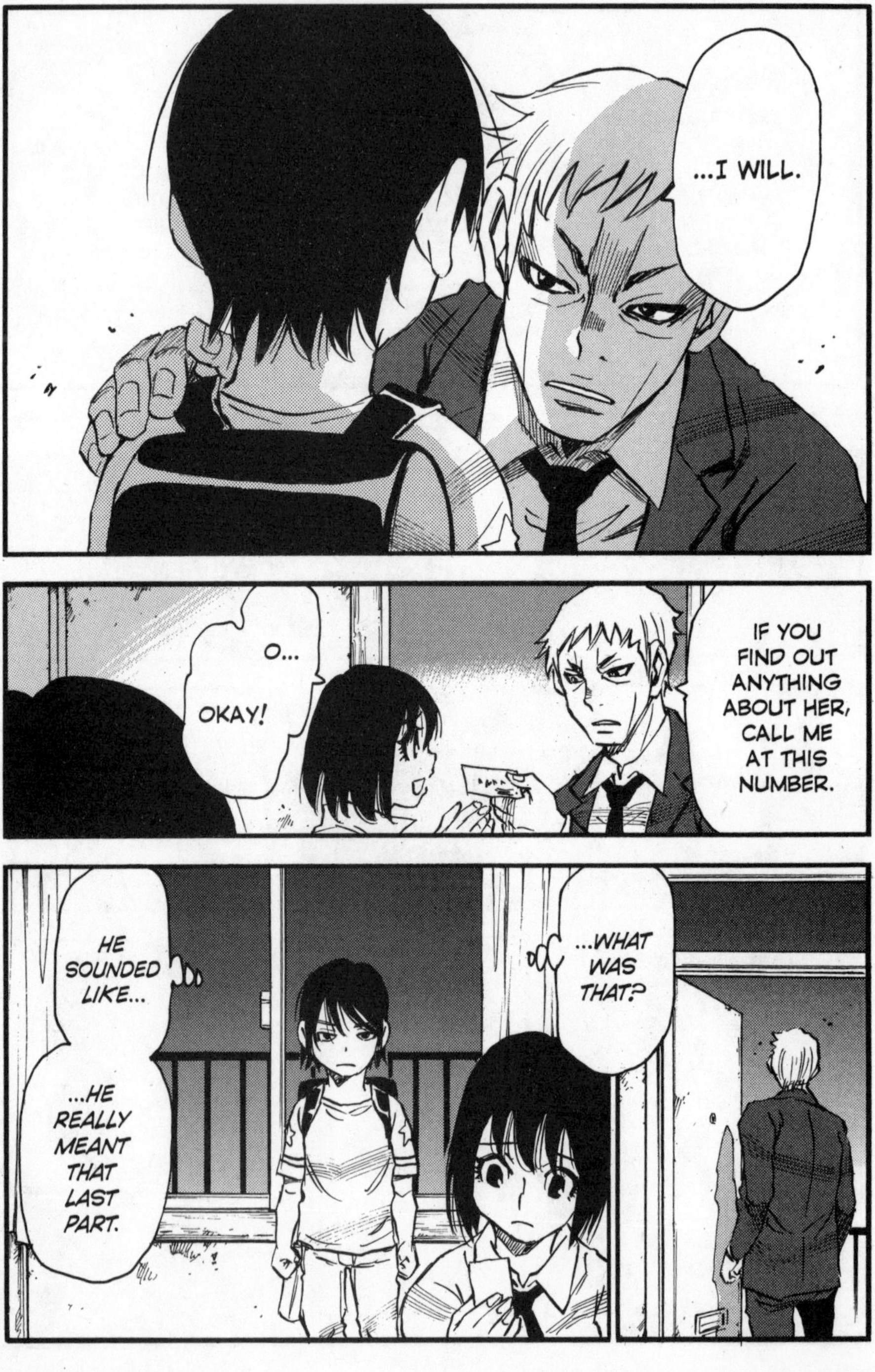
...I WILL.
IF YOU FIND OUT ANYTHING ABOUT HER, CALL ME AT THIS NUMBER.
O... OKAY!
...WHAT WAS THAT?
HE SOUNDED LIKE...
...HE REALLY MEANT THAT LAST PART.

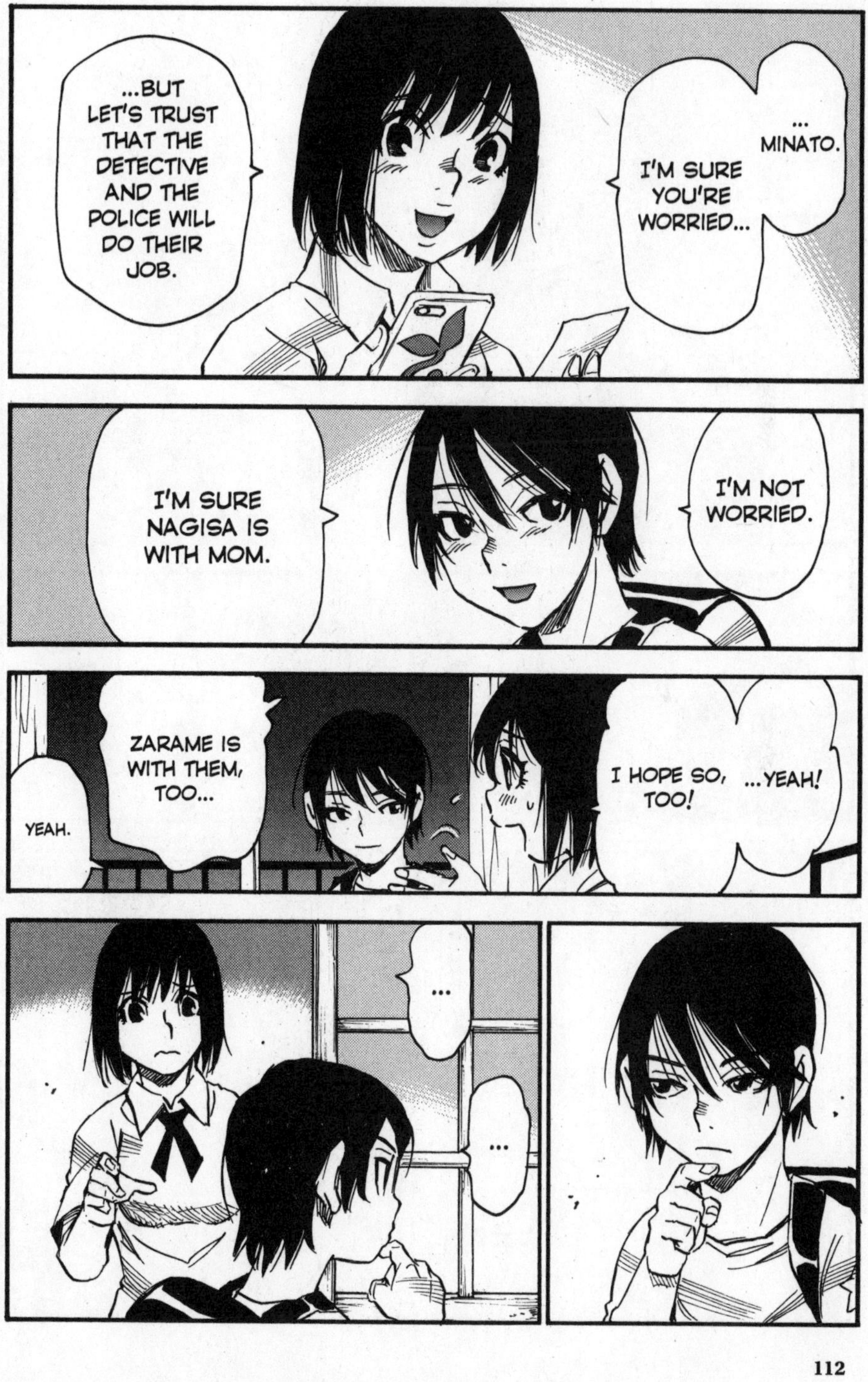
... MINATO.
I'M SURE YOU'RE WORRIED...
...BUT LET'S TRUST THAT THE DETECTIVE AND THE POLICE WILL DO THEIR JOB.
I'M NOT WORRIED.
I'M SURE NAGISA IS WITH MOM.
...YEAH!
I HOPE SO, TOO!
ZARAME IS WITH THEM, TOO...
YEAH.
...
...

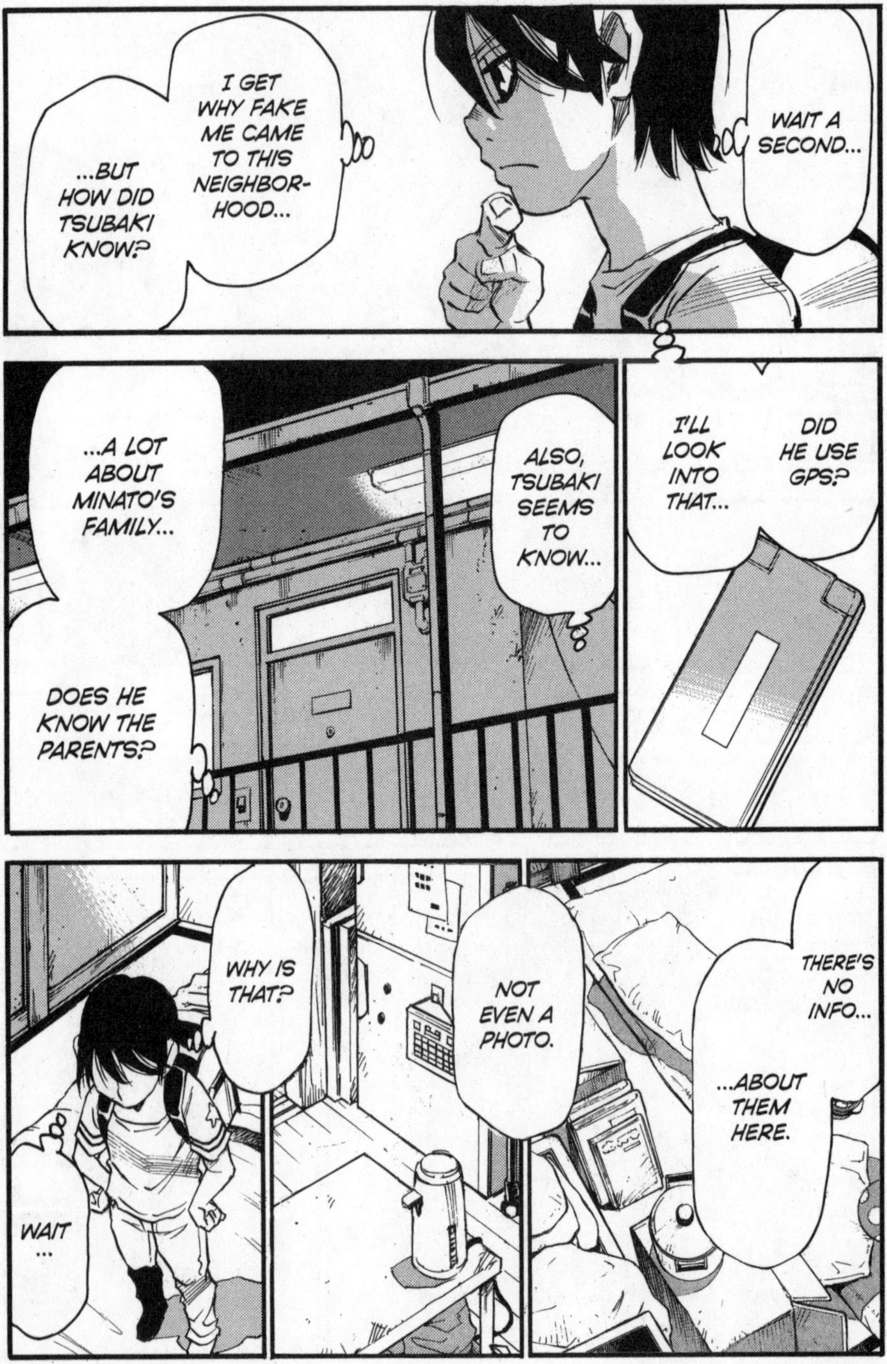
WAIT A SECOND...
I GET WHY FAKE ME CAME TO THIS NEIGHBOR-HOOD...
...BUT HOW DID TSUBAKI KNOW?
DID HE USE GPS?
I'LL LOOK INTO THAT...
ALSO, TSUBAKI SEEMS TO KNOW...
...A LOT ABOUT MINATO'S FAMILY...
DOES HE KNOW THE PARENTS?
THERE'S NO INFO...
...ABOUT THEM HERE.
NOT EVEN A PHOTO.
WHY IS THAT?
WAIT ...

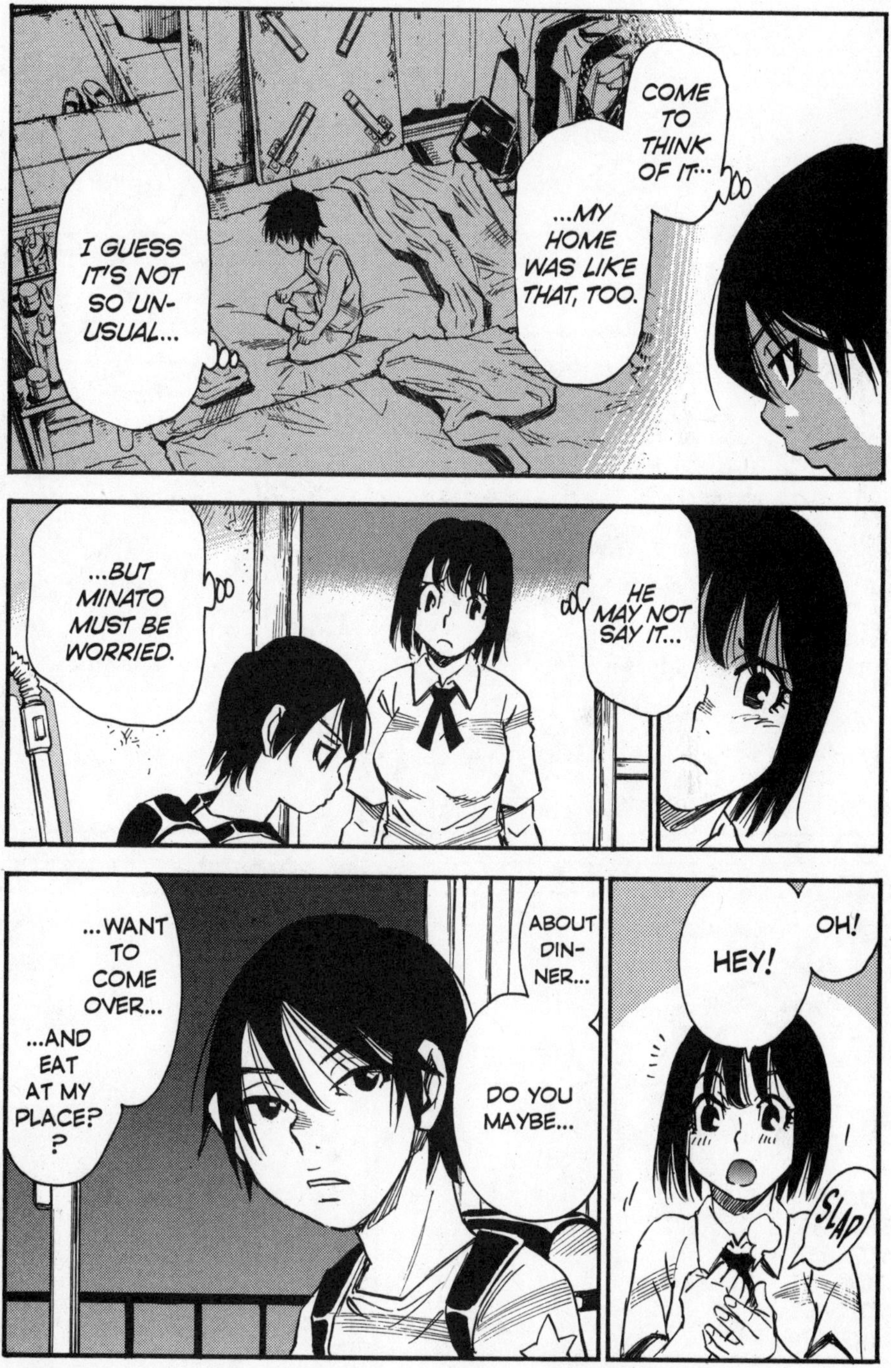
COME TO THINK OF IT...
...MY HOME WAS LIKE THAT, TOO.
I GUESS IT'S NOT SO UN-USUAL...
HE MAY NOT SAY IT...
...BUT MINATO MUST BE WORRIED.
OH!
HEY!
SLAP
ABOUT DIN-NER...
DO YOU MAYBE...
...WANT TO COME OVER...
...AND EAT AT MY PLACE?
?

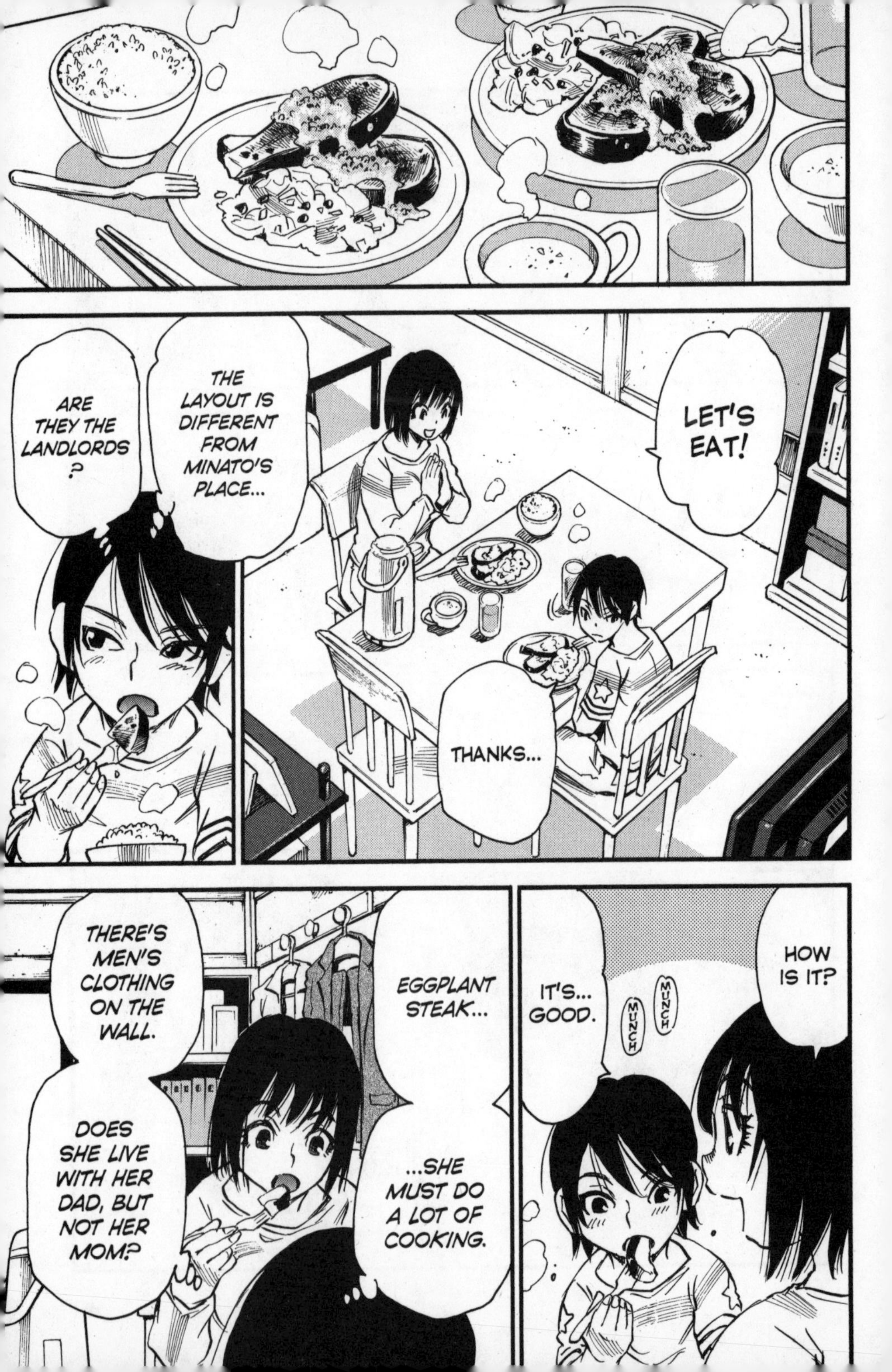
LET'S EAT!
THANKS...
THE LAYOUT IS DIFFERENT FROM MINATO'S PLACE...
ARE THEY THE LANDLORDS?
HOW IS IT?
MUNCH
MUNCH
IT'S... GOOD.
EGGPLANT STEAK...
...SHE MUST DO A LOT OF COOKING.
THERE'S MEN'S CLOTHING ON THE WALL.
DOES SHE LIVE WITH HER DAD, BUT NOT HER MOM?

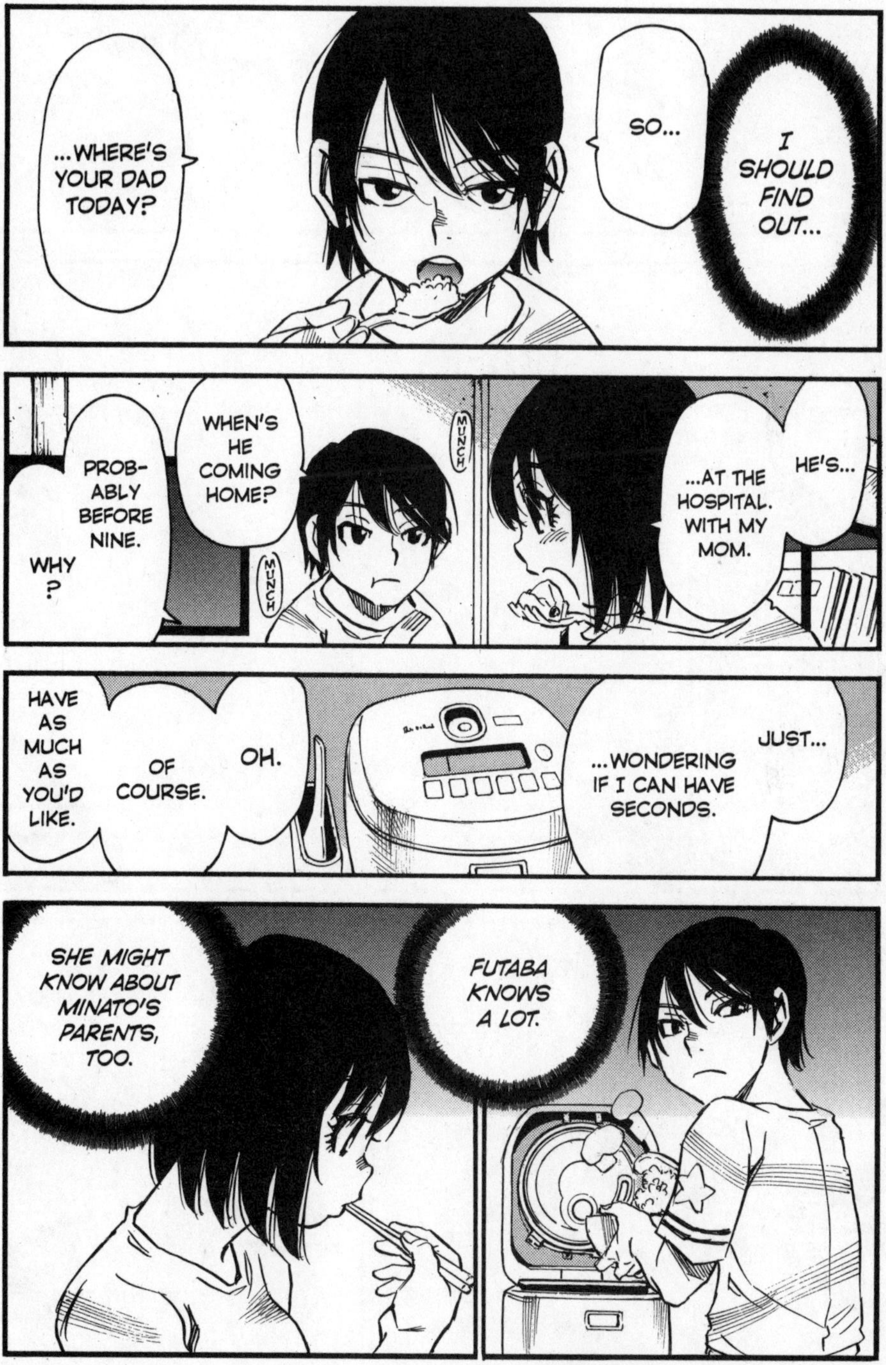
I SHOULD FIND OUT...
SO...
...WHERE'S YOUR DAD TODAY?
HE'S...
...AT THE HOSPITAL. WITH MY MOM.
MUNCH
WHEN'S HE COMING HOME?
MUNCH
PROBABLY BEFORE NINE.
WHY?
JUST...
...WONDERING IF I CAN HAVE SECONDS.
OH.
OF COURSE.
HAVE AS MUCH AS YOU'D LIKE.
FUTABA KNOWS A LOT.
SHE MIGHT KNOW ABOUT MINATO'S PARENTS, TOO.

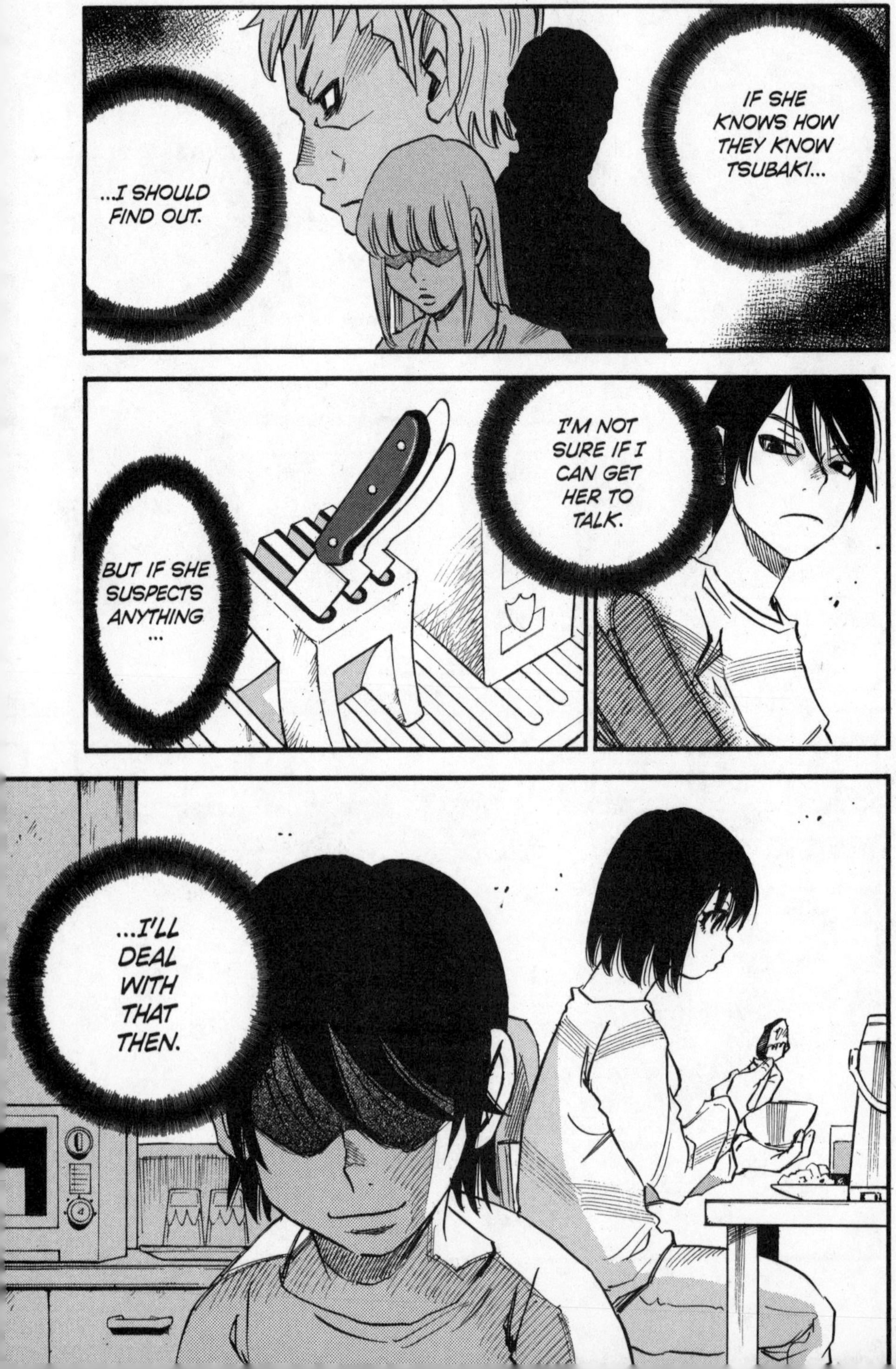
IF SHE KNOWS HOW THEY KNOW TSUBAKI...
...I SHOULD FIND OUT.
I'M NOT SURE IF I CAN GET HER TO TALK.
BUT IF SHE SUSPECTS ANYTHING ...
...I'LL DEAL WITH THAT THEN.

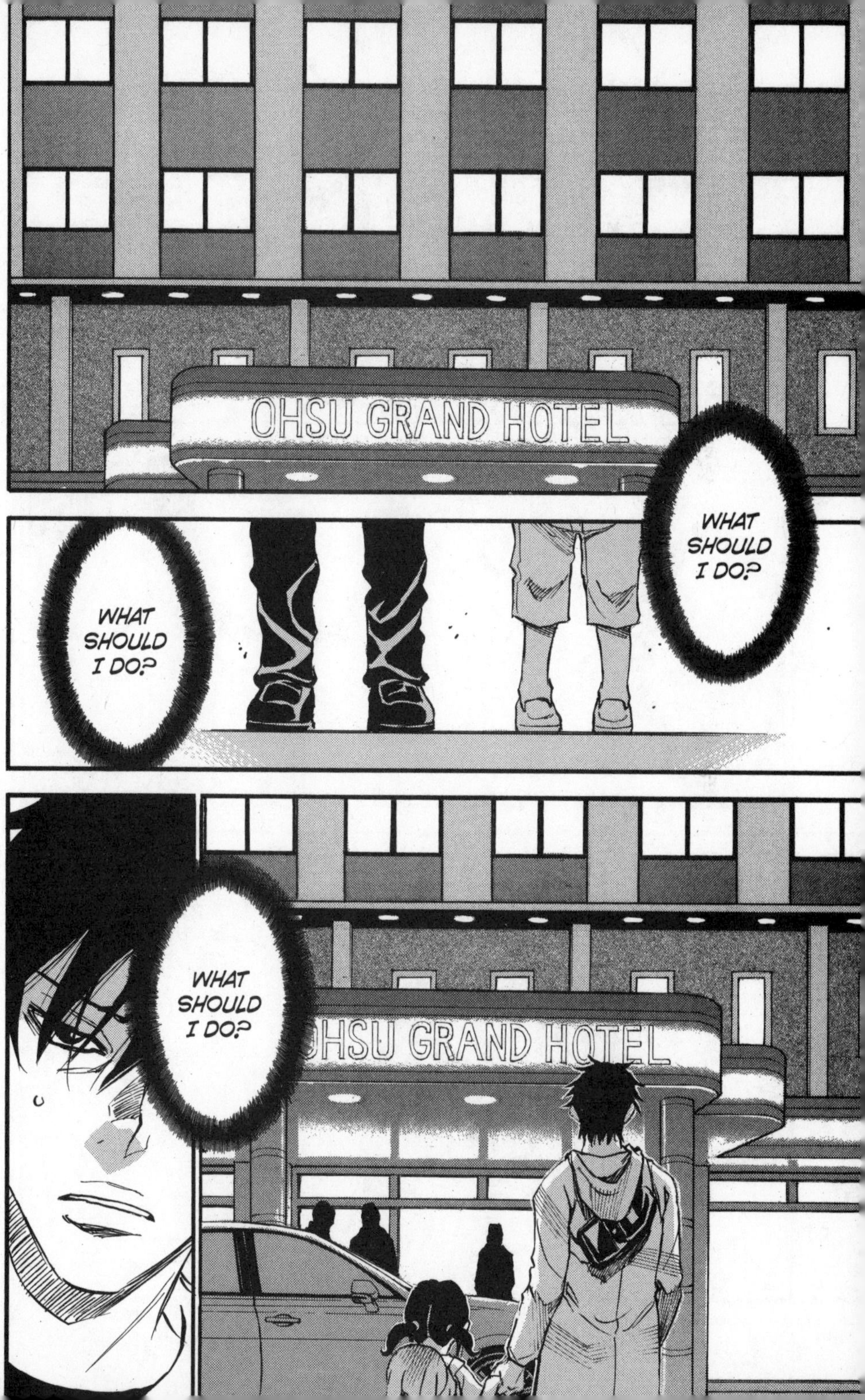
OHSU GRAND HOTEL
WHAT SHOULD I DO?
WHAT SHOULD I DO?
WHAT SHOULD I DO?
OHSU GRAND HOTEL

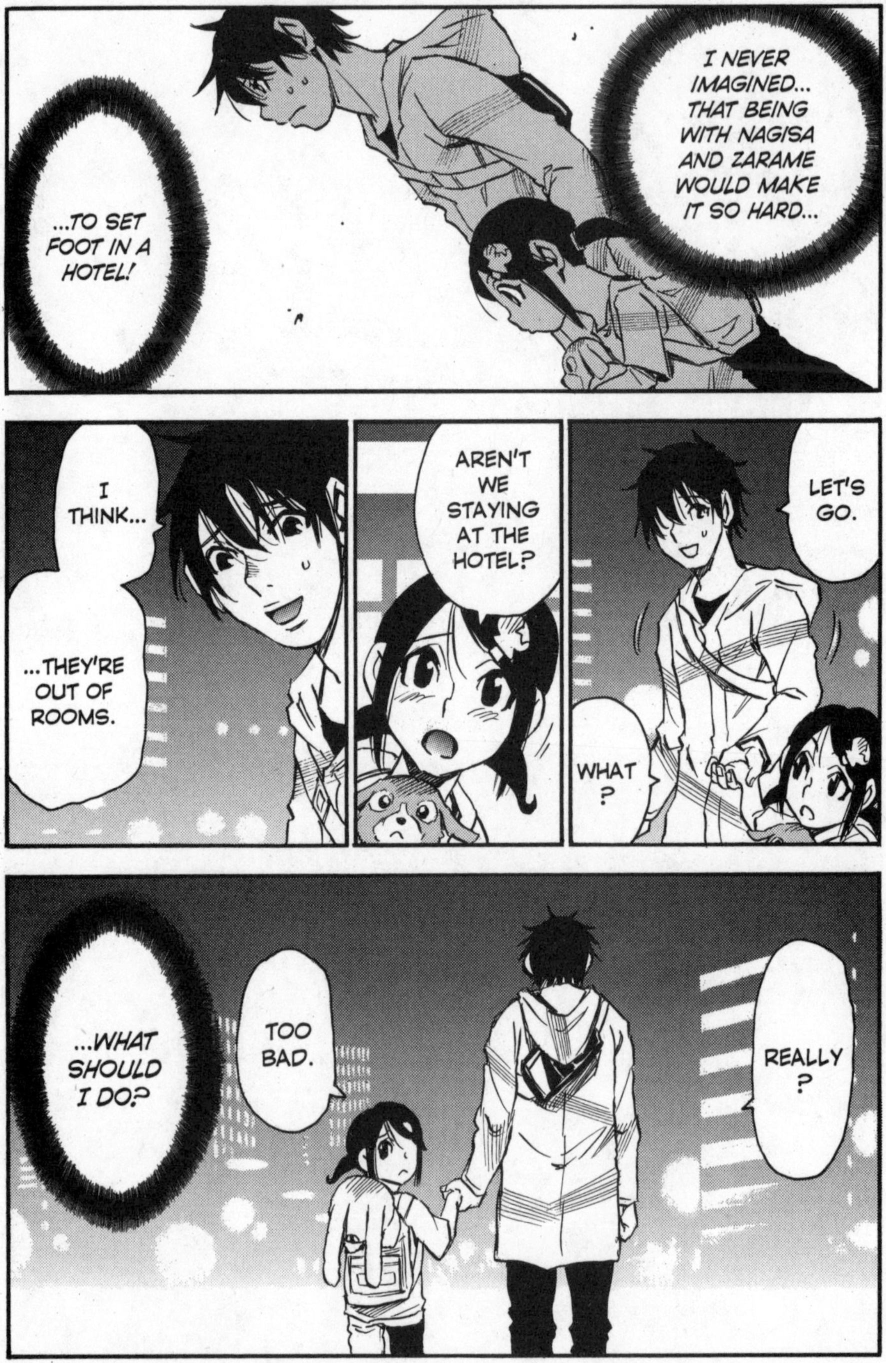
I NEVER IMAGINED... THAT BEING WITH NAGISA AND ZARAME WOULD MAKE IT SO HARD...
...TO SET FOOT IN A HOTEL!
LET'S GO.
WHAT?
AREN'T WE STAYING AT THE HOTEL?
I THINK...
...THEY'RE OUT OF ROOMS.
REALLY?
TOO BAD.
...WHAT SHOULD I DO?

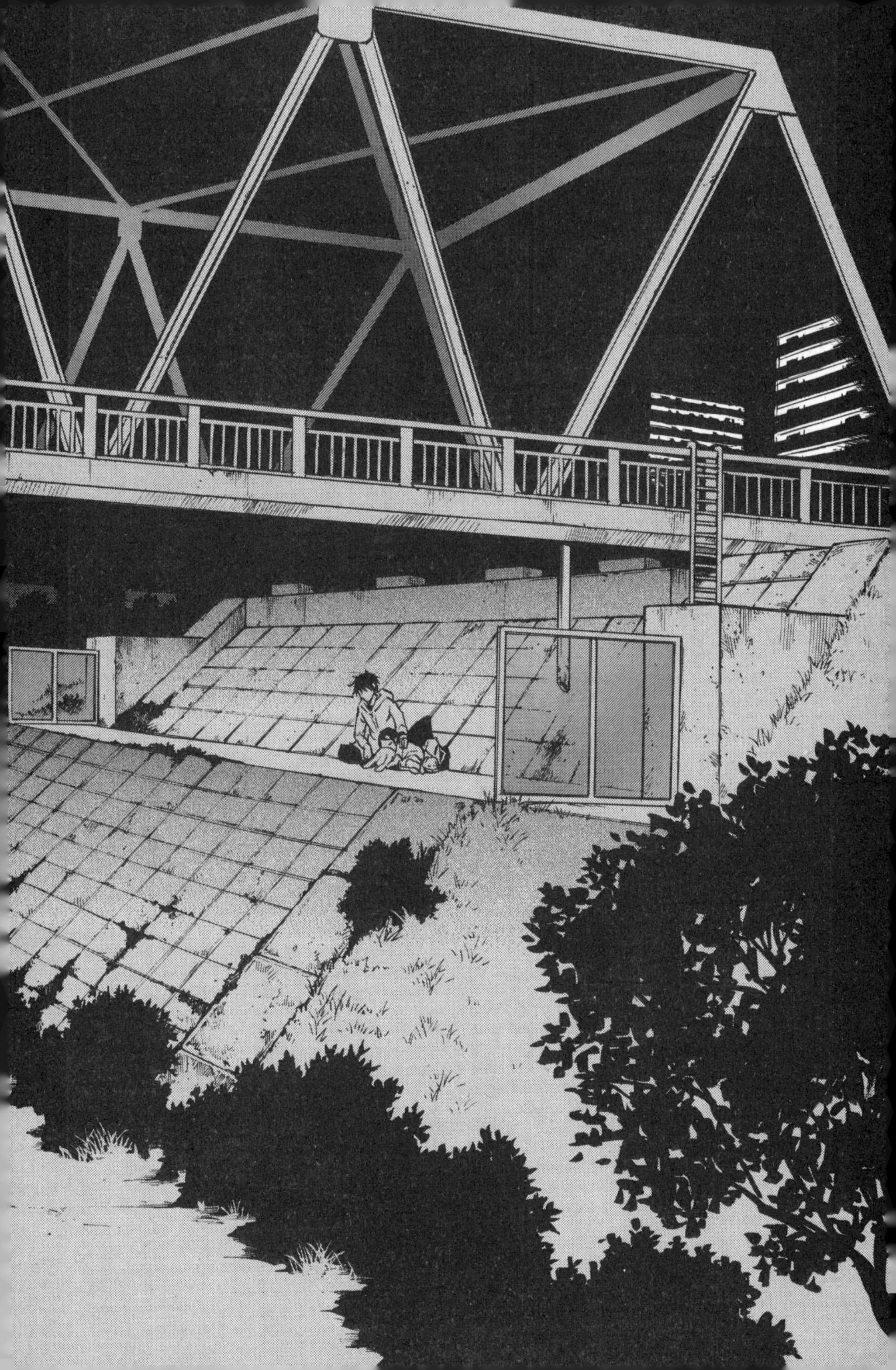

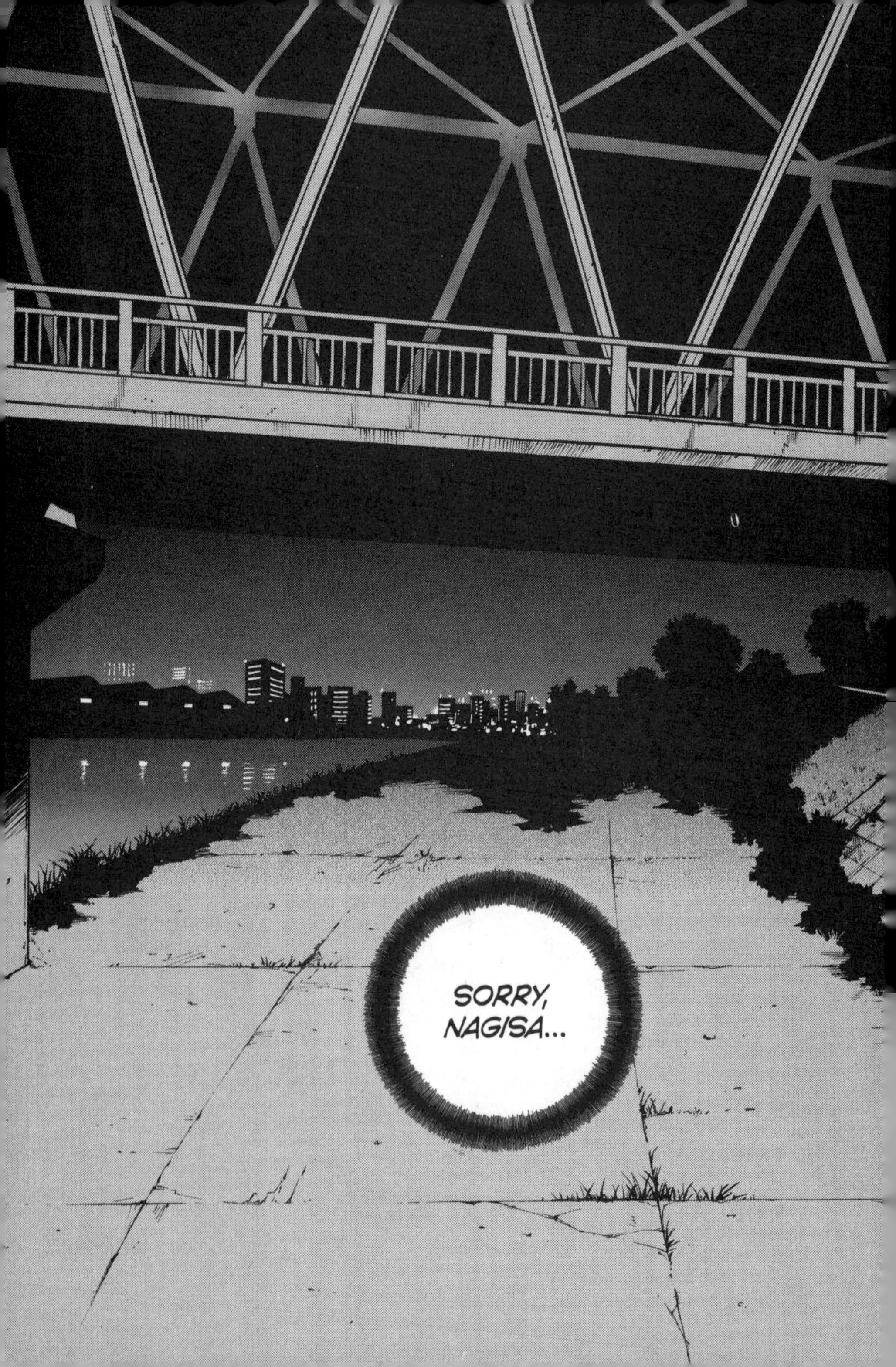
SORRY, NAGISA...

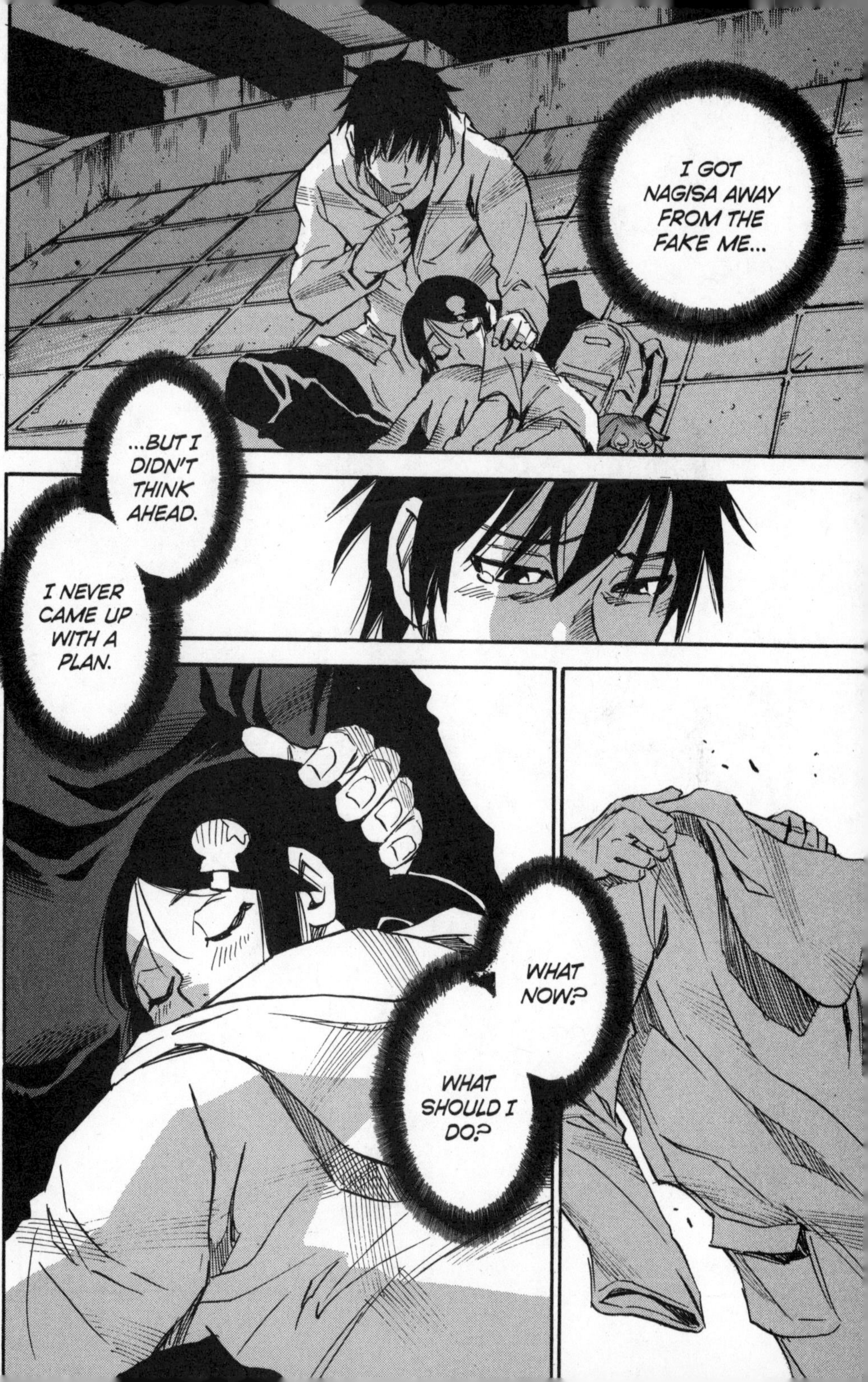
I GOT NAGISA AWAY FROM THE FAKE ME...
...BUT I DIDN'T THINK AHEAD.
I NEVER CAME UP WITH A PLAN.
WHAT NOW?
WHAT SHOULD I DO?

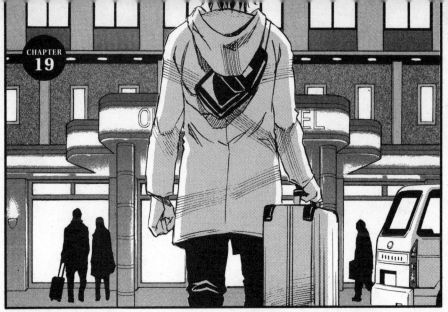

CHAPTER
19

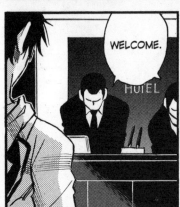

WELCOME.

HOTEL

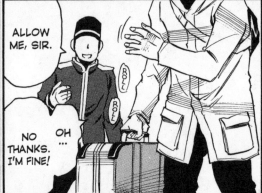

ALLOW ME, SIR.

NO THANKS. I'M FINE!

OH ...

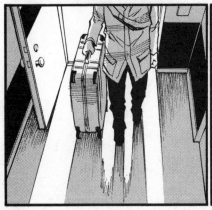

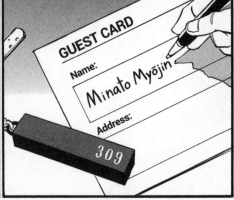

GUEST CARD

Name:

Minato Myōjin

Address:

309

CHAPTER 19
Nagisa Knew

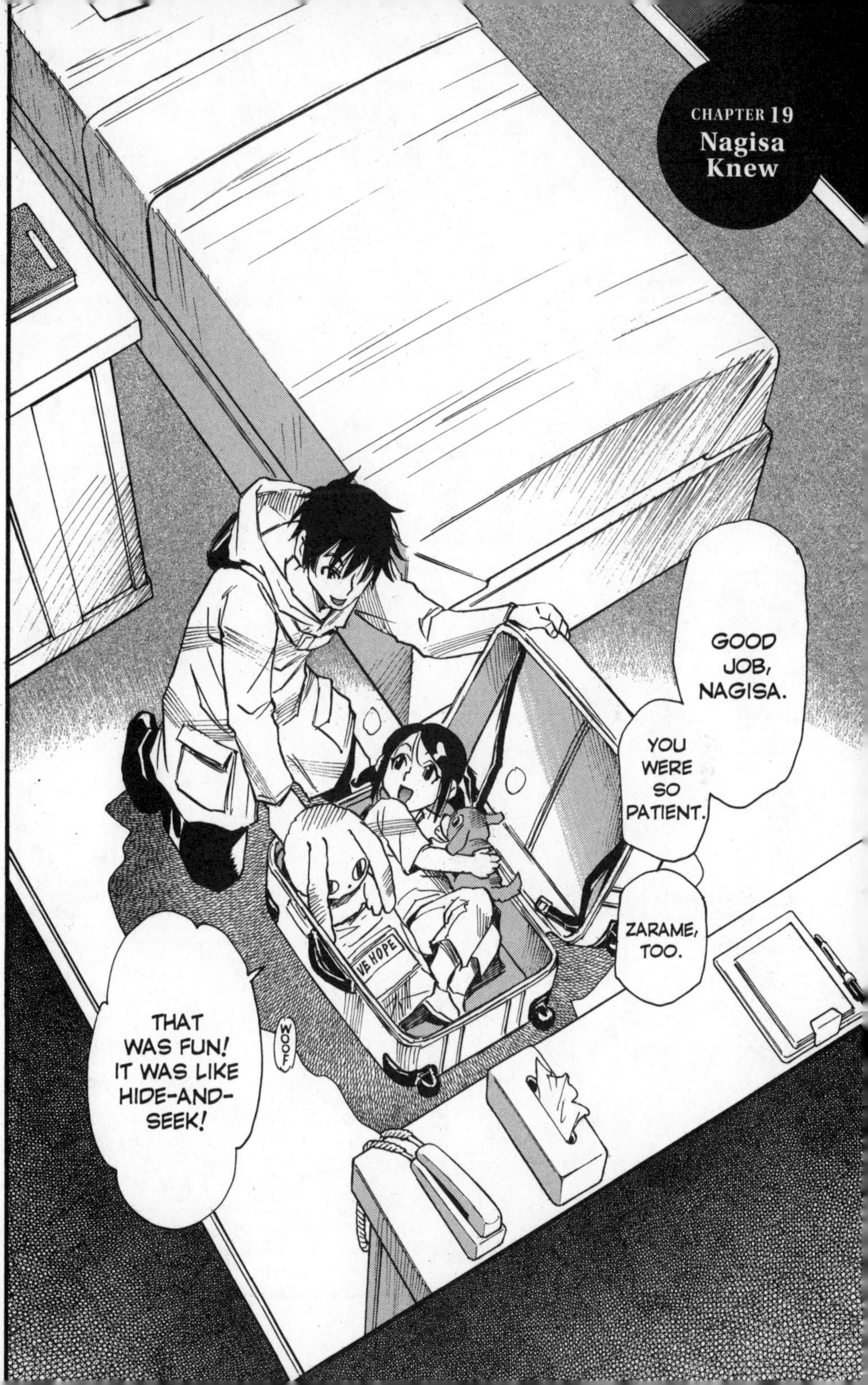
GOOD JOB, NAGISA.
YOU WERE SO PATIENT.
ZARAME, TOO.
THAT WAS FUN! IT WAS LIKE HIDE-AND-SEEK!
WOOF

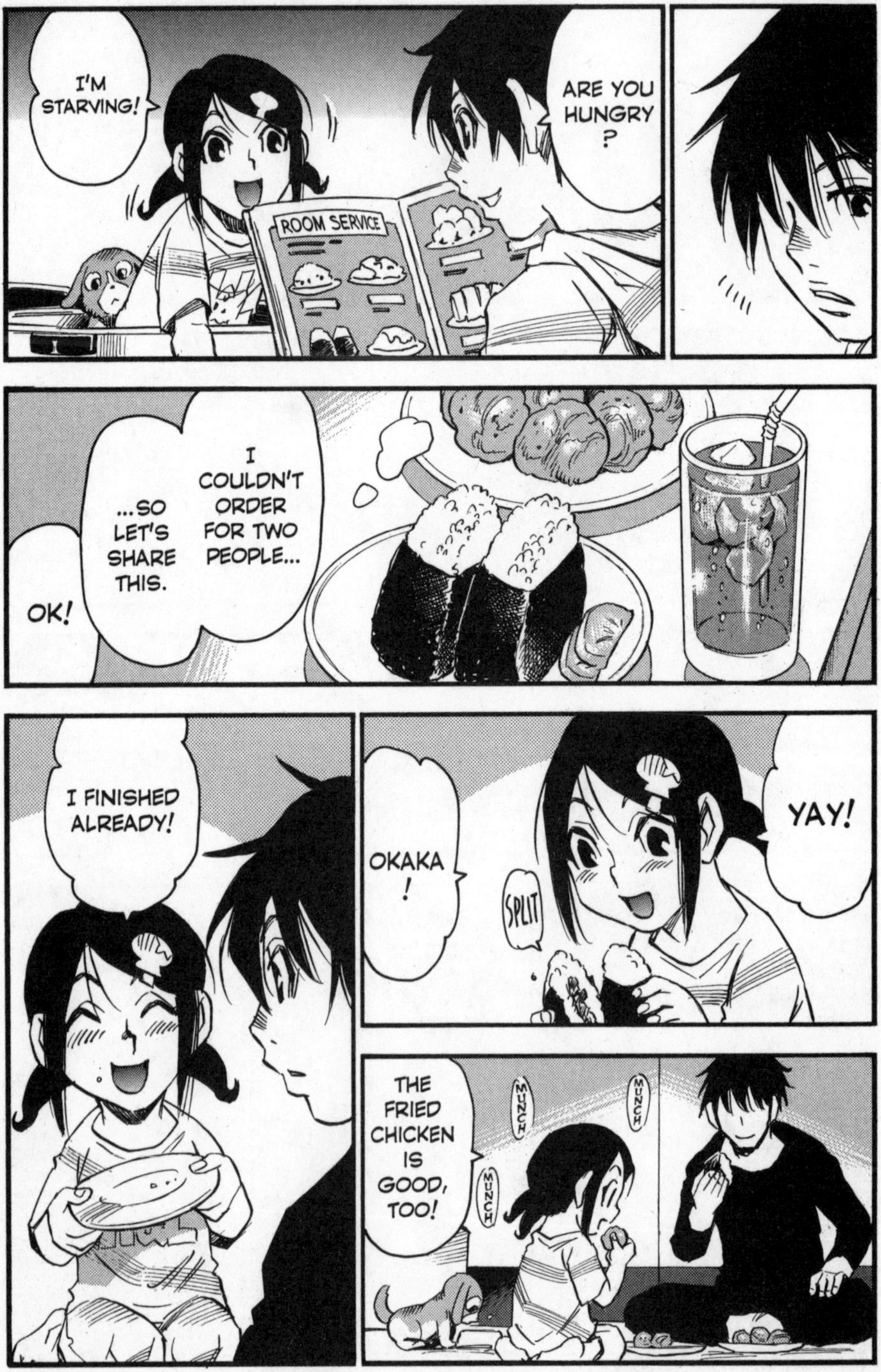
ARE YOU HUNGRY?
I'M STARVING!
ROOM SERVICE
I COULDN'T ORDER FOR TWO PEOPLE...
...SO LET'S SHARE THIS.
OK!
YAY!
SPLIT
OKAKA!
MUNCH
MUNCH
THE FRIED CHICKEN IS GOOD, TOO!
MUNCH
I FINISHED ALREADY!

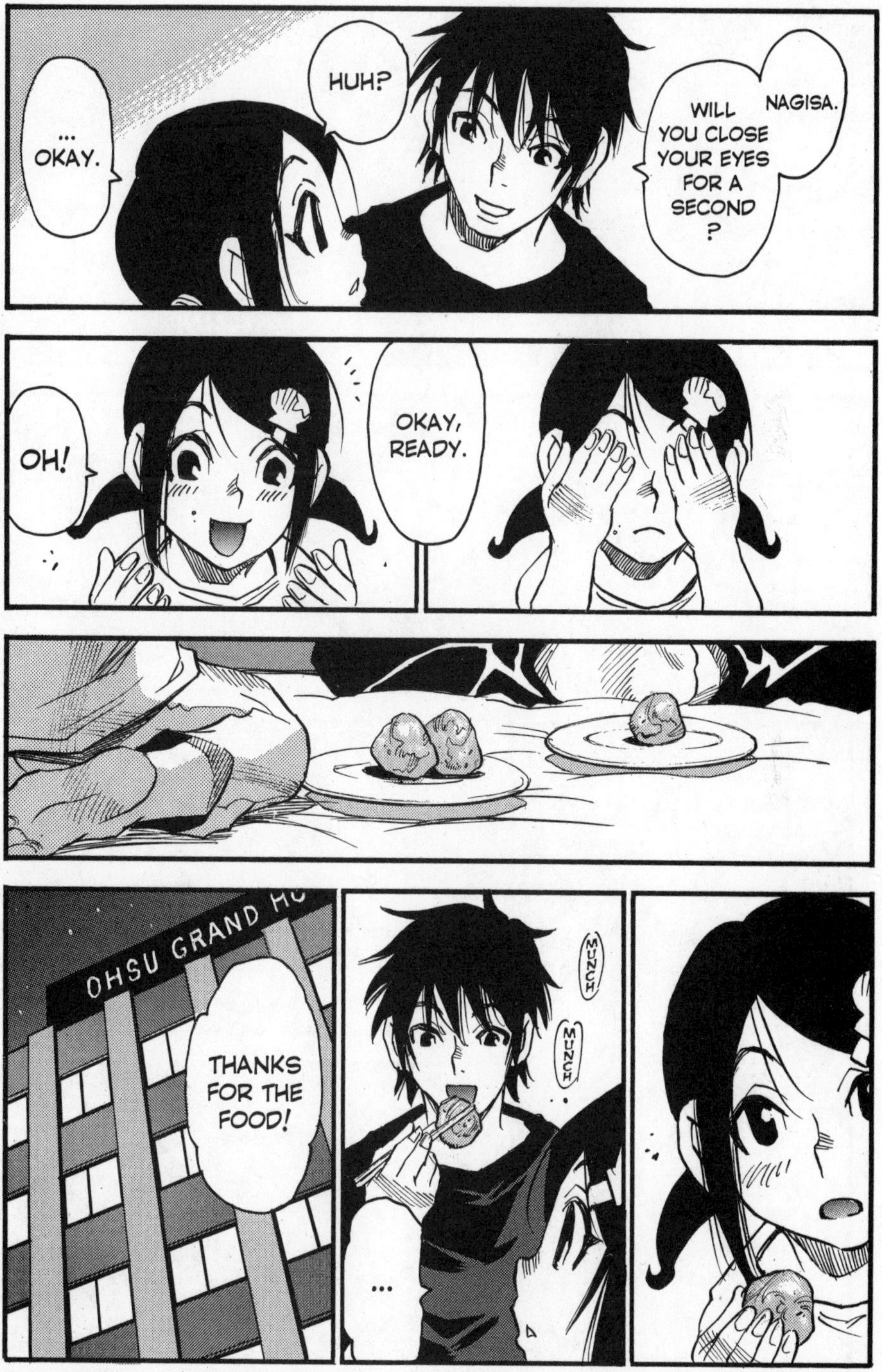
NAGISA.
WILL YOU CLOSE YOUR EYES FOR A SECOND?
HUH?
... OKAY.
OKAY, READY.
OH!
MUNCH
MUNCH
...
OHSU GRAND H
THANKS FOR THE FOOD!

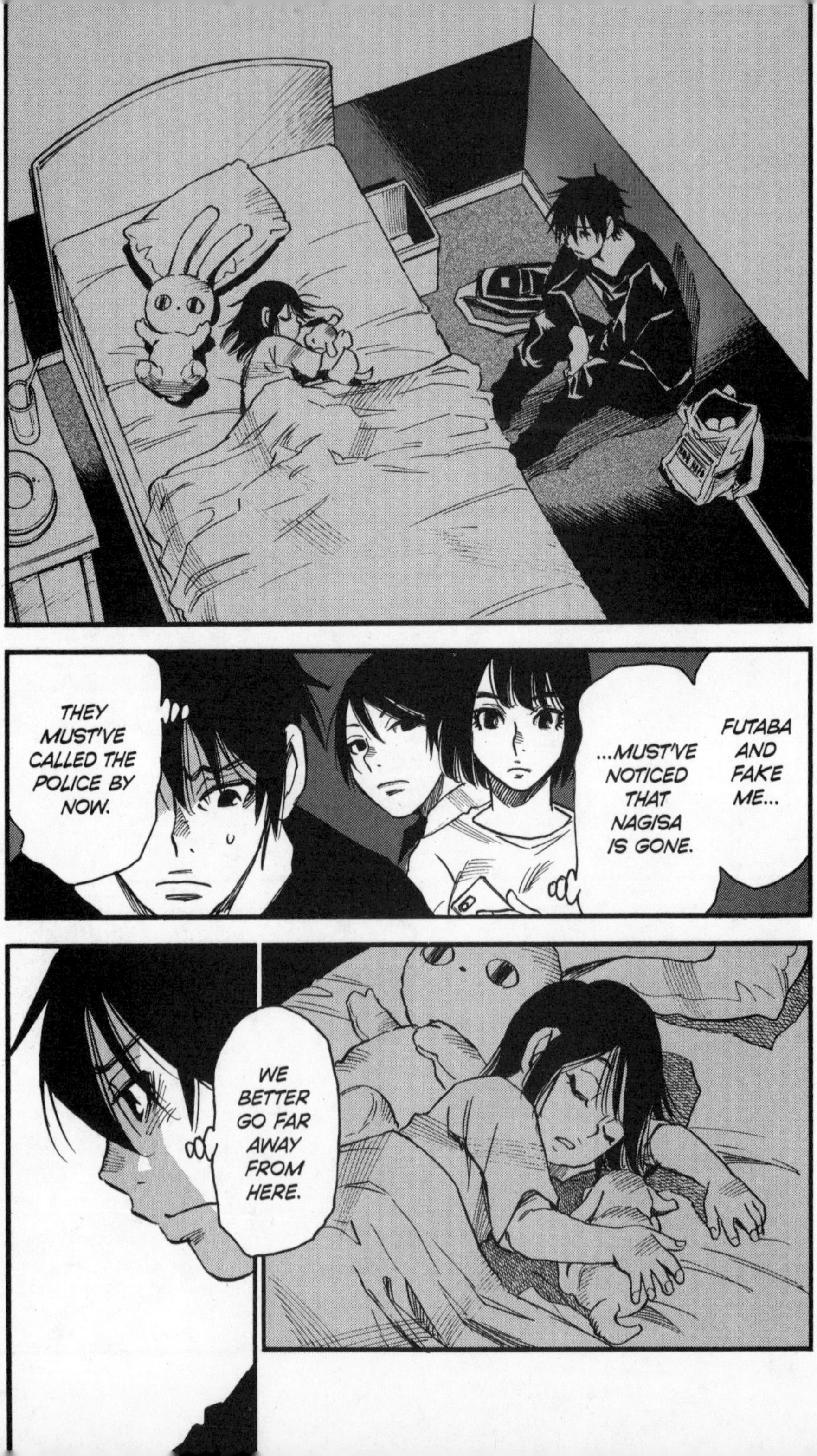
FUTABA AND FAKE ME...
...MUST'VE NOTICED THAT NAGISA IS GONE.
THEY MUST'VE CALLED THE POLICE BY NOW.
WE BETTER GO FAR AWAY FROM HERE.

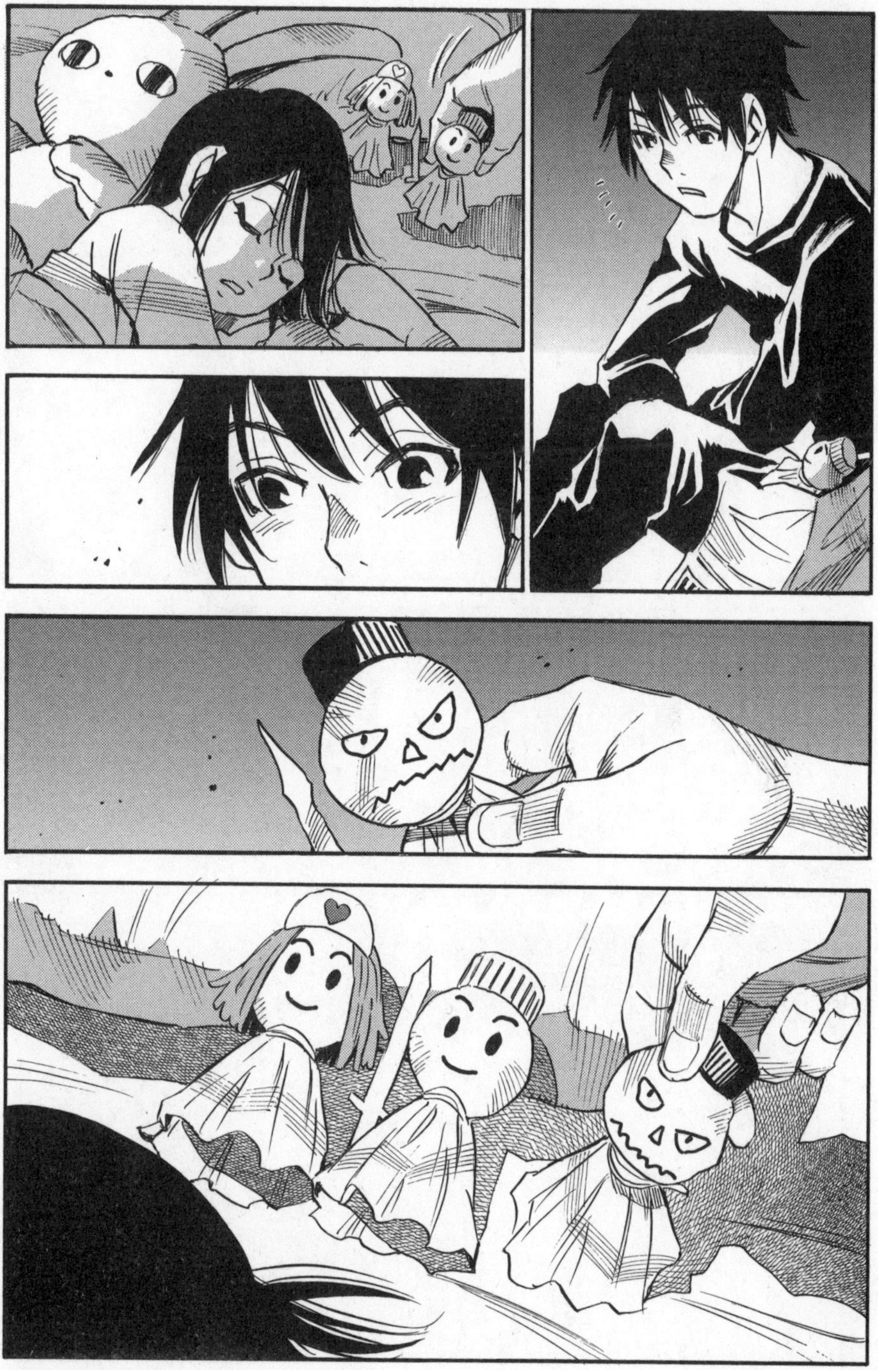

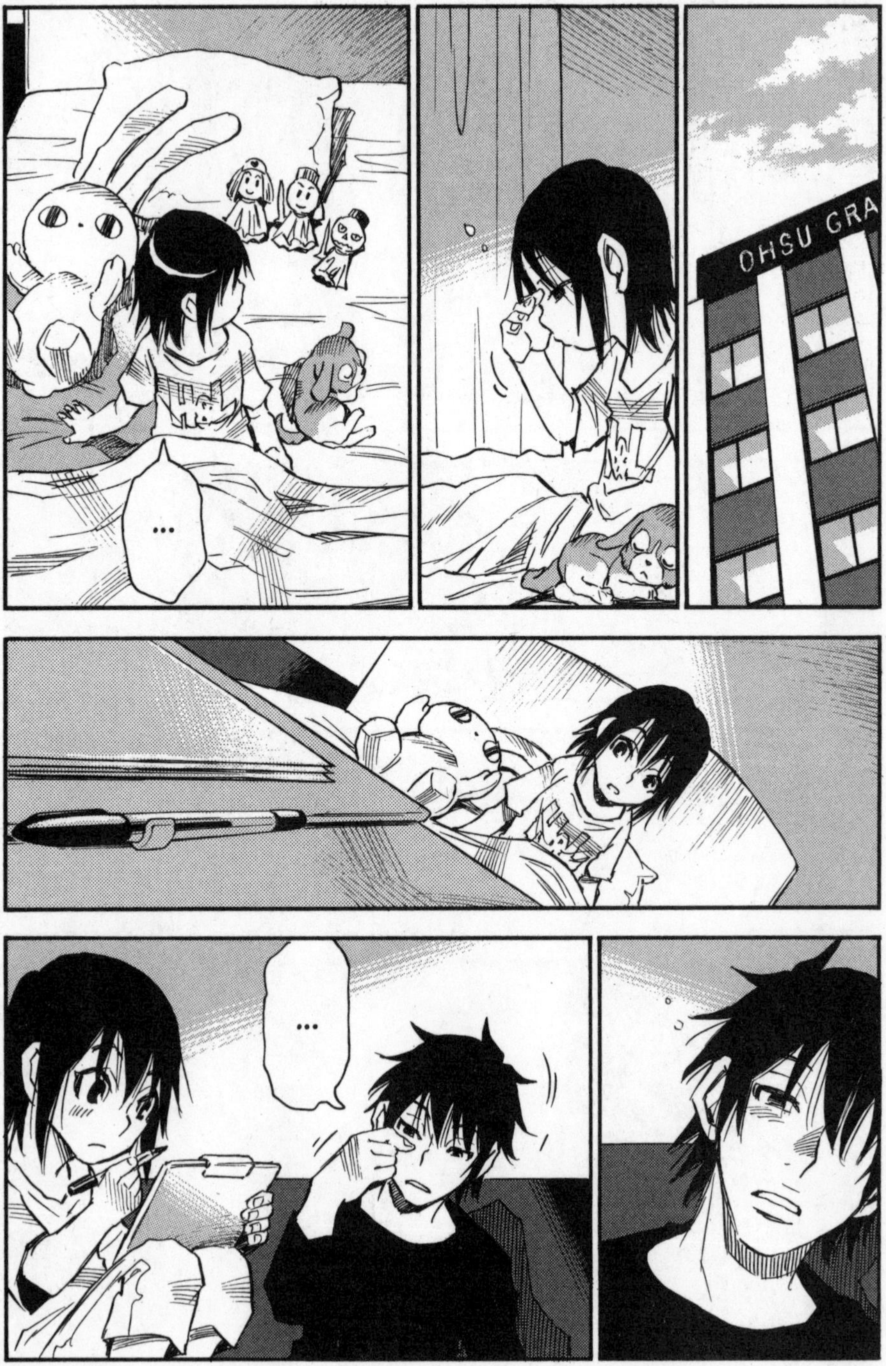
OHSU GRA
...
...

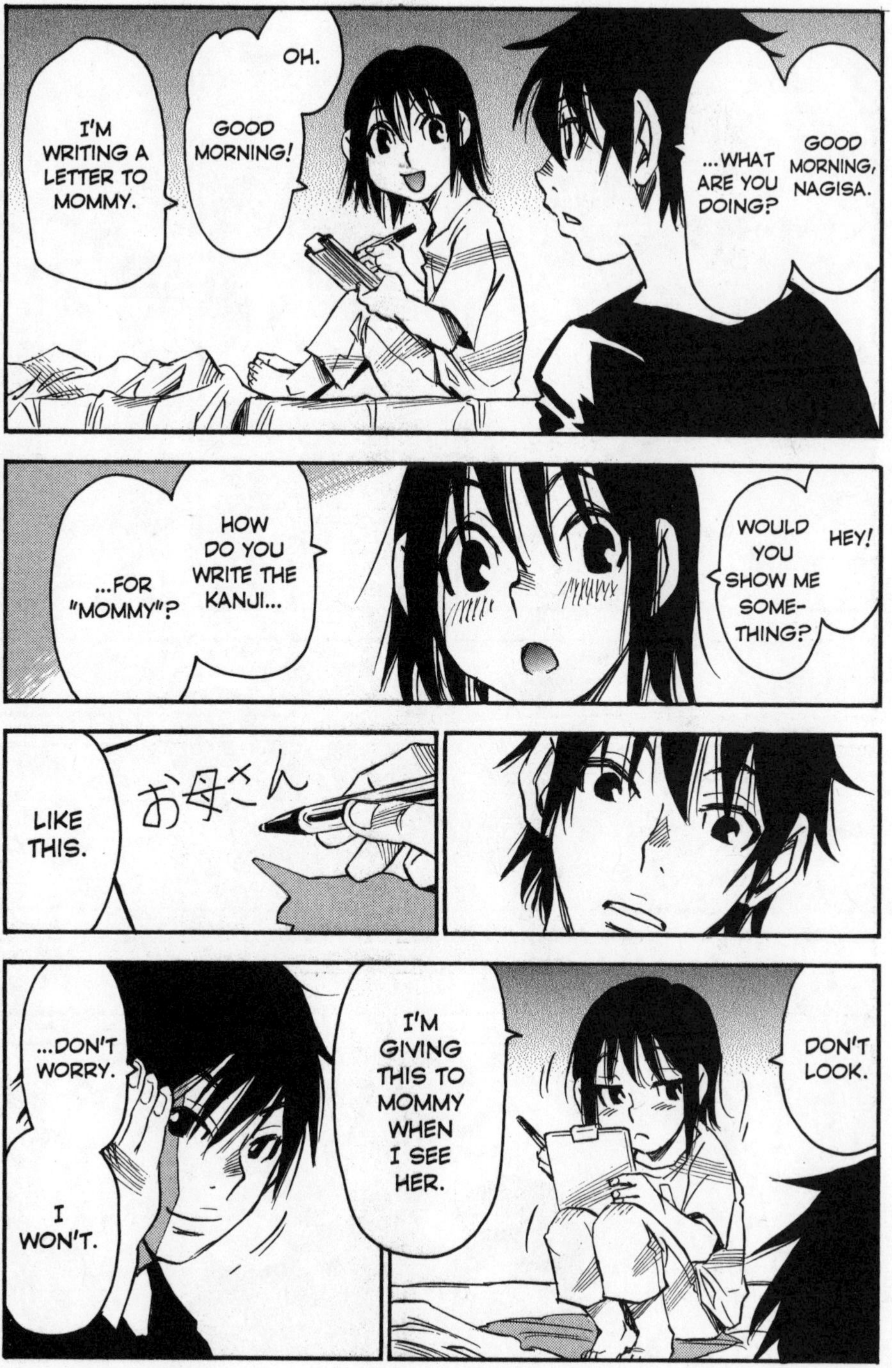
GOOD MORNING, NAGISA.
...WHAT ARE YOU DOING?
OH.
GOOD MORNING!
I'M WRITING A LETTER TO MOMMY.
HEY!
WOULD YOU SHOW ME SOME-THING?
HOW DO YOU WRITE THE KANJI...
...FOR "MOMMY"?
お母さん
LIKE THIS.
DON'T LOOK.
I'M GIVING THIS TO MOMMY WHEN I SEE HER.
...DON'T WORRY.
I WON'T.

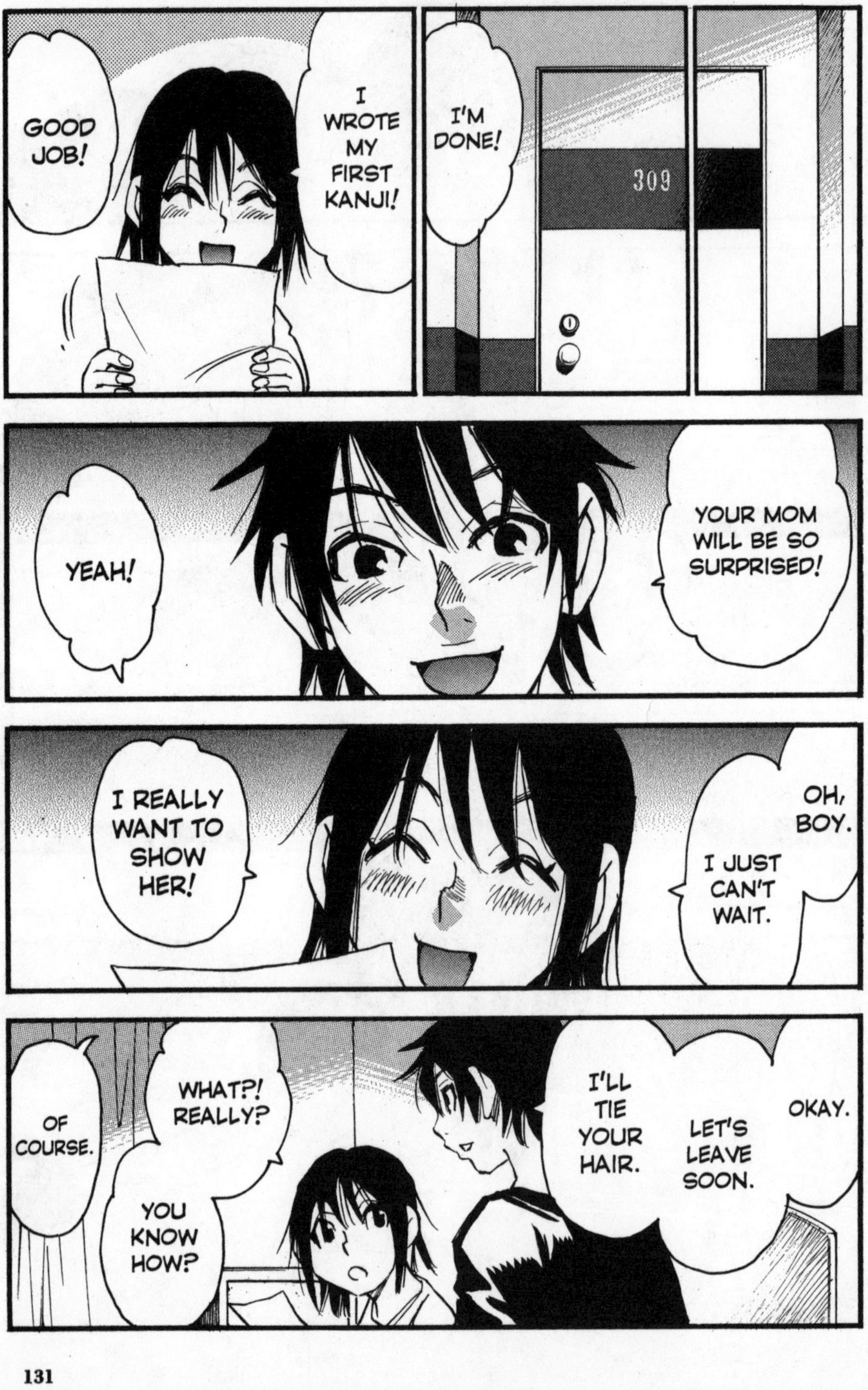
309
I'M DONE!
I WROTE MY FIRST KANJI!
GOOD JOB!
YOUR MOM WILL BE SO SURPRISED!
YEAH!
OH, BOY.
I JUST CAN'T WAIT.
I REALLY WANT TO SHOW HER!
OKAY.
LET'S LEAVE SOON.
I'LL TIE YOUR HAIR.
WHAT?! REALLY?
YOU KNOW HOW?
OF COURSE.

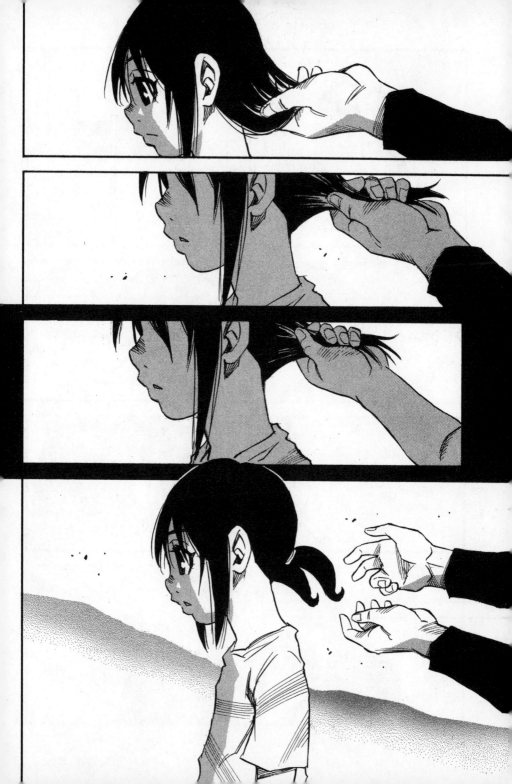

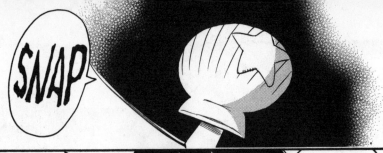

SNAP

IS THAT OKAY?

...I NEED YOU TO GO IN THE SUITCASE AGAIN.

OKAY, SO...

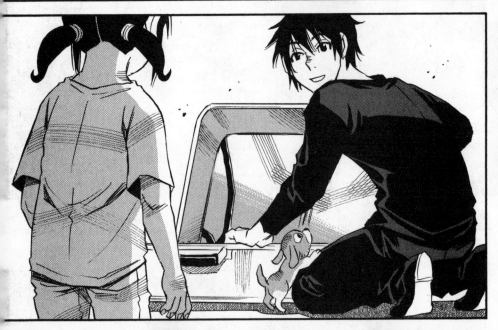

I DON'T MIND ONE BIT.

YUP.

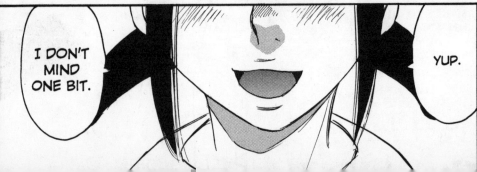

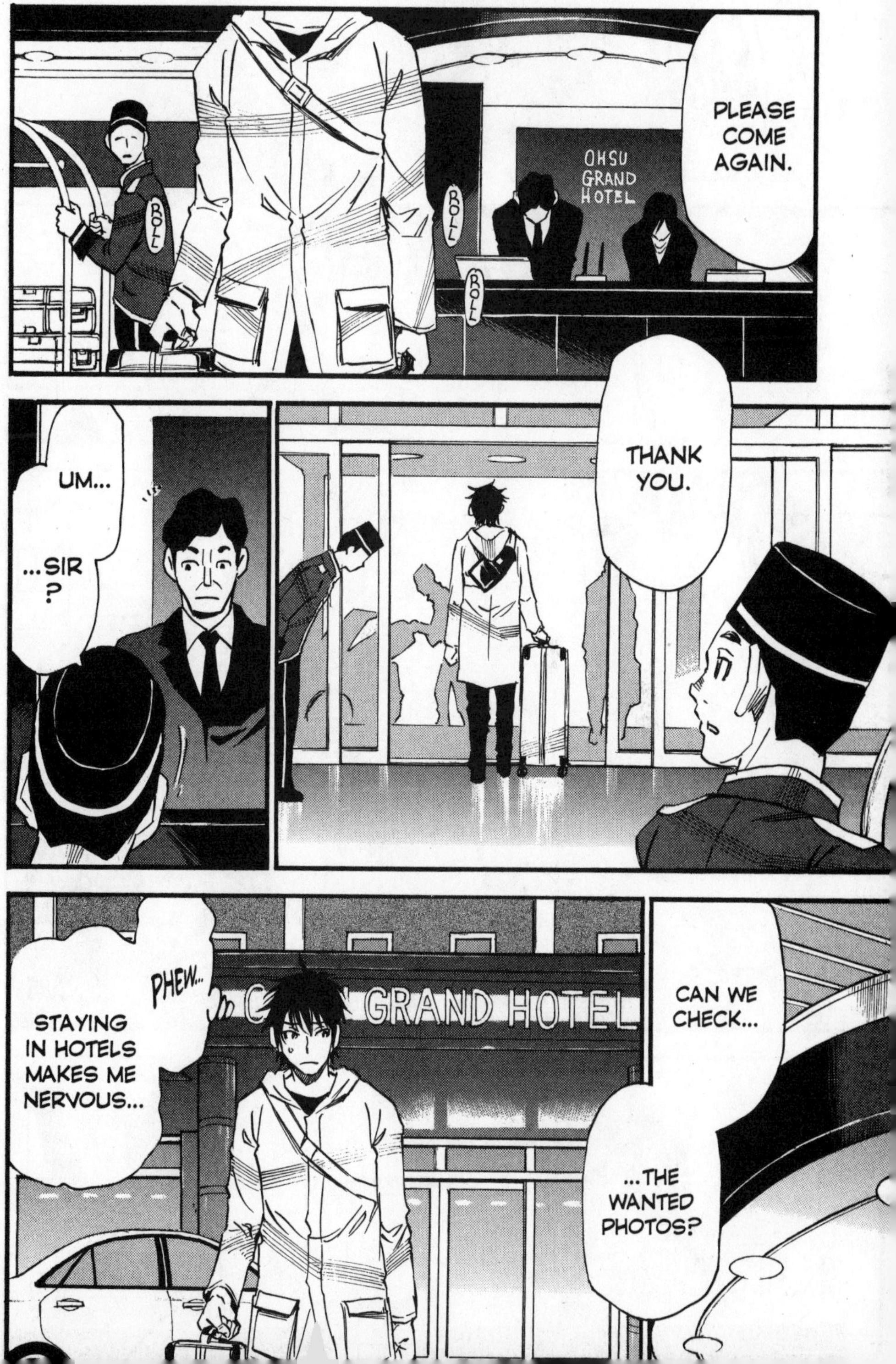
PLEASE COME AGAIN.
OHSU GRAND HOTEL
ROLL
ROLL
ROLL
THANK YOU.
UM...
...SIR?
CAN WE CHECK...
...THE WANTED PHOTOS?
PHEW...
STAYING IN HOTELS MAKES ME NERVOUS...
GRAND HOTEL

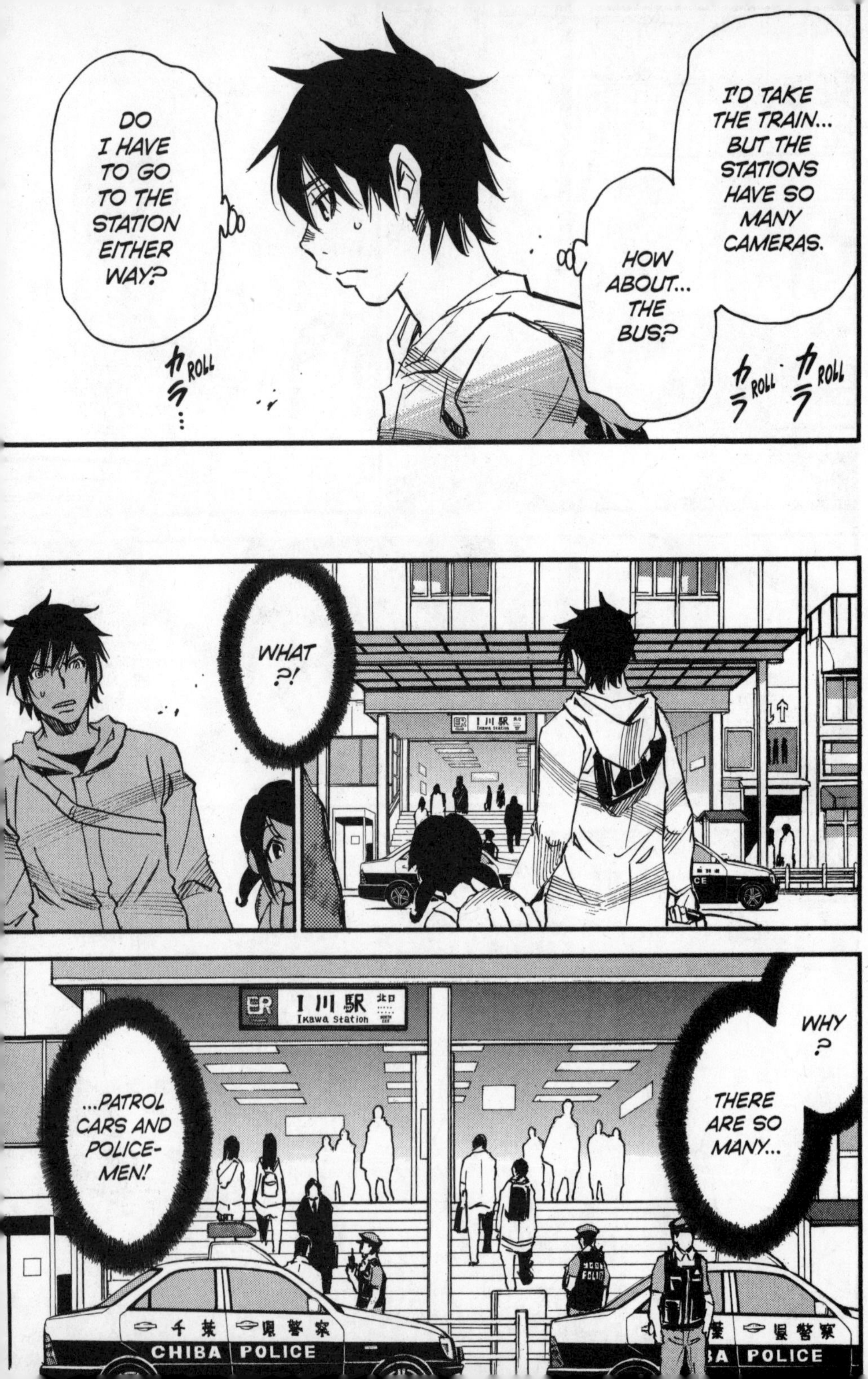

I'D TAKE THE TRAIN... BUT THE STATIONS HAVE SO MANY CAMERAS.
カラ ROLL
カラ ROLL
HOW ABOUT... THE BUS?
DO I HAVE TO GO TO THE STATION EITHER WAY?
カラ ROLL
I川駅 Ikawa Station
WHAT?!
I川駅 北口 Ikawa Station NORTH EXIT
WHY?
THERE ARE SO MANY...
...PATROL CARS AND POLICE-MEN!
千葉県警察
CHIBA POLICE
BA POLICE

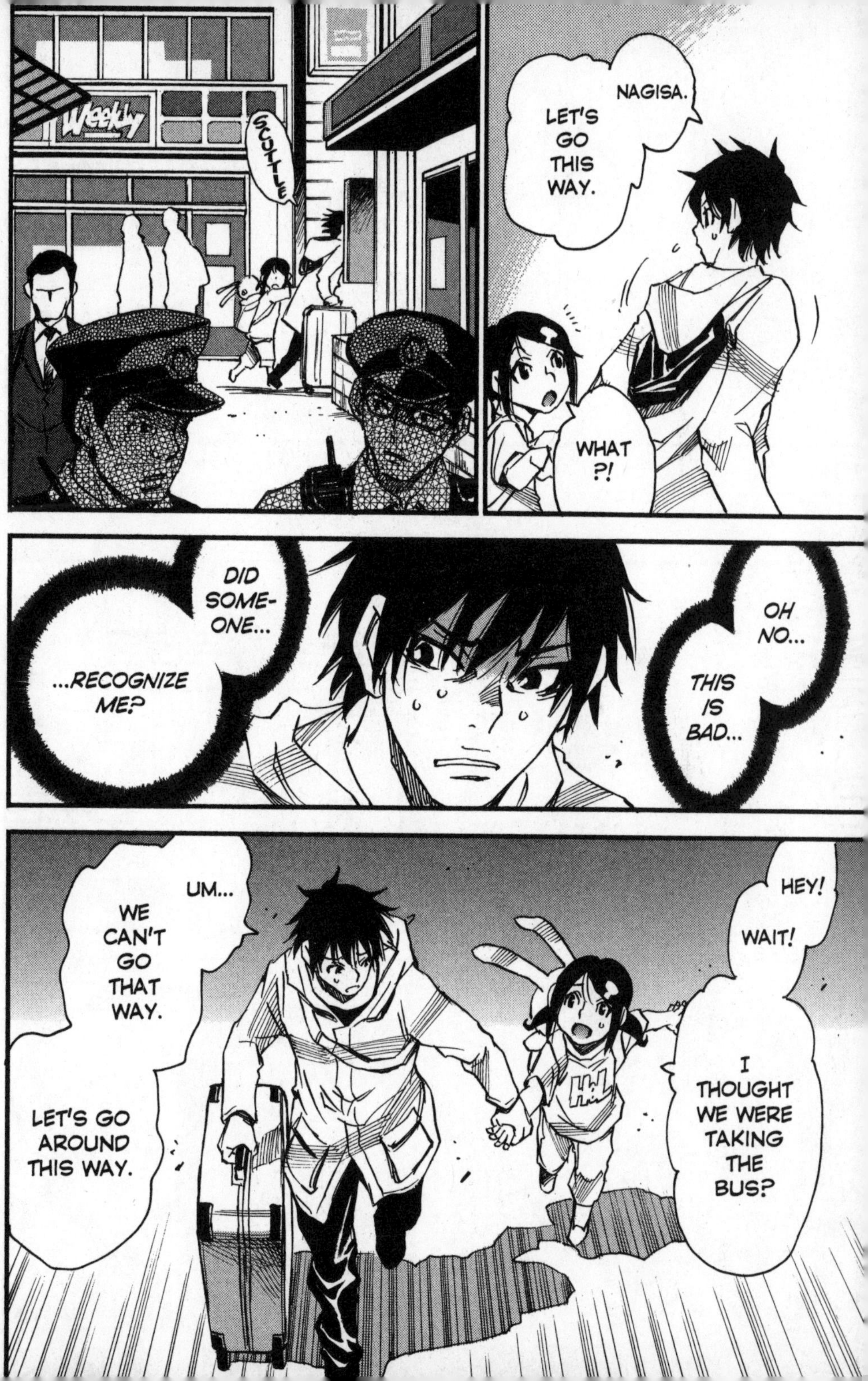
NAGISA.
LET'S GO THIS WAY.
WHAT ?!
SCUTTLE
OH NO...
THIS IS BAD...
DID SOME-ONE...
...RECOGNIZE ME?
HEY!
WAIT!
I THOUGHT WE WERE TAKING THE BUS?
UM...
WE CAN'T GO THAT WAY.
LET'S GO AROUND THIS WAY.

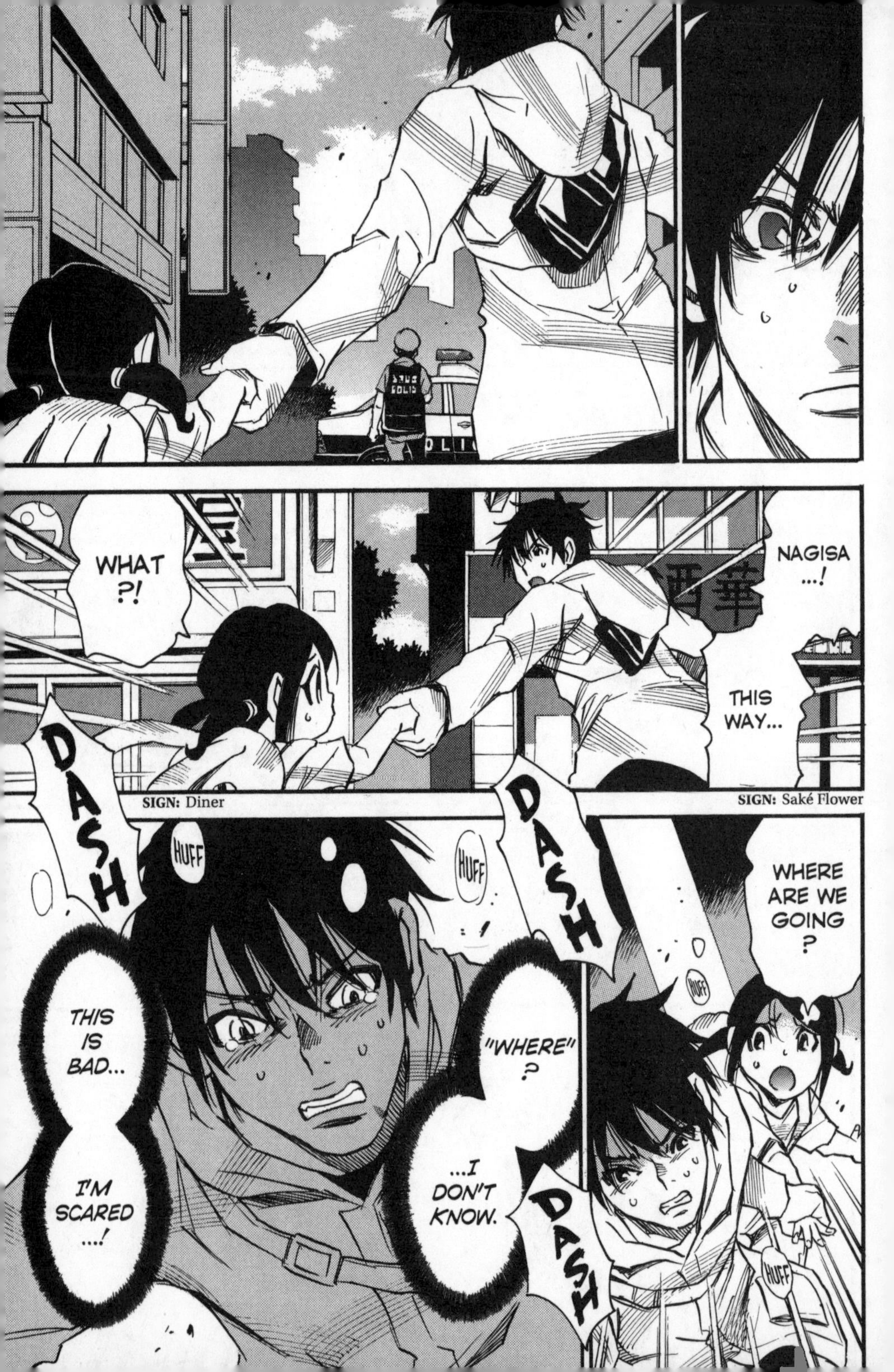

NAGISA ...!
THIS WAY...
WHAT ?!
SIGN: Saké Flower
SIGN: Diner
WHERE ARE WE GOING ?
HUFF
DASH
"WHERE" ?
...I DON'T KNOW.
DASH
HUFF
HUFF
HUFF
DASH
THIS IS BAD...
I'M SCARED ...!

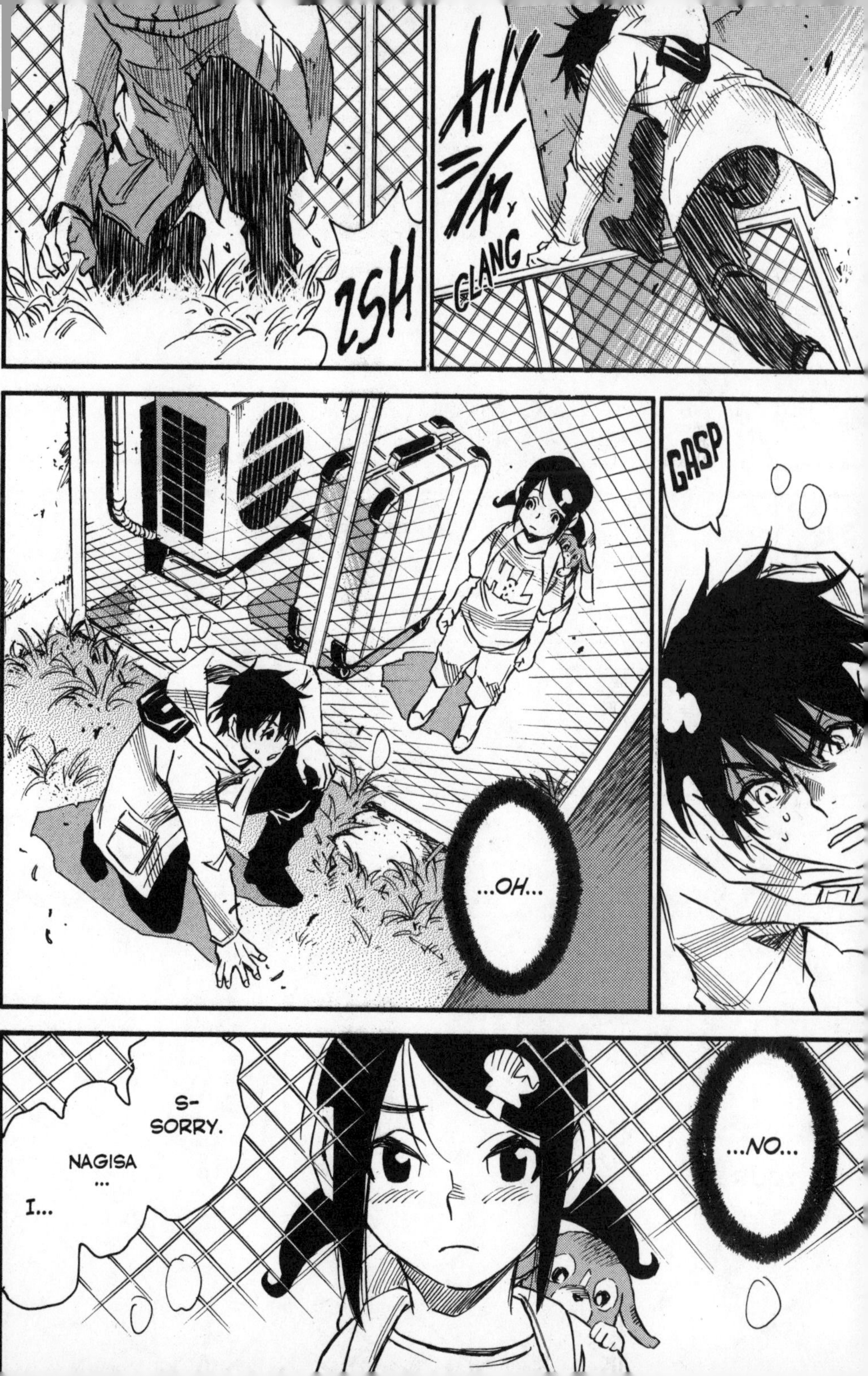

CLANG
ZSH
GASP
...OH...
...NO...
S-SORRY.
NAGISA...
I...

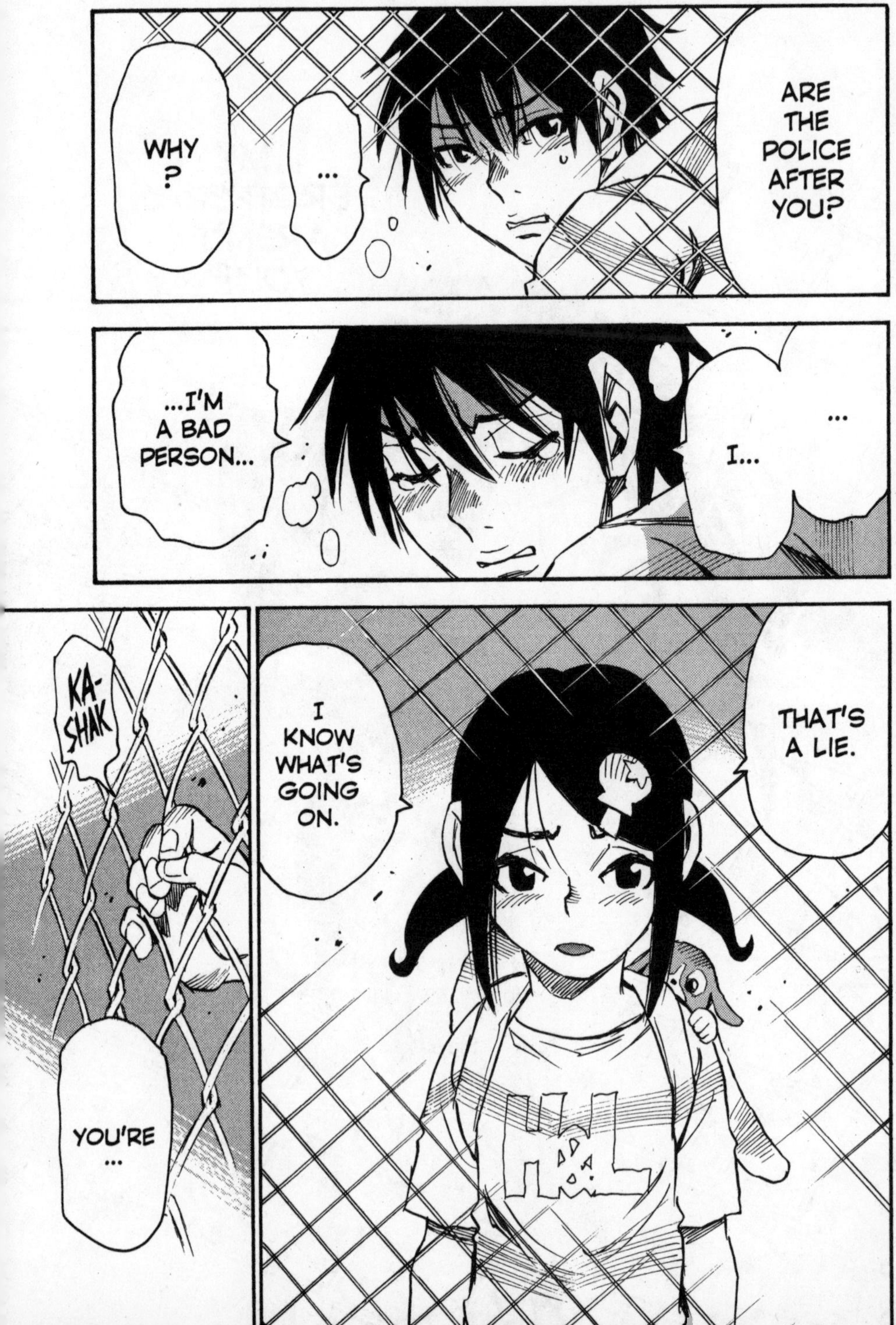
ARE THE POLICE AFTER YOU?
...
WHY?
...
I...
...I'M A BAD PERSON...
THAT'S A LIE.
I KNOW WHAT'S GOING ON.
KA-SHAK
YOU'RE ...

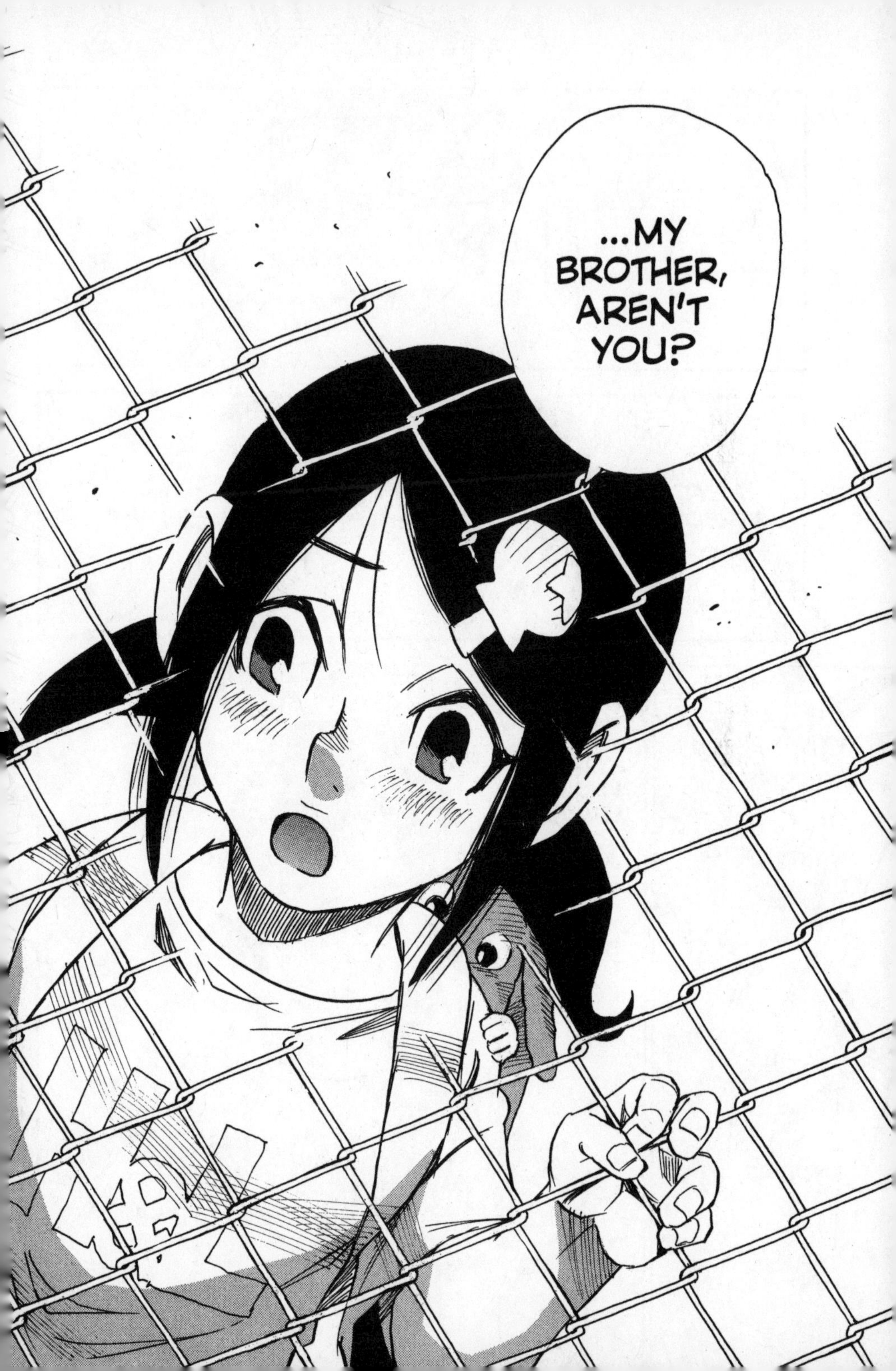
...MY BROTHER, AREN'T YOU?

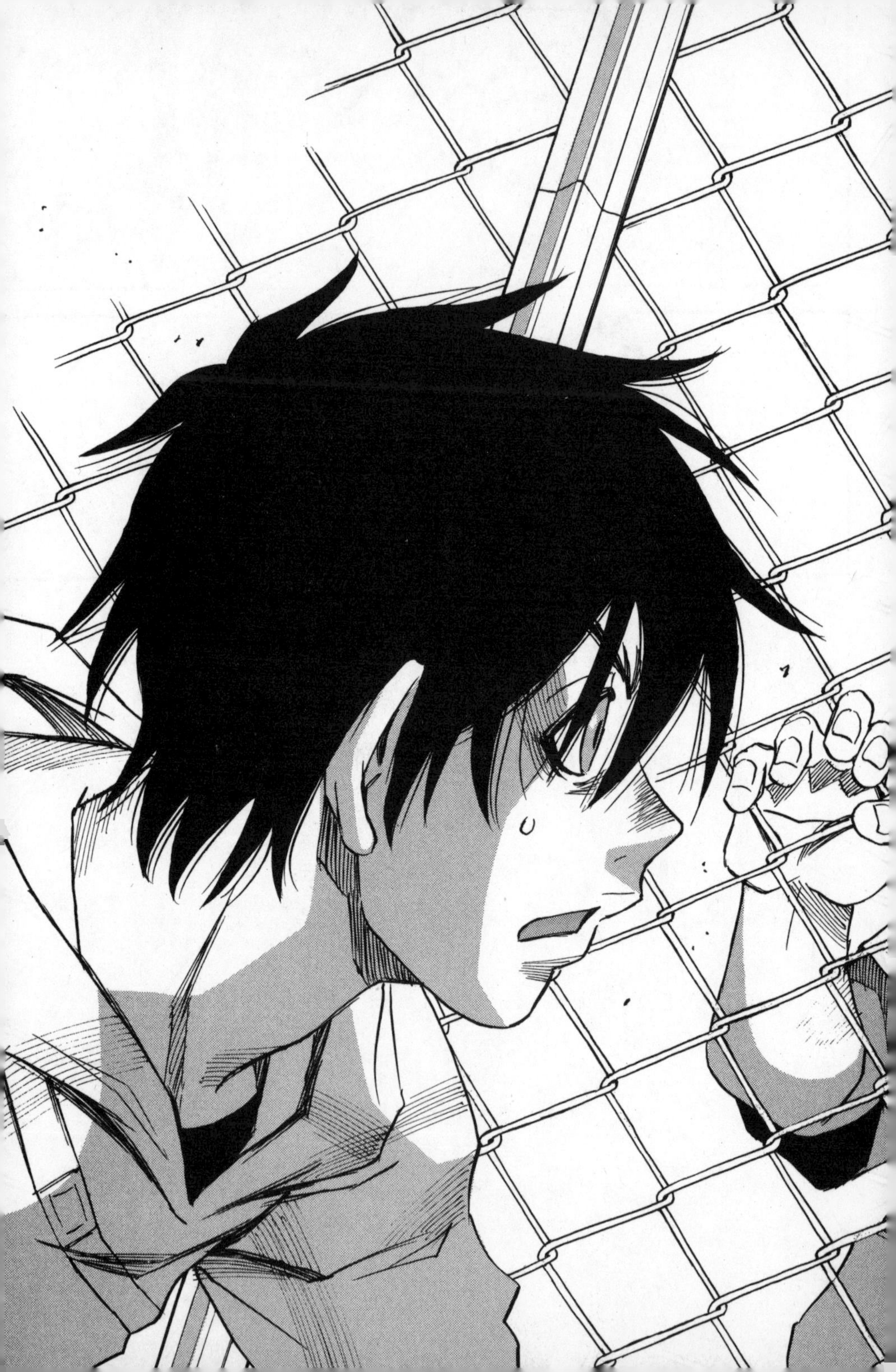

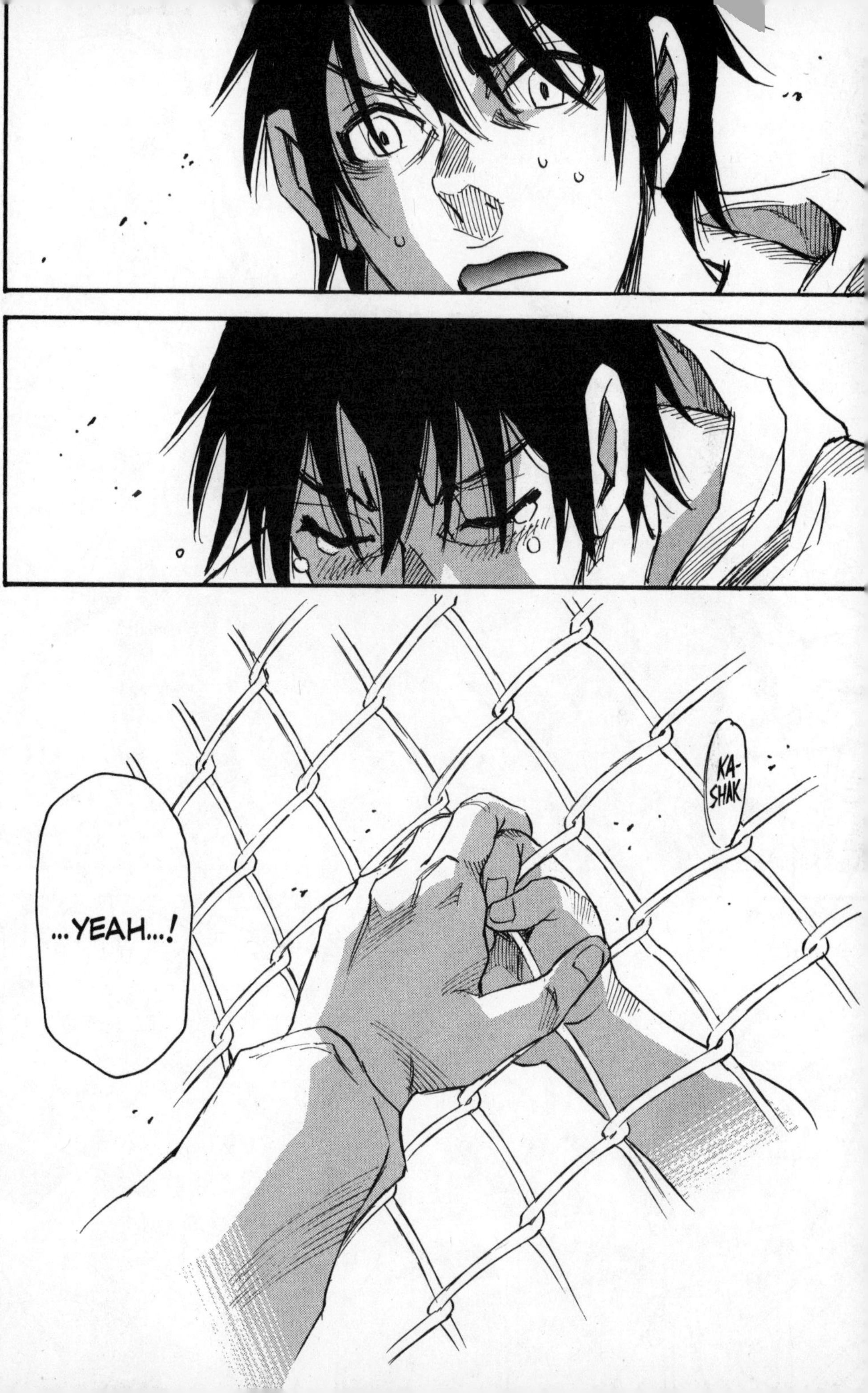
KA-SHAK
...YEAH...!

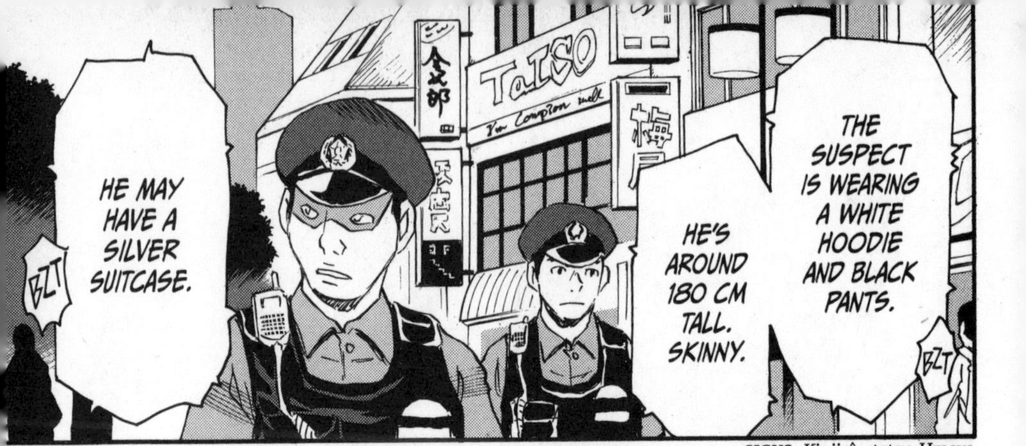
THE SUSPECT IS WEARING A WHITE HOODIE AND BLACK PANTS.
BZT
HE'S AROUND 180 CM TALL. SKINNY.
HE MAY HAVE A SILVER SUITCASE.
BZT

SIGNS: Kinjirô, -tatsu, Umeya

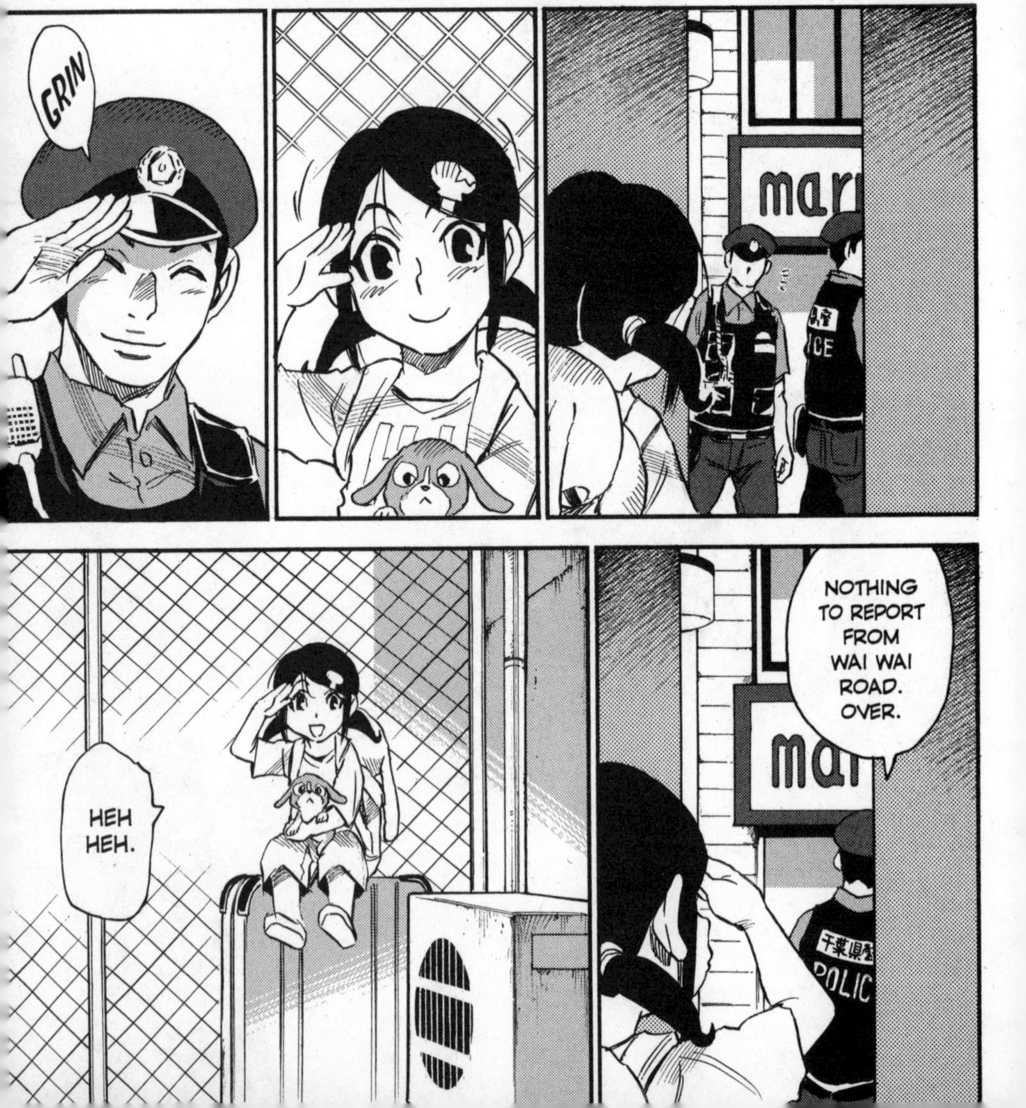
GRIN
NOTHING TO REPORT FROM WAI WAI ROAD. OVER.
HEH HEH.

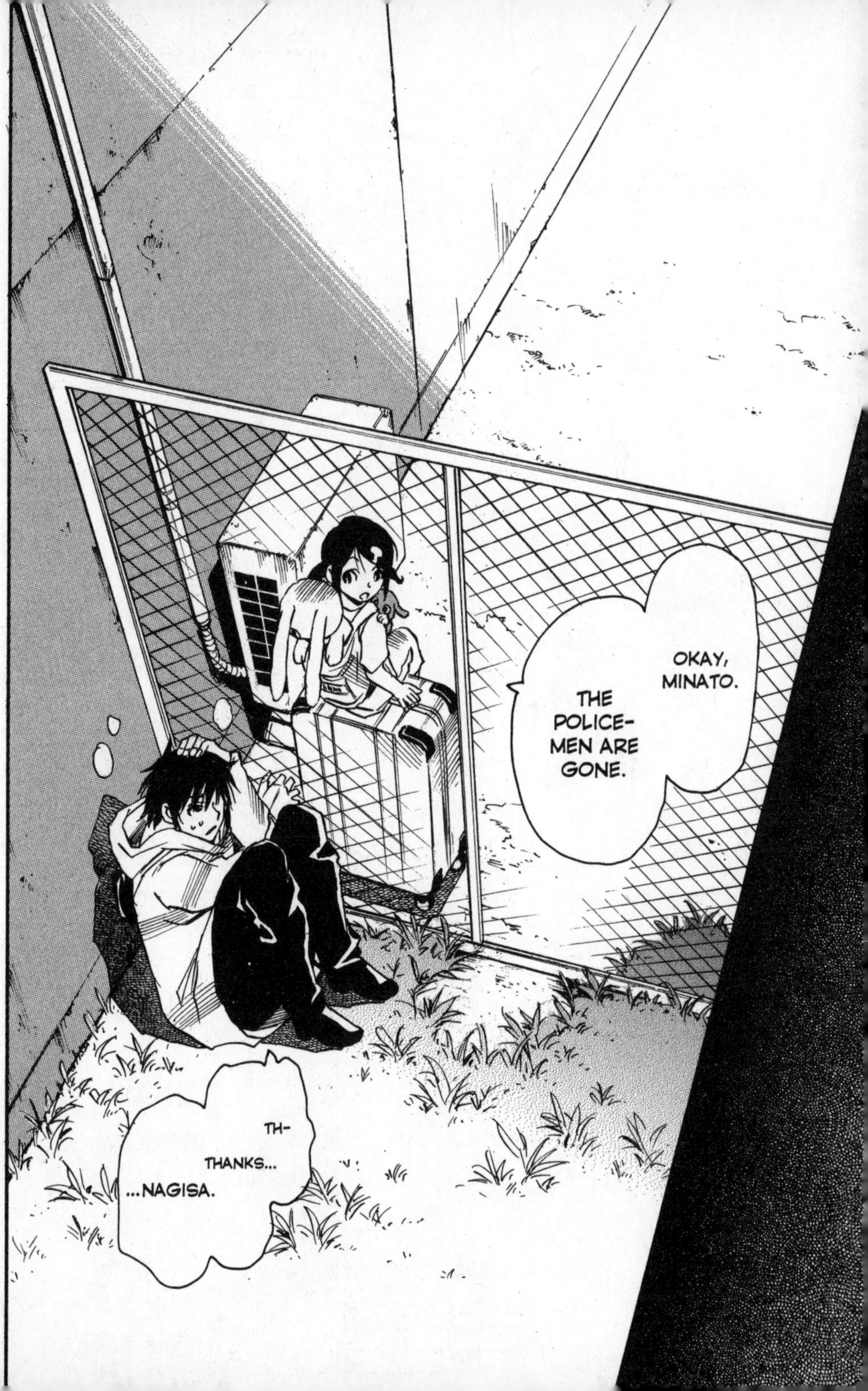
OKAY, MINATO. THE POLICE-MEN ARE GONE.
TH- THANKS... ...NAGISA.

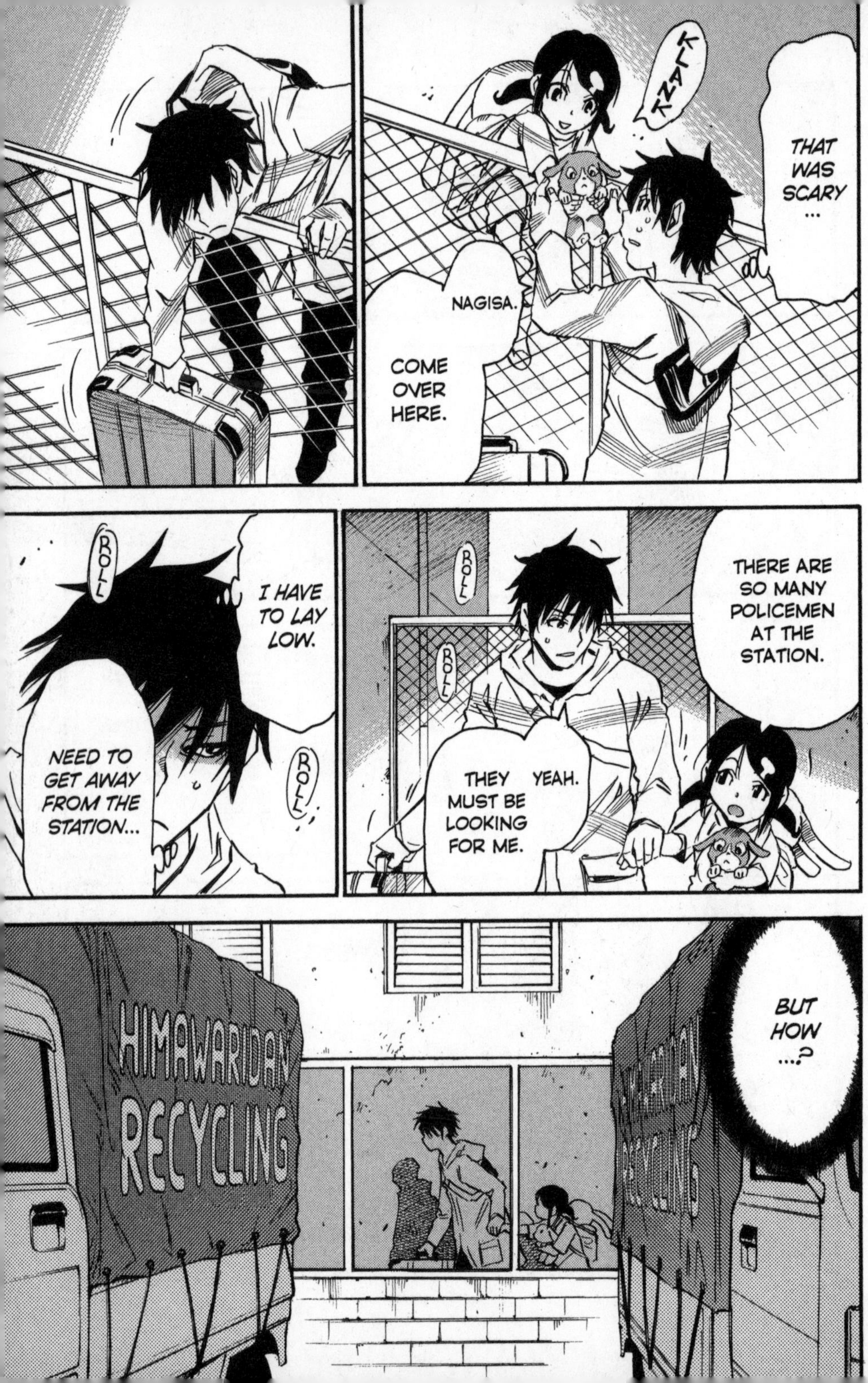

THAT WAS SCARY ...
KLANK
NAGISA.
COME OVER HERE.
THERE ARE SO MANY POLICEMEN AT THE STATION.
YEAH.
THEY MUST BE LOOKING FOR ME.
ROLL
ROLL
I HAVE TO LAY LOW.
NEED TO GET AWAY FROM THE STATION...
ROLL
ROLL
BUT HOW ...?
HIMAWARIDAI RECYCLING

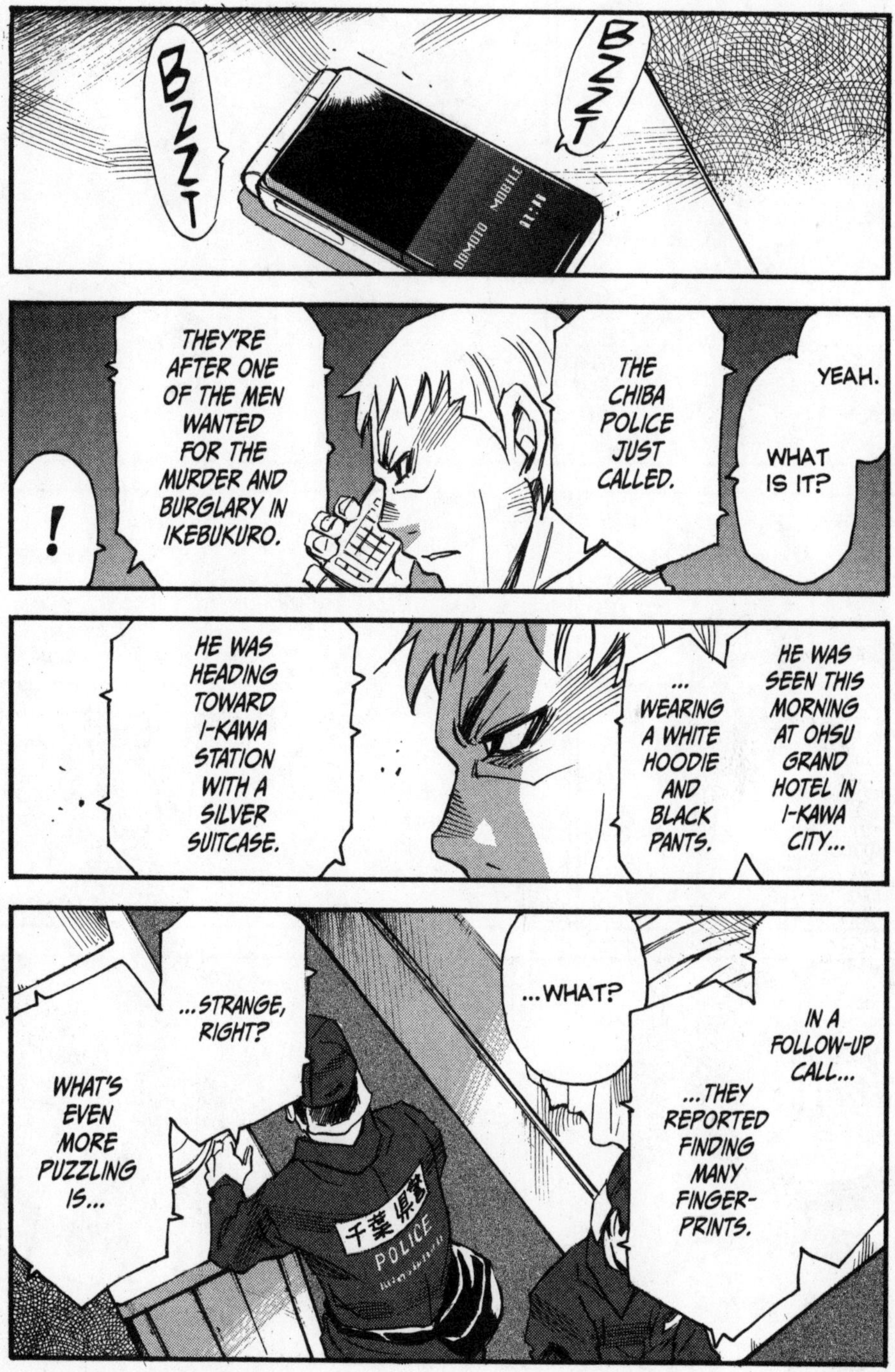
BZZZT
BZZT
YEAH.
WHAT IS IT?
THE CHIBA POLICE JUST CALLED.
THEY'RE AFTER ONE OF THE MEN WANTED FOR THE MURDER AND BURGLARY IN IKEBUKURO.
!
HE WAS SEEN THIS MORNING AT OHSU GRAND HOTEL IN I-KAWA CITY...
...WEARING A WHITE HOODIE AND BLACK PANTS.
HE WAS HEADING TOWARD I-KAWA STATION WITH A SILVER SUITCASE.
IN A FOLLOW-UP CALL...
...THEY REPORTED FINDING MANY FINGER-PRINTS.
...WHAT?
...STRANGE, RIGHT?
WHAT'S EVEN MORE PUZZLING IS...
千葉県警
POLICE

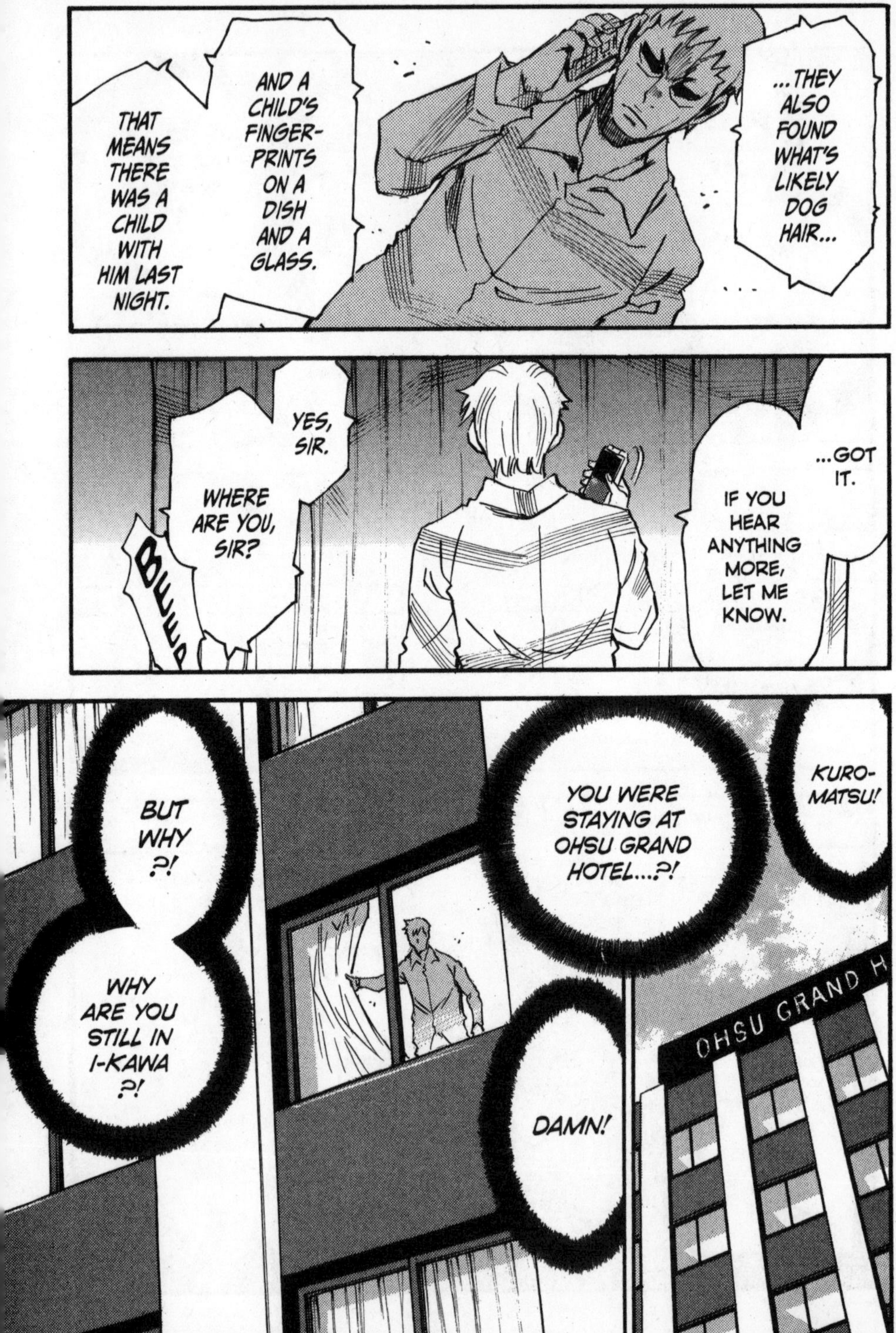
...THEY ALSO FOUND WHAT'S LIKELY DOG HAIR...
AND A CHILD'S FINGER-PRINTS ON A DISH AND A GLASS.
THAT MEANS THERE WAS A CHILD WITH HIM LAST NIGHT.
...GOT IT.
IF YOU HEAR ANYTHING MORE, LET ME KNOW.
YES, SIR.
WHERE ARE YOU, SIR?
KURO-MATSU!
YOU WERE STAYING AT OHSU GRAND HOTEL...?!
BUT WHY ?!
WHY ARE YOU STILL IN I-KAWA ?!
DAMN!
OHSU GRAND H

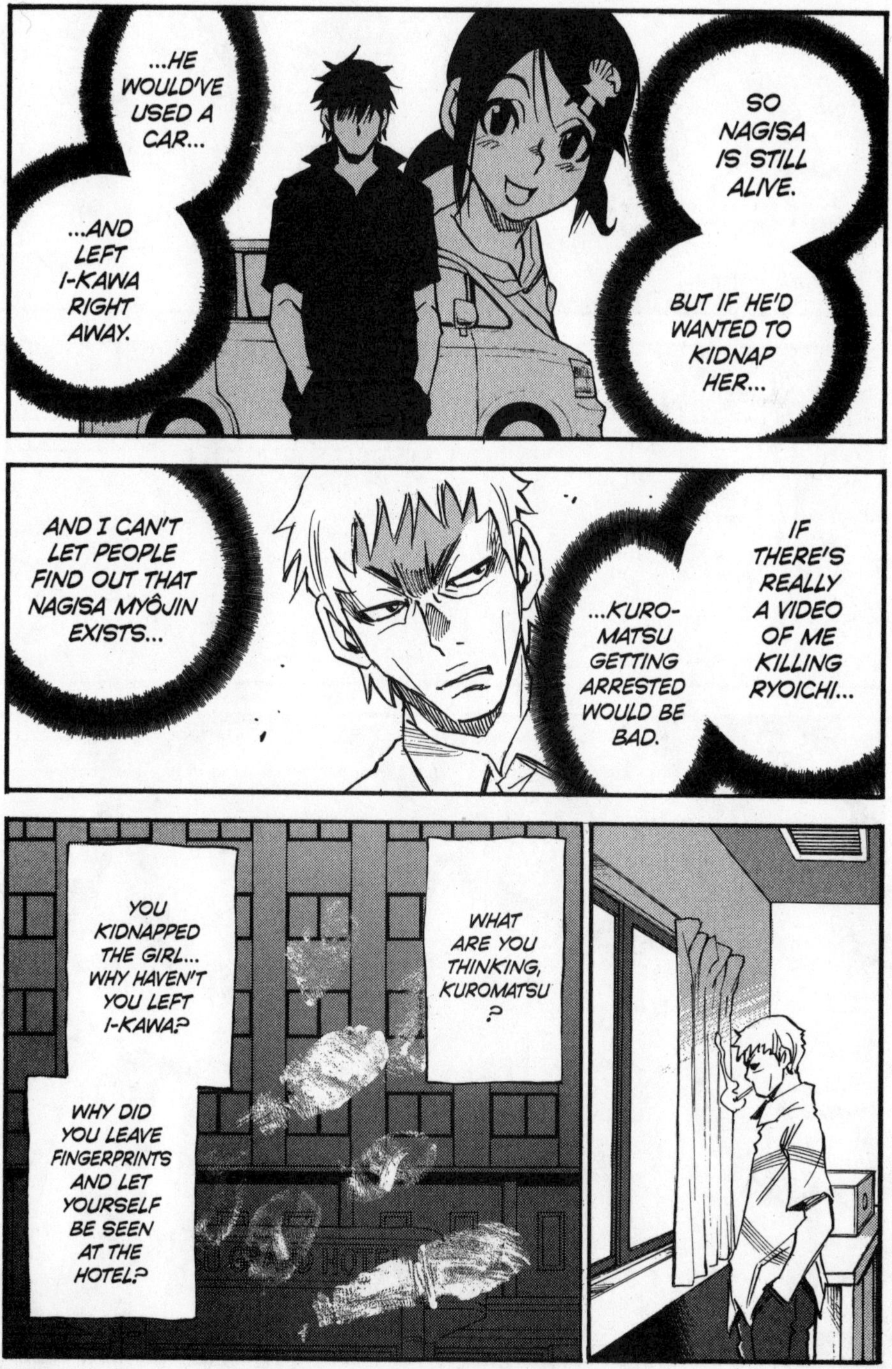
SO NAGISA IS STILL ALIVE.
BUT IF HE'D WANTED TO KIDNAP HER...
...HE WOULD'VE USED A CAR...
...AND LEFT I-KAWA RIGHT AWAY.
IF THERE'S REALLY A VIDEO OF ME KILLING RYOICHI...
...KURO-MATSU GETTING ARRESTED WOULD BE BAD.
AND I CAN'T LET PEOPLE FIND OUT THAT NAGISA MYÔJIN EXISTS...
WHAT ARE YOU THINKING, KUROMATSU?
YOU KIDNAPPED THE GIRL... WHY HAVEN'T YOU LEFT I-KAWA?
WHY DID YOU LEAVE FINGERPRINTS AND LET YOURSELF BE SEEN AT THE HOTEL?

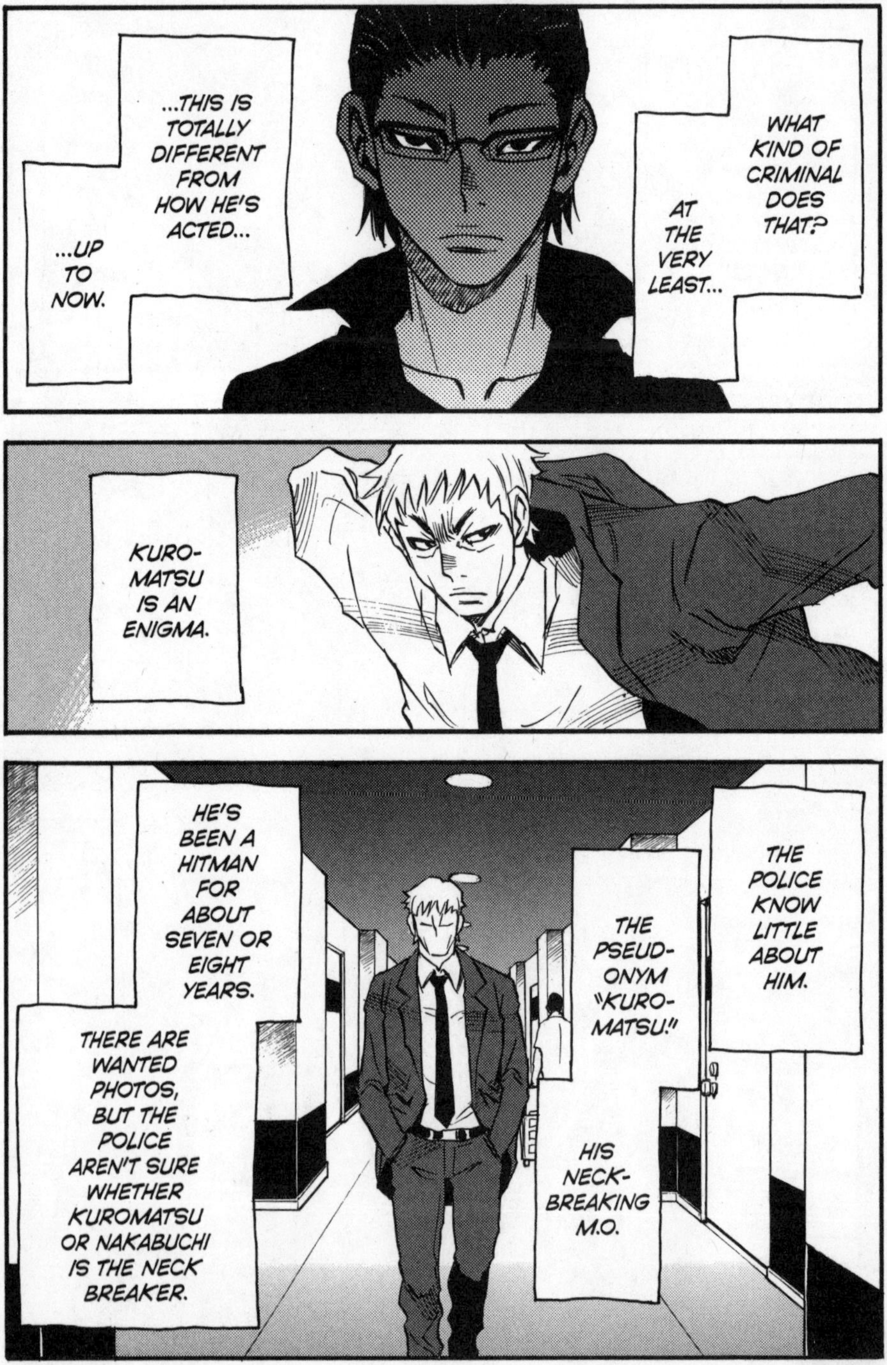
WHAT KIND OF CRIMINAL DOES THAT?
AT THE VERY LEAST...
...THIS IS TOTALLY DIFFERENT FROM HOW HE'S ACTED...
...UP TO NOW.
KURO-MATSU IS AN ENIGMA.
THE POLICE KNOW LITTLE ABOUT HIM.
THE PSEUD-ONYM "KURO-MATSU."
HIS NECK-BREAKING M.O.
HE'S BEEN A HITMAN FOR ABOUT SEVEN OR EIGHT YEARS.
THERE ARE WANTED PHOTOS, BUT THE POLICE AREN'T SURE WHETHER KUROMATSU OR NAKABUCHI IS THE NECK BREAKER.

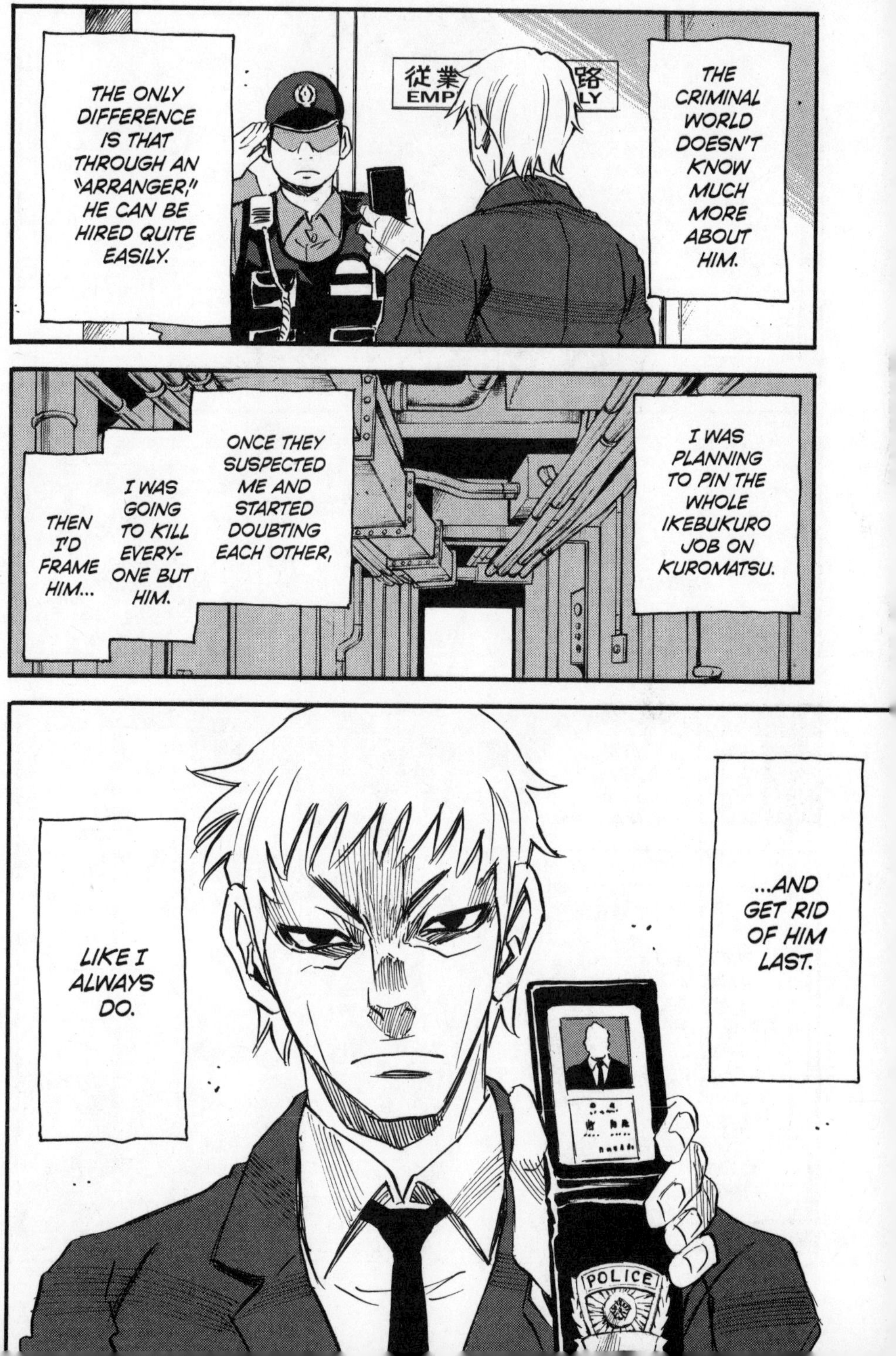
THE CRIMINAL WORLD DOESN'T KNOW MUCH MORE ABOUT HIM.
THE ONLY DIFFERENCE IS THAT THROUGH AN "ARRANGER," HE CAN BE HIRED QUITE EASILY.
I WAS PLANNING TO PIN THE WHOLE IKEBUKURO JOB ON KUROMATSU.
ONCE THEY SUSPECTED ME AND STARTED DOUBTING EACH OTHER,
I WAS GOING TO KILL EVERYONE BUT HIM.
THEN I'D FRAME HIM...
...AND GET RID OF HIM LAST.
LIKE I ALWAYS DO.
POLICE

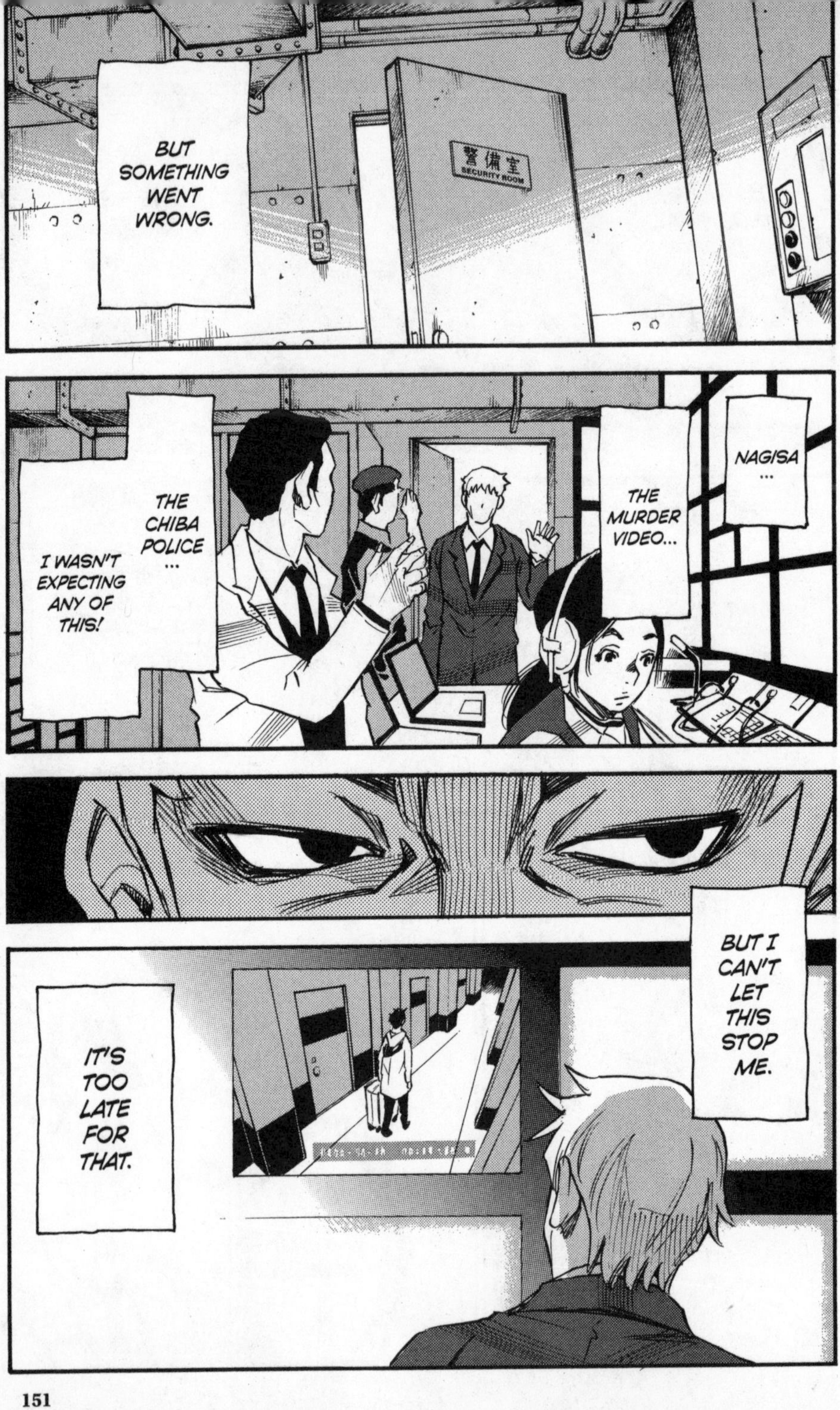
BUT SOMETHING WENT WRONG.
警備室
SECURITY ROOM
NAGISA...
THE MURDER VIDEO...
THE CHIBA POLICE...
I WASN'T EXPECTING ANY OF THIS!
BUT I CAN'T LET THIS STOP ME.
IT'S TOO LATE FOR THAT.

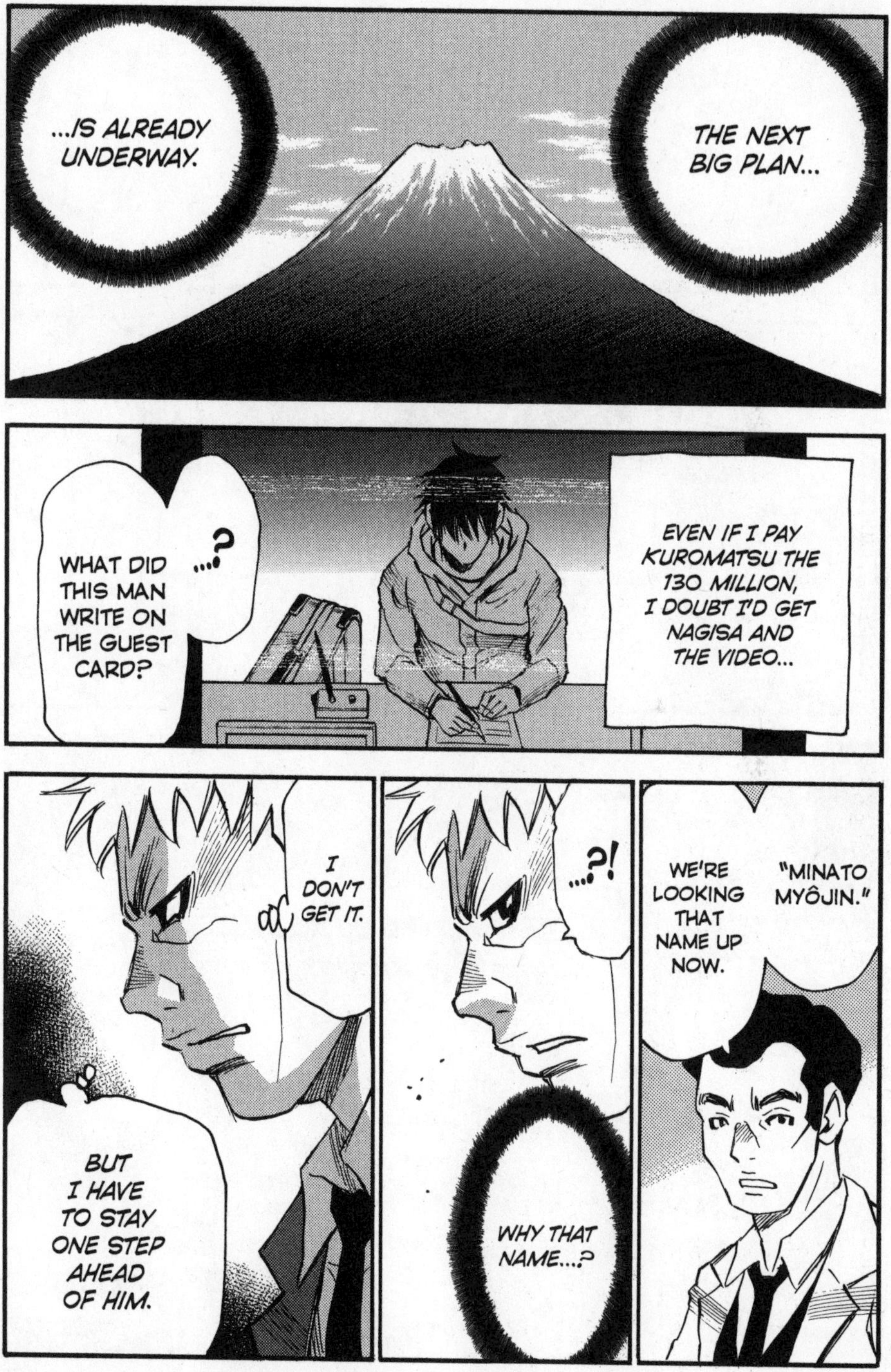
THE NEXT BIG PLAN...
...IS ALREADY UNDERWAY.
EVEN IF I PAY KUROMATSU THE 130 MILLION, I DOUBT I'D GET NAGISA AND THE VIDEO...
...?
WHAT DID THIS MAN WRITE ON THE GUEST CARD?
"MINATO MYÔJIN."
WE'RE LOOKING THAT NAME UP NOW.
...?!
WHY THAT NAME...?
I DON'T GET IT.
BUT I HAVE TO STAY ONE STEP AHEAD OF HIM.

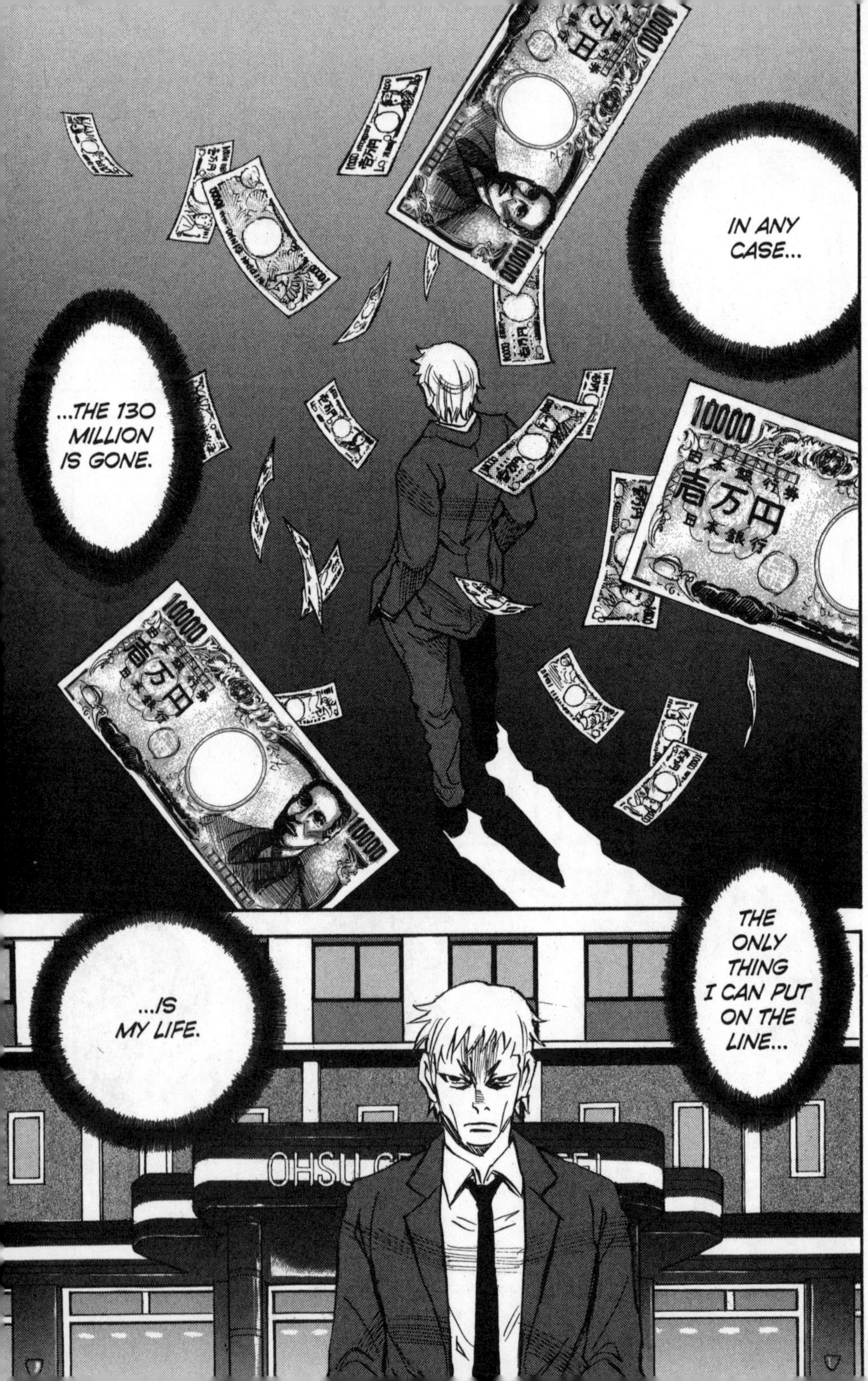
IN ANY CASE...
...THE 130 MILLION IS GONE.
THE ONLY THING I CAN PUT ON THE LINE...
...IS MY LIFE.

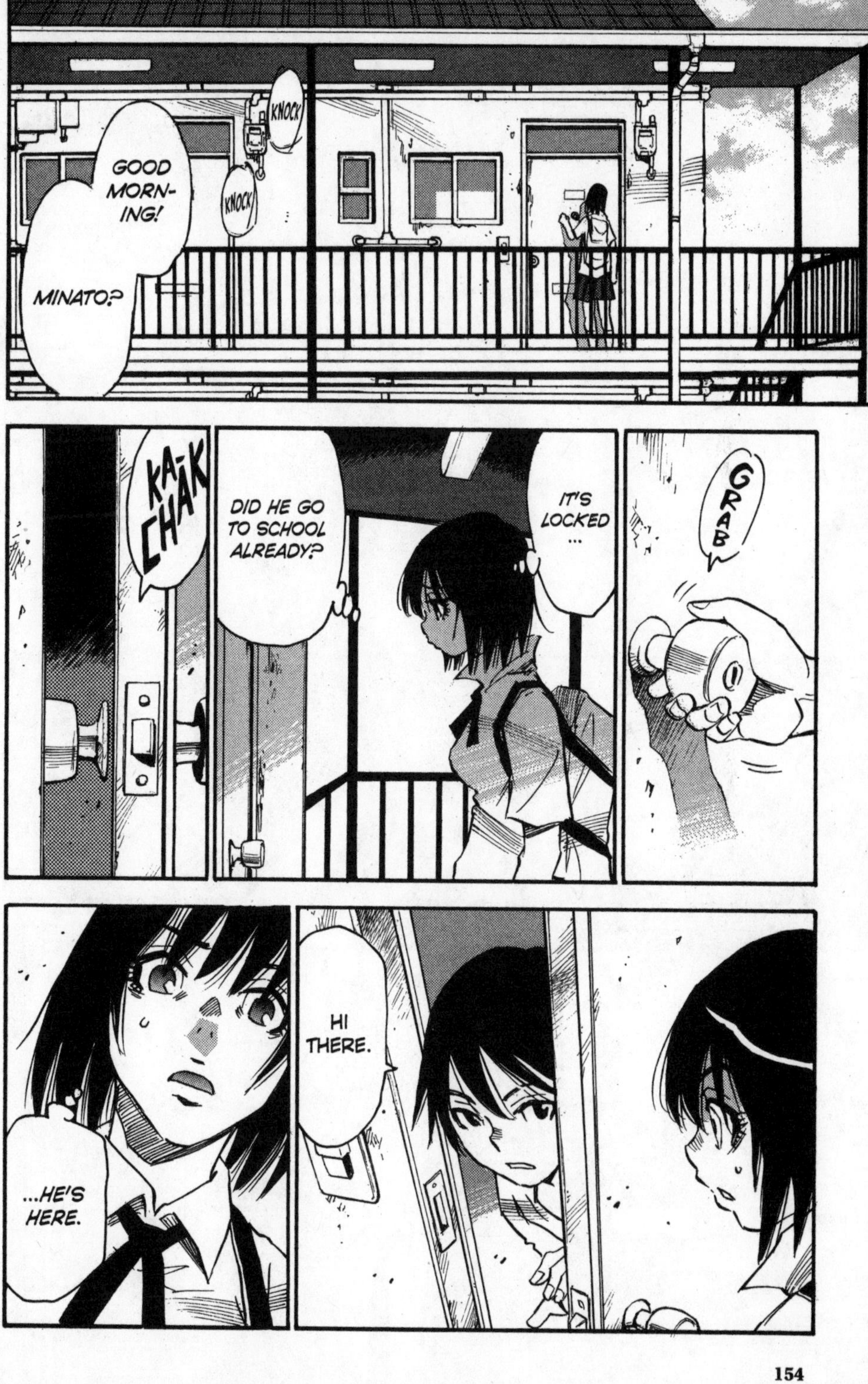
KNOCK
KNOCK
GOOD MORNING!
MINATO?
GRAB
IT'S LOCKED ...
DID HE GO TO SCHOOL ALREADY?
KA-CHAK
HI THERE.
...HE'S HERE.

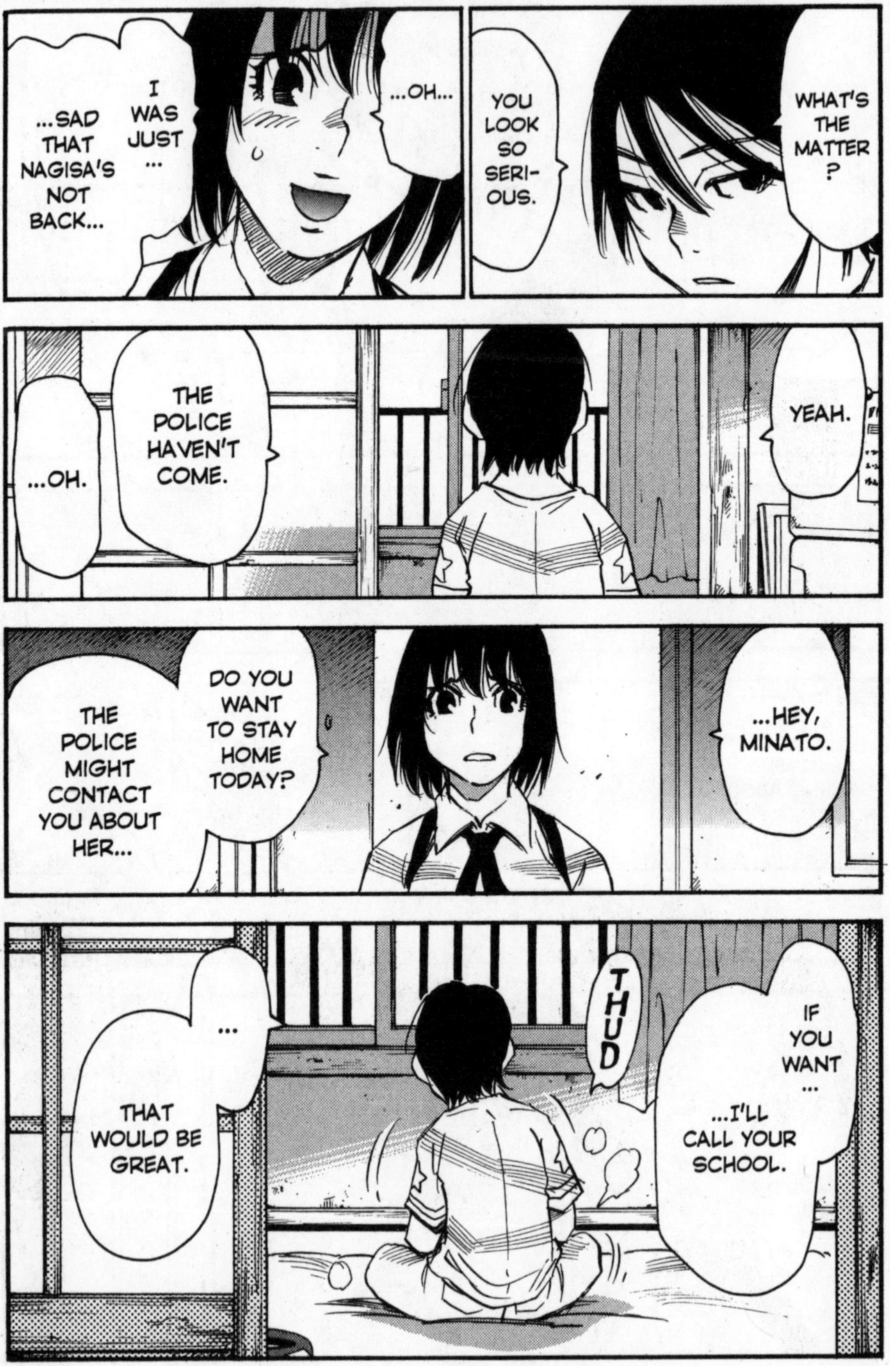
WHAT'S THE MATTER?
YOU LOOK SO SERI-OUS.
...OH...
I WAS JUST ...
...SAD THAT NAGISA'S NOT BACK...
YEAH.
THE POLICE HAVEN'T COME.
...OH.
...HEY, MINATO.
DO YOU WANT TO STAY HOME TODAY?
THE POLICE MIGHT CONTACT YOU ABOUT HER...
IF YOU WANT ...
...I'LL CALL YOUR SCHOOL.
THUD
...
THAT WOULD BE GREAT.

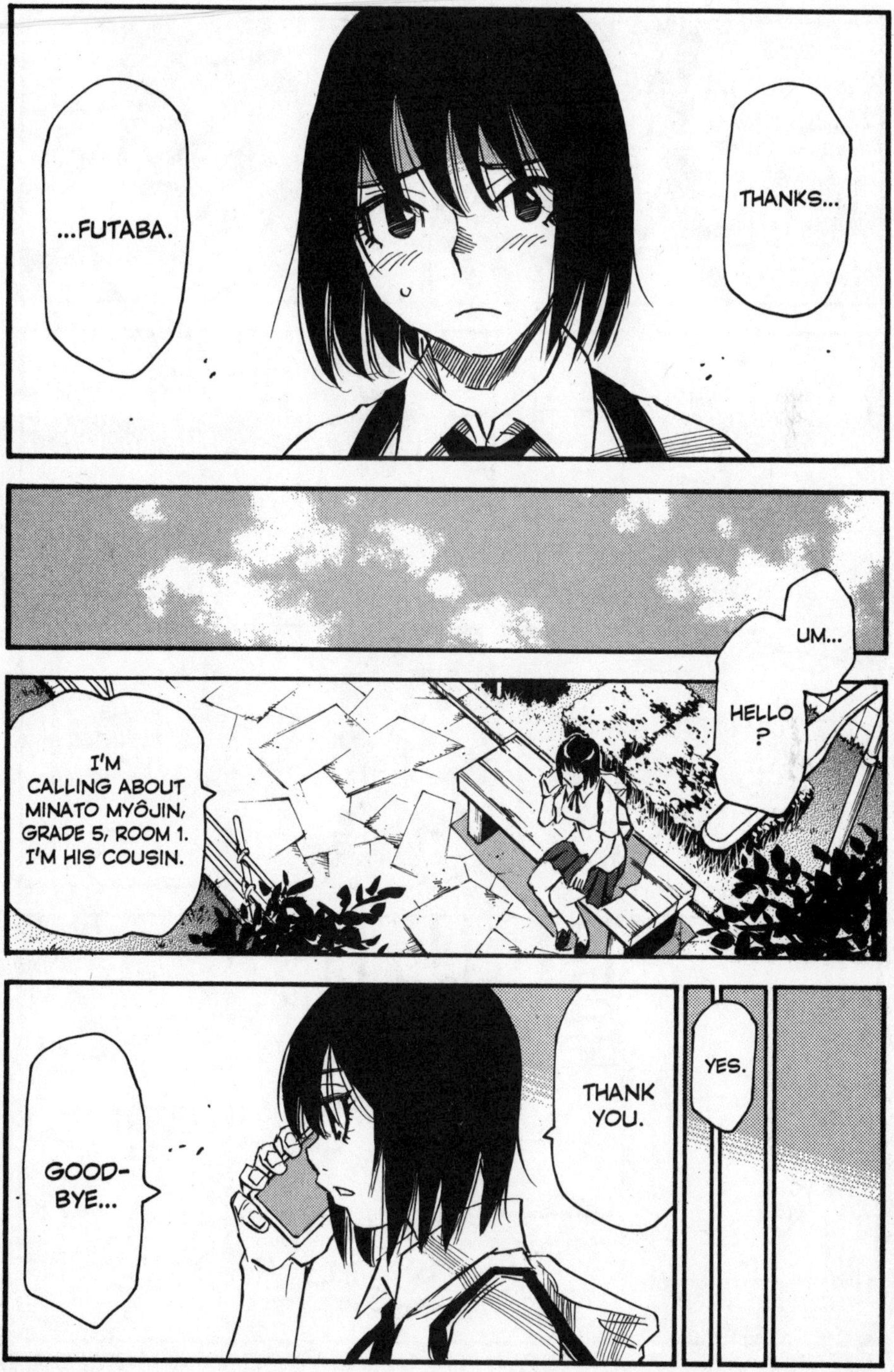
THANKS...
...FUTABA.
UM...
HELLO?
I'M CALLING ABOUT MINATO MYÔJIN, GRADE 5, ROOM 1. I'M HIS COUSIN.
YES.
THANK YOU.
GOOD-BYE...

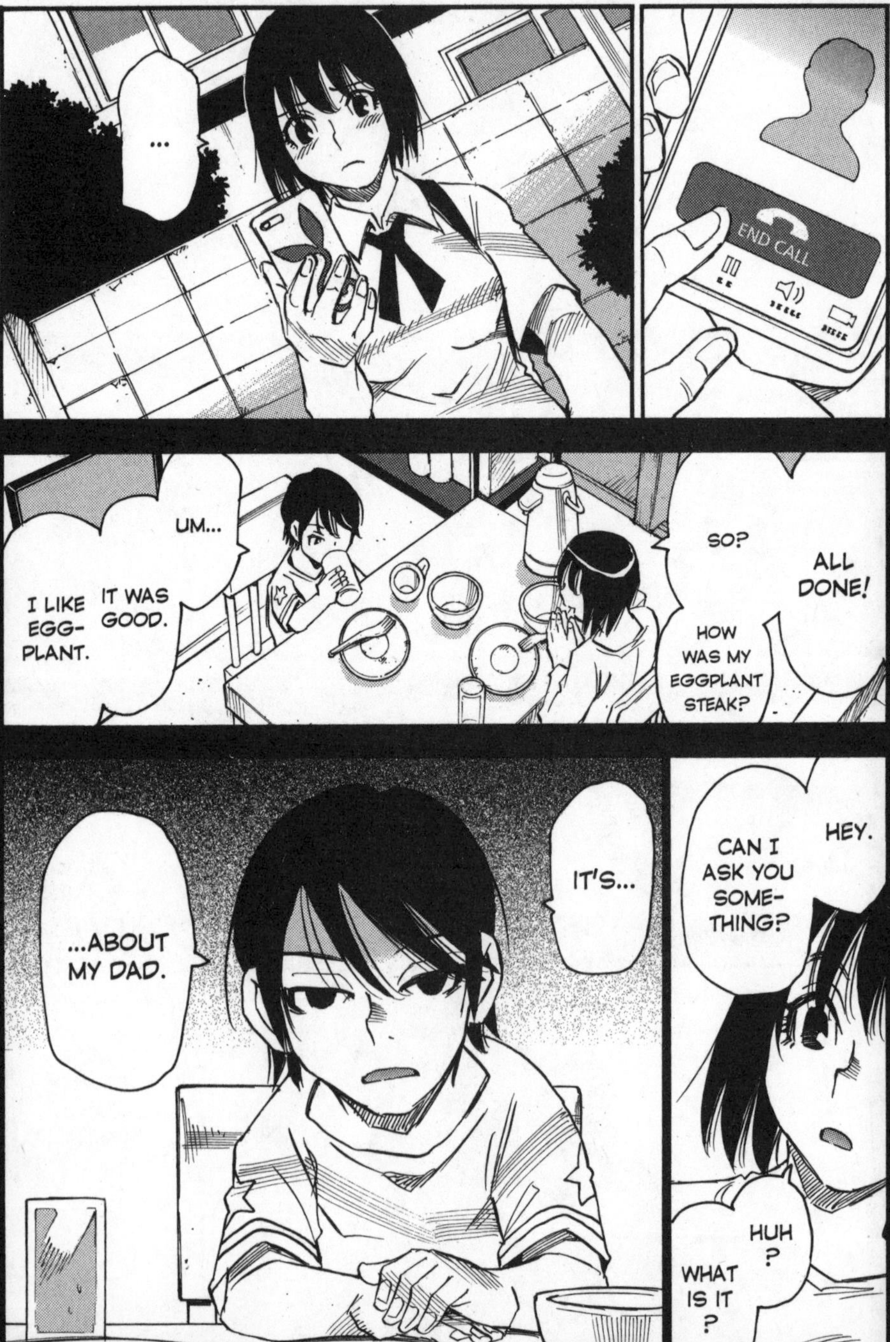
END CALL
...
ALL DONE!
SO?
HOW WAS MY EGGPLANT STEAK?
UM...
IT WAS GOOD.
I LIKE EGGPLANT.
HEY.
CAN I ASK YOU SOMETHING?
HUH?
WHAT IS IT?
IT'S...
...ABOUT MY DAD.

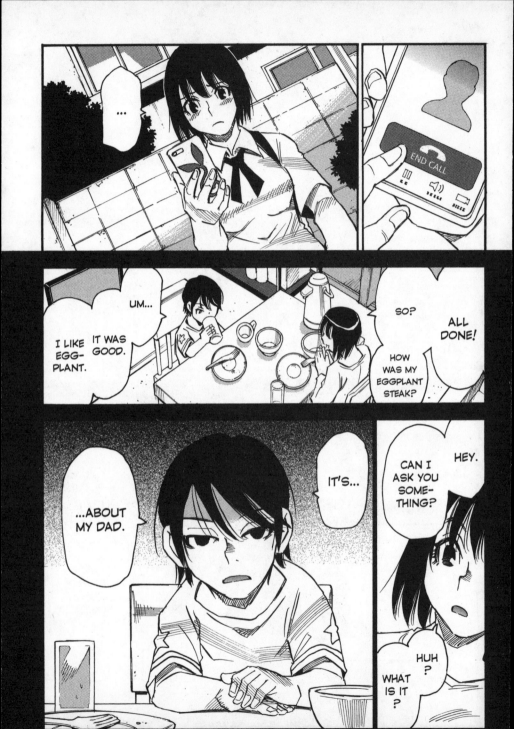

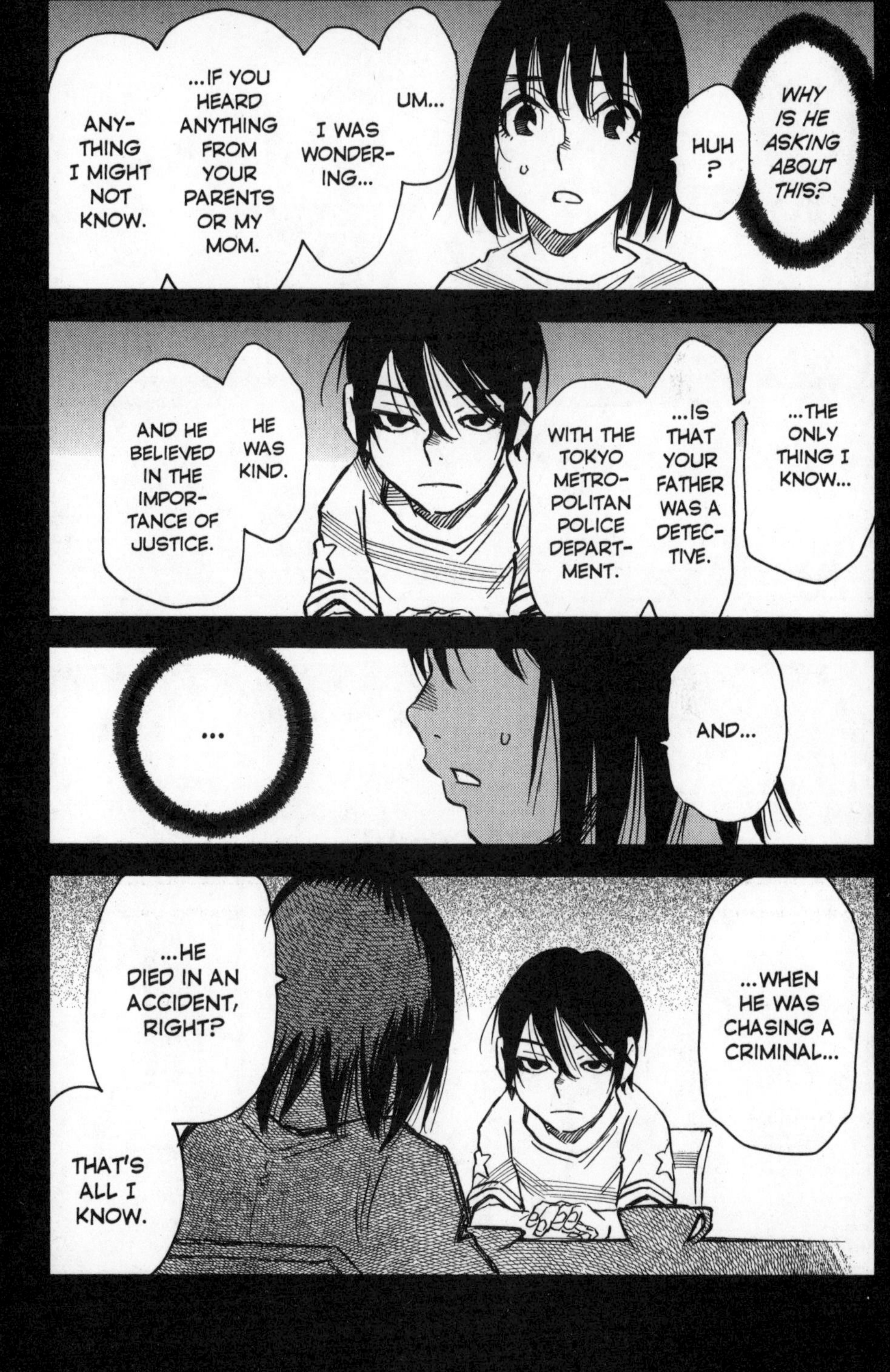
WHY IS HE ASKING ABOUT THIS?
HUH?
UM...
I WAS WONDERING...
...IF YOU HEARD ANYTHING FROM YOUR PARENTS OR MY MOM.
ANYTHING I MIGHT NOT KNOW.
...THE ONLY THING I KNOW...
...IS THAT YOUR FATHER WAS A DETECTIVE.
WITH THE TOKYO METROPOLITAN POLICE DEPARTMENT.
HE WAS KIND.
AND HE BELIEVED IN THE IMPORTANCE OF JUSTICE.
AND...
...
...WHEN HE WAS CHASING A CRIMINAL...
...HE DIED IN AN ACCIDENT, RIGHT?
THAT'S ALL I KNOW.

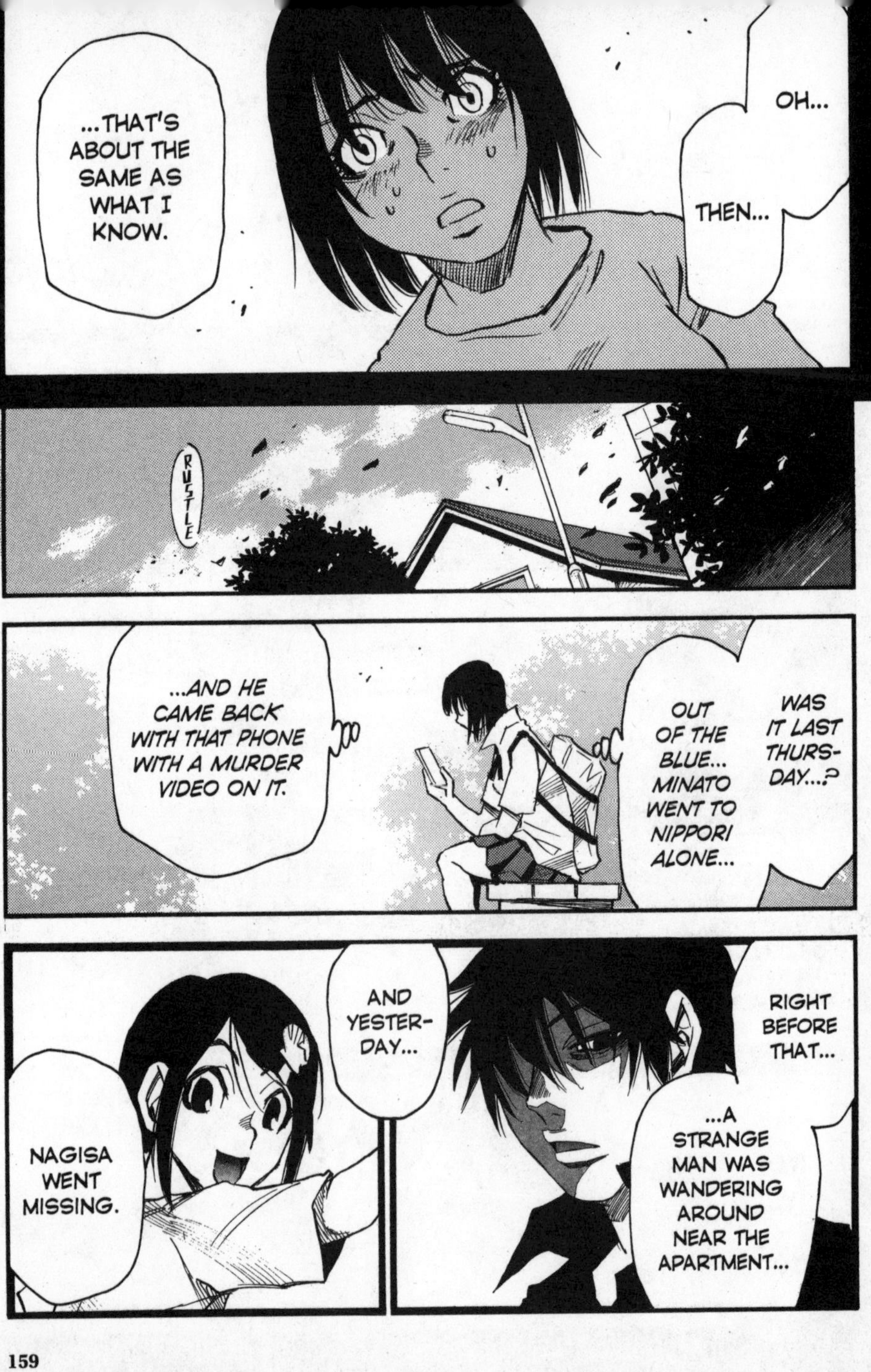
OH...
THEN...
...THAT'S ABOUT THE SAME AS WHAT I KNOW.
RUSTLE
WAS IT LAST THURS-DAY...?
OUT OF THE BLUE... MINATO WENT TO NIPPORI ALONE...
...AND HE CAME BACK WITH THAT PHONE WITH A MURDER VIDEO ON IT.
RIGHT BEFORE THAT...
...A STRANGE MAN WAS WANDERING AROUND NEAR THE APARTMENT...
AND YESTER-DAY...
NAGISA WENT MISSING.

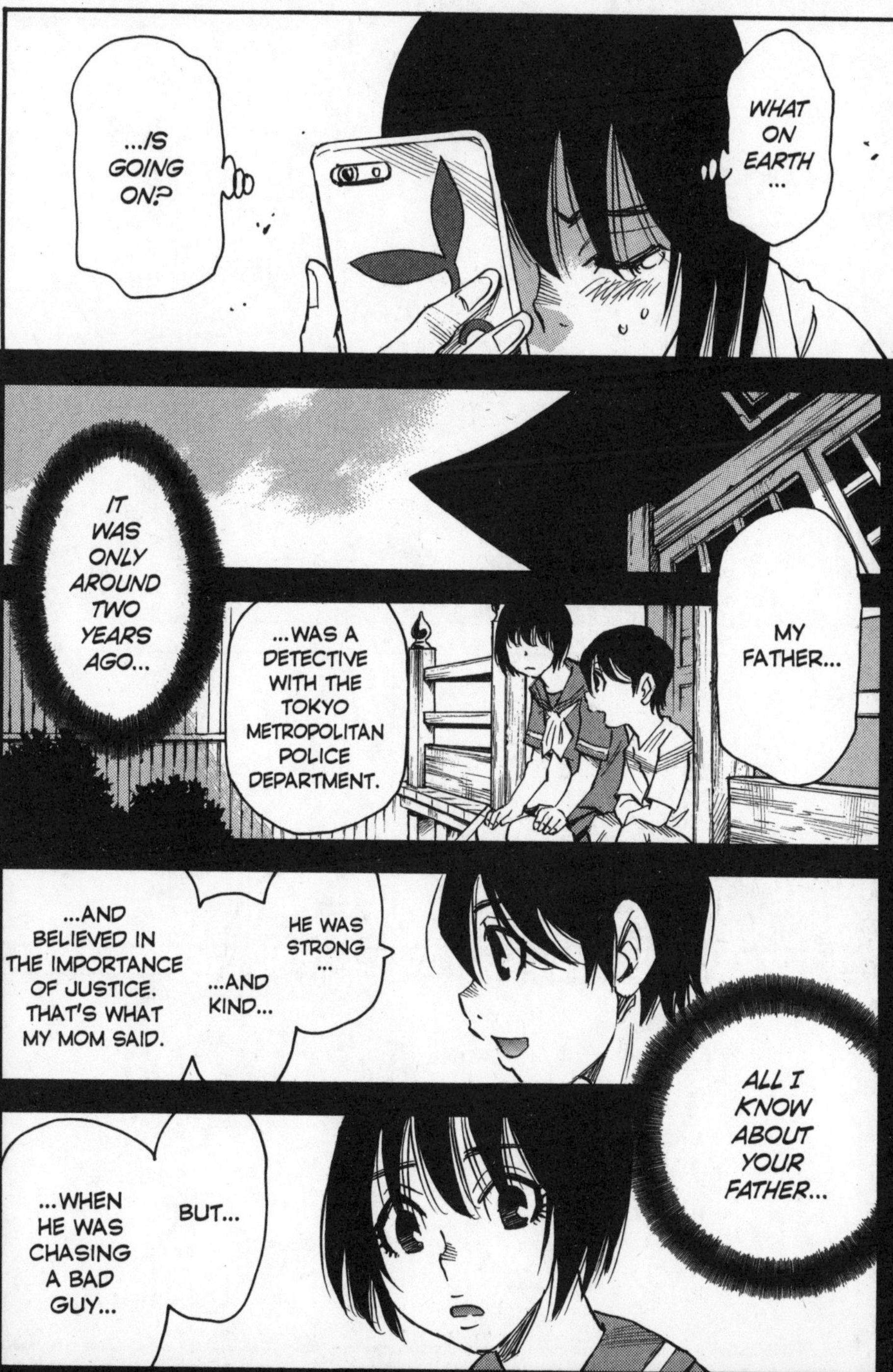
WHAT ON EARTH ...
...IS GOING ON?
MY FATHER...
...WAS A DETECTIVE WITH THE TOKYO METROPOLITAN POLICE DEPARTMENT.
IT WAS ONLY AROUND TWO YEARS AGO...
HE WAS STRONG ...
...AND KIND...
...AND BELIEVED IN THE IMPORTANCE OF JUSTICE. THAT'S WHAT MY MOM SAID.
ALL I KNOW ABOUT YOUR FATHER...
BUT...
...WHEN HE WAS CHASING A BAD GUY...

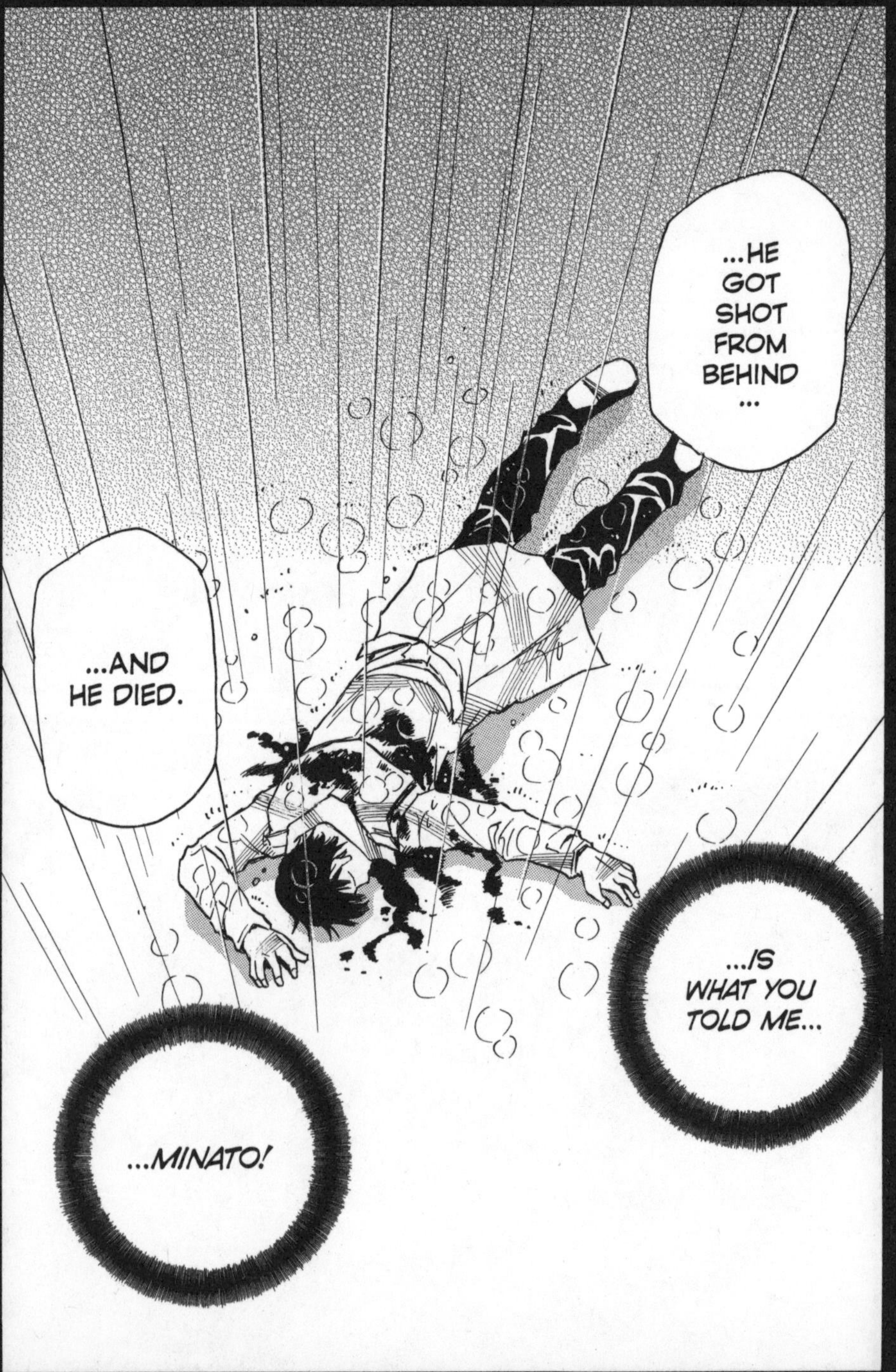
...HE GOT SHOT FROM BEHIND ...
...AND HE DIED.
...IS WHAT YOU TOLD ME...
...MINATO!

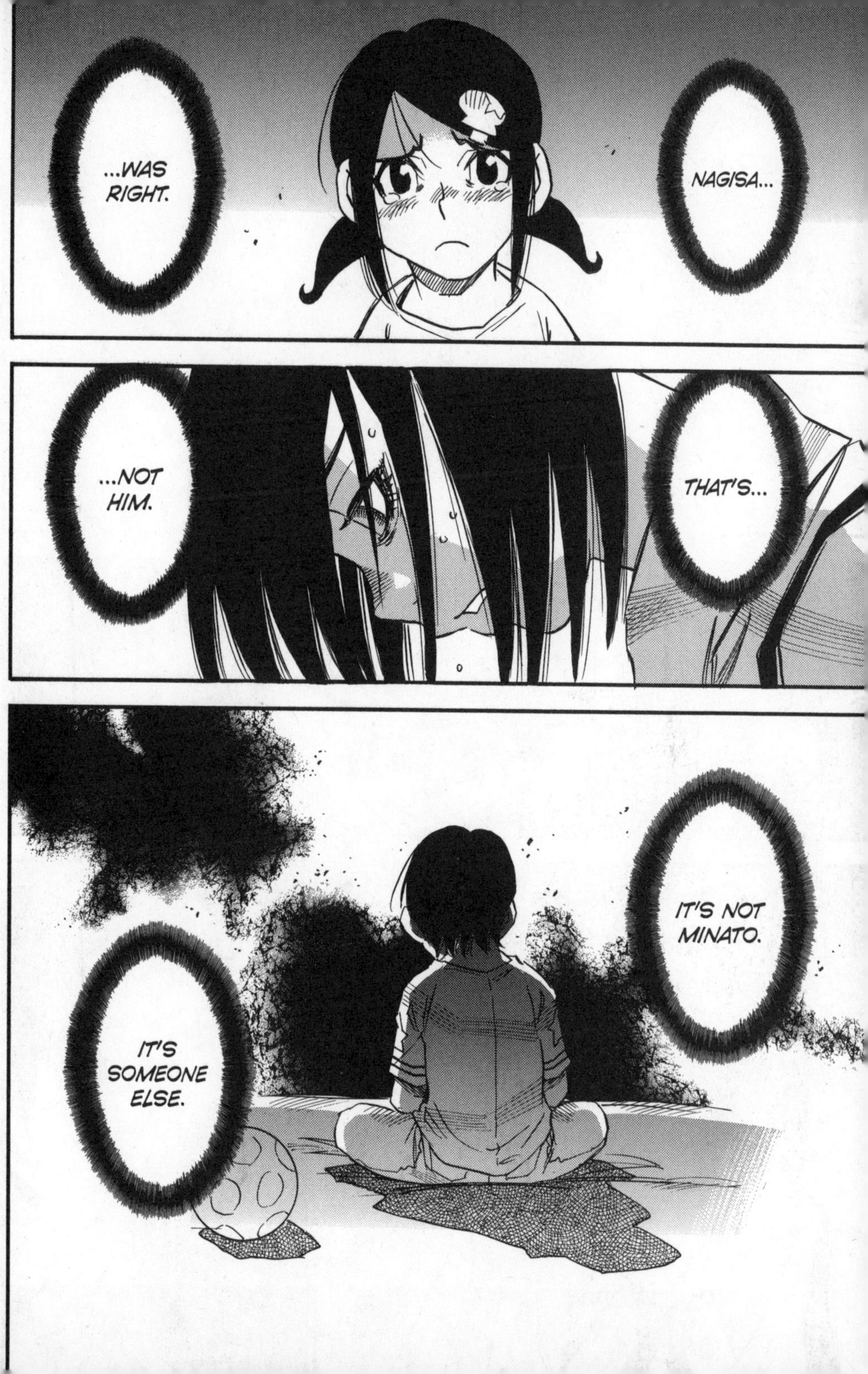
NAGISA...
...WAS RIGHT.
THAT'S...
...NOT HIM.
IT'S NOT MINATO.
IT'S SOMEONE ELSE.

CHAPTER 20

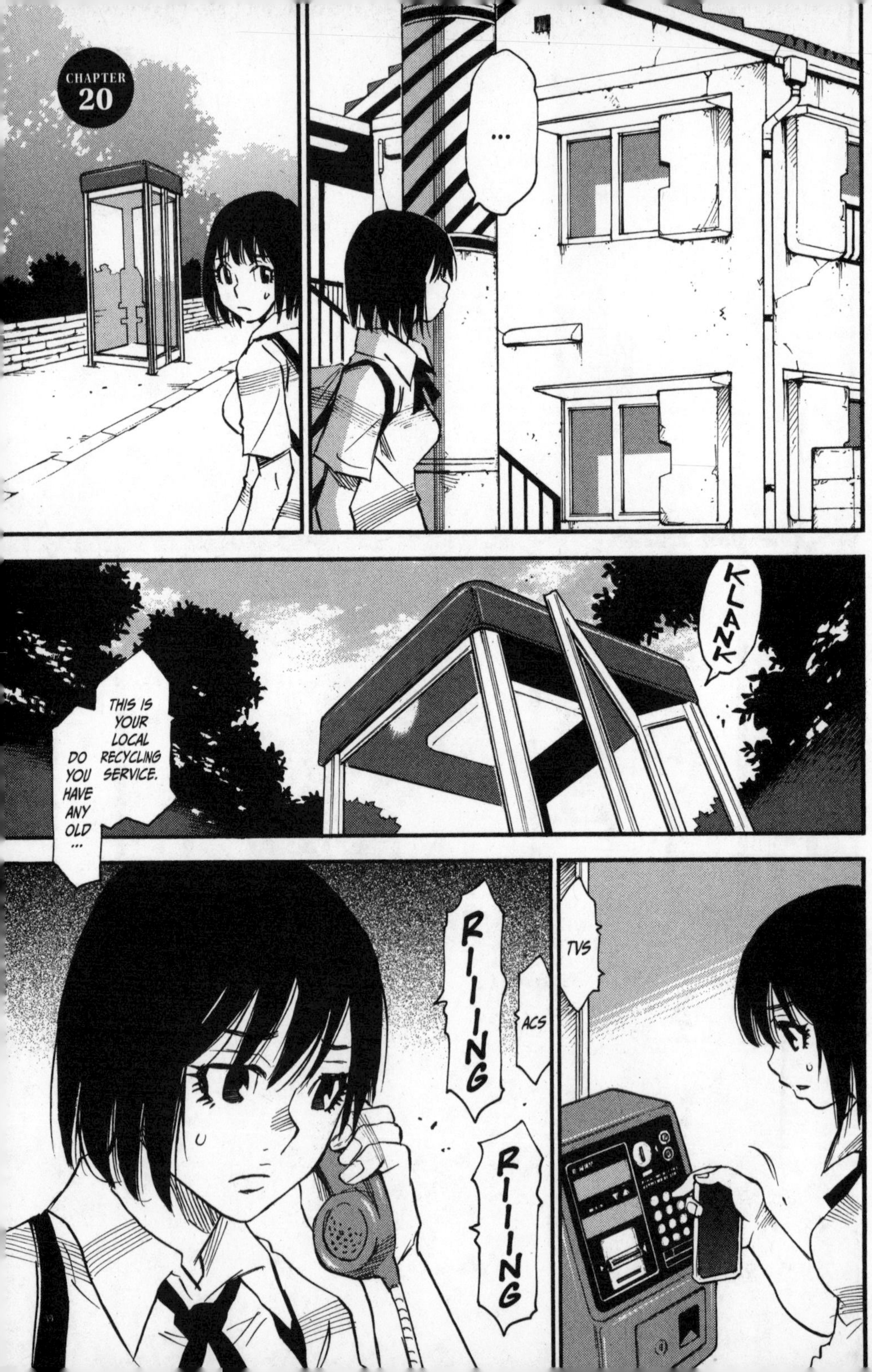
...
KLANK
THIS IS YOUR LOCAL RECYCLING SERVICE.
DO YOU HAVE ANY OLD ...
TVS
ACS
RIIING
RIIING

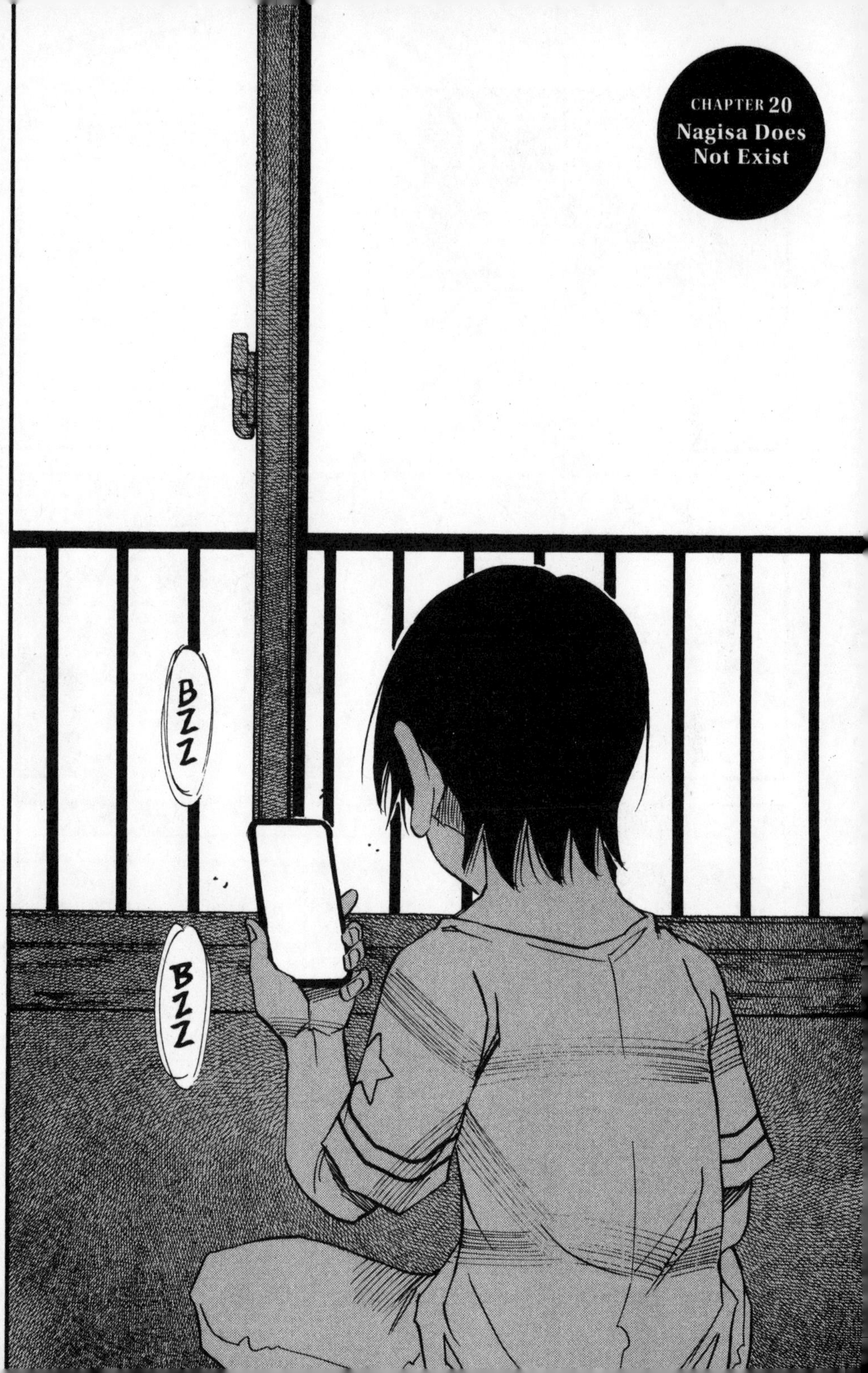
CHAPTER 20
Nagisa Does Not Exist
BZZ
BZZ

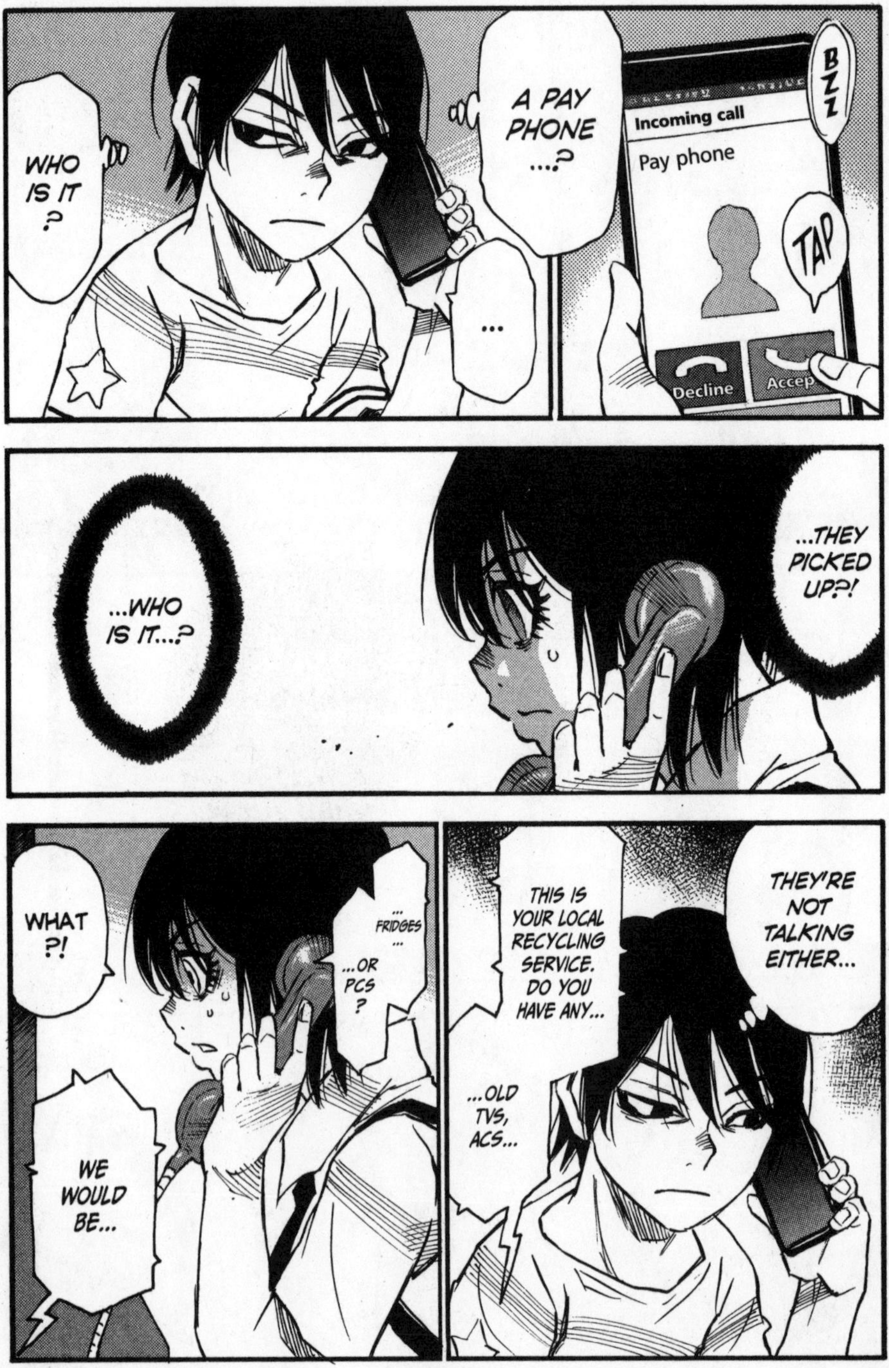
BZZ
Incoming call
Pay phone
TAP
Decline
Accep
A PAY PHONE ...?
...
WHO IS IT ?
...THEY PICKED UP?!
...WHO IS IT...?
THEY'RE NOT TALKING EITHER...
THIS IS YOUR LOCAL RECYCLING SERVICE. DO YOU HAVE ANY...
...OLD TVS, ACS...
... FRIDGES ...
...OR PCS ?
WHAT ?!
WE WOULD BE...

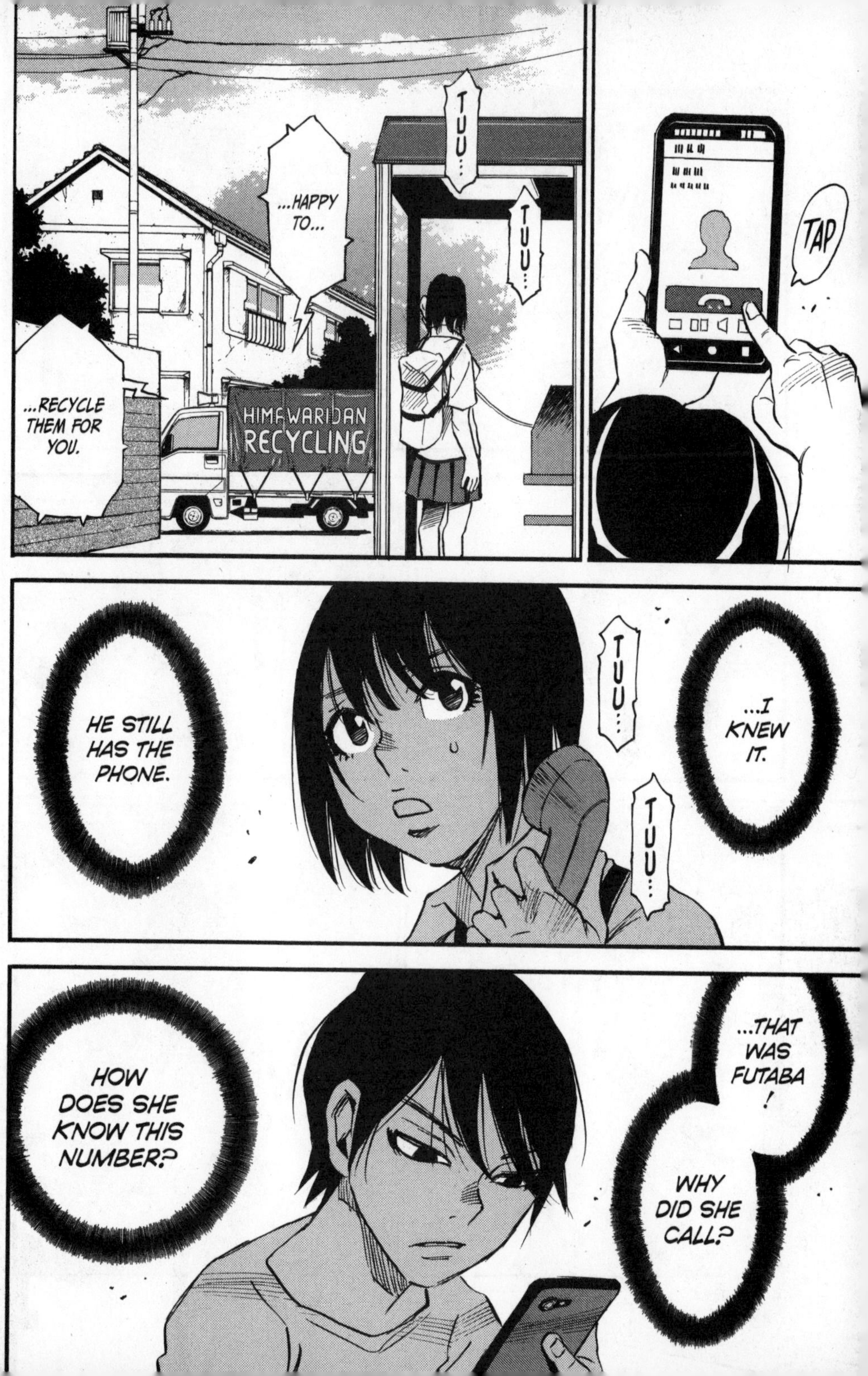
TAP
TUU...
TUU...
...HAPPY TO...
...RECYCLE THEM FOR YOU.
HIMAWARIDAN RECYCLING
...I KNEW IT.
TUU...
TUU...
HE STILL HAS THE PHONE.
...THAT WAS FUTABA!
WHY DID SHE CALL?
HOW DOES SHE KNOW THIS NUMBER?

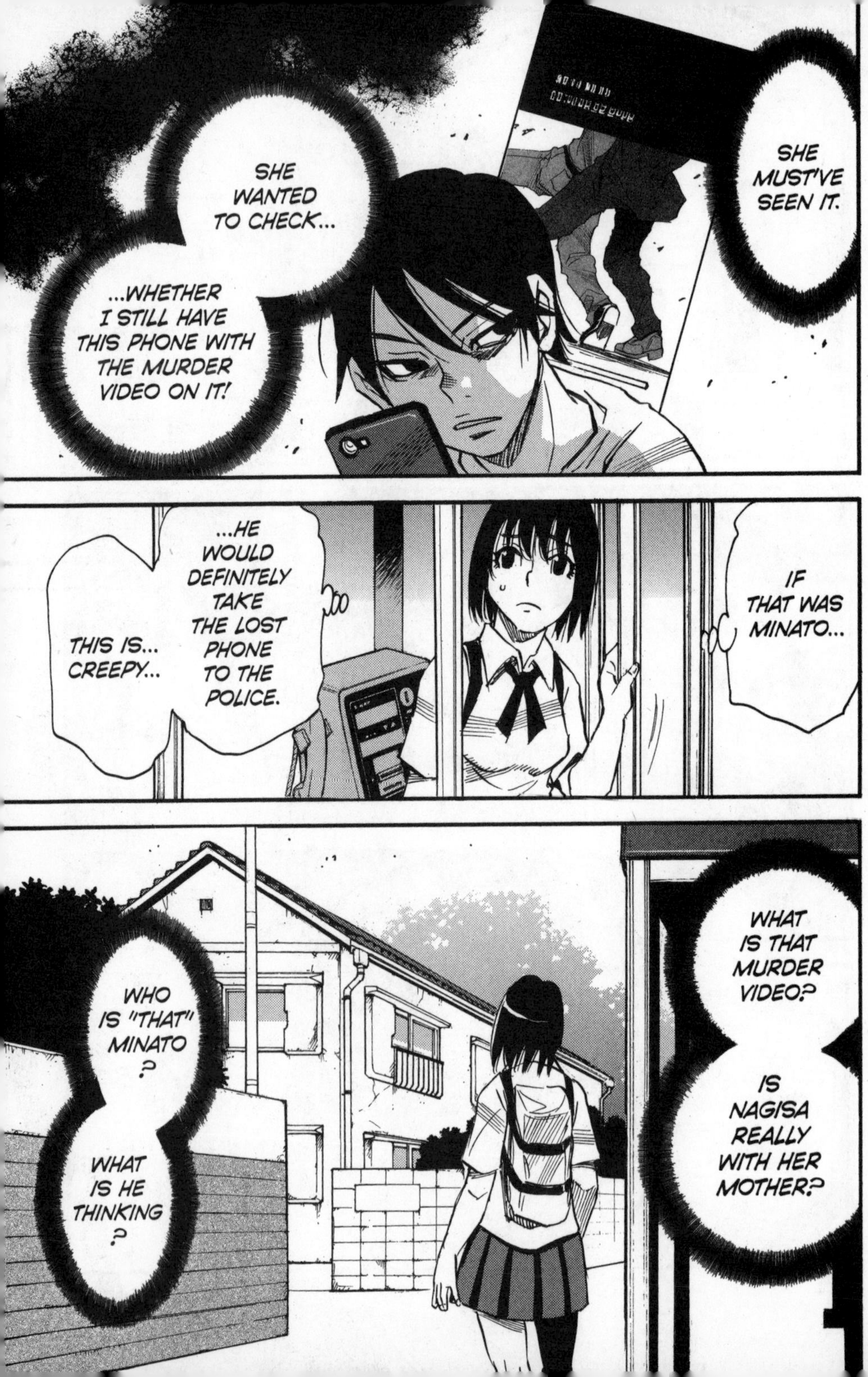
SHE MUST'VE SEEN IT.
SHE WANTED TO CHECK...
...WHETHER I STILL HAVE THIS PHONE WITH THE MURDER VIDEO ON IT!
IF THAT WAS MINATO...
...HE WOULD DEFINITELY TAKE THE LOST PHONE TO THE POLICE.
THIS IS... CREEPY...
WHAT IS THAT MURDER VIDEO?
IS NAGISA REALLY WITH HER MOTHER?
WHO IS "THAT" MINATO?
WHAT IS HE THINKING?

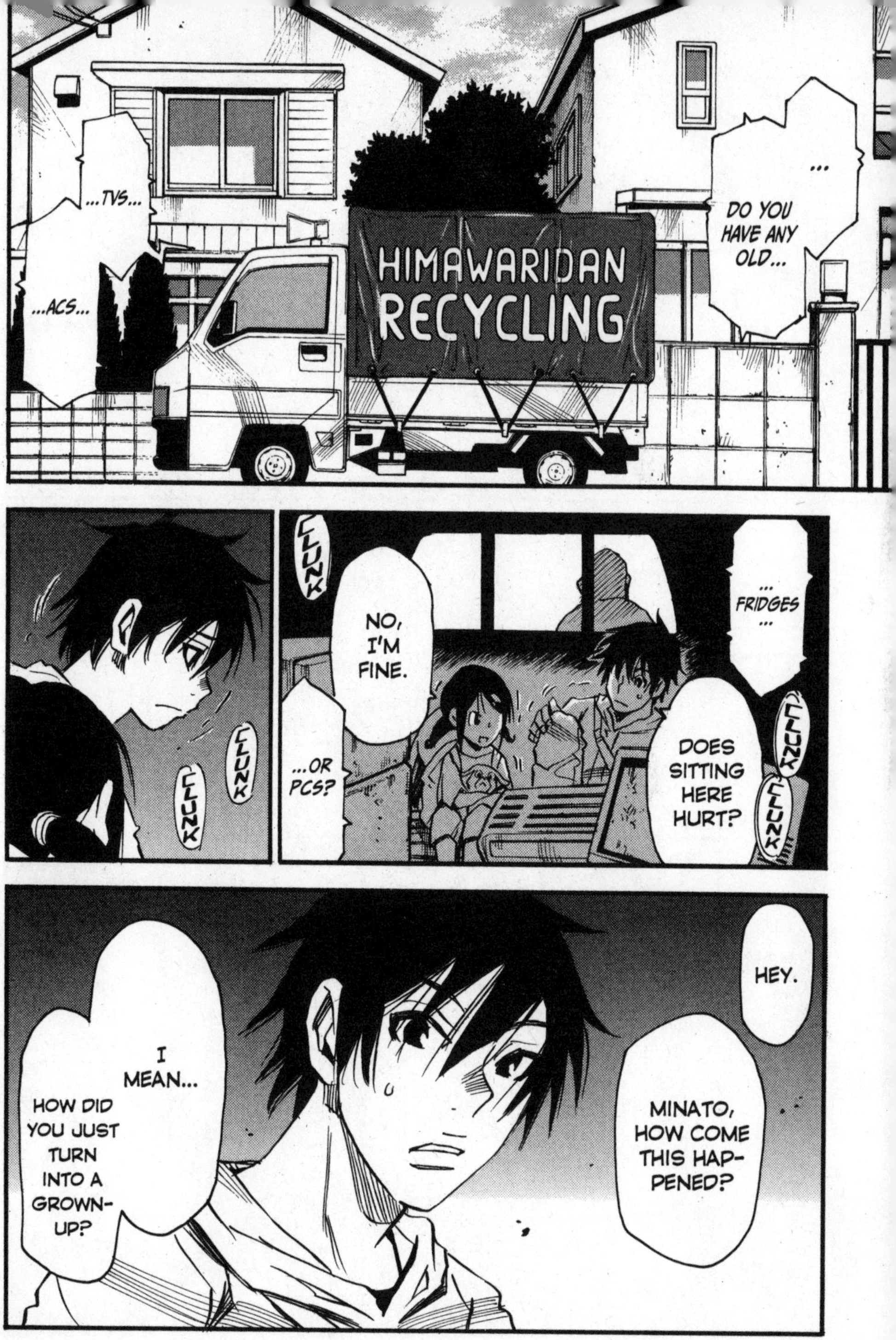
... DO YOU HAVE ANY OLD...
HIMAWARIDAN RECYCLING
...TVS...
...ACS...
... FRIDGES ...
CLUNK
CLUNK
DOES SITTING HERE HURT?
CLUNK
NO, I'M FINE.
...OR PCS?
CLUNK
CLUNK
HEY.
MINATO, HOW COME THIS HAPPENED?
I MEAN... HOW DID YOU JUST TURN INTO A GROWN-UP?

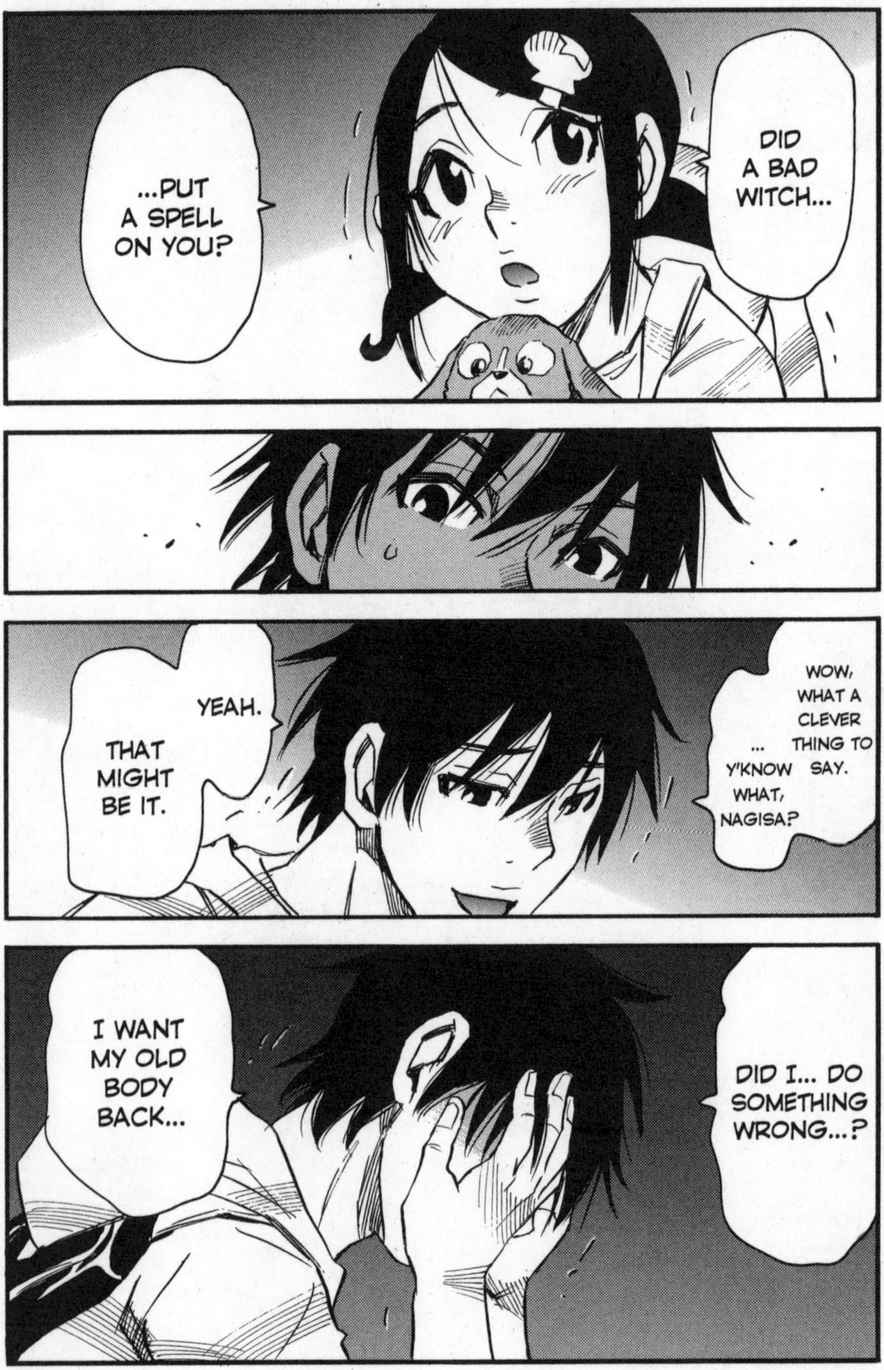
DID A BAD WITCH...
...PUT A SPELL ON YOU?
WOW, WHAT A CLEVER THING TO SAY.
... Y'KNOW WHAT, NAGISA?
YEAH.
THAT MIGHT BE IT.
DID I... DO SOMETHING WRONG...?
I WANT MY OLD BODY BACK...

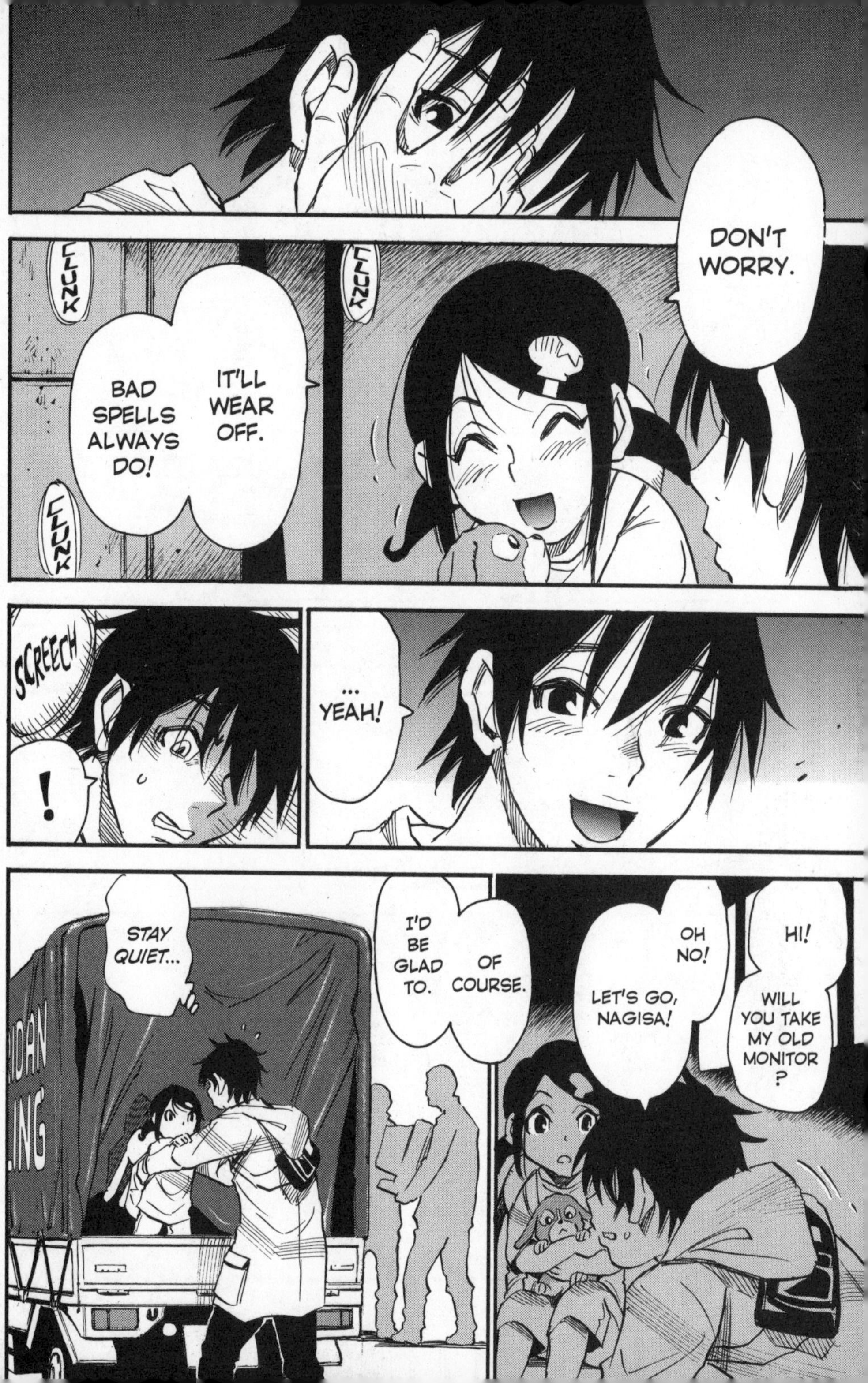
DON'T WORRY.
CLUNK
IT'LL WEAR OFF.
BAD SPELLS ALWAYS DO!
CLUNK
CLUNK
... YEAH!
SCREECH
!
HI!
WILL YOU TAKE MY OLD MONITOR?
OH NO!
LET'S GO, NAGISA!
OF COURSE.
I'D BE GLAD TO.
STAY QUIET...

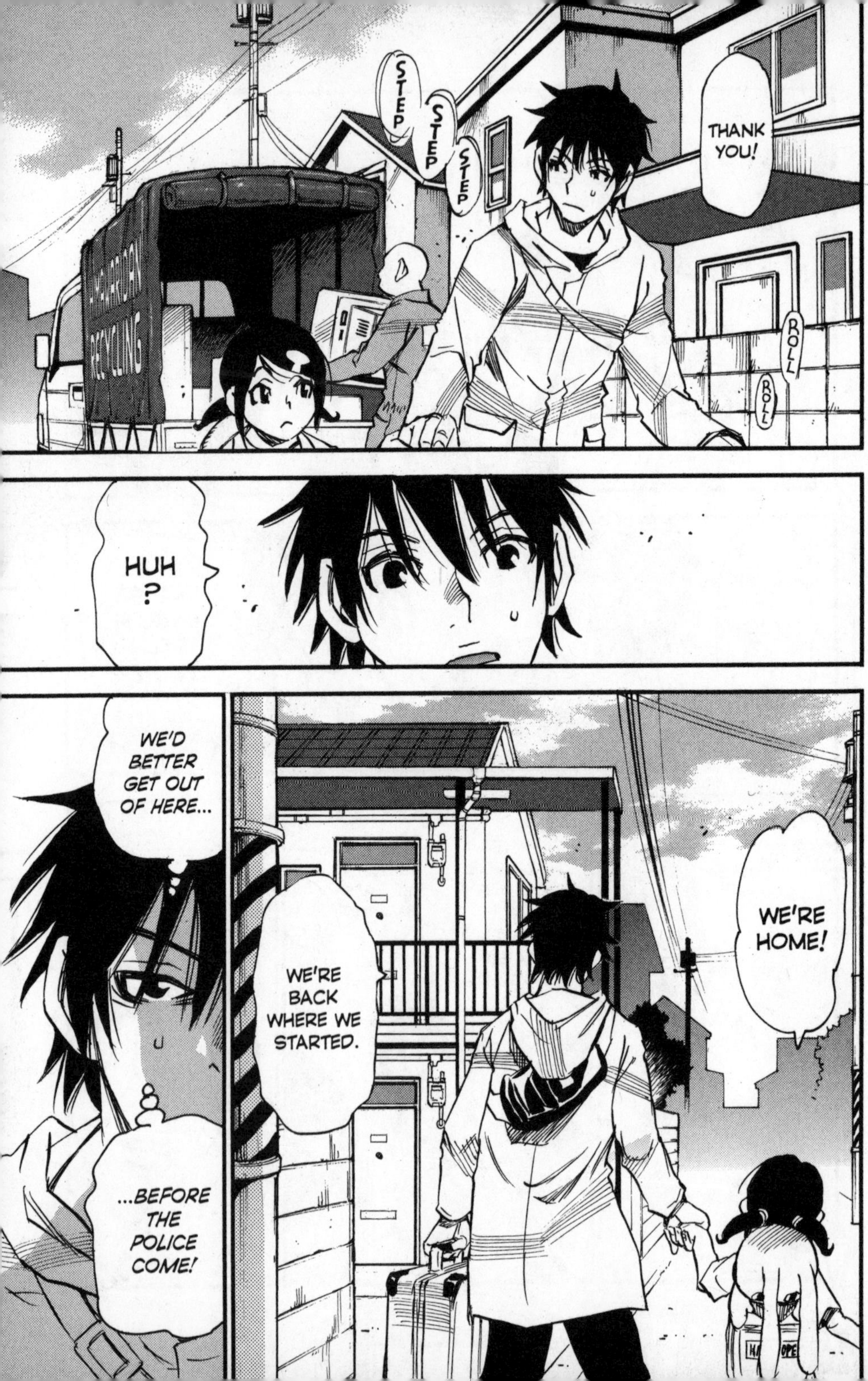
THANK YOU!
ROLL
ROLL
STEP
STEP
STEP
RECYCLING
HUH?
WE'RE HOME!
WE'RE BACK WHERE WE STARTED.
WE'D BETTER GET OUT OF HERE...
...BEFORE THE POLICE COME!

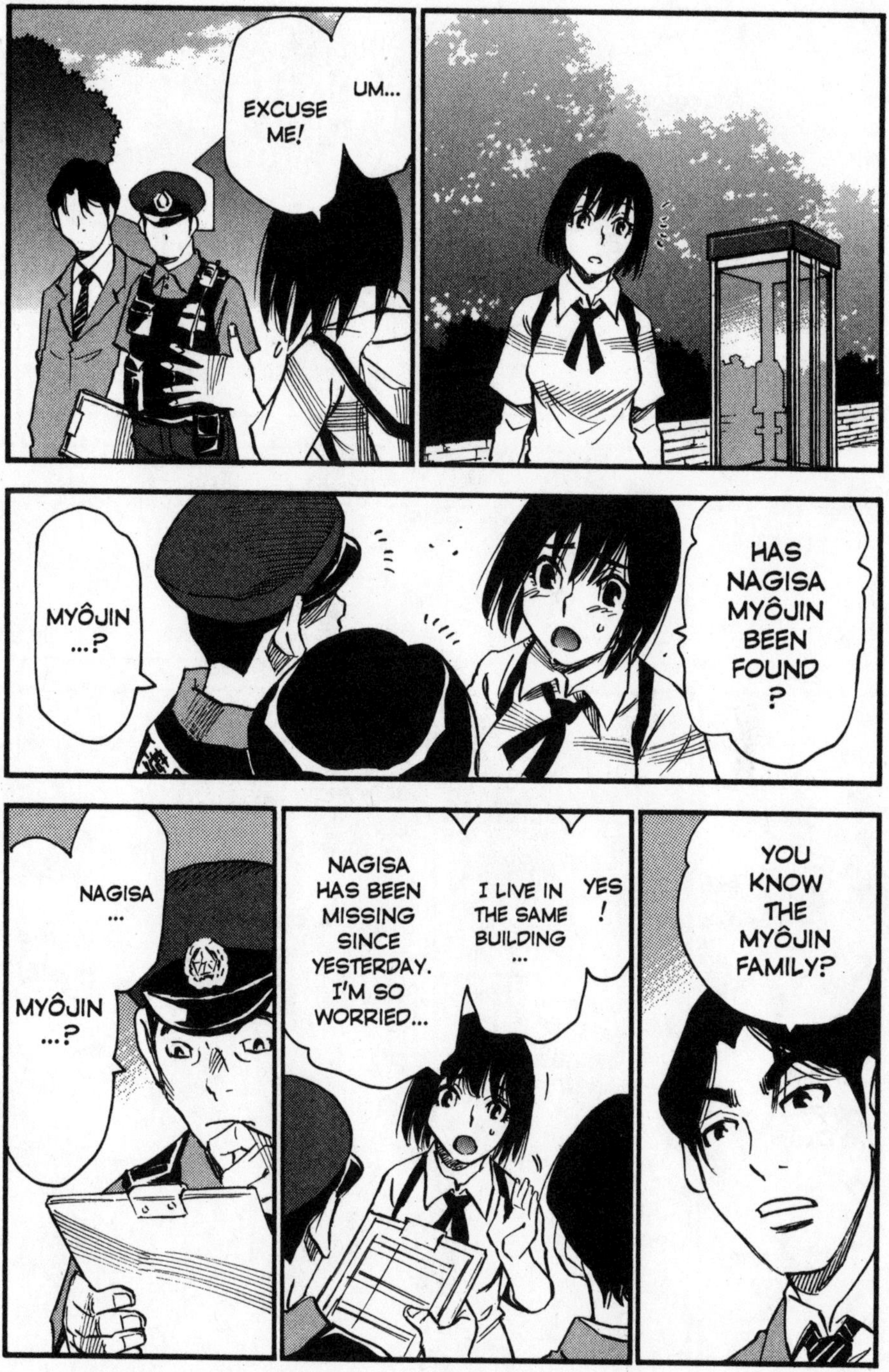
UM... EXCUSE ME!
HAS NAGISA MYÔJIN BEEN FOUND?
MYÔJIN ...?
YOU KNOW THE MYÔJIN FAMILY?
YES!
I LIVE IN THE SAME BUILDING ...
NAGISA HAS BEEN MISSING SINCE YESTERDAY. I'M SO WORRIED...
NAGISA ...
MYÔJIN ...?

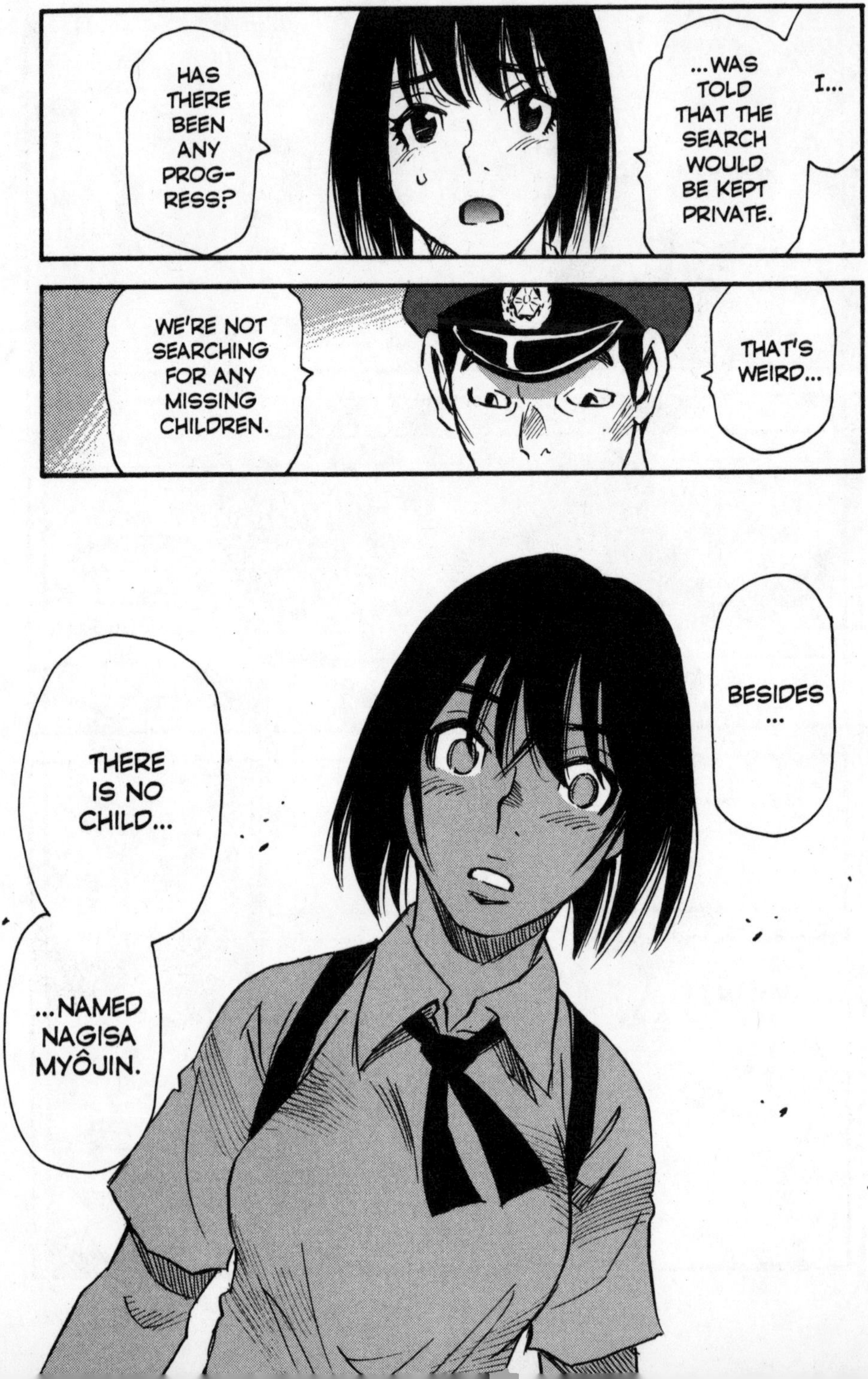
I...
...WAS TOLD THAT THE SEARCH WOULD BE KEPT PRIVATE.
HAS THERE BEEN ANY PROG-RESS?
THAT'S WEIRD...
WE'RE NOT SEARCHING FOR ANY MISSING CHILDREN.
BESIDES...
THERE IS NO CHILD...
...NAMED NAGISA MYÔJIN.

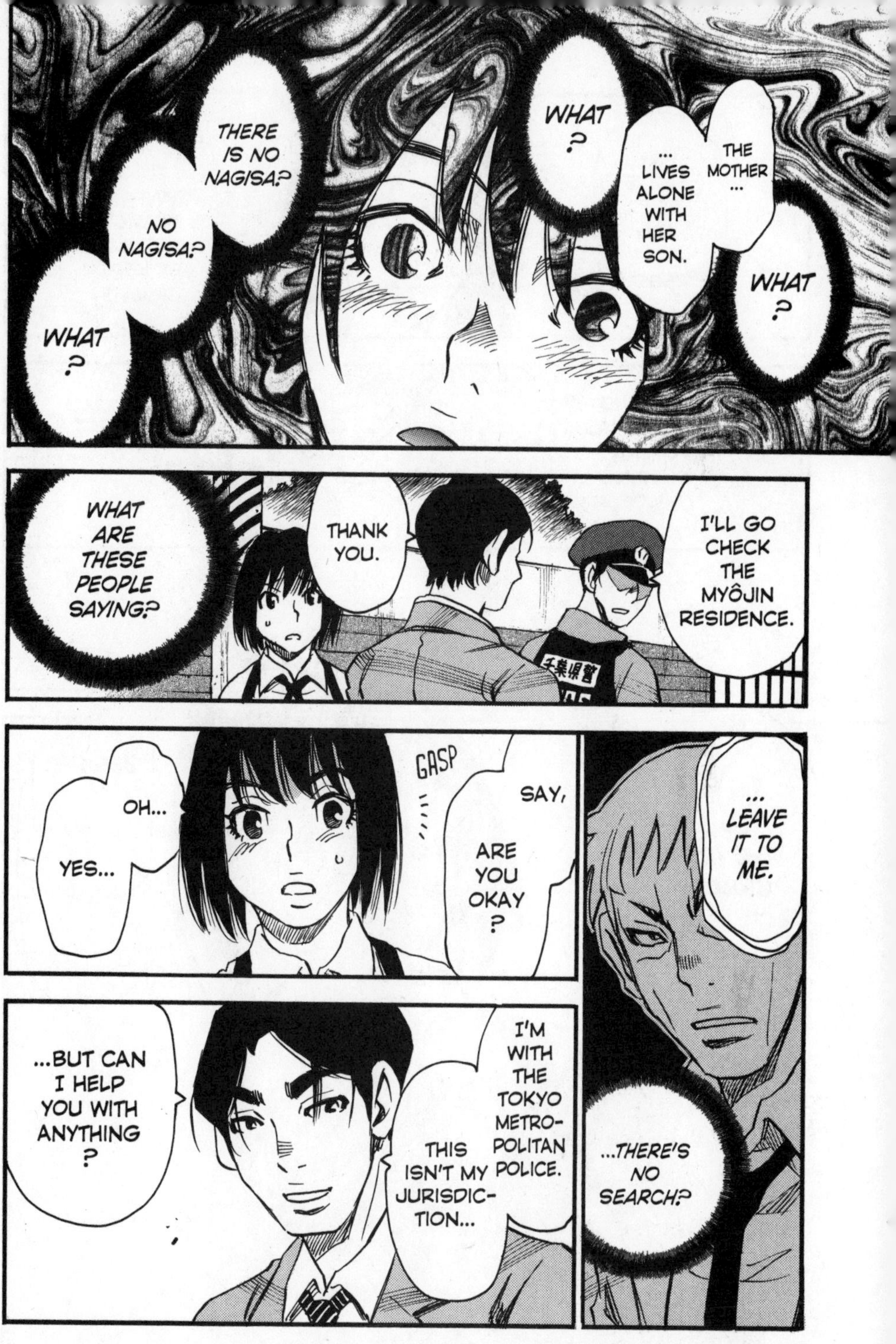
THE MOTHER...
...LIVES ALONE WITH HER SON.
WHAT?
WHAT?
THERE IS NO NAGISA?
NO NAGISA?
WHAT?
I'LL GO CHECK THE MYÔJIN RESIDENCE.
千葉県警
THANK YOU.
WHAT ARE THESE PEOPLE SAYING?
...LEAVE IT TO ME.
...THERE'S NO SEARCH?
SAY, ARE YOU OKAY?
GASP
OH... YES...
I'M WITH THE TOKYO METROPOLITAN POLICE.
THIS ISN'T MY JURISDICTION...
...BUT CAN I HELP YOU WITH ANYTHING?

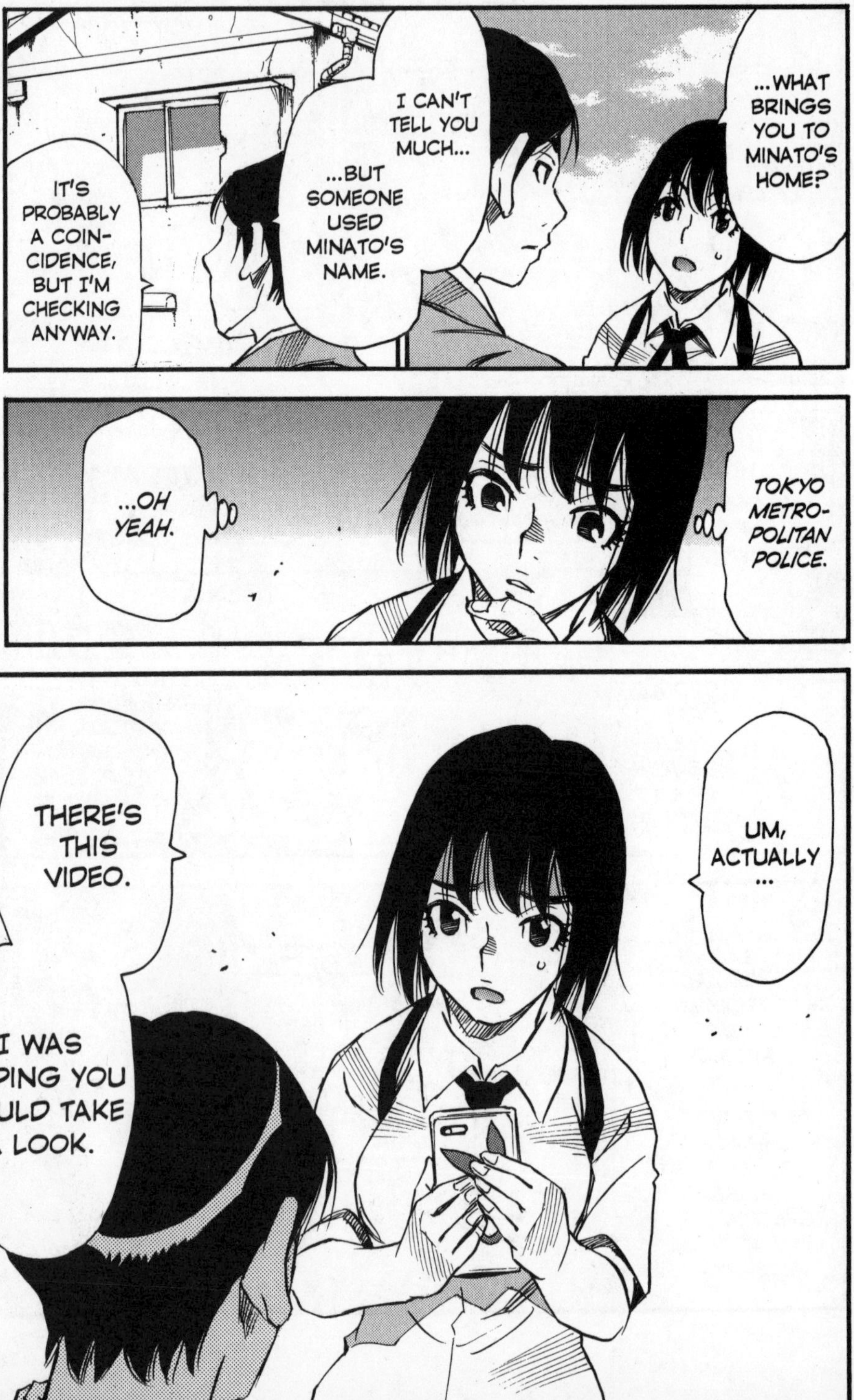
...WHAT BRINGS YOU TO MINATO'S HOME?
I CAN'T TELL YOU MUCH...
...BUT SOMEONE USED MINATO'S NAME.
IT'S PROBABLY A COINCIDENCE, BUT I'M CHECKING ANYWAY.
TOKYO METROPOLITAN POLICE.
...OH YEAH.
UM, ACTUALLY...
THERE'S THIS VIDEO.
I WAS HOPING YOU COULD TAKE A LOOK.

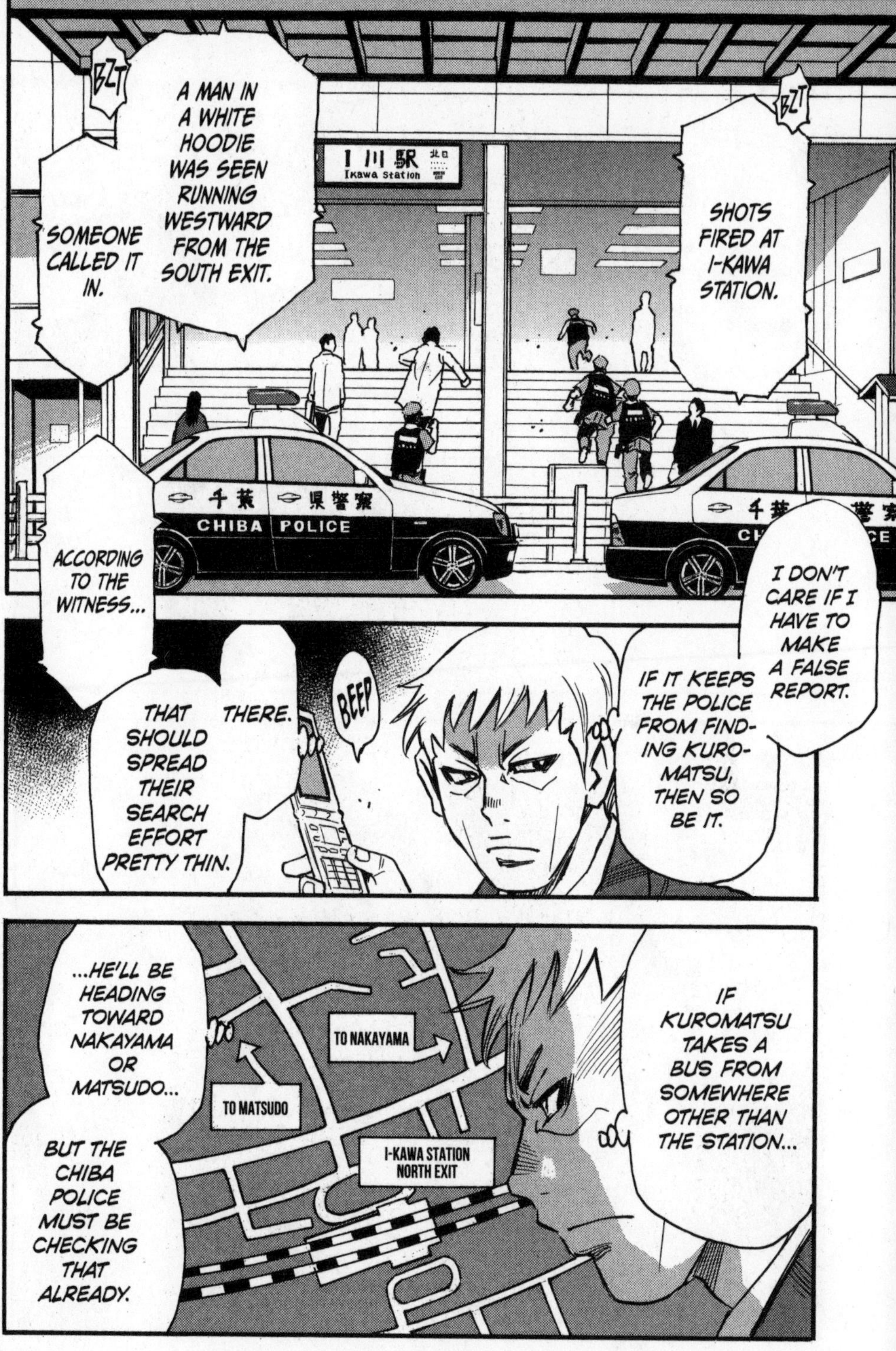
BZZT
SHOTS FIRED AT I-KAWA STATION.
I川駅 Ikawa Station
BZZT
A MAN IN A WHITE HOODIE WAS SEEN RUNNING WESTWARD FROM THE SOUTH EXIT.
SOMEONE CALLED IT IN.
千葉県警察
CHIBA POLICE
ACCORDING TO THE WITNESS...
I DON'T CARE IF I HAVE TO MAKE A FALSE REPORT.
IF IT KEEPS THE POLICE FROM FINDING KUROMATSU, THEN SO BE IT.
BEEP
THERE.
THAT SHOULD SPREAD THEIR SEARCH EFFORT PRETTY THIN.
IF KUROMATSU TAKES A BUS FROM SOMEWHERE OTHER THAN THE STATION...
TO NAKAYAMA
TO MATSUDO
I-KAWA STATION NORTH EXIT
...HE'LL BE HEADING TOWARD NAKAYAMA OR MATSUDO...
BUT THE CHIBA POLICE MUST BE CHECKING THAT ALREADY.

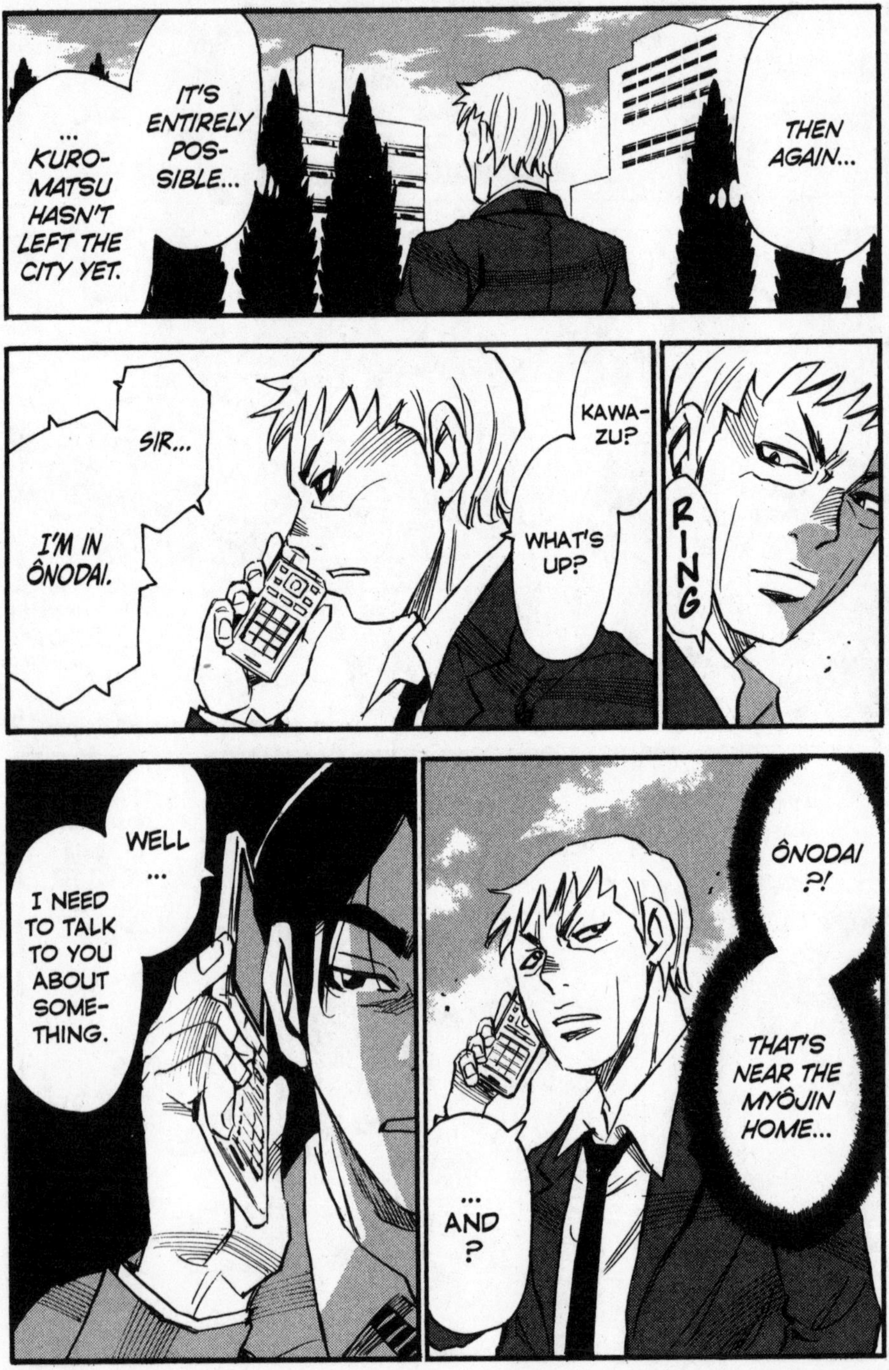
THEN AGAIN...
IT'S ENTIRELY POS-SIBLE...
... KURO-MATSU HASN'T LEFT THE CITY YET.
RING
KAWA-ZU?
WHAT'S UP?
SIR...
I'M IN ÔNODAI.
ÔNODAI ?!
THAT'S NEAR THE MYÔJIN HOME...
... AND ?
WELL ...
I NEED TO TALK TO YOU ABOUT SOME-THING.

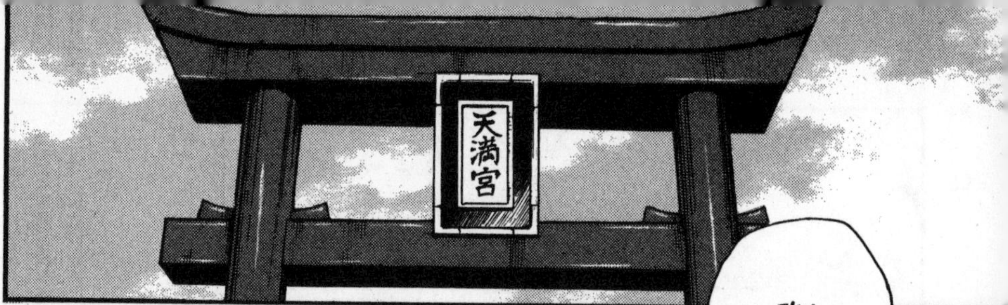
天満宮

SHRINE GATE: *Tenmangu.*

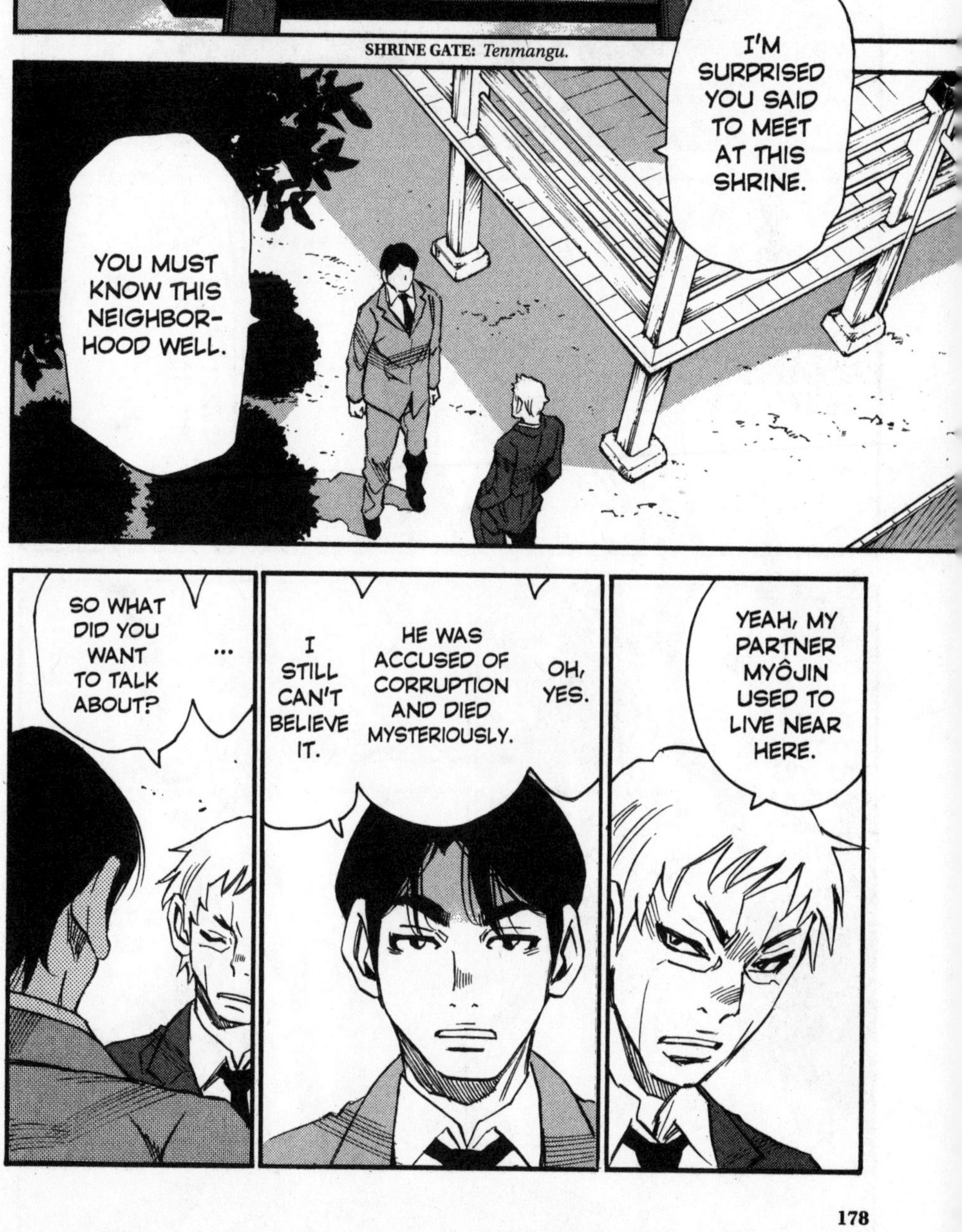
I'M SURPRISED YOU SAID TO MEET AT THIS SHRINE.
YOU MUST KNOW THIS NEIGHBOR-HOOD WELL.
YEAH, MY PARTNER MYÔJIN USED TO LIVE NEAR HERE.
OH, YES.
HE WAS ACCUSED OF CORRUPTION AND DIED MYSTERIOUSLY.
I STILL CAN'T BELIEVE IT.
...
SO WHAT DID YOU WANT TO TALK ABOUT?

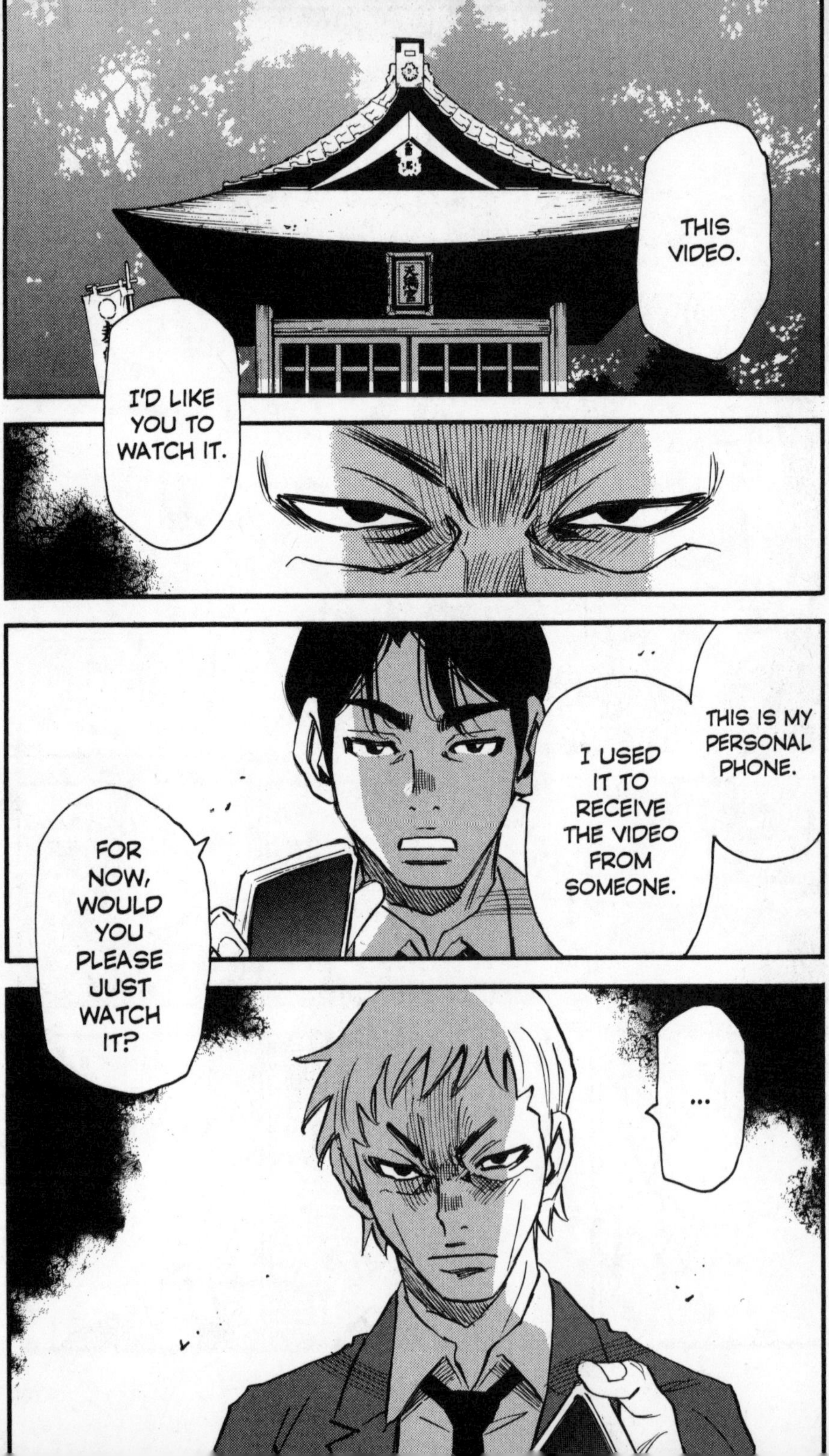
THIS VIDEO.
I'D LIKE YOU TO WATCH IT.
THIS IS MY PERSONAL PHONE.
I USED IT TO RECEIVE THE VIDEO FROM SOMEONE.
FOR NOW, WOULD YOU PLEASE JUST WATCH IT?
...

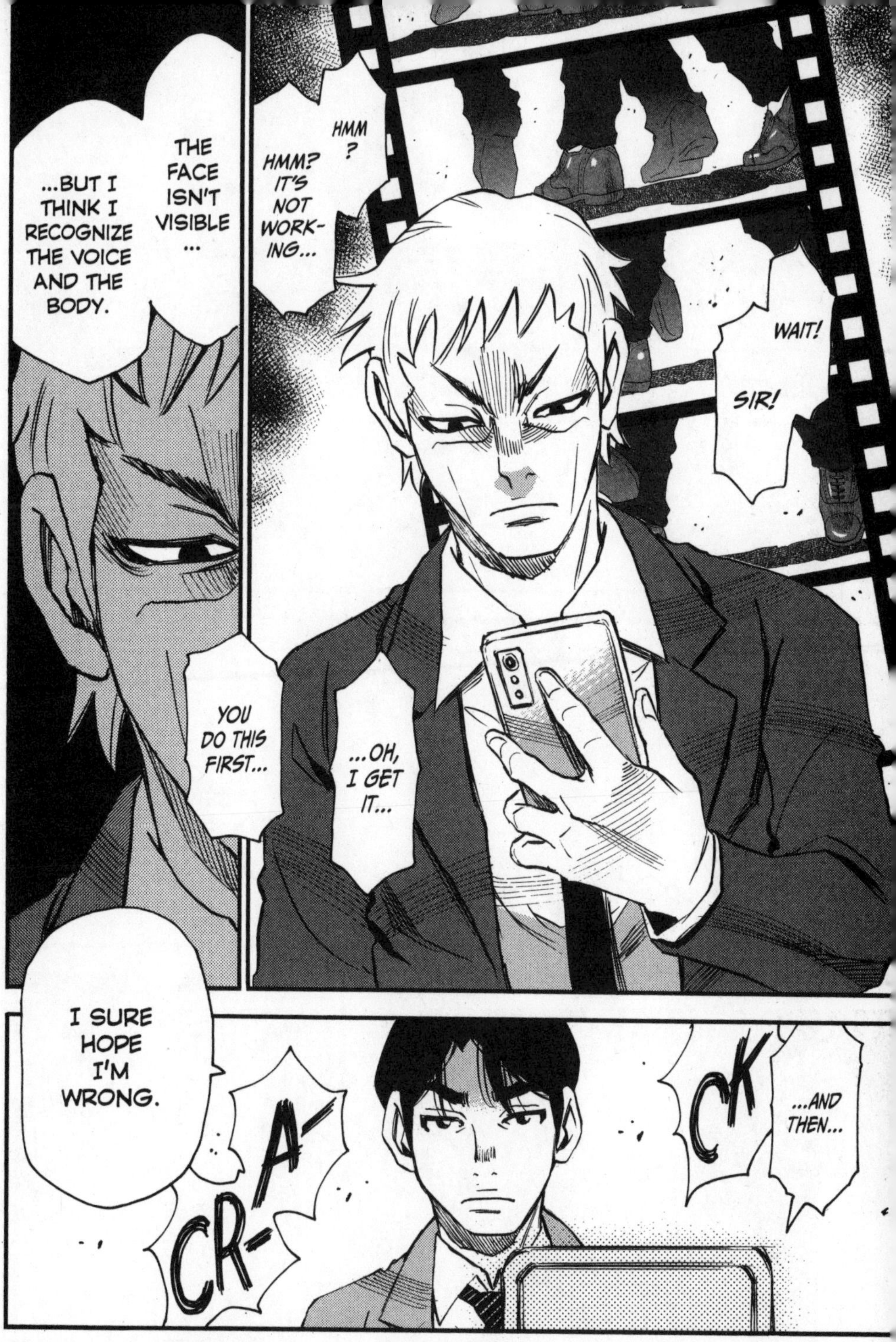
WAIT!
SIR!
HMM? IT'S NOT WORKING...
HMM ?
YOU DO THIS FIRST...
...OH, I GET IT...
THE FACE ISN'T VISIBLE ...
...BUT I THINK I RECOGNIZE THE VOICE AND THE BODY.
...AND THEN...
CR-A-CK
I SURE HOPE I'M WRONG.

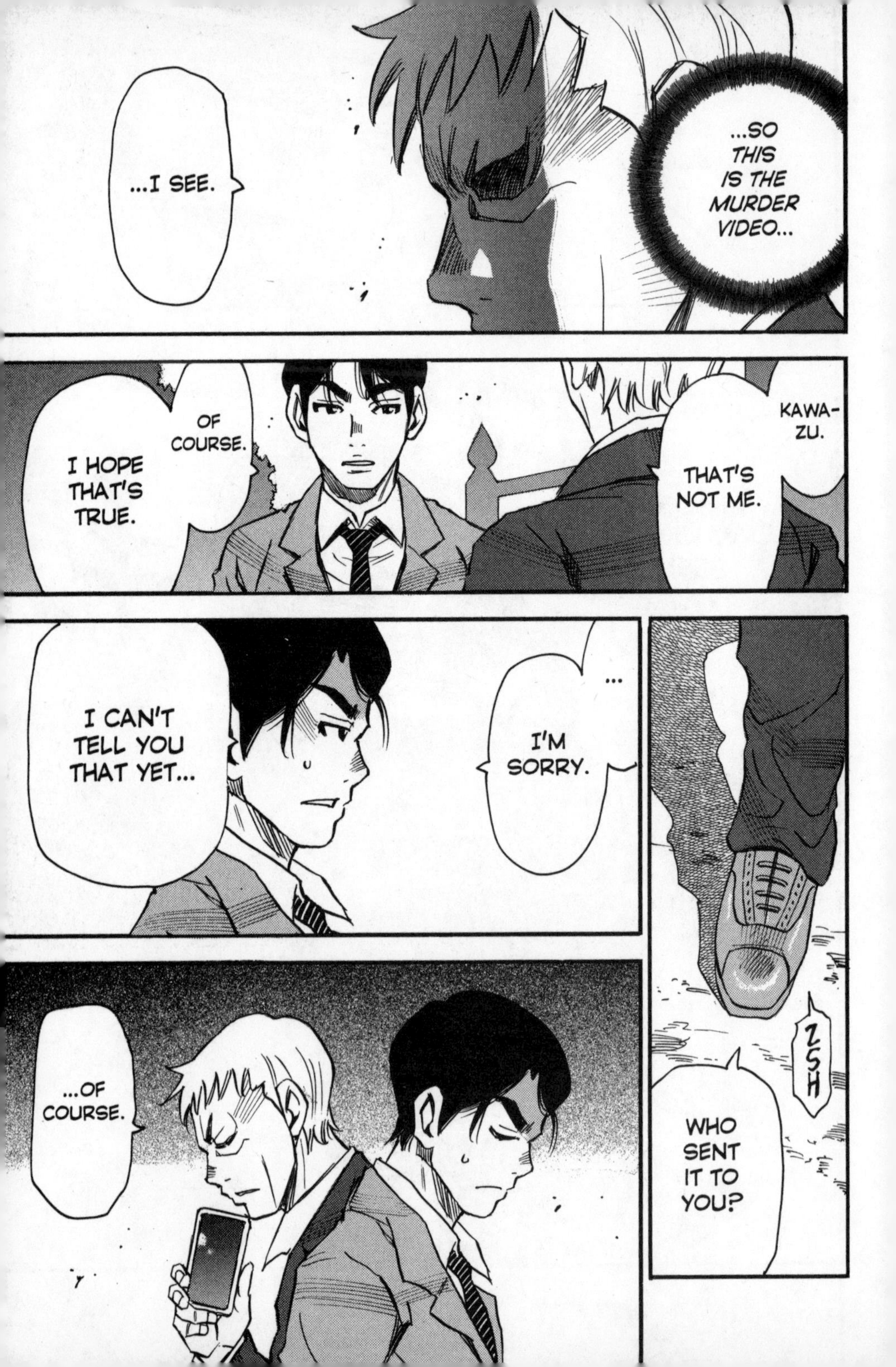
...SO THIS IS THE MURDER VIDEO...
...I SEE.
KAWAZU.
THAT'S NOT ME.
OF COURSE.
I HOPE THAT'S TRUE.
ZSH
WHO SENT IT TO YOU?
...
I'M SORRY.
I CAN'T TELL YOU THAT YET...
...OF COURSE.

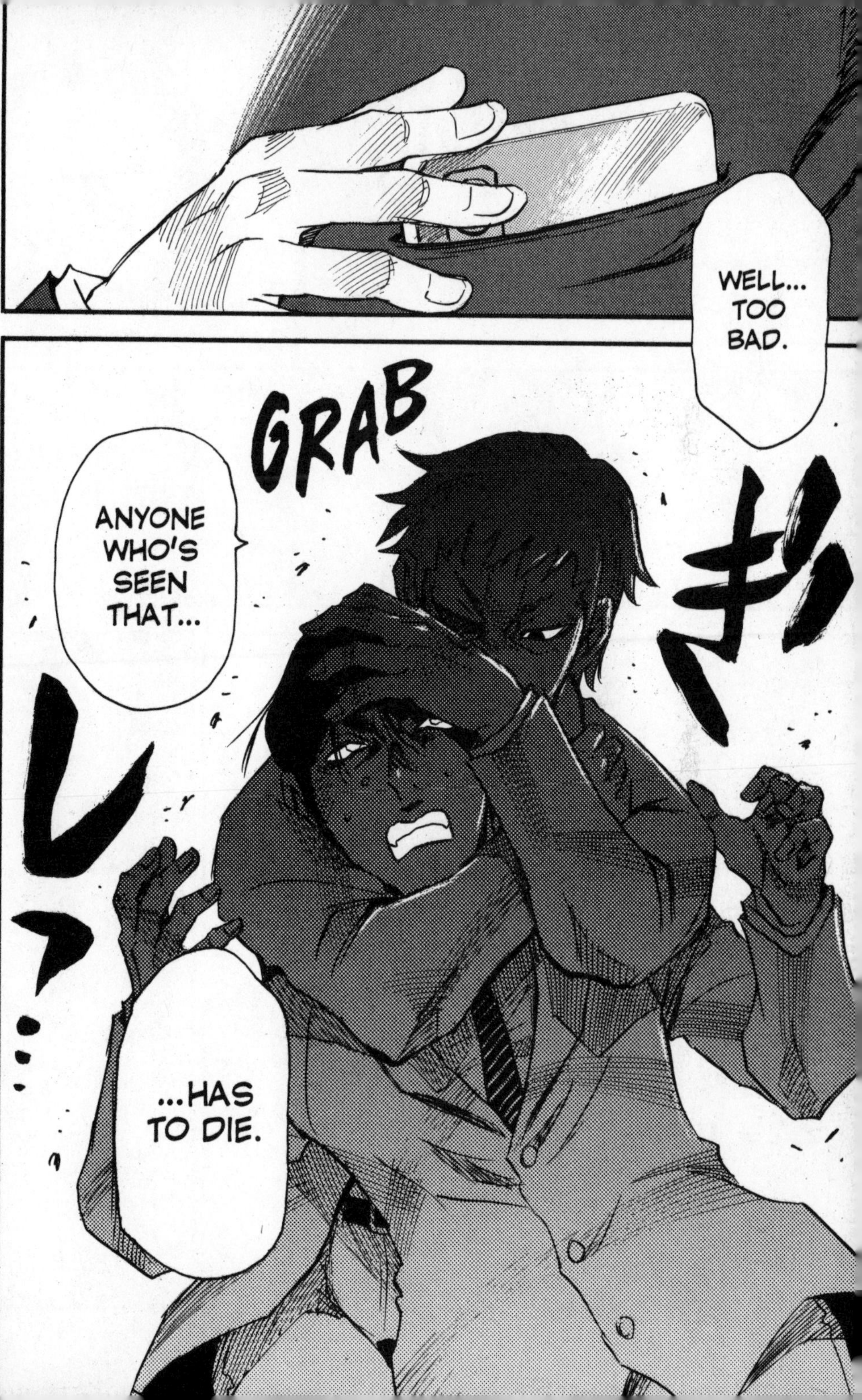
WELL... TOO BAD.
GRAB
ANYONE WHO'S SEEN THAT...
...HAS TO DIE.

STAFF

Kei Sanbe $^{\theta}$

Yoichiro Tomita
Manami, 18 years old
Koji Kikuta
Yasunobu

Keishi Kanesho

SPECIAL THANKS
Naginyo

BOOK DESIGN
Yukio Hoshino
VOLARE inc.

EDITORS
Naofumi Muranaka
Jun'ichiro Kito
Hiroshi Nishimura
Toshihiro Tsuchiya

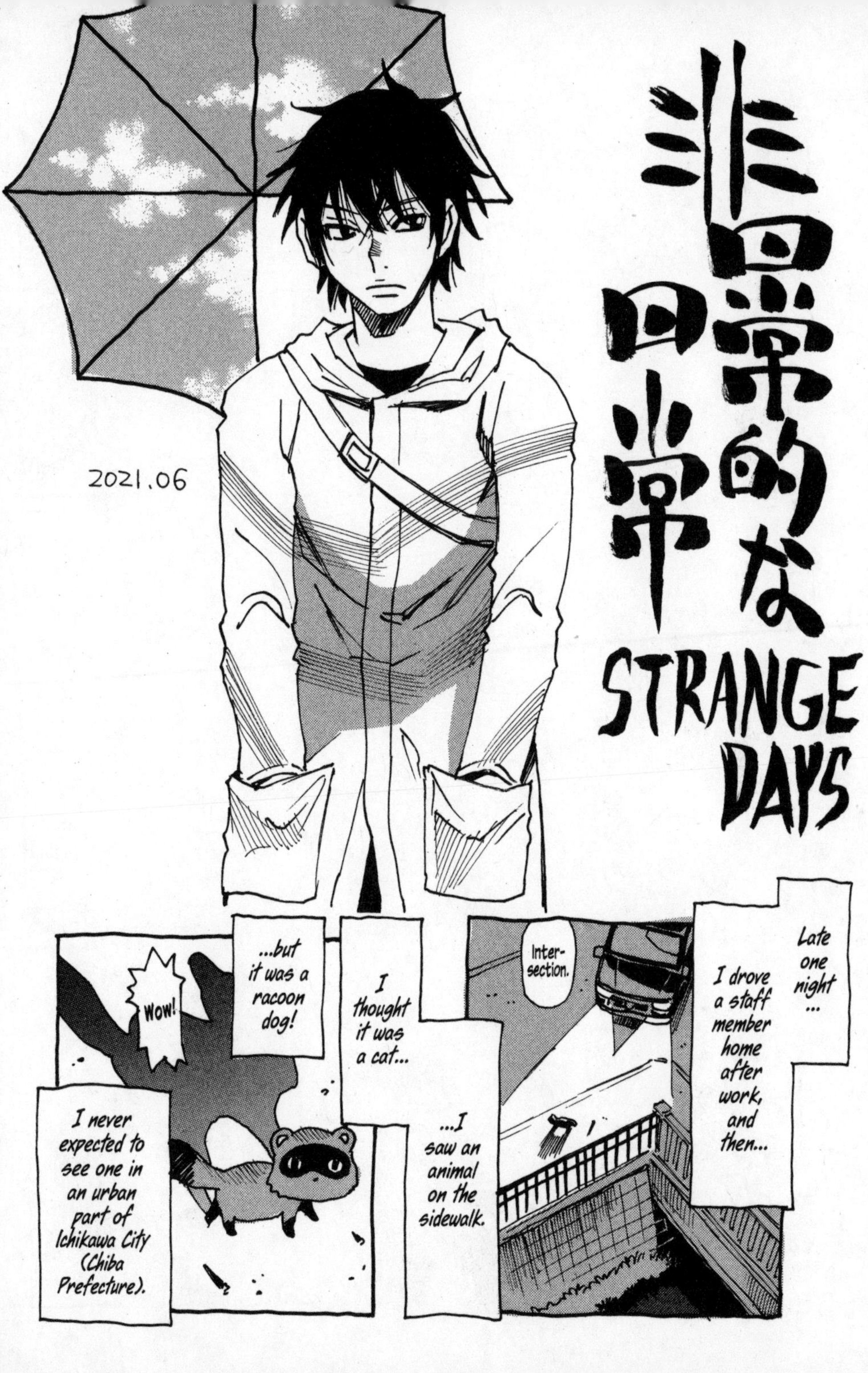

非日常的な日常
STRANGE DAYS
2021.06
Late one night...
I drove a staff member home after work, and then...
Inter-section.
...I saw an animal on the sidewalk.
I thought it was a cat...
...but it was a racoon dog!
WOW!
I never expected to see one in an urban part of Ichikawa City (Chiba Prefecture).

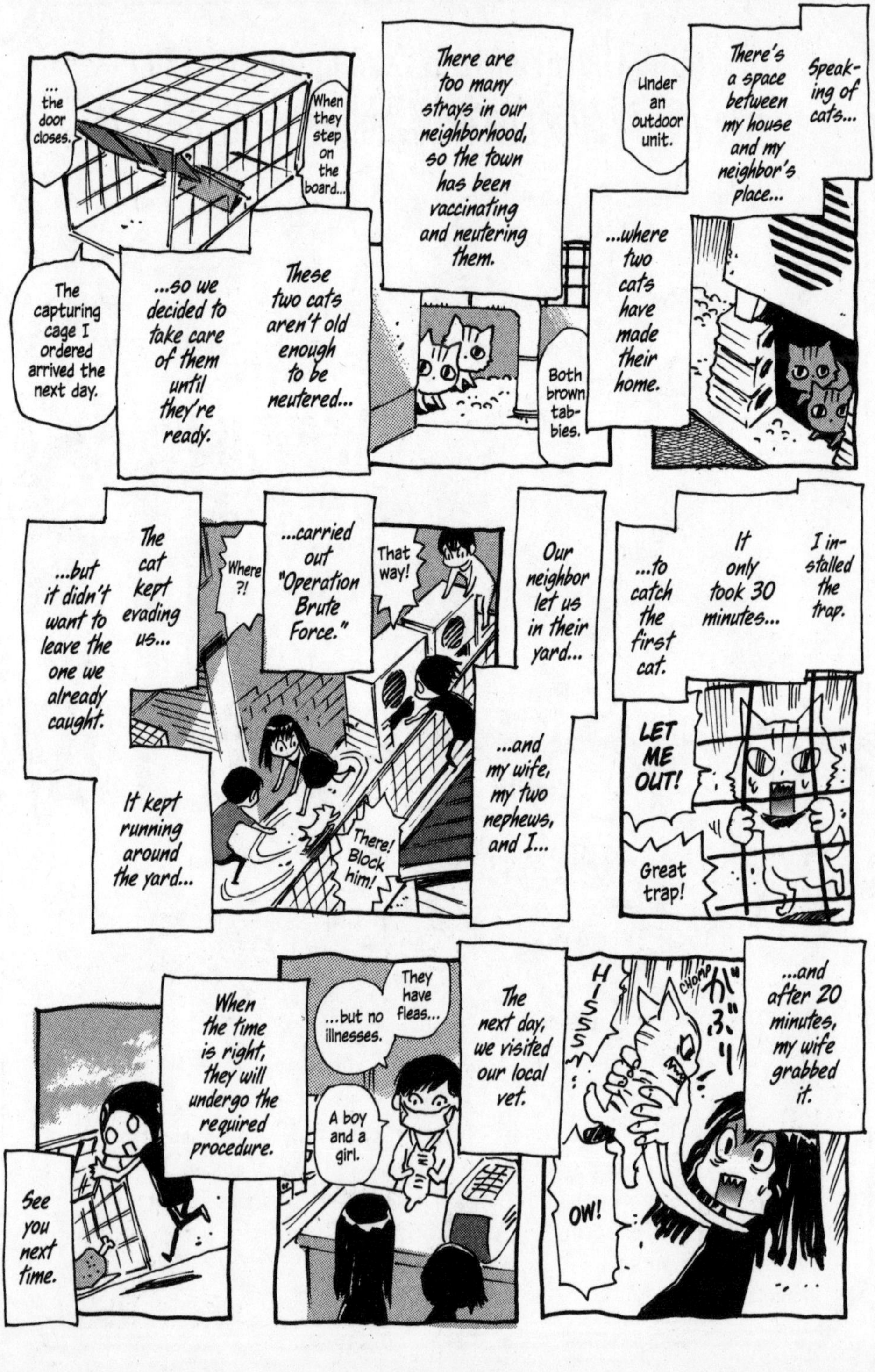

Speak-ing of cats...
There's a space between my house and my neighbor's place...
...where two cats have made their home.
Under an outdoor unit.
There are too many strays in our neighborhood, so the town has been vaccinating and neutering them.
Both brown tab-bies.
These two cats aren't old enough to be neutered...
...so we decided to take care of them until they're ready.
The capturing cage I ordered arrived the next day.
When they step on the board...
...the door closes.
I in-stalled the trap.
It only took 30 minutes...
...to catch the first cat.
LET ME OUT!
Great trap!
Our neighbor let us in their yard...
...and my wife, my two nephews, and I...
...carried out "Operation Brute Force."
That way!
Where?!
There! Block him!
The cat kept evading us...
It kept running around the yard...
...but it didn't want to leave the one we already caught.
...and after 20 minutes, my wife grabbed it.
CHOMP
がぶり
HISSS
OW!
The next day, we visited our local vet.
They have fleas...
...but no illnesses.
A boy and a girl.
When the time is right, they will undergo the required procedure.
See you next time.

Young characters and steampunk setting, like *Howl's Moving Castle* and *Battle Angel Alita*

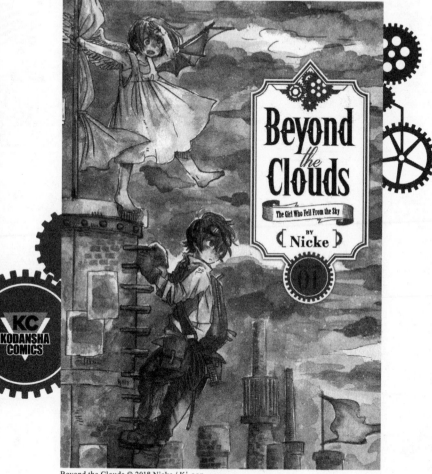

Beyond the Clouds © 2018 Nicke / Ki-oon

A boy with a talent for machines and a mysterious girl whose wings he's fixed will take you beyond the clouds! In the tradition of the high-flying, resonant adventure stories of Studio Ghibli comes a gorgeous tale about the longing of young hearts for adventure and friendship!

One of CLAMP's biggest hits returns in this definitive, premium, hardcover 20th anniversary collector's edition!

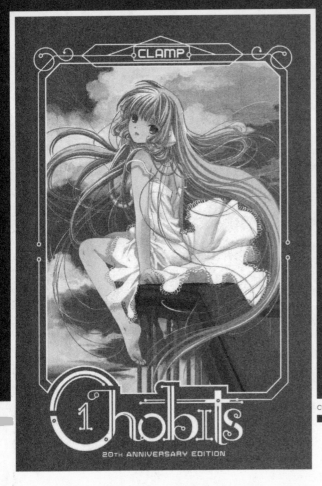

Chobits © CLAMP·ShigatsuTsuitachi CO.,LTD./Kodansha Ltd.

Poor college student Hideki is down on his luck. All he wants is a good job, a girlfriend, and his very own "persocom"—the latest and greatest in humanoid computer technology. Hideki's luck changes one night when he finds Chi—a persocom thrown out in a pile of trash. But Hideki soon discovers that there's much more to his cute new persocom than meets the eye.

KC KODANSHA COMICS

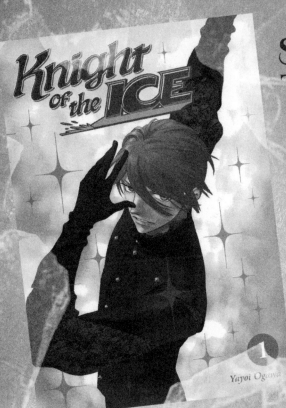
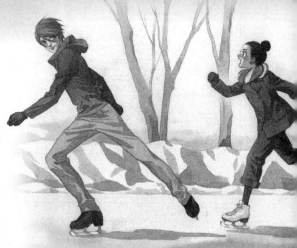

A SMART, NEW ROMANTIC COMEDY FOR FANS OF *SHORTCAKE CAKE* AND *TERRACE HOUSE!*

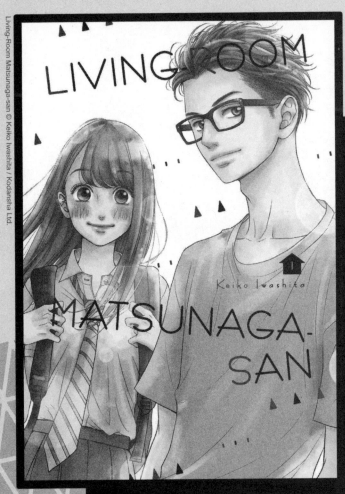

A romance manga starring high school girl Meeko, who learns to live on her own in a boarding house whose living room is home to the odd (but handsome) Matsunaga-san. She begins to adjust to her new life away from her parents, but Meeko soon learns that no matter how far away from home she is, she's still a young girl at heart — especially when she finds herself falling for Matsunaga-san.

PERFECT WORLD

Rie Aruga

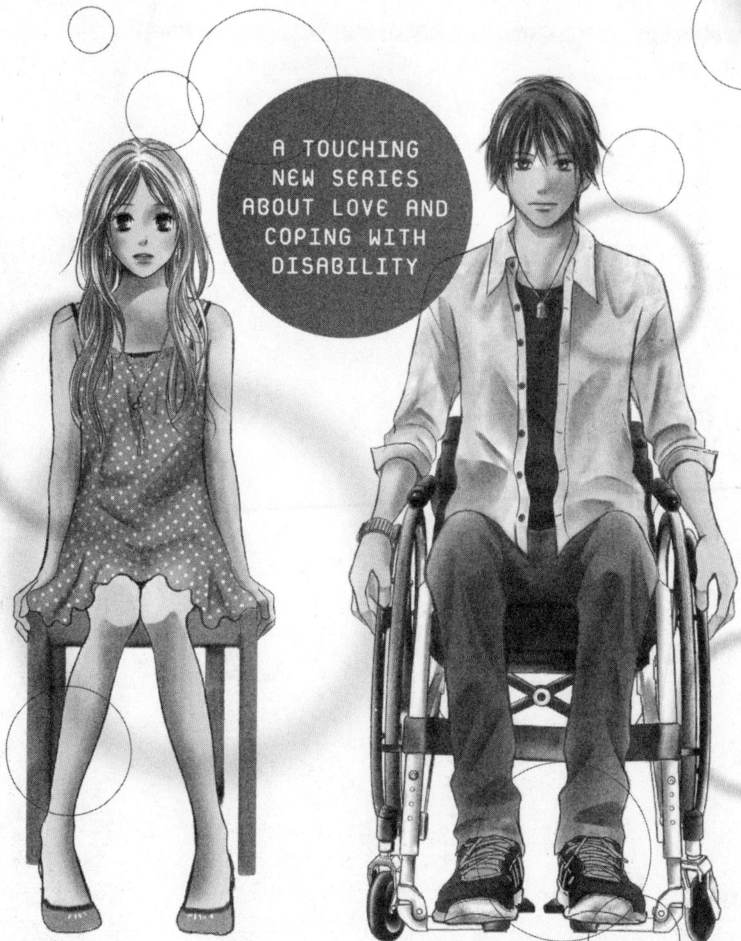

A TOUCHING NEW SERIES ABOUT LOVE AND COPING WITH DISABILITY

An office party reunites Tsugumi with her high school crush Itsuki. He's realized his dream of becoming an architect, but along the way, he experienced a spinal injury that put him in a wheelchair. Now Tsugumi's rekindled feelings will butt up against prejudices she never considered — and Itsuki will have to decide if he's ready to let someone into his heart...

"Depicts with great delicacy and courage the difficulties some with disabilities experience getting involved in romantic relationships... Rie Aruga refuses to romanticize, pushing her heroine to face the reality of disability. She invites her readers to the same tasks of empathy, knowledge and recognition."
—Slate.fr

"An important entry [in manga romance]... The emotional core of both plot and characters indicates thoughtfulness... [Aruga's] research is readily apparent in the text and artwork, making this feel like a real story."
—Anime News Network

The boys are back, in 400-page hardcovers that are as pretty and badass as they are!

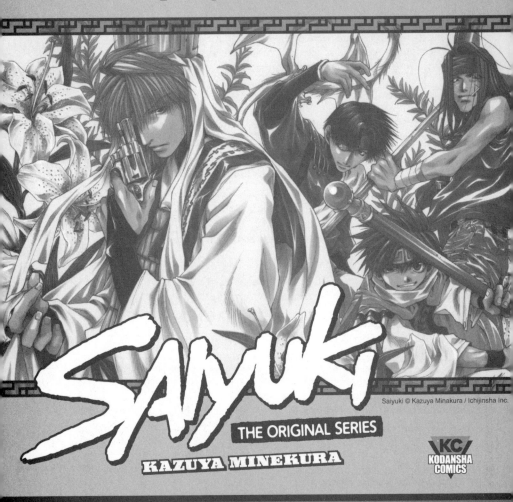

Saiyuki © Kazuya Minakura / Ichijinsha Inc.

SAIYUKI

THE ORIGINAL SERIES

KAZUYA MINEKURA

"AN EDGY COMIC LOOK AT AN ANCIENT CHINESE TALE." —YALSA

Genjo Sanzo is a Buddhist priest in the city of Togenkyo, which is being ravaged by yokai spirits that have fallen out of balance with the natural order. His superiors send him on a journey far to the west to discover why this is happening and how to stop it. His companions are three yokai with human souls. But this is no day trip — the four will encounter many discoveries and horrors on the way.

FEATURES NEW TRANSLATION, COLOR PAGES, AND BEAUTIFUL WRAPAROUND COVER ART!

Island in a Puddle 4 is a work of fiction. Names, cl[illegible] and incidents are the products of the author's imagination or are used fictitiously. Any resemblance to actual events, locales, or persons, living or dead, is entirely coincidental.

A Kodansha Trade Paperback Original

Published in the United States by
Kodansha USA Publishing, LLC, New York.

Publication rights for this English edition arranged through
Kodansha Ltd., Tokyo.

First published in Japan in 2021 by Kodansha Ltd., Tokyo
as *Mizutamari ni ukabu shima*, volume 4.

ISBN 978-1-64651-462-5

Printed in the United States of America.

1st Printing

Translation: Iyasu Adair Nagata
Lettering: Evan Hayden
Editing: Greg Moore
Kodansha USA Publishing edition cover design by Adam Del Re

Publisher: Kiichiro Sugawara

Director of Publishing Services: Ben Applegate
Director of Publishing Operations: Dave Barrett
Associate Director of Publishing Operations: Stephen Pakula
Publishing Services Managing Editors: Madison Salters, Alanna Ruse,
with Grace Chen
Production Manager: Jocelyn O'Dowd

KODANSHA.US

KODANSHA

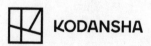